THE
RUSSIAN
CIVIL
WAR

EVAN MAWDSLEY

PEGASUS BOOKS
NEW YORK

*Although it was six in the morning, night was yet
heavy and chill. There was only a faint unearthly
pallor stealing over the silent streets, dimming
the watch-fires, the shadow of a terrible dawn
grey-rising over Russia.*

—John Reed, Petrograd, October 26, 1917

THE RUSSIAN CIVIL WAR

Pegasus Books LLC
45 Wall Street, Suite 1021
New York, NY 10005

Library of Congress Cataloging-in-Publication Data is available.

ISBN: 978-1-933648-15-6

10 9 8 7 8 6 5 4 3 2 1

Printed in the United States of America
Distributed by Consortium

CONTENTS

Glossary and Abbreviations   v

PART 1
1918: Year of Decision

1. The Triumphal March of Soviet Power: The Bolshevik Takeover in
   Central Russia, October 1917–January 1918   3

2. The Railway War: Spreading the Revolution,
   November 1917–March 1918   16

3. The Obscene Peace: Soviet Russia and the Central Powers,
   October 1917–November 1918   31

4. The Allies in Russia, October 1917–November 1918   45

5. The Volga Campaign, May–November 1918   56

6. Sovdepia: The Soviet Zone, October 1917–November 1918   70

7. The Cossack Vendée, May–November 1918   85

8. Siberia and the Urals, February–November 1918   99

PART 2
1919: Year of the Whites

9. The Revolution on the March: Sovdepia and the Outside World,
   November 1918–June 1919   115

10. Kolchak's Offensive, November 1918–June 1919   132

11. Omsk and Arkhangelsk: Kolchak, June–November 1919;
    North Russia, November 1918–March 1920   148

12. The Armed Forces of South Russia, November 1918–September 1919   161

13. The Armed Camp: Sovdepia, November 1918–November 1919   178

14. The Turning Point, September–November 1919   194

PART 3

1920: Year of Victory

15. The End of Denikin, November 1919–March 1920;
    The Caucasus, 1918–1921   219

16. Storm over Asia: Siberia, November 1919–October 1922;
    Central Asia, 1918–1920   230

17. Consolidating the State: The Soviet Zone,
    November 1919–November 1920   242

18. The Polish Campaign, April–October 1920   250

19. The Crimean Ulcer, April–November 1920   262

Conclusion   272
Maps   291
Notes   301
Bibliography   312
Supplementary Bibliography   344
Index   355

GLOSSARY AND ABBREVIATIONS

AFSR. Armed Forces of South Russia; the united White forces of the Volunteer Army and the southern cossacks.

Army Group. *Front,* several armies.

AR-PG. All-Russian Provisional Government; the Omsk "Directory" of late 1918.

Ataman. Chieftain, head of cossack host.

Central ExCom. (All-Russian) Central Executive Committee (*VTsIK*); nominally the permanent embodiment of a congress of soviets.

CC. Central Committee (of the Bolshevik party, etc.).

Cheka. Soviet political police.

FER. Far Eastern Republic; Soviet puppet government in eastern Siberia, 1920–1922.

Kadet. Constitutional Democrat (liberal party).

Kombedy. Committees of the Village Poor.

Komuch. Committee of Members of the Constituent Assembly; SR anti-Bolshevik government on the Volga in 1918.

Menshevik. Moderate subgroup of Russian Marxism.

Military District. Region, made up of several provinces, responsible for raising, supplying, and training troops; *voennyi okrug.*

Narkom. see People's Commissar.

People's Commissar. "Cabinet Minister" *(Narkom),* member of *Sovnarkom.*

ProvExCom. Provincial Soviet Executive Committee *(Gubispolkom)*; the chief state institution at province level.

ProvCom. Provincial (Bolshevik) Party Committee *(Gubkom).*

PSG. Provisional Siberian Government (Omsk, mid-1918).

RevCom. Revolutionary Committee *(Revkom)*; extraordinary military-civil administrative organ.

RevMilCouncil. Revolutionary Military Council *(Revvoensovet)*; a commander and several commissars in charge of an army group or army.

RSFSR. Russian Socialist Federative Soviet Republic; the official name of Soviet Russia.

Sovnarkom. Council of People's Commissars; the supreme executive of the congress of soviets, the Soviet "cabinet."

SR. Socialist-Revolutionary (peasant party).

Stavka. Army general headquarters.

UkSSR. Ukrainian Socialist Soviet Republic.

I

1918: YEAR OF DECISION

It is obvious that Soviet power is organized civil war against the landlords, the bourgeoisie, and the kulaks.

L. D. Trotsky, June 1918

1

THE TRIUMPHAL MARCH OF SOVIET POWER: THE BOLSHEVIK TAKEOVER IN CENTRAL RUSSIA, October 1917–January 1918

Citizens:
The counter-revolution has raised its criminal head. The Kornilovites are mobilizing their forces in order to crush the All-Russian Congress of Soviets and to wreck the Constituent Assembly. At the same time the pogrom-makers may attempt to cause trouble and slaughter in the streets of Petrograd.

The Petrograd Soviet of Workers' and Soldiers' Deputies takes upon itself the defense of revolutionary order against attempts at counter-revolution and pogroms.

Petrograd MRC Announcement, 24 October 1917

October

Historians of modern Russia have not come to a clear verdict on when the Civil War started. Many are vague. Others, probably a majority, date the Civil War from the summer of 1918, usually linking it to an uprising by Czechoslovak troops in May. Dating the Civil War from the summer of 1918 has important implications: it suggests a peaceful start to Soviet power, increases the weight of "foreign intervention" (the Czechoslovaks), and links radical Bolshevik policies to the outbreak of fighting.

My own view, shared with a respectable minority of writers (both Western and Soviet), is that the Civil War began with the October

3

Revolution. The events described in the following two chapters will show that the victory of Soviet power in the winter of 1917–1918 went hand in hand with internal fighting of an intensity that can only be called "civil war."

The Russian Civil War, then, began in the autumn of 1917. To be precise, it began on 25 October during the evening. The specter of Russian fighting Russian had lurked in the background since the Tsar was toppled in February, but what set off the final apocalyptic struggle, one that would last three years and cost over seven million lives, was the seizure of power in Petrograd by the Bolshevik Party. Detachments of armed workers, sailors, and soldiers took control of the capital and arrested Kerensky's Provisional Government. They were organized by the Bolsheviks but acted in the name of the soviets—the workers' and soldiers' councils; the Second All-Russian Congress of Soviets met on the night of 25 October. Resistance was weak—the "storming" of the Winter Palace is something of a myth—but real bloodshed came a few days later with an attempted counterrevolt.

The events taking place around Petrograd from 28 October to 1 November were the overture of the Civil War, demonstrating themes that would recur. The same forces, even some of the same leaders, were involved. Young officer-cadets ("junkers") rose within Petrograd; small cossack detachments under General Krasnov (a future Don Cossack leader) tried to break into the city across the scrubland of the southern outskirts. On the Soviet side were armed workers and revolutionary soldiers and sailors, loosely coordinated by two future heroes of 1918, Antonov-Ovseenko and Lieutenant Colonel Muraviev. In the end the junkers were crushed, and the cossacks were stopped at Gatchina. As in the later Civil War the civilian opponents of the Bolsheviks, people of the moderate Left and Right, lacked effective combat forces of their own and played no part.

The October events are sometimes called a coup, but their deeper roots can be seen in what Lenin termed the "Triumphal March of Soviet Power," the rapid takeover of the Russian Empire. In Moscow, the second city of the Empire, a few days of confused and bloody street fighting, complete with artillery bombardment and massacre, ended with rebel victory. In most of the big towns of central and northwestern Russia—the crucial future core of Soviet territory—and also in the Urals, the local soviets took power within a couple of weeks. Nowhere in these regions was there serious fighting, even on the scale of Petrograd and Moscow. By the new year an even vaster region, the great majority of the Empire's seventy-five province and region (*oblast'*)

4

centers, stretching from the Polish borderlands to the Pacific, was in the hands of the revolutionaries; the main areas outside nominal Soviet control were the Transcaucasus, Finland, four Ukrainian provinces, and the Don, Kuban, and Orenburg Cossack Regions.

The end of the easy (for the Bolsheviks) first phase of the Civil War came on 5 January, with the meeting in Petrograd of the All-Russian Constituent Assembly. National elections held in early November had shown the peasant-based Socialist-Revolutionary (SR) Party, not the Bolsheviks, to be the most popular group. The Bolsheviks allowed the Assembly to meet for one night, and then armed sailors closed the hall and locked the delegates out. With this ended the last serious political challenge to Bolshevism in central Russia. "Soviet" power was then confirmed by the Bolshevik-dominated Third Congress of Soviets.

Bolsheviks and Soviets

The Bolshevik victory in the winter of 1917–1918 was neither a conspiracy nor an accident. The hopes and fears of the mass of the Russian people were involved in it, and these hopes and fears were to some extent measurable through a unique national test of political attitudes, held at the decisive moment: the November 1917 elections to the All-Russian Constituent Assembly.

The overall voting in the Assembly elections showed, above all, peasant opinion; over two-thirds of the electorate were peasants. What was striking about these overall returns was the strength of the *socialist* vote. Some 40 percent of the total vote went to the main peasant socialist party (the SRs) and 27 percent to Marxists (nearly all Bolsheviks); popular ethnic-minority parties, often with a socialist element, took another 15 percent. In contrast to other countries, there was no strong non-socialist farmers' party. So about four voters out of five chose parties calling for radical land reform; this in turn reflected a basic fact of Russian politics—the peasant desire for land reform at the expense of the landowning nobility.

Relatively few of the Empire's population lived in towns, perhaps 26 million out of 160 million. The main non-socialist party, the Constitutional Democrats (Kadets), polled only 24 percent of the urban vote (in sixty-eight of the largest towns); the socialist vote was 61 percent. Socialism was a deeper red in the towns than in the electorate as a whole. The extreme Left, the Bolsheviks, won 36 percent of the votes,

5

making them the largest party. In Petrograd the Bolsheviks took 45 percent, in Moscow 50 percent. The urban Bolshevik votes accounted for only about 1.4 million of the 40 million civilian votes cast, but because power was based on the towns they represented crucial nuggets of strength. The radical nature of the urban electorate had several causes. The mix in the factories of experienced workers and people fresh from the countryside was an explosive one. Trade unions had had little base in Russia and could not act as a channel for discontent. The war brought special hardships to the towns. The unemployment and food shortages of late 1917 created a mood of desperation and a desire for maximalist solutions. "Workers' control" was demanded, and the workers' militia (Red Guard) gave the physical force to back up demands.

The vast Russian armed forces were the third element of mass upheaval. The army did not drain away to nothing under the Provisional Government. A census of 25 October 1917 put the current strength of the field army at 6,300,000, with a further 750,000 men in rear military districts (the navy would add another 750,000).[1] *Soldati*—NCOs and ordinary soldiers—made up 85 percent, say six million. As a group they were much larger than the middle class and twice the industrial working class. And this mass was a unique social force, thanks to the collapse of officer control and the growth of soldiers' committees. By the autumn of 1917 the soldiers' main wish was to end the war and go home. The Constituent Assembly elections show the soldiers (five million of them voted) to have overwhelmingly supported Russian socialist parties: 82 percent voted for the SRs or the Bolsheviks. (The centrist Kadets took two percent, the nationalists one percent.) The SRs, with 41 percent of the total army vote, were the strongest party, but the Bolsheviks also took 41 percent in the army (compared to 24 percent in the population as a whole). And the Bolsheviks did even better among troops near the center of political power. In the Northern and Western Army Groups their vote was over 60 percent (and the SR vote under 30 percent), and they did extremely well in the crucial rear garrisons: 80 percent in Petrograd (12 percent for the SRs) and 80 percent in Moscow (six percent SR).

Public opinion, then, was predominantly socialist, but it did not follow that socialism would take Bolshevik form. The Bolshevik Party's success is sometimes explained by its organization and program. The leader of the Bolshevik wing of Russian Marxism was, of course, Vladimir Ilich Lenin, who had organized the break of the Bolshevik wing from the Russian Marxist party (the RSDRP). For a decade and a half in exile he had been, if not the total master of the Bolshevik group, at least the single most important influence on doctrine and organization. Lenin called for the creation of a "vanguard party" in his *What Is to Be Done?* of 1902: "Give us an organization of revolutionaries and we will turn Russia upside down!"[2] The Bolsheviks entered 1917 with a core of dedicated, experienced, and radical activists, hardened by Tsarist repression, committed to a maximalist political and economic program, and completely hostile to any vestige of the old regime. The Bolsheviks were better organized than the other socialists. They had in Lenin a remarkable leader, whose political daring in 1917 exceeded that of his closest lieutenants and matched the radical activists. His insistence on an uprising just *before* the (October) Second Congress of Soviets allowed him to present the congress with power and to form a "Soviet" cabinet (*Sovnarkom*, the Council of People's Commissars) made up entirely of Bolsheviks.

But Bolshevik strengths can easily be exaggerated. Lenin's party was no monolith; the myth of the tightly organized Bolshevik party has rightly been called a "cruel mockery." Membership did indeed swell to 300,000 in October 1917, but from a tiny base of no more than 24,000 in February 1917[3]; this meant that eleven out of twelve Bolsheviks had only a few months' *stazh* (experience). Communications between the party center and its new branch membership were poor. The very seizure of power would deal a near mortal blow to the party "machine," as the attention of the most active members was turned to their new state, the soviet network. And party organizations were concentrated in a few radical regions, such as Petrograd, the Central Industrial Region (including Moscow), and the Urals; even here the party's reach did not extend beyond the boundaries of towns and industrial settlements. Bolshevik "voters" in the Assembly elections were 35 times party membership, some 10,661,000, but a total of 44,433,000 people voted. And the eight provinces where the party got more than 50 percent of the votes were restricted to a Red heartland in central and western Russia; here too were the military formations that gave more than half their votes to the party—two of the five army groups, and the Baltic Fleet.

Neither the Bolshevik program *in its pure form* nor the Bolshevik leaders' assessments of the situation were a guarantee of victory or even of support across a wide social spectrum. The small working class was ready, it is true, to support the Bolsheviks; the vague Bolshevik solutions to the economic crisis—workers' control and the expropriation of the capitalists, state control of trade, and the replacement of the market with state-controlled barter—were popular enough in the factories. But the great majority of the Russian people were peasants,

7

and the Bolsheviks were a town-based Marxist party. Until well into 1917 Bolshevik agrarian policy had called for turning the landowners' estates into large socialist farms, not simply dividing them up among the peasants. In addition, the Leninist view of a peasantry split between rich and poor would prove unworkable in the years to follow. On the question of war, Lenin's goal was not simple pacifism but the transformation of World War into international civil war. All the Bolsheviks placed their faith in the myth of a European revolution that would save them in Russia. They believed, too, that if attacked by the "imperialists" they could defend themselves by means of "revolutionary war." The Bolsheviks' political tactics were also out of step; at a time when the country's mood still favored socialist cooperation, Lenin's dominant faction among the Bolshevik leaders refused to work with other socialists. And unlike most of the population, the Bolsheviks wrote off the Constituent Assembly as a parliamentary sham much inferior to the soviets. Finally, the Bolsheviks, with their stress on the class struggle, were opposed in principle to the idea of independence for the national minorities, who made up half the population. Many strands of Bolshevik policy, then, did not meet the hopes of war-weary, rural, multinational Russia—and much of the program was simply not viable.

The organization and the ideology of the Bolsheviks are not enough to explain their success. What counted was the concept of "Soviet Power." The common name, the "Bolshevik Revolution," is in this sense misleading. Power was seized not in the name of the Bolshevik Party but in that of "Soviet Power," of the much broader soviet movement. Workers' and soldiers' councils (sovety) had appeared in most towns at the start of 1917. Their success did not come from some special creativity of the Russian workers and soldiers (not the peasants) who elected them. The power of the soviets came partly from the lack of any alternative broadly based local government; under the Tsar the towns had been run by appointees and a wealthy elite. But the soviets, elected directly by factories and military units, did provide a remarkably direct (if administratively ineffective) means of giving political institutions to a wider range of people than ever before. The Second All-Russian Congress of Soviets, which met in late October, was not entirely dominated by the Bolsheviks, but it did show dissatisfaction with the slow pace of change under the Provisional Government. More important, the leaders of the October uprising in Petrograd claimed to be acting in defense of the soviet congress in the face of a counterrevolutionary threat from the Provisional Government. This threat was claimed to be a repetition of the August attempt by General Kornilov, the army Supreme Commander-in-Chief, to overthrow the Petrograd

8

Soviet. At the very top of the Bolshevik Party, where the idea of insurrection was indeed born, the counterrevolutionary bogey was a piece of self-conscious manipulation. But even among middle-ranking party activists the tales of Prime Minister Kerensky's scheming were believed—and it was the "defense" of the congress that got so many supporters of the soviets out into the streets in October. And this action was organized not directly by the Bolsheviks but by the Petrograd Soviet's Military-Revolutionary Committee (MRC).

The soviets not only gave an excuse for an uprising but also provided the skeleton of an administration to run the country. Indeed, the soviets had been increasing their power for months and, as has been suggested, the October Revolution was here more a "shifting of gears, an acceleration of tempo" than a decisive break.[4] After October the Bolsheviks had control of the Central Executive Committee (Central ExCom—*VTsIK*—the standing body of the Soviet congress) and of Sovnarkom. The political cooperation of the Left faction of the agrarian-socialist SR Party gave the Central ExCom and Sovnarkom some claim to speak for the peasant majority. The nationwide network of nine hundred soviets made possible the quick spread of the revolution from town to town, and on to the most distant parts of the Empire. Once "Soviet" power had been proclaimed in the capital, local soviets across Russia formed their own MRCs, ejected representatives of the Provisional Government, and took sole power in their own hands—with the support of much of the population.

What might be called the "Soviet program"—as opposed to the Bolshevik program—was also of great importance. A series of sweeping social reforms announced by the new soviet government seemed to justify popular confidence. Of the various planks of the Bolshevik program, it was those related to industry and trade that were put into effect in the most full-blooded form: workers' control of the factories was announced, a Supreme Economic Council (*VSNKh*) set up to run the economy, the banks were nationalized (there was as yet no official nationalization of industry, although many factories were taken over "from below," by the workers). In other areas of policy, however, the hard ideological cutting edge of radical Marxism was softened into a program more suited to 1917 Russia. The Decree on Land divided the landowners' big estates among millions of individual peasant families (rather than keeping them as "model farms"); the Bolsheviks had simply adapted a draft SR land program. The Decree on Peace offered negotiations with the fighting powers. Talks with the Central Powers began, and on 2 December an armistice was signed. As the armies were sent home nothing more was heard of a revolutionary war against imperialism.

Three issues were of greatest importance to all social groups in the winter of 1917–1918: peace, salvation from economic catastrophe, and social change. The Soviet program promised to deal with these issues, and it won wide support in the first two or three months after October, especially after the failure of the Provisional Government even to make gestures. The program won popular support, too, for the Bolshevik domination of the Soviet regime.

Alternatives

The outcome of October and the success of the Triumphal March were also due to the weakness of alternative forces. The Tsarist political elite seemed within eight months of February 1917 to have almost completely disappeared. The Romanovs had done little to rouse political support of a modern sort. Romanov statesmen and their rightist supporters looked on *any* politics as the negation of autocracy. Organized popular backing for the Right was small despite such bogeymen (for the Left) as the "Black Hundreds." The regime had relied on the inertia of the masses, the passive support of the educated elite, and, in the last resort, the brute power of the police and the army. The political Right could not function once Russia had wide suffrage, and it played no effective part in 1917's politics; there were no right-wing delegates to the Constituent Assembly. The Russian Orthodox Church, a second conservative force, also had little influence. Close links to the Tsar both compromised the church and left it no tradition of independent action. The first *sobor* (general assembly) for two centuries recreated the Patriarchate, and after October Patriarch Tikhon anathematized the Bolsheviks and condemned their peace policy. Few concrete steps, however, were taken. There was no political base of church-organized parties or trade unions (as existed elsewhere in Europe), and the church had to put its hopes in a vague "upsurge" of the faithful. The Bolsheviks, for their part, had neither the strength nor the need to assault the church head on. The Metropolitan of Kiev was murdered in January 1918, but this was an exceptional case. Early attacks were concentrated on the hierarchy, and were mainly verbal; meanwhile the church was further weakened by the loss of its wealth, schools, and state functions.

The third leg of the conservative tripod, the army, was also useless. The army was particularly interesting, however, since it would be the basis for the eventual White counterrevolution. The autocracy had been

10

so strong that the army officer corps had historically played a small political role. The army's last political action had been an attempted junior officers' coup in 1825, the Decembrist Uprising. But there were other short-term reasons for the army's political impotence. The old regular army had been destroyed in battle in 1914–1915 and then flooded with new recruits and wartime officers. Only one officer in ten was a regular in 1917, and the corporate sense of the officer corps was gone. Then came the revolution. Committee control of units, condoned by the Provisional Government, corroded the army's ability to fight or to keep internal order. The June 1917 offensive failed disastrously, and with it the gamble that active combat would restore discipline. At the end of August 1917 General Kornilov, the army Supreme Commander-in-Chief, ordered troops to move on Petrograd. Whether Kornilov was trying to curb the power of the soviets or to replace Kerensky's Provisional Government with a military dictatorship is not clear. In any event the Kornilov affair was a catastrophe for both the generals and Kerensky. The advancing troops were easily stopped by soviet agitators; Kornilov was arrested; the army command lost whatever cohesion had survived the February Revolution. Prime Minister Kerensky, a lawyer by profession, became Supreme Commander-in-Chief, but with no support from senior officers, who felt he had betrayed Kornilov. Simultaneously the Bolsheviks accused Kerensky of having plotted with Kornilov, and eight weeks later they raised—with decisive success— the specter of another military coup, this time against the Second Congress of Soviets. So at the critical moment of the October uprising the Bolshevik-dominated Military-Revolutionary Committee controlled the Petrograd garrison, whose units either maintained neutrality or actively backed the rebels.

The army's disintegration sped up after October. With the decapitation of the Provisional Government a young general named Dukhonin became the acting Supreme Commander-in-Chief. He existed in limbo, physically isolated at the Mogilev *Stavka* (General Headquarters), four hundred miles from Petrograd. Some of the moderate socialist leaders arrived, hoping to create a rival center of government, but they lacked the will to proceed, and Dukhonin lacked the real support to back them. On 20 November—twenty-six days after the uprising—trainloads of Red Guards and Baltic sailors finally reached the Stavka with the new Soviet-appointed Supreme Commander-in-Chief, a Bolshevik sub-altern named Krylenko. Dukhonin presented himself at Krylenko's coach, where he was attacked by a mob and bayoneted to death. Krylenko had even less authority than Dukhonin or Kerensky; by mid-November no one controlled the army. Southwestern and Rumanian

11

Army Groups now ignored the Stavka; Northern and Western Army Groups, while more loyal to the Soviet cause, broke up all the more rapidly. In mid-December the Soviet government passed a law on elected commanders and on the end of ranks; it also put forward a phased demobilization.

Ten miles south of Mogilev were the monastery prison of Bykhov and the generals who had acted in August 1917: Kornilov, Lukomsky, Denikin, Markov, and others. They saw that central Russia held no hope for them. The day before Krylenko reached Mogilev they slipped away and set out on a 600-mile journey to the Don Cossack Region in southeast Russia. Counterrevolution was not dead. The Right would eventually mount the main challenge to Bolshevism. Nationalist army officers—and particularly the Bykhov prisoners—created the White armies. The church blessed them, and rightist politicians gave them their main political personnel. But that would only be from the *end* of 1918 until 1920. In 1917, in the supercharged democratic atmosphere of the times, all these forces were helpless.

The liberals *should* have had a better chance against Bolshevism than the conservatives; they believed in parliamentarism, and the February Revolution catapulted them into power. In reality, however, a feature of the revolution—and of the Civil War that followed—was the impotence of the center parties. In the Assembly elections the main center group, the Constitutional Democrats (Kadets), got less than five percent of the vote. Liberalism began with great handicaps. The middle class was small, perhaps six million in all. The first Russian parliament was created only twelve years before the Revolution. After the 1905 Revolution the autocracy began to grasp back its power. The liberals responded with great caution (to save what had been granted) and with an attempt to find some common ground with the government; as a result they did not establish themselves as a popular opposition. February 1917, and power, only served to discredit the centrists. The dominant faction of the Kadets rejected comprehensive social reform and gave priority to the war and to law and order. Although they saw themselves as the natural ruling elite, the liberals lacked administrative experience and any real base in local government (they could not take part in the soviets). By the winter of 1917–1918 the Kadets were identified in the popular mind with reaction—and at the same time they were hated by the reactionaries, who saw them as disloyal to the Tsar and responsible for the sorry condition of the country.

The Right and Center were often lumped together as the *tsenzovoe obshchestvo* ("census society"), the propertied classes. Opposed to them was the broad spectrum of the self-styled *revoliutsionnaia demokratiia* ("revolutionary democracy"). In the first half of 1917 the *demokratiia* dominated the soviets from top to bottom, and shared power with the liberals in the coalition Provisional Governments. Russian public opinion was socialist; socialists of one kind or another won, as we have seen, 80–90 percent of the Constituent Assembly vote. Nevertheless, the united "revolutionary democracy" was another loser in October, when political mastery passed to a minority socialist group, Lenin's Bolsheviks.

The Mensheviks can be dismissed quickly. As orthodox Marxists they needed a proper "bourgeois" revolution before the socialist revolution. This led them first to support the Provisional Government, and then to form a coalition with the liberals. By October they had lost an early leading role in the local soviets and were deeply divided. Their following was small; the Assembly elections gave them a disastrous result of under three percent. A new leftist Menshevik leadership emerged in the autumn—too late to make good the loss of support. After October the Mensheviks did little; they would neither oppose a "workers' " government nor join an anti-Bolshevik coalition.

Much more remarkable was the failure of the Socialist–Revolutionary (SR) Party, the heart of the *demokratiia*. If any group had a "right" to rule Russia it was the SRs: logically because they were *the* peasant party in a peasant country, a party with a tradition dating back to the Populists of the 1860s; and legally because they won the elections to the Constituent Assembly. And yet they failed. In part this was because the SR Party was such a *good* reflection of Russian reality. The SR electorate was the Russian peasantry, and political power was decided by the urban minority. Numbers could not be translated into power. It is not enough to say that peasants are bound to lose, or to argue—with the Marxists— that the "petty bourgeois" peasant class were doomed to play a subsidiary part. The SR failure was a failure too of leadership. Their historian, Radkey, laid the blame ultimately on the intellectuals who led the party. The ri_ght wing replaced the revolutionary passion of 1905 with a passion for national defense. The Center wanted to avoid a split with the party Right, and at the same time came under the powerful influence of Kadet professors and Menshevik theorists. The more radical wing was unable to push through its policy of rapid social reform. The SRs joined the Provisional Government coalition in May 1917 and became identified with it; Kerensky, prime minister from July, was closer to them than any other party. Constantly outbid by the Bolsheviks, the SR Party lost its influence among workers and soldiers.

When the October Revolution came, the SRs mounted no effective challenge. They relied on the powerless Constituent Assembly to give them power, and they lacked armed support. The SRs' growing loss of confidence in their Provisional Government coalition partners led them to form a "Committee for the Salvation of the Revolution" on their own. But it would take five months of disastrous Bolshevik economic and foreign policy failures, plus outside support from the Czechoslovak Corps, before the SRs created their counter-government. From the late autumn of 1917 the SRs' problems were made worse by splits in their ranks. The leadership was politically cut off from many of its members in the crucial towns and garrisons of central Russia, who had become as radical as the Bolsheviks. The (November) All-Russian Congress of Peasants' Soviets was no alternative to the Bolshevik-dominated (October) Second Congress of Workers' and Soldiers' Soviets; it was marked mainly by factional fighting among the SRs. The party split, when it came in November, helped Bolshevik hegemony. The splitters, the "Left SRs," had the combination of a mass following and a radical policy but lacked the experience to use it. Far from being a challenge, the Left SRs supported the Bolsheviks and in December became the junior partners in a left-socialist coalition.

The real end of the *demokratiia* was the meeting of the Constituent Assembly. The Assembly was a key event—the climax of SR efforts in 1917 and the symbol they would rally around in 1918. As we know, the Bolsheviks closed it after one night's sitting (5–6 January), but the closure was a *symptom* of SR weakness, not a *cause*. The SR Party lacked the local following to physically defend the Assembly building (Petrograd's Tauride Palace) and there was no support from the rest of Russia. Radkey argues convincingly that the rump SR Party lacked a working majority: they had lost the Left SR delegates, and the Ukrainian SRs did not attend; even without Lenin the Assembly "would have fallen of its own weight."[5] I would add that even if the SRs had protected the Tauride Palace, even if they had used their simple majority in the Assembly, they could not have had their will fulfilled across the country. The key instruments of local power, the urban soviets, were mostly hostile to them.

The Constituent Assembly was the last of the great illusions of 1917, and with its closure began the cold dark year of 1918. The Bolsheviks began the Civil War in October 1917; ten weeks later, by January 1918, they had achieved something of decisive importance for that war's eventual outcome. They had won control over the Russian heartland, a vast base from which they would never be driven.

14

There is an interesting historical parallel between central Russia in 1917–1918 and Germany in 1918–1919. Germany, despite the end of the monarchy, mutinies, local soviets (*Räte*), and the Berlin Spartacist revolt, had no civil war; the extreme Left never came near to power. This was no accident. The elections to the Russian and German Constituent Assemblies showed that public opinion was more socialist in Russia, and the radical element stronger. (The German version of the Constituent Assembly was also not delayed; it was elected and convened within thirteen weeks of the revolution.) There were similarities: the Right and Center-Right were weak (about five percent of the vote in Russia, 15 percent in Germany); the main moderate socialist party (the SRs and the German "Majority" Social Democrats) won the largest share of the vote, but not an absolute majority (40 and 38 percent). But in Germany there was much more of a political Center and Center-Left, including the church-based Center Party; as a result the coalition led by the moderate socialists had a working majority of 76 percent. In Russia a radical Marxist party won 24 percent (as compared to eight percent for Germany's "Independent" Social Democrats); the local nationalists who took 20 percent of the "Russian" vote would not contribute to a working coalition. The assembly vote reflected the greater problems facing the Russians. Social differentiation was sharper, people feared for their very survival, the peasantry could not serve as a stabilizing force, and the issue of war and peace had not been resolved. The state and the army, moreover, had collapsed in Russia, while the Center-Left "Weimar" coalition in Germany was able to use these elements to impose its will.

The Russian Bolsheviks, with a popular program and a skeleton structure provided by the soviets, were able to take power without great difficulty. But it remained to be seen how *they* would solve the problems that the Provisional Government could not solve. Meanwhile, the Civil War was extended to the periphery of the Empire.

2

THE RAILWAY WAR:
SPREADING THE REVOLUTION,
November 1917–March 1918

There remain only the *peoples of Russia*, who have suffered and are suffering under arbitrary oppression, whose emancipation must be begun at once, and whose liberation must be carried out resolutely and with finality.

Declaration of Rights of the Peoples of Russia, 2 November 1917

The Great Russian Periphery

In October 1917 the revolutionary Russian Empire was the largest country on the earth's surface, stretching five thousand miles from the western trenches to the Pacific coast. In the sixteen weeks between the October Revolution and a renewed German-Austrian offensive (in mid-February 1918), Soviet power triumphed not just in the core territories of northern European Russia and in the Urals but right across the vast land mass.

Many of the people on the Imperial periphery were of Great Russian nationality. For them events often unfolded much as in the Great Russian center, but delayed a little by the vast distances involved. The North and Siberia made up the largest area, and they were alike in many ways. The population was very widely scattered and nearly wholly rural; because there were no large estates rural tension was not high. The towns were mostly small and isolated; the few workers were employed in the railways or the docks, and the army garrisons were small. In the North the port of Arkhangelsk (750 miles from Petrograd)

16

eventually declared for Soviet power, but only in February 1918. The Constituent Assembly vote in Arkhangelsk's province had gone heavily for the SRs (63 percent, against 22 percent for the Bolsheviks). But the province capital had given its votes to the Bolsheviks, and that was where political power lay. Armed support from the center was not needed. The Allied ships docked in the Arkhangelsk harbor made—as yet—no difference. The pattern was repeated in Siberia. The town of Krasnoiarsk came under Soviet control as early as 29 October, Irkutsk and Vladivostok followed in November, and Tomsk and Khabarovsk in December. By February Soviet power was victorious in the last remaining link, between Lake Baikal and Vladivostok. The only serious fighting was in Irkutsk. The SRs won their highest percentage of votes in Siberia, but the Bolsheviks had captured the urban voters. The minorities—the Iakuts and Buriats were the largest group—lived in scattered settlements; they showed little interest in politics or nationalism. Even among the dominant Great Russian part of the population there was no powerful sense of particularness. The "regionalists" (oblastniki) were poorly organized in 1917 (they had no Assembly candidates).

Not all of the periphery was so easily won for Soviet power. It was here that the so-called "eshelonaia war," war by railway train (eshelon), came in. In the "railway war" trainloads of revolutionaries became a deciding factor, traveling long distances from the industrial cities to put down centers of opposition in the periphery; the most important of these centers were in the (Great Russian) cossack lands and in the (nationalist) Ukraine.

The cossacks (kazaki) were one exception to the rapid and unopposed spread of Soviet control over the Great Russian parts of the empire; they were to be a crucial element in the Civil War as a whole. The cossacks numbered 4.5 million people, and their men were professional warriors; 300,000 fought in the World War.[1] Cossack military units were less vulnerable to revolutionary disruption than others, due to their sense of apartness, their internal cohesion (with cossack officers), and their traditional service loyalty. Their thirteen "host regions" (voiska) had been sited to guard the borders of the Empire, so they were far from the revolutionary urban centers. Within these lands, self-government and privileges made the cossack a conservative force.

The small hosts in Siberia caused no immediate worry to the Petrograd government. Farther west, however, where Siberia, European Russia, and Central Asia meet, the Orenburg Host became one of a handful of anti-Soviet centers. Ataman (chieftain) Dutov declared his

17

opposition to the Bolshevik government, overthrew the Orenburg town soviet, and began to spread his authority. The "Dutovshchina" was opposed by the local non-cossack population, but the main enemy were detachments of revolutionary workers sent from faraway pro-Soviet areas as part of the "Railway War." There were detachments from Central Asia, the Urals, and Saratov, and even a Northern Flying Column of soldiers and sailors who traveled 1100 miles from Petrograd. Coordinating operations was an Extraordinary Commissar of the Soviet government. Dutov could not match all this. Only the older cossacks, the *stariki*, were prepared to fight for him; the younger men, coming home from the front (the *frontoviki*) wanted peace and quiet, and adopted a policy of *neitralitet* (neutrality); a few had even been radicalized. Orenburg was taken on 31 January 1918. Dutov's few active supporters were pushed back to the remote southern Urals and then, in April, into the emptiness of the Kirgiz steppe.

The cossacks of southeastern European Russia—the Don, Kuban, and Terek Hosts—were even more prominent in the first winter. The Don, in particular, was for fifteen weeks *the* center of resistance to Soviet rule. The Don cossacks' figurehead was Ataman Kaledin, a much more experienced man than Dutov; a fighting general, Kaledin had commanded a Tsarist army. On the day of the October Revolution he assumed power in the Don region—pending the Provisional Government's re-establishment of order. The Don Cossack Host had great potential strengths. From May 1918 to January 1920 it proved capable not only of defending itself but also of driving north into non-cossack "Soviet" territory.

In the last months of 1917, however, Kaledin found it impossible to rally effective forces. One underlying problem was that the cossacks were not a majority in the Don Region. Many non-cossack peasants—*inogorodnie* ("outsiders")—had arrived in the last half century; they were poorer and less privileged than the cossacks, and had to rent land from them. In the Assembly elections 45 percent of the Don Region votes were for the cossack list, but 34 percent were for the SRs and 15 percent were for the Bolsheviks; there were some industrial towns, and 38 percent of the Rostov (town) vote was Bolshevik. Ataman Kaledin attempted only as a last resort (in early January) to broaden his political base by forming a "United Host Government" including the *inogorodnie*. But more important as a source of weakness was the inactivity of the cossacks themselves. In part this came from the newness of Soviet power; in 1918–1919 there would be the most bitter hatred towards the Bolshevik regime to the north, but at the end of 1917 few cossacks wanted armed struggle, especially against the rest of Russia and in the name of Kerensky. The returning *frontoviki* had no stomach for more fighting, and some hoped for a Don revolution. Kaledin could not raise anything except small detachments to fight along the railways.

Some 950 miles to the northwest, the Petrograd revolutionary government quickly focused on the Don as its most serious threat. The cossacks were old enemies of the revolution, and leading counterrevolutionaries were known to be rallying behind Kaledin. The Don Host, with a cossack population of 1,460,000, occupied a territory larger than England and Wales, and thrusting deep into European Russia. This territory was within striking distance of the mines and factories of the Donets River Basin (Donbas) and the eastern Ukraine. The Don towns of Rostov and Novocherkassk blocked the main rail line to the Caucasus.

The campaign to cope with this danger was the first one fought by Soviet forces. In late November detachments began to leave central Russia for the Don. In December no less a person than Vladimir Antonov-Ovseenko, then Sovnarkom's "People's Commissar for War" (War Minister), was given operational command. Antonov was already famous as a leader of the October uprising, the man who arrested the Provisional Government in the Winter Palace; now, as "Main Commander-in-Chief for the Struggle with Counter-Revolution in South Russia," he had to master not just streets and corridors but a theater of operations the size of France, mounting a vast campaign along the southern railways. To the south of the Don were revolutionized troops returning from the Caucasus front; to the west were detachments of workers and miners from the Donbas; to the east was the revolutionary town of Tsaritsyn. Petrograd added trainloads of reinforcements. There was much confusion. The Red Army did not formally exist. Many of the commanders were not Bolsheviks. Antonov, though a Marxist, had only joined the Bolshevik faction in mid-1917. His chief of staff, Lieutenant Colonel Muraviev, was an SR (who would betray the Bolsheviks in 1918), as were two of his commanders, Lieutenant Colonel Egorov (the future Stalinist Marshal) and Ensign (*praporshchik*) Sablin.

Progress was slow, and as the fighting went back and forth between key junctions there were frequent pauses for negotiation. Key decisions were made at mass meetings—continuing the 1917 tradition of *mitingovanie*. Some mutinous detachments had to be disbanded. Others were diverted to cope with a "war" in the Ukraine. The cossacks, however, were no better organized. An open split appeared in early January,, when revolutionary *frontoviki* set up a Don Military-Revolutionary Committee under Podtelkov, an SR subaltern. Antonov's forces pressed in from all directions. Rostov fell on 23 February, and Novocherkassk—

the cossack capital—on the 25th. The few loyalists fled into the Sal steppe. Kaledin had shot himself through the heart two weeks before, despairing at his beloved cossacks' disloyalty. His successor was executed. A Don Soviet Republic was set up in March, with Podtelkov as head of its Sovnarkom. (The republic only survived until early May when, with the help of the German-Austrian advance, the loyalists rode back; then it was Podtelkov's turn to hang.)

The Kuban Cossack Host was nearly the same size (1,340,000) as the Don Host, but more of a backwater. There was no counterrevolutionary figurehead, no Dutov or Kaledin to attract Petrograd's wrath, and indeed a form of "dual power" came to exist. The Kuban, bordered on the north by the Don Region and on the south by the Caucasus mountains, was protected against Red detachments. But the cossacks were a minority (46 percent), many *frontoviki* had been radicalized, and the *inogorodnie* wanted more power. On 13 March 1918 the cossack leaders and some supporters had to flee the Kuban capital, Ekaterinodar (now Krasnodar), and the last major cossack stronghold went over to Soviet power. (To the southeast a Terek Soviet Republic had been declared in the Terek Host on 3 March; there the weakness of the loyalist cossacks was complicated by struggle with the local minorities.)

It was clear by the beginning of 1918 that the cossacks were not going to be a center of resistance to the "triumphal march of soviet power." The previous November, however, the cossack lands had seemed to conservatives to be the one patch of firm ground in the swamp of revolutionary Russia. In early November, when fighting had just ended on Petrograd's outskirts, General Mikhail Alekseev arrived in Novocherkassk, the Don capital, to organize a counterrevolutionary base. Alekseev had been de facto commander of the Russian armies since 1915 (as Nicholas II's chief of staff); he was nationally known, acceptable to a wide political spectrum, and respected by the Allied missions. The "Alekseev Organization" was joined within a month by the senior officers arrested after General Kornilov's August "action"; they had made their way incognito across the Russian turmoil from the Bykhov prison. Kornilov himself was the best known, a charismatic war hero of humble origins who had actively opposed the Left in 1917 and become the darling of the Right. After some friction Kornilov became military commander and Alekseev the political chief.

A few "eaglets," young officers not demoralized by defeat and revolution, broke through to join the generals on the Don, and the nucleus of an armed force was created. The men of the Volunteer Army—as the Alekseev Organization became—saw themselves as patriots reacting to national humiliation and the October Revolution. As General Denikin—a founder of the Volunteer Army and Kornilov's successor—put it:

> If at that tragic moment of our history there had not been among the Russian people individuals ready to rise up against the madness and crime of Bolshevik power and to offer their blood and lives for the motherland which was being destroyed—then it would have been not a people, but dung for fertilizing the boundless fields of an old continent which were doomed to colonization by strangers from West and East.
> Fortunately we belong to the tortured but great *Russian people*.

But twelve weeks in Rostov and Novocherkassk produced little in the way of an anti-Bolshevik movement. A few politicians arrived, and Russian business circles and the Allies gave moral support and some cash, but none of this had real impact. In the end what counted was the collapse of the Don Host. On 24 February 1918, the day before Rostov fell to the Soviet railway detachments, Kornilov led the Volunteer "Army," still only four thousand strong, out into the frozen steppe. "We went," Denikin recalled, "from the dark night and spiritual slavery to unknown wandering—in search of the bluebird."[2] The bluebird, the fairytale symbol of hope, summed up the fantastic quality of the venture. This was the most important little band in the Civil War, for it would grow into an army of 100,000 combat troops, the force that came closest to defeating the Bolsheviks.

The "Ice March" lasted from late February to mid-May 1918. It was perhaps *the* epic of the Civil War, a march through cruel empty steppe in midwinter; the survivors would eventually be awarded a medal in the form of a crown of thorns pierced by a sword. The Volunteers first went south in the hope of finding a new base in the Kuban. Stronger Bolshevik detachments chased them. Railways and settlements had to be avoided. The greatest shock came after seven weeks of wandering, when the Volunteers tried to take Ekaterinodar, now the capital of the Kuban Soviet Republic. The attack began on 10 April and was fiercely resisted. Disaster struck early on the morning of the 13th, when Soviet artillery made a lucky hit on Kornilov's farmhouse headquarters. Kornilov, the symbol of the counterrevolutionary cause, was killed. Denikin took over command, called off the siege, and pulled the Volunteers back into the steppe. Kornilov, in death, could not escape; the jubilant Reds dug up his body and dragged it to the main square before burning it on a rubbish dump.

The anti-Bolsheviks had failed in Petrograd, in the central provinces, and now even here on the edge of civilized Russia. Kornilov's death was a great victory, Lenin told the Moscow Soviet (ten days after the event): "It can be said with certainty that, in the main, the civil war has ended." There might be skirmishes, "but there is no doubt that on the internal front reaction has been irretrievably smashed by the efforts of the insurgent people." "We are leaving for the steppe," General Alekseev had written in January. "We will be able to return only with God's mercy. But a lamp must be lit, so that there will be at least one spot of light in the darkness that has covered Russia."[3] Now the light had been snuffed out.

National Integration

The spread of Soviet power into the borderlands also affected large numbers of people who were not Great Russians. The ethnic minorities were a significant factor in the Civil War; this is not surprising given that they made up half the total population. Of 160 million people in the unoccupied provinces in 1917 only about 78 million were Great Russians (this figure and the ones below must be taken as approximations).[4]

The Empire's minorities were widely varied. Two of the most important were the Ukrainians and the Belorussians, numbering in 1917 about 32 million and five million, respectively. Like the Great Russians they were Slavs, and the three peoples were similar in language, culture, and religion. Conquest and reconquest over a thousand years had, however, given each a distinct identity. Much of the territory inhabited by the Ukrainians and Belorussians was brought into the Muscovite state as it expanded to the west and south in the 1600s, the rest was taken in the following century. Earlier Muscovite expansion into the eastern part of what is now European Russia gained smaller numbers of non-Slav peoples. By 1917 these were scattered among the Russians and relatively assimilated; they included 2.5 million Volga Tatars, 2.5 million Mordvinians and other Finno-Ugric peoples, and a million each of Chuvash and Bashkirs,

The Russian Empire became even more diverse from the time of Peter I and Catherine II. Further expansion to the west and south between 1700 and 1815 brought in a number of peoples culturally very different from—and sometimes more advanced than—the Great Russians. In 1917 Russia's Baltic lands included 3 million Finns, a million Estonians, and .5 million Latvians. (A further .5 million Latvians, 1.5 million Lithuanians, as well as eight million "Russian" Poles, lived in western territory lost in 1914–1916.) The three million Jews and million ethnic Germans in 1917 also came from recent expansion. Toward the Black Sea, southern expansion in the eighteenth and nineteenth centuries added lands in which lived, by 1917, a million Rumanians (Moldavians) and (in the Transcaucasus) two million Georgians, 1.5 million Armenians, two million "Tatars" (Azerbaidzhanis), and a bewildering mix of smaller groups. Russia in Asia also had a mixed population. In Siberia the majority of people were Great Russian settlers, but scattered across the huge territory were small and backward groups, the most numerous being the (Mongolian) Buriats and Iakuts (together totaling .5 million). Central Asia, conquered only in the late nineteenth century, had by 1917 only a small Great Russian population. The "natives" included 4.5 million Kazakhs, four million Uzbeks, and a million Turkmens, all of whom shared the Moslem religion and Turkic languages; in addition there were a further million Moslem Tadzhiks.

The very diversity of peoples was an underlying reason for Great Russian predominance, either in its Tsarist or its Soviet form. The number of groups meant that nearly all were much smaller than the 78 million Great Russians. The *third largest* nationality (the Belorussians) numbered only five million, then there were five groups with between four and two million, and eight with between two and one million; *eighty* other groups were smaller still. Cultural and political backwardness also furthered Great Russian domination. The educational level of many minorities was low, and even the more developed were peasant nations. Few had any history of national independence, and the autocratic, centralized, and Great Russian–dominated Tsarist Empire had given no opportunity for them to form a political identity. Even some of the larger groups were widely scattered, and most were mixed in with other minorities; it was usually hard to define national territory, and the minorities often resented one another more than the Great Russians. Great Russians or "Russified" members of the minorities dominated the towns, the garrisons, and communications, and with this the administration and the economy.

Finally, the special situation of 1917 also helped the Petrograd/ Moscow Soviet central government keep control of the national regions. The Soviet program won some support in the minority regions because it acknowledged the right of self-determination. But other aspects of early government policy were more important still. Peace and social reform were as popular to the minorites as they were to the Great Russians. And on the other hand the Bolshevik government had no inhibitions about crushing "bourgeois nationalism"; for them it was not a serious force—the workers and peasants of the minorities would

23

naturally want to join hands with the Great Russian proletariat. The Bolsheviks' local supporters, often transplanted Great Russians, identified the revolution with Great Russia.

The advance of Soviet power was different in each area. Central Asia was an extreme case, where fewer than three million Russians dominated eleven million Moslems through control of the towns. The soviets were as popular in the "Russian" towns of Central Asia as they were in those of European Russia, and power was seized in Tashkent, the regional center, only seven days after Petrograd. In western Russia, on the other side of the Empire, the largest single group were the Belorussians, but they were mostly peasants with little national consciousness or organization. The region's population was mixed, the towns being dominated by Great Russians, Jews, or Poles. In Minsk Province, core of the future Belorussia, only 23 percent of the civilian Constituent Assembly votes went to nationalist parties, while an extraordinary 63 percent went to the Bolsheviks. The town of Minsk declared for Soviet power on the same day as Petrograd. The radicalized soldiers of Western Army Group (voting 67 percent Bolshevik) had an important effect.

Further north were the Baltic Provinces, where the Estonians and Latvians had had little chance to develop politically under the double curse of Russian officials and German landowners. Social tensions, wartime dislocation, and closeness to revolutionary centers combined to produce a population as much interested in the social struggle as the national one. In Estliand Province (the future Estonia) the Bolsheviks got 40 percent of the Assembly vote, compared to 32 percent for the nationalists. Lifliand Province (Livonia, later eastern Latvia) gave the highest Bolshevik share (72 percent) of any civilian electoral district; the nationalist vote was 23 percent. The major towns in the Baltic had all declared for Soviet power by the first week of November. Northern Army Group, based in the Baltic, was also very radical.

Most of these non-Russian areas were won over with little direct pressure from outside. The Railway War, however, was important in the Ukraine, which posed the greatest potential challenge to the Soviet government. There were 32 million Ukrainians (by far the largest non-Russian ethnic group), and they had a clear majority in more than half a dozen provinces in south Russia. A separate authority, the Ukrainian-dominated Central *Rada* (Council), existed in Kiev (the main city). It took only six weeks for hostility between the Central Rada and the new Bolshevik government to come into the open. Petrograd sent an ultimatum to the Central Rada on 4 December 1917, and followed it with an invasion. The ultimatum spelled out the grievances: moving Ukrainian troops, disarming Soviet forces, and not cooperating against the "Kadet-Kaledin revolt" on the Don. There were deeper causes, too. Soviet Russia would have had great trouble surviving without control over Ukrainian grain and raw materials. Bolshevik internationalists believed that the Rada was basically artificial, or at best founded on the politically "backward" Ukrainian peasantry. And from the Bolshevik point of view there was no middle ground between support and opposition; the Ukrainians' desire to follow their own course put them in the enemy camp.

In Kiev the Rada's fate hung in the balance. Its program was popular enough; it was dominated by Ukrainian SRs and SDs (Marxists); the Ukrainian People's Republic, which it set up, accepted the gains of the 1917 social revolution and wanted an end to the war. Political development, when it really began in 1917, had been rapid. In the "Ukrainian" provinces (the eight for which Assembly returns are available) national minority parties, mostly Ukrainian, won 62 percent of the vote, as against 11 percent for the Bolsheviks. But the Ukrainians were mainly peasants, and it was hard to bring peasants into active support for the new and abstract notion of Ukrainian nationalism. South Russia also had a large non-Ukrainian minority, and this minority was strategically placed. In the eastern Ukraine the workers in the new industrial centers were mostly Great Russians, and in the west, too, even in Kiev, the city people were mostly Great Russians and Jews. In 1917 there was the additional element of the Great Russian soldiers of the Southwestern and Rumanian Army Groups. Ukrainian administrative and political experience was very limited.There had been no separate political entity in south Russia since the 1700s. Ukrainian political parties dated only from the 1900s, and even in the Duma period made little mark. The Central Rada, which appeared in Kiev in March 1917, remained a shadow government with no institutional base, despite long arguments with the Provisional Government. (These arguments led it to do nothing to help the Kerensky government in October.)

Lacking traditions and institutions, the Rada could not impose its will. "We were like the gods . . .," recalled Vinnichenko, the head of the Rada, "attempting to create from nothing a whole new world."[5] In any event, the Rada did not even declare full independence until its Fourth Universal of 11 January 1918. Nationalist soldiers had been among the Rada's strongest supporters, and civilians had formed bands of armed volunteers, but neither source gave mobile and effective troops for the Rada; the Ukrainian detachments, known as *Haydamaki* (*Gaidamaki*) after eighteenth-century cossack freebooters, were of little use. There could be no help from outside. The Allied missions, frantic to keep the Eastern Front active, were prepared to offer the Ukraine a measure of recognition, but they had little to give in the way of resources.

The Soviet side, too, lacked strength in the Ukraine. An all-Ukrainian congress of soviets, a Left alternative to the Rada, met in Kiev at the time of Petrograd's December ultimatum. Unlike the October all-Russian soviet congress in Petrograd, the local Bolsheviks were out-numbered. They were forced to move 250 miles east to the friendlier climate of Kharkov, where they formed a "Ukrainian Republic of Soviets." Even in the eastern Ukraine, however, they only controlled a few Great Russian–dominated towns. (Kharkov *Province* gave only ten percent of its Assembly vote to the Bolsheviks.)

In the end it was armed detachments, organized in the Great Russian north and diverted from Antonov-Ovseenko's railway war against the cossack counterrevolution, which were decisive. Several thousand men under Lieutenant Colonel Muraviev made up the main group. Muraviev, an SR, had led the defense of Soviet Petrograd in October. Six months later he would be gunned down after attempting a grand mutiny against Bolshevik power on the Volga, but in January 1918 he made an effective if ferocious commander. Muraviev's advance was slowed more by damaged railway lines than by *haydamak* resistance. The towns en route declared for Soviet power. In Kiev itself Russian workers in the Arsenal plant rose in revolt, only to be put down by the Rada. (Dovzhenko made a classic film about this in the 1920s.) Then Muraviev arrived, bombarding Kiev from across the Dnepr River for several days.

On the night of 26 January the last Rada forces slipped away, and on the following day the Reds took control. The battle for the city and Muraviev's subsequent reign of terror against officers and nationalists was the bloodiest episode of the Civil War so far. Muraviev's Order No. 14 put the situation at its starkest: "Here is the power which we have brought from the far north at the point of our bayonets."[6] A few thousand armed Russians had decided—at least for the moment—the fate of the Ukraine.

National Liberation

About five percent of the 1917 population *did* take decisive steps toward independence (before the February 1918 German–Austrian invasion). They were exceptions to the rule of nationalist failure. Tsarist expansion had usually been so successful that minorities were swallowed whole. The 1.5 million Rumanians (Moldavians) in the southwest were different: they could look across the border to an independent motherland. In January 1918 a Moldavian People's Republic was established in Bessarabia Province, where ethnic Rumanians made up the majority; Rumania, despite its wartime defeats, was able to send soldiers into Bessarabia in support. Petrograd held Rumania's ambassador hostage and seized her gold reserve, the Odessa Soviet Republic sent troops, but in April 1918 Bessarabia merged with Rumania, and stayed Rumanian until 1940.

In the case of the Transcaucasian minorities the crucial factors allowing secession were the distance from the Russian heartland, the small number of Great Russians (about five percent), and a relatively strong national identity. Effective local organizations existed in the form of the Georgian Mensheviks, the Armenian Dashnaks, and the "Tatar" (Azerbaidzhani) Musavat Party. The Assembly elections produced only a five percent Bolshevik vote, compared to a nationalist 58 percent and a remarkable Menshevik 30 percent. Local power passed to a Transcaucasian Commissariat in Tiflis (Tbilisi) in November 1917. This government was reluctant to quit Russia, partly from (Christian) Armenian and Georgian fears of what the Turks might do, but on 22 April 1918 an independent Transcaucasus Democratic Federative Republic was set up.

Unlike Bessarabia, Finland had no neighboring motherland, and unlike the Transcaucasus it was not remote from the Great Russian core; in Finland what counted was a more "modern" political and social tradition. Indeed, the struggle in the north is worth looking at in some detail because in a way Finland was the exception that proved the rule. Factors operated in Finland that did not operate in the more backward parts of the empire, and it was those factors that allowed the victory of conservative nationalists over the radical Left. "Modern" politics did not, however, rule out the most bitter struggle. In January 1918 the Left seized power in the main towns. Lenin, late that month, was confident: "In Finland the victory of the Finnish workers' government is rapidly being consolidated, and the forces of the counterrevolutionary White Guard have been pushed back to the north, the workers' victory over them is certain." In reality the defeat of the Finnish workers was only three months away. Over 30,000 "Red Finns" and "White Finns" would die[7]—a great number in a population of 3,400,000. (This includes 12,000

27

who died from neglect in White-run concentration camps; of the rest, more were executed than killed on the battlefield.)

Of all the areas still under "Russian" control at the start of 1917 (this leaves out German-held Poland), Finland was most distinct. Finland was taken from Sweden only in 1809. Few Russians moved in, and there was wide autonomy in the nineteenth century. Attempted Russification after 1899 provoked active resistance, and in Helsinki the February Revolution led more quickly than in other parts of "Free Russia" to demands for the loosest ties. Finnish politics were more like those of Western Europe than those of Russia. A Finnish Parliament (Diet) had existed long before 1917 (the only example of regional self-government in the Russian Empire, albeit within narrow limits). The October 1917 elections gave more than half the seats in the Parliament to non-socialists. Most Finns saw the Parliament as the center of political life; the Red Finns overthrew the Parliament in January 1918, and the White Finns gained much support by acting in its name.

The Finnish parties were different from those elsewhere in Russia. The political Center and Right had experience and wide support; fear of social disorder, the October Revolution in Petrograd, and the November general strike in Finland made them act together. And nationalism was a potent force in the Finnish "War of Liberation." The Russian Bolsheviks had no large following of their own in Finland, in contrast to other areas. The local Marxist organization, the *Sosialidemokraattisen* Party (SDP), was much larger in per capita terms than the Bolsheviks were in Russia, and the biggest single party in Finland. The leadership, however, were divided between advocates of the revolutionary and parliamentary roads, while the rank and file were pushed toward action by radicals of the Red Guard movement. The SDP failed to seize power in the general strike, and then dithered for two more months. (This despite Stalin coming out to quote Danton at them: "Audacity, audacity, and again audacity!")

Across Russia workers' militias and mutinous soldiers gave the October revolutionaries a great advantage in physical force. In Finland *both* sides created large armies: the Red Finns had as many as 140,000 and the Whites 80,000.[8] (In the spring of 1918 Moscow's whole Red Army numbered only 196,000). The conservatives had begun formation of their Home Guard in early 1917. In the following winter they were greatly helped by the secret return of 1200 young Finnish nationalists who had trained in Germany; the "Jägers" formed the shock force and training cadres of the White Army. The Whites were also fortunate in their commander: Carl Gustav Mannerheim, a Tsarist general, was a first-class military expert; he ignited the war in central Finland, mobilized and trained the bulk of the army, and led it to victory. The Reds had a larger army, but it was static, undisciplined, and poorly trained. Since the Finns had been exempt from conscription, there were no revolutionized "frontoviks" coming home to support the Red cause.

The action—or inaction—of the Russians was crucial. The Red Finns at first got arms and some military advice from the Russian garrisons, but these quickly withdrew and took no part in the fighting. And no trainloads of Red Guards, soldiers, and sailors arrived to help their Finnish comrades, although the distance from Petrograd to Helsinki was only a third of that even from Petrograd to Moscow. The eleven-week delay in the Red Finns' seizure of power was important; by mid-January the Bolshevik government was preoccupied with the Brest peace negotiations and the southern railway war. By the time of the critical battles of March–April 1918 the Bolsheviks had made peace with Germany (3 March) and had bound themselves to keep out of Finnish affairs. The White Finns, meanwhile, did get help from outside. German units landed on the south coast in early April, and it was they who actually took Helsinki (on 13 April). But the back of the Reds' army had already been broken when the White Finns took Tampere in central Finland on 6 April.[9]

Bessarabia, the Transcaucasus, and Finland were exceptions; by mid-February 1918 nearly all the enormous Empire was under Soviet control. The Ukrainian Rada; the Don, Kuban, and Orenburg cossacks; the Volunteer Army—all had been driven into a physical and political wilderness. "A wave of civil war swept all of Russia," Lenin said in early March 1918, "and everywhere we won victory with extraordinary ease." Trotsky poured scorn on his enemies: "a pitiful lot, without ideas, talent or strength, who are not dangerous, who have been everywhere defeated by improvised detachments of workers and sailors."[10] Trotsky was mainly talking about Russian counterrevolutionaries, but the nationalities, too, seemed—except for the Finns—a "miserable lot." If central Russia can be contrasted with Germany, the Empire as a whole can be compared with Austria–Hungary. There, within days of the final crisis beginning in Vienna, independent governments were in being under the Czechs in Prague, the Hungarians in Budapest, the Poles in Cracow, the Croats in Zagreb, and even the Ukrainians in Lvov. In Russia, even eight months after the February Revolution no nationality had tried to break away; three months after that—in February 1918—the Petrograd government still controlled nearly all the periphery.

Enthusiasm for the Soviet program was an important factor in winning over the population of the periphery—both the Great Russians and the minorities—just as it was in the center. But there were important differences between the two zones. The Constituent Assembly vote shows the Bolsheviks' limited support on the periphery, and the political potential of other forces. The continent-spanning march of Soviet power had been due in part to temporary factors, especially the confusion, the revolutionary garrisons, and the railway detachments from the central cities. And there was another difference: the central zone would stay under Soviet control throughout the Civil War, while the peripheral zone would be lost in 1918 and become the base of the anti-Bolshevik movement. The ease with which Soviet power was to be swept away in the borderlands was a sign of its weak foundations. But first of all a push from outside was needed.

3

THE OBSCENE PEACE:
SOVIET RUSSIA AND THE CENTRAL POWERS,
October 1917–November 1918

Unerhört! (Unheard of!)

General von Hoffmann, 28 January 1918

Germany, Austria-Hungary, Bulgaria and Turkey for the one part, and Russia for the other part, declare that the state of war between them has ceased. They are resolved to live henceforth in peace and amity with one another.

Peace of Brest-Litovsk, 3 March 1918

Brest-Litovsk

The famous Decree on Peace, proclaimed on the revolutionary night of 25 October, was a vital element in the success of the Bolsheviks' struggle for power. It was one thing, however, to promise peace, another to secure it. The Bolshevik government got no response from Russia's allies, and it found itself treating only with her enemies. From the start the Central Powers used their position of military strength; they chose the place for negotiations, the ruined fortress-town of Brest-Litovsk, deep behind German lines in occupied Poland. There, on 2 December, an armistice was signed between Russia and the Central Powers, but an actual peace treaty would need a further two and half months of confused negotiations and confrontation.

Once peace negotiations proper began, the Central Powers demanded that Russia give up Poland, Lithuania, and western Latvia, territory

31

already occupied by Germany in 1914–1916. These were harsh terms, but predictable given the Central Powers' military superiority, and better than those Soviet Russia would eventually have to sign. In early January 1918, however, the majority of the Bolshevik CC decided not to accept the enemy terms. The Brest negotiations were to be drawn out, but if they broke down, Russia would adopt a policy of "Neither War nor Peace," declaring a halt to the war but not concluding a formal peace. The Bolsheviks took this line despite their military inferiority and despite the desire of the mass of the Russian population, and especially the soldiers, for *any* end to the war's burden. The Bolsheviks were not a conventional government, trying to bargain their way to the least damaging peace terms. Bolshevik activists loathed giving up to "imperialism" *any* people or territory. And they believed that the Brest negotiations should be used not just to make peace; they assumed that the capitalist world was tottering on the brink of revolution, and they believed Russian defiance would rouse the oppressed masses of Europe to give the final push.

Leon Trotsky, the People's Commissar for Foreign Affairs (foreign minister), shared the utopian notions of his comrades; "What diplomatic work will we have?" he asked. "We will publish a few revolutionary proclamations to the peoples, and then shut up shop."[1] Trotsky was the leading advocate of the policy of "Neither War nor Peace," and it fell to him to try and put this policy into practice. Trotsky had made a name for himself with the Russian Left as the last chairman of the 1905 St. Petersburg soviet; he held the same post in 1917 and was among the leaders of the Bolsheviks' uprising. But it was his appearance at Brest-Litovsk that made him an international figure. He soon had the chance to use his powers of oratory in an extraordinary confrontation; on one side were the revolutionary socialists of Soviet Russia, on the other the diplomats and generals of the Central Powers. The climax for Trotsky came on 28 January when he announced that the trifling was over: Socialist Russia was declaring the end of the war. "*Unerhört* (Unheard of)!" General von Hoffmann, the representative of the German High Command, murmured to the stunned gathering.[2]

The Central Powers had the last laugh. On 18 February 1918, eight days after Trotsky's *coup de théâtre*, they resumed a state of war. (The confusion of dates comes from the change in the Russian calendar at this time; 31 January [old style] was followed by 14 February [new style], bringing Russia into line with the Western calendar.) The German attack rolled with little opposition across the now empty Russian trenches. Berlin presented greater demands: an end to Soviet control in the Ukraine, Finland, and all the Baltic provinces. In the

Bolshevik Party many, perhaps a majority, still opposed peace (and especially the harsher terms); the principles of the revolution were not easily given up. A faction of the younger Bolshevik leaders called the proposed terms "the obscene peace"; some even wanted "revolutionary war."

It was at this point, however, that Lenin intervened, and Brest-Litovsk was one of three or four central episodes that showed his political strength. He had always stressed the international dimension. When he demanded a political overturn in October 1917 he claimed Germany was close to revolution. But even in early January 1918 Lenin had urged that the initial German terms be accepted. He was already then less confident of revolution in the West; "Germany is only just pregnant with revolution and we have already given birth to a completely healthy child." It was also crucial that within Russia the fate of the revolution was unresolved and Bolshevik strength was still limited; "We must make sure of throttling the bourgeoisie, and for that we need both hands free." About the same time he wrote that "the peasant army, exhausted to the limit by war, will after the very first defeats [in a revolutionary war] . . . overthrow the socialist workers' government."[3] When the Soviet delaying tactics failed, when the Germans increased their demands and resumed their advance, Lenin threw his entire reputation into the debate. On 23 February, five days after the German offensive, he threatened to quit the CC and Sovnarkom if the final terms were not accepted. Given his prestige, given the support of senior leaders such as Zinoviev, Kamenev, and Stalin, and given the enemy's successes, Lenin had his way. A new Bolshevik delegation agreed to the February terms and signed the Peace of Brest-Litovsk on 3 March 1918; in a last futile gesture of revolutionary principle they refused to formally read the document.

The final terms of the Treaty of Brest-Litovsk were, from the Russian point of view, a combination of dismemberment and emasculation. The Bolsheviks accepted a vast amputation of territory—one unprecedented in great-power relations. Russia completely gave up Poland, Lithuania, and western Latvia. She agreed to make peace with the Ukrainian nationalists, in effect recognizing the Ukraine as an independent state. Russian forces were to be pulled out of Estonia, western Latvia, Finland, and the southern Transcaucasus, and the implication was that these territories could and would decide to break away from the Russian state; in fact they were to be occupied by the Central Powers' troops. Russia also had fully to demobilize her army and refrain from any agitation or propaganda; the first point had little practical effect, but the second seemed to rule out the revolutionary propaganda that the Bolsheviks considered so important.

In the eyes of the leadership—including Lenin—the acceptance of the Brest terms was only a temporary setback, dictated by weakness. But the future would show that the decision made by the Bolshevik leadership on 23 February 1918 had been a sea change. Revolutionary dreams had been abandoned for diplomatic reality. Although European revolution was a major Bolshevik objective in 1919 and 1920, the program had lost its original purity. Symbolic of the immediate defeat was the transfer of the capital to Moscow; Petrograd was now too exposed to attack. (Before October the Bolsheviks had pilloried Kerensky for wanting to give up the Baltic capital.) Lenin's famous arrival at Petrograd's Finland Station in April 1917 was now followed by its ignominious consequence, his departure during the night of 12 March from the Tsvetochnaia Ploshchadka, a freight depot in the southern outskirts of Petrograd, well out of the public eye. Protected by Latvian Riflemen, the only reliable troops the Bolsheviks had, Lenin and the government train left for the interior.

Revolutionary War

Strange as it may seem, while the Bolsheviks were negotiating with the Central Powers they had also been overseeing the destruction of the Russian army. They did this partly because they reflected the soldiers' desire to go home and partly because they held militarism in contempt. Ensign Krylenko's main tasks as Supreme Commander-in-Chief were democratization and demobilization. The final blow was Krylenko's demobilization of the whole army (announced on 29 January). It was the logical consequence of "Neither War nor Peace." General Bonch-Bruevich, Krylenko's "professional" chief of staff, was appalled at the flow of decrees that brought in elected commanders, ended all ranks, and sent home class after class; the army melted like snow before his eyes. But for the Bolsheviks, given the way they saw the world, the loss of the Imperial Russian Army did not much matter. Any invasion would be defeated by revolutionary outbreaks in the enemy's homelands and the internal decay of his armies. If any fighting was required it would be done by the Russian masses with minimal organization.

The test was the Germans' Operation *Faustschlag* (Thunderbolt), launched at noon on 18 February—after Trotsky walked out of the peace talks. The Germans quickly showed that they too were masters—on a grand scale—of *der Eisenbahnfeldzug* (Railway War). "It is the most comical war I have ever known," wrote General von Hoffmann. "We put a handful of infantrymen with machine guns and one gun onto a train and rush them off to the next station; they take it, make prisoners of the Bolsheviks, pick up a few more troops, and so on. This proceeding has, at any rate, the charm of novelty." The Germans pushed to a depth of 125 miles or more, along a front stretching from the Baltic to the Carpathians, during what Lenin called "The Eleven Days War."[4] (The main fighting actually lasted fourteen days, but the Soviet delegation arrived at Brest to sue for peace on the eleventh day.)

The key Dvinsk junction was taken on the very first day of *Faustschlag*. Within six days the Germans were as far east as Pskov; on 4 March (after Brest) they secured, at Narva, the other anchor of the natural defenses between Estonia and Russia. German troops now stood within 100 miles of Petrograd. Further south, in Belorussia, the invaders reached Minsk on 21 February, capturing the headquarters of Western Army Group. From Minsk another long bound gained the Dnepr River. Here, at Mogilev, the personnel of the revolutionary Stavka, the all-Russian army headquarters, saved themselves at the last minute by commandeering a train. The broad advance to the Dnepr also cut through the remains of Southwestern Army Group. Ukrainian railwaymen helped the Germans take Zhitomir on 24 February. Kiev, further east, was taken on 2 March; detachments loyal to the nationalist Rada had reached the city the day before.

The Bolshevik capitulation, the signing of the Brest treaty of 3 March, only ended the enemy advance on a line running down from Narva on the Baltic to the northern edge of the Ukraine. At Brest the Soviet central government gave up any right to intervene in south Russia, and the Central Powers marched on for 500 miles and several months to occupy and garrison the whole Ukraine—and some territory beyond. The depth of the German-Austrian push was partly explained by the weakness of local resistance. Authority in south Russia was splintered among four quasi-independent Soviet governments. The first, the Odessa Soviet Republic, quickly vanished; German and Austro-Hungarian troops took Odessa on 14 March and then went on to Nikolaev and Kherson. When the Germans approached the "Soviet Socialist Republic of the Tauride [Crimea]," in mid-April, the Crimean Tatars rose and killed the local Sovnarkom. The Sevastopol naval base was captured by the Germans on May Day, along with the Black Sea Fleet; some ships (including the dreadnought *Free Russia*) found a temporary refuge off the Kuban but were scuttled there in June.

The main fighting was farther north. The third government, the Ukrainian Socialist Soviet Republic, had only been installed in Kiev for a few weeks before it was driven out. Local mobilizations failed. All the fighting had to be done by Antonov-Ovseenko and the detachments that had beaten the Rada and the Don Cossacks. Lenin urged that these detachments be Ukrainianized and that their commander be referred to by the Ukrainian-sounding name of "Ovseenko." But the defenders had only about 10,000 mobile troops, and even popular commanders such as Muraviev, Sablin, and Sivers could do nothing against superior numbers of regular—if second-line—enemy troops. The Reds were forced back along the routes they had followed in January. Kharkov, the main city of the eastern Ukraine, fell on 8 April 1918. Farther east the Donets-Krivoi Rog Soviet Republic (the fourth government) in the Donbas refused to help the UkSSR, and then it in turn was overrun. The Red Guards from the local mines and factories put up some resistance before Lugansk was taken on 29 April. Then the defenders withdrew in one of those epic Civil War marches, 250 miles farther east across the hostile Don Cossack Region; they rallied at Tsaritsyn on the Volga, where they would later form the nucleus of the famous Red Tenth Army.

The Central Powers reached Rostov on 8 May. With this they completed the transformation of South Russia. The Ukraine had been cleared of Bolshevik detachments. In the Don Region the counter-revolutionary cossack leadership took over and established friendly relations with the Central Powers. The Kuban Region was for the moment still in Soviet hands, but its main railway link to the Soviet heartland had been cut.

The Eleven Days War and the Ukrainian campaign were demonstrations of Soviet impotence. They had a profound effect on the internal development of the Soviet state. For one thing, the fiasco led to the first steps to organize regular armed forces. Revolutionary War was an illusion. (The last flickers were the uprisings organized in the late summer by the Ukrainian Bolsheviks; they came to nothing.) Lenin had been right to mock the "cardboard swords" of the radicals. Now properly organized units of a new model Red Army were to be raised in the interior, while the "frontiers," facing the enemy-occupied Belorussia and Ukraine, were to be covered by detachments of the Western and Southern "Screens."

Brest was also a turning point in Soviet Russia's political life. Between January and March war and peace had led to open argument in the soviets and within the Bolshevik Party itself. Many Bolsheviks, perhaps a majority, had been opposed to making peace on German terms. After Brest was signed Lenin and Iakov Sverdlov (the best

36

political organizer in the party) used their skills at political manipulation to win ratification at the Seventh Party Congress and the Fourth
Congress of Soviets. Lenin prevented a split between idealists and
pragmatists that would surely have destroyed the Bolsheviks, and in the
process he secured his position as unrivaled leader. From then on
political debate was much more restrained. Never again would such a
major issue be fought out in public, never again would Lenin be so
deeply challenged. Indeed, five days after Brest the Seventh Party
Congress secretly resolved that a general tightening up was essential.
The party leadership recognized

> that the primary and fundamental task of our party, of the whole conscious
> proletarian vanguard, and of Soviet power, is the taking of the most energetic,
> ruthlessly decisive and Draconian measures to raise the self-discipline and
> discipline of the workers and peasants . . . for the creation everywhere of
> soundly co-ordinated mass organizations held together by a single iron will
> . . . and, lastly, to train systematically and comprehensively in military
> matters and military operations the entire adult population of both sexes.[5]

This was, in theory at least, the charter of the totalitarian state. It came
not with the fighting in the following summer against counterrevolutionary forces but as a direct consequence of failure in the Eleven Days
War.

Selbstbestimmung

Brest-Litovsk is normally seen as a ferocious *Diktat* that robbed Russia
of much territory and population and a large percentage of its farms and
factories. On paper, however, the terms were a triumph for what the
Germans called *Selbstbestimmung* (self-determination), the principle with
which they had supposedly begun the negotiations. No territory
peopled mainly by Great Russians was lost by the Russian (Bolshevik)
government. Finland, Estonia, Latvia, Lithuania, Poland, Belorussia,
and the Ukraine were freed from its control. It is true that had Germany
won the war most of these territories would probably have become
political and economic satellites of Berlin's *Mitteleuropa* system—but the
actual outcome would be something else again. Brest gave the border
territories a certain chance to develop, clear for the first time of Great
Russian (if not of foreign) influence.

In Finland self-determination was real. The conservatives did eventually invite a Hessian prince to rule the country, an ill-timed gesture in

the autumn of 1918, but their government was independent. The situation on the south shore of the Gulf of Finland was different. Events in Estliand, Lifliand, and Kurliand Provinces (Estonia and Latvia) were heavily influenced by the local Germans—ten percent of the population and the largest landowners; Berlin's intervention in February 1918 had come partly from a desire to protect "Baltic barons" arrested by the local Soviet governments. The most enthusiastic expansionists wanted to include the *Baltikum* in a Greater Reich. But even here nine months of relative stability gave a chance for national consolidation. The Germans also encouraged the formation of White Russian units, notably the Pskov-based Northern Army, which would be a significant force in the following year under General Iudenich.

Of all the areas affected, none was more important than the Ukraine. The Germans had had no long-range plans to absorb the region. Only the unexpected total collapse of Russian power made this conceivable; the negotiations and treaties between the Germans and the Ukrainian nationalist Rada were improvisations. The Austro-German garrison force of several tens of thousands of overage soldiers was not enough to secure effective control of the countryside, but it could ensure that the "government" in Kiev was one that would keep up the supply of raw materials to blockaded Central Europe and not challenge German hegemony. The socialist republic of the Rada was overthrown by a coup on 29 April. It was the Rada's second catastrophe in three months: first it had been overthrown by Bolshevik detachments from the north and the workers of the eastern Ukraine; now it was overthrown by the local conservatives with German approval. Although essentially it grew from a popular movement, the Rada did not have deep enough roots.

Power passed to General Pavel Skoropadsky, who took the archaic title of *Hetman* (Chieftain). He had a famous name—a Skoropadsky had been one of the last active Hetmans (in the eighteenth century)—and the general himself had in 1917 commanded one of the first "Ukrainianized" corps. Skoropadsky was a wealthy member of the imperial establishment. Most senior commanders looked down on the nationalists of "Little Russia"—as the Ukraine was known—as "separatists," *samostiyniki*. Skoropadsky himself said that he would rather be a samostiynik than a Bolshevik. But whatever Skoropadsky's motivation, the Hetmanate ultimately failed. The Rada's "Ukrainian People's Republic" had become the "Ukrainian State (*Derzhava*)," but Skoropadsky's regime was not able to found strong state institutions or even an effective army, and it lacked the popular appeal of the socialist Rada. Once German and Austrian protection ended in November 1918 the Hetmanate would be swept away. The regime that followed—

effectively the reborn Rada—would inherit little of use in holding off a second Bolshevik invasion in the winter of 1918–1919. On the other hand, Austro–German occupation was important because it also gave the Bolsheviks no chance to consolidate *their* hold over the region. As a result, chaos would reign in the Ukraine for thirteen months after the German defeat.

Moscow and Berlin

Brest-Litovsk, the central fact in Russia's foreign relations in 1918, was followed by some strange political events. Between January and March the issue of war or peace nearly tore the Bolshevik party apart, but in August a harsh Soviet-German Supplementary Treaty was signed without a murmur of discontent. Brest did lead to the formation of a Left Communist faction, but by the summer this had disappeared. There were various reasons why foreign policy ceased to be a major issue for the Bolsheviks. Political habits changed after the party crisis of February–March 1918 and after Lenin's reassertion of control. The Left lacked powerful leaders, especially after Nikolai Bukharin withdrew, and many of its economic demands (including greater nationalization) were put into practice during the summer. There was the fait accompli of enemy occupation, with the failure of revolutionary war and the European revolution. And the Bolsheviks, high and low, were preoccupied with civil war and economic crisis.

The other parties could not be as flexible as the Bolsheviks. A key political term of the time was "orientation" (*orientatsiia*). Russian and Ukrainian conservatives in the German-occupied Ukraine took a "German orientation", as did General Krasnov's Don Cossacks. In the Soviet zone a few individuals on the extreme Right were in contact with Berlin, but hardly enough to form an alternative administration. Most of the Right and Center-Right political groups operating underground in the Soviet zone took an "Allied orientation," as did the Kuban-based Volunteer Army. The Center-Left was also oriented toward the Allies. The (mainstream) Socialist-Revolutionaries had supported "revolutionary defensism" in 1917, and after October they were still against the Central Powers. The Mensheviks, too, were anti-German (although also anti-Allied, which widened the gap between the two moderate socialist parties). The only all-Russian party that really took the German orientation—if not openly—were the Bolsheviks. This had two import-

39

ant effects. First, it strengthened the Soviet government's position with the Germans. There was no alternative government to install in Moscow. "We do not have any friends worth mentioning in Russia," pointed out the German Foreign Minister in August 1918.[6] And second, the German orientation blocked Bolshevik agreement with the other socialists. The (mainstream) SRs in particular moved more and more into direct opposition; they looked for Allied support and even intervention; in turn their exclusion from Soviet political life was completed.

The separate peace made cooperation impossible even on the extreme left of Russian politics. This was shown in a spectacular way by the Left SRs. Generally sympathetic to the October Revolution, they had finally, in December 1917, agreed to work within the Bolshevik-dominated Sovnarkom. But Brest-Litovsk was for them a betrayal; at the Fourth Congress of Soviets (March 1918) they voted against ratification of the treaty, and their "ministers" quit the Sovnarkom. They remained active in the Central ExCom, the local soviets, the Red Army, and even the Cheka (Political Police), but from that time on their relations with the Bolsheviks worsened. They disagreed over agrarian policy and use of the death penalty, but most of all they were dismayed by the government's inaction as German and Austrian troops rolled across the Ukraine and consolidated their hold along the southern border.

The arrival in Moscow in late April 1918 of a German ambassador, Count Mirbach, presented a physical symbol of imperialist oppression. On the afternoon of 6 July two young Left SRs went to the German embassy in Moscow, used Cheka credentials to gain access to Mirbach, and murdered him. Great confusion followed. The Left SR leadership admitted that they had killed Mirbach, but only to force a change in the government's policy. They certainly hoped to influence the Fifth Congress of Soviets, which was in session in the Bolshoi Theater; the Fifth Congress formed a backdrop for the July Uprising, just as the Second Congress did for the October Revolution. Left SR detachments began to seize government buildings in what looked like a coup d'état. They claimed that they were forced to take wider action to protect themselves from Bolshevik reprisals *after* the assassination. In any event, everything came to depend on who held the streets of Moscow.

The Bolsheviks were caught by surprise. They had limited forces. A number of the government's armed detachments in Moscow—including some from the Cheka—supported the Left SRs. Dzerzhinsky, the head of the Cheka, was captured. The economy had gone into a much steeper decline after October 1917, and the Bolsheviks were no longer able to mobilize factory workers and Red Guards. The mutinous soldiers who had supported them in 1917 had gone home. Much of the surviving Moscow garrison was intended to reinforce the anti-German screens; unwilling to take part in "internal" fighting, these troops declared their neutrality.

The saviors of Soviet power in Moscow, and perhaps in the country as a whole, were the Latvian Riflemen. Regiments of Riflemen (*Strelki*) had formed during the world war, rare examples in the Tsarist army of "national" units. In 1917 the Latvian Riflemen showed extreme commitment to the Bolsheviks' revolution; they also kept military discipline and efficiency. The sources of this unique combination included the radical local tradition, German occupation of Latvian-populated districts, and insulation, by language, from the rest of the army. By the late spring of 1918 the Latvian Rifle Division consisted of 18,000 fighting men, a small enough number, but the ten regiments represented the largest concentration of armed strength in Soviet Russia. One Latvian regiment formed the Kremlin garrison, and elements of three others were stationed in Moscow. The division commander, Colonel Vatsetis, was summoned to a dark and empty Kremlin on the night of 6–7 July. "Comrade," asked Lenin, "can we hold out until morning?"[7] Fortunately the Left SRs failed to take the offensive when the Kremlin was lightly defended. By the morning of the 7th their chance was gone. Vatsetis had gathered his men. The end came at noon after heavy fighting in the Kitai-Gorod district. The Latvians moved up a 152 mm howitzer and fired it point-blank at the Left SR headquarters. The rebels scattered, and the building was taken. The Left SRs were broken as a party. They were now banned from the soviets, and with this began the one-party Soviet state. There was a parallel here with General Bonaparte and the Paris riots of 1795. The "whiff of grapeshot" that broke up the Left SR uprising also made Colonel Vatsetis's career; Lenin had found his "General Vendémiaire." Three days later Vatsetis was appointed commander of the new army group fighting on the Volga River; soon he would become the first Main Commander-in-Chief of the whole Red Army.

Of all the foreign governments that intervened in Russian affairs in 1917–1920, Germany (Austria-Hungary and Turkey were junior partners) had the best chance of destroying the Soviet regime. Of course, Russia is not easily conquered. The German army had only one hundred miles to go from Narva to Petrograd, but three hundred from Mogilev to Moscow. The occupation of the Bolshevik-controlled zone would have been a huge task: it was vast even after the loss in the summer of 1918 of the east and north to the Czechoslovaks and the

Allies. And from the late summer the Germans were preoccupied with the great Allied successes on other fronts. The Battle of Amiens on the Western Front—Ludendorff's "Black Day of the German Army" (8 August 1918)—was a decisive defeat; the collapse of the Balkan front in September marked the beginning of the final desperate months when the Central Powers had no troops to spare. (The Allies, then, would be the ultimate saviors of Soviet Russia.)

It was not Soviet powers of resistance that kept the Germans away. The Bolsheviks initially planned to survive a Central Powers attack by developing the Red Army (the Screens) and preparing a withdrawal into the depths of Eurasia. All this came to nothing in the summer, when the Czechoslovak rebellion overran western Siberia and the Urals, and the new Eastern Army Group swallowed up the few available Red Army units. In north Russia and the Far East, moreover, Soviet Russia was virtually at war with the Allies. Until at least August–September 1918 the strength of the Central Powers and the weakness of the Red Army would have assured the success of a narrow thrust against Moscow and Petrograd and, probably, the destruction of the Bolshevik central government. Moscow's best defense, then, was making concessions to Berlin.

In late August—three weeks after the German army's "Black Day"—Soviet Russia and Germany (only) signed a Supplementary Treaty. Moscow recognized the loss of Estliand, Lifliand, and Georgia and agreed to make large payments; the exchange of notes that accompanied the treaty gave details of cooperation against the Allies. (This was the Bolsheviks' first recourse to that secret diplomacy they had so violently attacked the year before.) The treaty reflected the new foreign policy adopted in February 1918. From general Europe-wide revolution, the Bolshevik government's immediate aim became one of saving the one country that had a radical socialist regime. Symbolic of the change was Trotsky's replacement as foreign commissar by G. V. Chicherin; the revolutionary firebrand was replaced by a former Menshevik and an aristocrat with experience of the Tsarist Foreign Ministry. But the skilfulness of the Soviet Foreign Commissariat, *Narkomindel*, should not be exaggerated. The Bolshevik government could not negotiate from strength, and it could not play its enemies off against one another. Soviet policy was appeasement.

Bolshevik appeasement was a factor in convincing Berlin not to smother the monster infant. In Germany both the foreign office and the army looked on the newborn Soviet regime as a monstrosity, but the dominant opinion was that it was one that would not live long enough to be a threat or to require a counterrevolutionary crusade. The Moscow government was despised, but its great appeal was precisely its weakness and unpopularity. When General Ludendorff suggested active operations against the Bolsheviks, the Foreign Ministry replied with the essence of Germany policy:

> What, after all, do we want from the East? The military paralysis of Russia. The Bolsheviks are doing a better and more thorough job of this than any other Russian party, and without our devoting a single man or one mark to the task. We cannot expect them or other Russians to love us for milking their country dry. Let us rather be content with Russia's impotence.[8]

Neither the assassination of Mirbach nor reactionary-minded German generals were able to shake this logic. The only serious plans for German action in Russia involved measures against Allied forces that had taken up position in north Russia after Brest, and such action would have helped the Soviet government rather than hurt it.

Moscow's rewards for appeasement were great. Most important, Germany never moved against the Soviet capital. Lenin actually got his "breathing space." Also, the Bolsheviks were able to concentrate on the Civil War. The crucial moment came in early August, when Moscow faced a most acute internal crisis after the fall of the Volga town of Kazan to the Czechoslovaks and anti-Bolshevik Russians. Lenin was able to order that the Red Army be moved from its screens on the western front to tip the balance in the east. Lenin, as he had hoped, had "both hands free" to throttle the internal enemy.

The military operations of the Central Powers from February to May 1918 were the most important foreign intervention in the Civil War. Hundreds of thousands of German, Austrian, and Turkish troops were involved; seventeen Russian provinces (as well as Poland) were occupied. Allied intervention in 1919 would be on comparatively tiny scale.

The Bolsheviks should not bear sole responsibility for this catastrophe. They reflected a general war-weariness that made a strong Russia impossible. And the rank-and-file Bolsheviks and many of their leaders were at least consistent with their principles; they believed in the myth of an imminent international revolution. But of all the political groups operating in Russia the Bolsheviks were, in two respects, most to blame. First, they consciously amplified Russian defeatism in 1917; they, and Lenin especially, must bear more responsibility than any other party for destroying the means with which Russia might have defended itself against foreign aggression. And second, their ideological preconceptions led them to make almost the worst peace possible— short of complete enemy occupation; the majority, between December

1917 and February 1918, rejected enemy terms that would have allowed Soviet control of much more of the old Empire. Lenin was right when he said that a much cheaper peace could have been bought.

The confrontation with the Central Powers marked, Lenin told the Seventh (March) Party Congress, a great turning point:

> From the continuous triumphal march of October, November, December [1917] on our internal front, against our counter-revolution . . . we had to pass to an encounter with real international imperialism. . . . From the period of the triumphal march it was necessary to pass to the period of an extraordinarily difficult and painful situation.[9]

At Brest the Soviet government gave up Finland, the Baltic provinces, Belorussia, and the Ukraine. As an indirect result of Brest it also, as we shall see, lost control of the Don, the Kuban, north Russia, the Urals, and Siberia. The Bolsheviks were not the only ones to gain a breathing space as a result of the separate peace with the Central Powers. National movements in the borderlands had a chance to consolidate. So did the counterrevolutionary Russian groups that had been overrun in the Bolsheviks' "Triumphal March." Furthermore, any broader socialist coalition that might have softened the problems of Soviet rule was made impossible. And by aligning Bolshevik Russia with the Central Powers, Brest led the Allies to establish military bridgeheads and to support anti-Bolshevik groups.

4

THE ALLIES IN RUSSIA,
October 1917–November 1918

It can be said with certainty that, in the main, the Civil War has ended.

Lenin, 23 April 1918

At first sight it might seem incomprehensible that some Czechoslovak Corps, which has wound up with us in Russia through the tortuous ways of the World War, should at the given moment prove to be almost the most important factor in deciding the questions of the Russian revolution. Nevertheless, that is the case.

Trotsky, 29 July 1918

Russia and the Allies

Common interest *might* have made the Allies and the Soviet government cooperate. Both Russia and France were being invaded by the Central Powers that spring. The Bolsheviks, however, had just made a revolution against "imperialism," and from top to bottom the new ruling party saw the Allies as hostile imperialists. Those most eager for revolutionary war against the Central Powers were least ready to take Allied aid. Bukharin, then leader of the Bolshevik Left, wept when the CC agreed—in principle only—to Allied help: "We are turning the party into a dung-heap." The dominant policy was Lenin's. His famous phrase about accepting "potatos and guns from the bandits of Anglo-French imperialism"[1] summed up his pragmatism, distrust, and contempt. Negotiation was possible to keep the Allies in contact (as a counter to Germany) but at arm's length. The main line of policy had to

45

be the appeasement of the Central Powers, who were clearly the greater threat—and a threat against which Soviet Russia (and the Allies) had no real power.

The bandits of Anglo-French imperialism, for their part, saw no reason to support a weak, repulsive, and transient regime. Bolshevik economic policy—rejection of foreign debts, nationalization of British and French-owned factories—was bound to cause tension, but far more important in the winter of 1917–1918 was the new Russian government's effort to get out of the World War. The first Allied reaction to the Bolshevik Revolution and the Decree on Peace had been to cast about for any group that might offer resistance to the Germans. In the early winter their agents gave support to Kaledin's Don Cossacks, Alekseev's Volunteer Army, the Ukrainian Rada, and to the Rumanian and Czechoslovak forces. ("Your Lloyd George," Trotsky hissed at a British diplomat, "is like a man playing roulette and scattering chips on every number."[2])

In early December (o.s.) Britain and France even divided Russia into areas of operations—Britain took the Caucasus, France took the Ukraine, the Crimea, and Bessarabia. Later, during the winter, the Allied ambassadors withdrew to Vologda (300 miles north of Moscow), leaving shadow representatives to talk to the unrecognized Soviet government. Some of these representatives tried to build links with the Bolsheviks, others conspired against them. When negotiations with the Soviets produced nothing for the war effort, Allied opinion hardened.

The Czechoslovaks

The Allies' policy might well have meant nothing in 1918 beyond the taking of a few remote ports. Bizarre circumstances gave them a weapon near the heart of Russia. The twenty-fifth of May 1918 was not, as is often argued, the starting point of the Civil War, but it was a key date. On that day fighting began in western Siberia between the Czechoslovak Corps and Soviet forces. Revolt flared along the powder trail of the Corps' scattered elements, stretching over 4900 miles of the Trans-Siberian Railway—from the Pacific to west of the Volga. Within two weeks the Czechoslovaks had taken several major towns and blocked the vital railway; within three months they had control of the whole Trans-Siberian, and with it two-thirds of Russia's land area. The regions they freed from Bolshevik control became key centers for

46

anti-Bolshevik movements: on the Volga for an SR government, and in Siberia for Kolchak's Whites.

The Corps had begun with some of the Czechs working in Russia in 1914. Their homeland was part of Austria-Hungary, but they decided to fight with the Russians—their "brother Slavs"—against the German-dominated empires. The force expanded with recruitment of Czech and Slovak POWs from the Austro-Hungarian army; in 1917 it reached corps strength—two divisions. When the end came for the old army in the autumn and winter of 1917–1918 the Czechoslovak Corps—based in the Ukraine—held together. Russia's revolution was not theirs, and a distinct culture cut them off from the general disintegration. For them, the world war seemed a struggle worth continuing, a route to national independence. Anyway, they could not just go home like the Russian soldiers, and they could not be caught in Allied uniforms by the advancing Central Powers. In March 1918 the Soviet government agreed to let the Corps, now numbering about 40,000 men, leave the country via the Trans-Siberian Railway.

Why, two months later, the Corps should have risen against Soviet power is a much-debated question. Lenin announced to the Central ExCom at the end of July 1918 that "the direct and immediate participation of Anglo-French imperialism in the Czechoslovak mutiny has long been established"; "it is completely clear to us . . .," Trotsky told the same meeting, "that here was a malicious, precisely worked out plan."[3] Soviet propagandists and, for many years, Soviet historians accepted this as the only truth. But although the revolt did work in the interests of the Allies, what happened in late May had little to do with their planning. During the winter of 1917–1918 the Allies had only slowly come to see the potential of the Czechoslovak Corps, and even then they disagreed about how to use it. The hard-pressed French wanted the Czechoslovaks *out* of Russia and on the Western Front. The British wanted them in Russia as part of a new Eastern Front, but they wanted a concentration at the northern port of Arkhangelsk, not on the Volga. As tension between Moscow and the Czechoslovaks mounted toward the end of May, the Allied representatives on the spot actually used their influence—fruitlessly—to try to *prevent* a final break.

The uprising *as it actually occurred* was something no one wanted. The immediate cause was an incident at Cheliabinsk, in the Urals, on 14 May 1918. The Czechoslovaks there had a deadly brawl with Hungarian POWs and afterward briefly took over the town. Moscow overreacted. The War Commissariat ordered the local soviets to disarm the Czechoslovaks, remove them from their trains, and put them into Red Army units or labor detachments; the Corps was to be disbanded. In turn a conference of Corps delegates at Cheliabinsk decided, ignoring the mediation of their Moscow representatives, to take matters into their own hands and—whatever the opposition—crash through east to Vladivostok.

But if there was little calculation, the revolt was not just an accident. The move across Siberia was almost *bound* to cause conflict. The Czechoslovaks were desperate to get out of Russia. The administrative problems of moving an army corps across 4900 miles of a country bubbling with revolution could not possibly be uncomplicated. The local soviets—which held what real power there was in early 1918— ignored the instructions of the center and squabbled among themselves; the center in turn had little local information or control. At all levels the soviets had other problems to worry about. And they had become used to dealing with problems by force. When the critical moment came in May they showed "Bolshevik" subtlety in dealing with the escalating crisis. The last straw came on 25 May with an order from Trotsky to the local soviets: "Every armed Czechoslovak found on the railway is to be shot on the spot."[4]

Underneath was a deeper incomprehension and mistrust. The Soviet authorities, both central and local, did not grasp the strength of Czechoslovak nationalism. They saw the Czechoslovak soldiers as deluded victims who could be won over; this belief was reinforced by the number of Czechs and Slovaks (largely outside the Corps) who became Bolsheviks. The Soviet attempt to recruit "Internationalists" for the new Red Army was one way in which the Soviet authorities can themselves be blamed for the uprising. And the same authorities saw the armed, pro-Allied Czechoslovak Corps—if not its individual soldiers—as a counterrevolutionary force threatening their totality of power. This was especially true once disagreements began with London and Paris over the Allied presence at Murmansk and Vladivostok. The Czechoslovaks, for their part, distrusted the Bolshevik government, and after Brest believed that, at worst, it would sell them out to the Germans and Austro-Hungarians.

Mistrust spiraled upward from these practical and political frictions. Week after week, argument raged about such critical issues as the Corps' permitted level of armament and its rate of progress. Czechoslovak suspicions were especially aroused in April when Moscow ordered the Corps split, with the units furthest west turning around and making for Arkhangelsk rather than Vladivostok. (The irony was that Moscow was here acting—unknown to the Czechoslovak troops—according to the wishes of the Allies.) When, in mid-May, relations reached an impasse, there seemed no alternative to the use of force by either side:

by the Soviet authorities to get rid of their unwanted guests and by the Czechoslovaks to fight their way east.

Why the Czechoslovaks mutinied to get *out* of Russia is an important question. Even more important is a second question: Why did they stay and fight? By early July they had officially decided to remain in Russia with the aim of "the establishment of an anti-German front in Russia in conjunction with the whole Russian nation and our allies."[5] There were the spiraling conflict with the Bolsheviks, the physical problems of extricating the Corps (it took three months to fight a way clear along the whole Trans-Siberian), and the realization that the Bolshevik opposition was so weak. Also important was sympathy for the local anti-Bolsheviks. Two weeks after the revolt began, the westernmost Czechoslovaks completed their withdrawal to Samara, the first province capital east of the Volga. They made the crucial decision to make a stand there when the local SRs—the Russian movement they had most sympathy for—set up an anti-Bolshevik government (*Komuch*). By this time the Allies (especially the French military mission) had began to appreciate the potential of the Corps' operations and were encouraging them in the war with the Bolsheviks; this was a vitally important change of Allied policy. The mutiny also provided a reason for further Allied involvement: to protect the Czechoslovaks. In particular, it encouraged the Americans to send units, and it made a more concerted Allied policy possible.

The third question is why 40,000 Czechoslovaks were able to have such extraordinary successes, but that will be answered later.

North Russia

The Czechoslovak Uprising was a windfall; events in north Russia showed a more deliberate policy, involving the Allies directly. The Allied interest in the area came partly from a fear of enemy influence, especially the danger of pro-German White Finns advancing to Murmansk. Meanwhile, there was thought to be a large amount of military stores at Arkhangelsk which might fall into unfriendly hands. And, most important, Murmansk and Arkhangelsk were the only ports (other than Vladivostok), that the Allies could reach during the World War; if they were going to act *anywhere* in European Russia it would have to be here. The Bolsheviks could do little to stop them. The Soviet regime had neither political support nor administrative grasp in the north.

49

Arkhangelsk Province was no revolutionary hotbed. It was hundreds of miles from the Bolshevik industrial centers. The Allies could move in small but effective forces by sea, and they offered a link with the outside world, including food supplies; the Soviets, on the other hand, could neither protect nor feed the north.

The town of Murmansk (in 1918 in Arkhangelsk Province) lies on a fjord 150 miles north of the Arctic Circle. In 1918 it was only a new, small settlement, mostly of railway workers and their families. During the February–March 1918 German invasion, Trotsky, then Foreign Commissar, ordered the local soviet to accept Allied aid (Stalinist historians would give this as an example of Trotsky's treachery). A landing party of 170 British marines came ashore on the day after Brest-Litovsk; it was a momentous little incident, the start of Allied military involvement in Russia. In late June 600 British reinforcements arrived. By this time Soviet-Allied relations were passing from distrust to open hostility. Moscow tried to assert its control over the northern port by ordering armed detachments up the Petrograd-Murmansk railway. Allied detachments moved south to intercept them. What followed was the first real fighting between troops of the main Allies (i.e., excluding the Czechoslovaks) and the Reds. The Allies got the better of these skirmishes and quickly secured a defensive line 300 miles down the railway.

Arkhangelsk, much bigger and older than Murmansk, was harder for the Allies to reach; it is on the White Sea, a deep bay that is frozen much of the year. (Although Murmansk and Arkhangelsk are the major ports of the Russian North, they are far apart—600 miles by sea and more overland.) The Bolsheviks had been aware for some time of the threat to the port, and had sent a fierce commissar to sort things out. He had little to work with, however, and when an Allied flotilla appeared off Arkhangelsk on 1 August, the big port quickly capitulated. The tiny operation at Arkhangelsk was the closest thing to an "opposed landing"—an actual invasion—in the history of the intervention; at Murmansk and Vladivostok in 1918, and in south Russia and the Baltic in 1919, Allied troops were sent to "friendly" ports. Fortunately for the Allies, the coastal batteries put up no effective resistance, and the Reds' local "specialists," a colonel and a rear admiral, changed sides. Soviet power in the city was overthrown. When the 600 French and British troops came ashore in the evening, the town was already in anti-Bolshevik hands.

Linked with the landing was one of the last serious internal uprisings within Soviet Russia. The inland town of Iaroslavl, capital of a province and headquarters of a big military district, was set strategically 525

miles south of Arkhangelsk on the only railway to Moscow. On 6 July
the town was seized by the SR "Union for the Defense of the Fatherland
and Freedom." The rebels killed many of the local Bolsheviks, including
the chairman of the Province ExCom. They were led by Boris Savinkov,
one of the most extraordinary characters of the Revolution. Savinkov
was acting with French support, but he had mistaken the timing and
strength of the Allied landings. Fortunately for Moscow, no Allied relief
force arrived; the landing at Arkhangelsk came ten days after the
Iaroslavl rising was crushed. The rebels were besieged by detachments
from the industrial towns farther south and by Red Army units using
artillery (and, apparently, poison gas); after two weeks Iaroslavl was
recaptured.

The Reds organized a hurried defense against the new threat from the
arctic ports. The principle of screen detachments was extended, with
the creation of a Northwestern Sector based on Petrozavodsk, Vologda,
and Kotlas; in early September this became Sixth Army (part of
Northern Army Group). Although the local strength had been doubled,
it was still a tiny force of 9000 men and 34 guns spread over a vast front.
Given the republic's meager military resources and the crucial battles
on the Volga, the north got only a trickle of help from the center.
Fortunately, the challenge to Soviet power from the north was never
large. From Arkhangelsk the nearest sizable town on the railway was
Vologda, 400 miles to the south; from Vologda it was 300 miles to
Moscow (via Iaroslavl) and 350 to Petrograd. Murmansk was over 750
miles from Petrograd, and the main link was a jerry-built wartime
railway. Arkhangelsk province was covered by great coniferous forests
and impassable swamps; the severe weather made movement across
country extremely difficult for much of the year. Olonets and Vologda
provinces, to the south, were little better. Invaders coming from the
north would have to cover enormous distances to get within range of
the Soviet heartland, and even then they would have only a couple of
single-track rail lines behind them. The Allies made good progress—
extending their lines about 150 miles inland from Arkhangelsk. But the
initial landings were not reinforced to allow a real offensive. The troops
on the spot were spread very thinly and by the winter had to keep to a
defensive strategy; their military position would not change much
throughout the Civil War.

Trotsky described what was happening at Arkhangelsk by recalling a
folk tale.[6] A soldier tricked an old woman into making him soup by
boiling an axe head and then "borrowing" the real ingredients for
flavoring; "the Anglo-French soup," Trotsky told the Central ExCom
with satisfaction at the end of September 1918, "is cooking much more

51

slowly than the Allies expected." It was certainly true that there were few recruits available. Poor soil, difficult terrain, and severe weather dictated human geography; fewer than 600,000 people inhabited the vast area of Arkhangelsk Province; the population density was about one one-hundredth of Moscow Province. There were no significant national minorities and no cossack organization—nothing to focus anti-Bolshevik organization.

The north Russian anti-Bolshevik government, which appeared after the Allied landing, did not get popular support. The first government was led by socialist Constituent Assembly delegates; the chairman was Chaikovsky, an active socialist since the 1870s. There was tension and distrust between this government, on the one hand, and Russian and British officers on the other. On the night of 5 September 1918, five weeks after the "Supreme Administration of the Northern Region" had been founded, it was overthrown by a military coup. The local British commander may have been involved, but the Allied diplomats secured the politicians' quick release. The affair, however, left relations even more strained between Left and Right; it humiliated the civilian government and showed where the real power lay. When a new government was formed, Chaikovsky was the only socialist in it. It was not this political maneuvering that prevented the creation of an effective anti-Bolshevik Russian movement in north Russia—there were just not the numbers for that. But it was telling in all-Russian terms that one of the first anti-Bolshevik governments was attacked by its own military. The trend would be continued strikingly with Admiral Kolchak's coup in Siberia two months later. Civilian socialists and the Russian military could not work together, and this would be a fundamental weakness of the anti-Bolshevik movement.

Meanwhile other Allied troops had been sent to eastern Siberia. The first Japanese and British marines established a presence at Vladivostok in early April 1918, ostensibly to maintain order; Bolshevik control of the city was ended by Czechoslovak troops three months later. British troops were also engaged in the Transcaucasus, partly due to German and Turkish activities there; this was the one other point on the edge of Russia that could be reached from the outside world. In August 1918 a small detachment, "Dunsterforce," crossed the Caspian Sea from Persia to Baku, where the local Bolsheviks had just been overthrown. The British troops were at the end of a very long supply line and had no contact with the Civil War fighting; from Baku to even the Kuban battlefields of the Volunteer Army it was 650 miles. In any event, the Turks drove the British out of Baku in September.

Allied-Soviet relations were never good. The Bolsheviks hated the Allies; for them the *Antanta* (Entente) meant imperialism. The Western statesmen despised what the revolution stood for, and, more important, were outraged by Russia's betrayal of the wartime alliance. During the summer of 1918 hostility turned into open warfare. The Allied presence at Murmansk (from March) and Vladivostok (from April) greatly increased Soviet distrust. The Czechoslovak revolt (end of May) gave the Allies new possibilities and increased the Bolshevik fear of conspiracy; the Iaroslavl rising (early July) made that fear even greater. The expansion of the Murmansk bridgehead in late June began the (small-scale) fighting. On 29 July Lenin told the Central ExCom that Russia was in a state of war (de facto) with the Anglo-French "predators," and the landing at Arkhangelsk three days later confirmed this. The Soviet reaction to the Allied incursions, justified or not, was counterproductive. The Cheka arrested many Allied citizens in early August. An (SR) attempt on Lenin's life in August was followed by the so-called "Red Terror." The British naval attache in Petrograd was murdered, and Lockhart, the unofficial "agent" in Moscow, was thrown into the Lubianka prison, accused of trying to suborn the Kremlin garrison. The spiral of distrust, intervention, and terror made good relations between Soviet Russia and the Allies impossible.

Few aspects of the Russian Civil War have been as much discussed as Allied intervention. Lenin, at least, had no doubts about what was happening. The Czechoslovaks, North Russia, the Transcaucasus—all were linked together. He told the Central ExCom in July 1918 that "what we are involved in is a systematic, methodical, and evidently long-planned military and financial counterrevolutionary campaign against the Soviet Republic, which all the representatives of Anglo-French imperialism have been preparing for months."[7] It is true that operations by Allied or pro-Allied forces were the immediate cause of the worsening relations. Still, Lenin's analysis is unconvincing. What happened was not systematic or long-planned—partly because the "planners" had such little information to go on, partly because the Allies disagreed among themselves, and partly because Russia had a low priority. The Czechoslovak uprising, which had by far the biggest effect, was not hatched in ministry buildings in Paris and London—it arose aboard the "echelons" (trainloads) of Czech and Slovak troops worried about their own survival.

This whole series of events was also not essentially anti-*Soviet*. The Allies made decisions to send small detachments to the accessible ports, and the British, at least, wanted to leave the Czechoslovaks as a fighting force in Russia. But this was to aid the struggle against the Central

Powers. The Soviet government had been unable to defend its newly claimed neutrality; large numbers of Central Powers' troops were operating in south Russia, the Baltic, and the Caucasus. The maritime powers seized the ports on the periphery as a response to the march of the continental powers toward the Russian heartland. The Allies (and the Central Powers) intervened in the aftermath of the Russian Revolution, not because the new government was socialist but because it was *weak*.

This weakness not only caused intervention but also explains its success. North Russia, Siberia, and much of the Volga region were lost to the Soviets. This did not happen because vast numbers of troops invaded Russia; in fact there were very few Allied troops in Russia— and only two divisions of Czechoslovaks. The results were achieved, again, because Soviet power was so limited. The regions lost were ones in which the Bolsheviks had had little support in 1917. There was as yet no centralized Red Army. Siberia, the Volga, north Russia were all political and military vacuums that tiny forces could control. Soviet power had meant control of a few urban centers by worker activists; this was destroyed by battalion-strength Czechoslovak forces and by small Allied landing parties. "The Czech conquest of Siberia," one observer noted, "was like the Spanish conquest of Mexico."[8] The same could be said about other territories that the Bolsheviks gained control of in the winter of 1917–1918 and then lost again so quickly.

It is sometimes argued that the Civil War proper only began in the summer of 1918, with Allied intervention, and especially with the Czechoslovak uprising. This was not the case. It *is* true that a distinct phase of the Civil War began and that the Bolsheviks felt more threatened. But armed civil conflict seethed in Russia in the winter of 1917–1918. The success of the "Triumphal March of Soviet Power" was ended not by the Czechoslovak uprising but by the Central Powers' invasion and the shortcomings of the Soviet regime. Lenin, it is true, was not wrong to say in the late spring that the internal civil war was more or less over. But the Soviet grip on much of the country was still extremely weak.

The immediate influence of small Allied landing parties was great; the longer-term impact was greater still. Allied intervention was aimed at beating the Central Powers; Allied victory over Germany in November 1918 might have led to a complete withdrawal from Russian affairs. That it did not was partly a product of how things had developed during the previous half year. "Red Terror," as we shall see, made the Allied governments less willing to come to terms with the Bolsheviks. And the Allied "wartime" commitment to the anti-Bolshevik governments made it morally more difficult to leave them to their fate. The result would be two more years of active Allied hostility to Soviet Russia.

5

THE VOLGA CAMPAIGN,
May–November 1918

Discipline cannot possibly be maintained without revolvers.

Trotsky to Lenin, August 1918

Komuch

When their Corps revolted in May 1918, the Czechoslovaks west of the Volga could easily have broken through to join their "brothers" (as the soldiers of the Corps called one another) in Siberia. Their trains did indeed begin to roll along the main rail line to the east. But as the Czechoslovaks passed through the Volga town of Samara, the leaders of the SR underground convinced them to pause and overthrow the local Bolsheviks. It was one of the decisive moments of the Civil War. Without this intervention Soviet power on the Volga would probably have survived; with it the SRs were able on 8 June to proclaim a rival to the Moscow government, the "Committee of Members of the Constituent Assembly," known by the abbreviation *Komuch*.

The few Red troops on hand were demoralized and of poor quality. If this were not enough, there was a mutiny at the top in the Volga command. After Samara's fall Mikhail Muraviev had been made Main Commander-in-Chief of the newly created Red Eastern Army Group. His qualities were unique: a lieutenant colonel *and* a militant Left SR. He was a charismatic leader, the Reds' best commander, the man who defeated Krasnov's cossacks before Petrograd and crushed the Ukrainian Rada. His first steps in the east were eminently sensible. At Kazan, his headquarters, he set up a regular army-group (*front*) administration, and from troops scattered from Ekaterinburg to Saratov he assembled the first four Soviet armies. To put an end to panic he ordered his men to leave their trains and fight on foot. Muraviev kept Lenin's confidence, even after the Left SR uprising in Moscow (6 July); he immediately quit the Left SRs, and Lenin merely ordered that the commissars keep him under close watch: "I am sure that if these conditions are observed it will be possible fully to make use of his excellent fighting qualities."[1]

Three days later Muraviev rose in revolt. On 10 July he and a thousand men sailed down the Volga from Kazan to Simbirsk. He now styled himself the "Garibaldi of the Russian people," and like the great Italian nationalist he hoped that his expedition would change history. His cause was renewed war with Germany, "the vanguard of world imperialism"; to this end Muraviev ordered fighting against the Czechoslovaks to cease and the Corps itself to turn west and join the common fight.[2] On the night of 10 July Communist rule on the Volga, and perhaps ultimately in all of Russia, hung by a thread. Had Muraviev kept control he would have taken with him the largest military force that the Bolsheviks had been able to assemble. The vital grain region of the Volga would have been lost to Moscow as well. The Germans might have been encouraged to act on the Soviet western front. The situation was saved by the Bolshevik chairman of the Simbirsk Province ExCom, a young Lithuanian worker named Vareikis (sent to the province in May). Vareikis set an ambush; he claimed later that Muraviev resisted arrest, Mauser in hand, but in any event he was killed. (It was reported that Muraviev committed suicide, but since his body had five bullet holes and several bayonet wounds this seems a little unlikely.)

Muraviev had been the heart of the uprising, and with his death it ended. But if catastrophe had been averted, the Volga war continued. Simbirsk only stayed in Red hands for two more weeks before falling to troops from the Czechoslovak Corps and a new "People's Army" formed by Komuch. The attackers numbered only 1500 but Red morale (even among the Latvian Riflemen) was low; the battle showed that the People's Army could fight and that it possessed, in Colonel V. O. Kappel, a daring strategist and a popular leader. Simbirsk was a province capital and the site of arms depots, munitions factories, and a key railway bridge; it was also Lenin's birthplace. The town's loss set the alarm bells ringing in Moscow. A Bolshevik Central Committee resolution of 29 July called the panicky surrender "an incredible crime"; "the fate of the revolution is being decided on the Volga and in the Urals," it proclaimed, and all possible forces were to be concentrated there.[3] The War Commissar, Trotsky himself, was sent to the Volga to sort things out.

Meanwhile, the new Commander-in-Chief of Eastern Army Group was another revolutionary colonel, Ioakhim Vatsetis. The stout, bullet-headed Vatsetis was no officer–aristocrat; his father had been a Latvian farmhand. He had proven his loyalty by crushing the Moscow Left SR uprising. His Latvian connection was vital; the Latvian Rifle Division, the only Red unit combining reliability and effectiveness, would be the spearhead of any counterattack. Like Muraviev, Vatsetis had been a front-line commander in the world war; unlike his predecessor, he had attended the General Staff Academy. Trotsky respected him more than cautious former staff officers who never stuck their necks out: "Vatsetis, on the contrary, issued orders and, in moments of inspiration, forgot about the existence of Sovnarkom and the Central ExCom." Vatsetis moved to Kazan in mid-July and began whipping his command into shape, chiding superiors and subordinates alike. The goal of this blunt energy was a general offensive. Fifth, Fourth, and First Armies would close in on the Samara-Simbirsk area from the north, south, and west (respectively); Third Army would recapture Ekaterinburg in the Urals; and Second Army would cut the Volga-Urals rail link.[4] Success would mean a secure front line far to the east, along the Asiatic slope of the Urals. But in reality this line would not be reached for twelve months.

The first reverse was a sudden attack by the enemy up the wide artery of the Volga—to the very heart of the Red eastern command, Kazan. Curiously enough, the height of anti-Bolshevik success in 1918 came about against the wishes of the Komuch leadership and Colonel Cecek, the local Czechoslovak commander. Both favored a cautious strategy; if there was to be any advance it should be to the south, *down* the Volga towards Saratov. The SRs had strong roots in Saratov Province, and it was believed that Alekseev's Volunteer Army was approaching Saratov from the other side. (In reality the Volunteers were just at this moment turning south to the Kuban, *away* from the Volga.) The Kazan attack went ahead because the local commanders disobeyed Cecek's orders and acted in the spirit of the Russian saying, "Victors are not court-martialed."

One participant described the expedition that suddenly descended on Kazan on the evening of 5 August as a "microscopic detachment." Tiny it was, three battalions of Czechoslovaks and People's Army troops, 2500 in all.[5] Their lightning advance was possible because they had mounted heavy guns on tugs and barges and gained control of the Volga. The first landing was driven off. There was bitter fighting in the streets the next day. But by the morning of 7 August Kazan had been taken. Vatsetis's new striking force, Fifth Army, melted away before his eyes. Most of the new Russian units, he later complained to Moscow, "turned out to be completely useless as a result of their poor training and indiscipline"; "the [local] workers could not shoot or attack, they could not even build barricades"; only the Latvians put up a fight. Vatsetis suffered the humiliation of being trapped in his headquarters after part of his staff went over to the enemy and began taking potshots at him. It was with the greatest difficulty, and under cover of fog and darkness, that the Main Commander-in-Chief of Eastern Army Group and a few dozen Latvian Riflemen made their escape from Kazan.[6]

The Red Army

The Volga thunderbolt caught the Reds still without an effective army, although the first steps had been taken. Red armed forces had existed since the October Revolution, in the form of the Red Guard and revolutionary soldiers and sailors from the "regular" army and navy. Their detachments had fought and won the "Railway War." The "Workers' and Peasants' Red Army" had officially been set up in mid-January 1918, and there was an attempt to raise larger forces during the February "Eleven Days War" with the Central Powers.

More important in the long run was Trotsky's reluctant agreement in March to turn his attention from "diplomacy" to the army. He was to stay on as "People's Commissar for the Army and Navy" until 1925, and here he would make his greatest practical contribution to the Soviet state. Before 1917 most Russian Marxists had loathed everything about warfare, but Trotsky at least had gained some military knowledge as a journalist covering the Balkan Wars and the Western Front. More important were his energy and political power. Before Trotsky the Red forces had been vaguely under a committee of lesser Bolsheviks; Trotsky introduced the principle of central control and tried to enforce it, and he had the power to make the party swallow unpalatable policies.

Greater use was now made of the Tsarist army's rich legacy. A central fact about the Red Army, one often forgotten, is that it was originally intended for use not against counterrevolutionaries but against the Germans and Austrians. As Trotsky told the Central ExCom in April 1918, a proper army was needed, not to fight "our *internal* class enemies, who are pitiful . . .", but against "the all-powerful *external* enemies, who utilize a huge centralized machine for their mass murder and extermination."[7]

59

An army defending what was left of Russia against traditional enemies, Germany and Austria-Hungary, would get vital help from the specialists of the old Tsarist army. The most important was an Imperial Guard officer who had held senior Tsarist Army staff posts, General M. D. Bonch-Bruevich. As head of the new Soviet "Supreme Military Council," Bonch was even more important than Trotsky in laying the foundations of the Red Army. (Bonch was trusted by the Bolsheviks because of a chance personal connection characteristic of late Imperial Russia; the general's brother was a veteran Bolshevik party member who after the October Revolution became Lenin's private secretary!)

Given its concern with the German threat, the "Red" high command· in March and April 1918 kept its eyes fixed firmly on the West. Bonch developed the concept of the screens: the Northern Screen covered Petrograd, the Western Screen Moscow. When Russia was divided into six new Military Districts the "border" districts faced the Germans and Austrians. Ironically, it was the "internal" Volga and Urals Military Districts where the front lines actually formed.

The new army was pointed backward, but at least the first steps had been taken. Sovnarkom had in late April, based on Bonch's plans, begun to plan for an army of a million men in 91 proper divisions. This westward-facing mass army had the advantages of professional organization. Kakurin, the 1920s historian of the Civil War, admitted that the central administration of the old army survived the Revolution more or less intact and provided the Bolsheviks with an invaluable tool.[8] The administrative heart of the Red Army came to look more and more like that of its predecessor. In early May 1918 an All-Russian Main Staff was set up; it was named after a Tsarist institution and manned by officers. Rear institutions appeared in the provinces of central Russia. The military activities of local soviets were replaced by provincial Military Commissariats under Moscow's control. This infrastructure of army organization would be indispensable wherever the fighting actually began.

At a lower level the use of Tsarist officers was extremely important, and this too was linked with the original orientation of the army against the Central Powers. In both the central administration and the new units of the "Workers' and Peasants' Red Army" one of the most striking features was the large number of Tsarist officers. Some 8000 were serving in the early months, by the end of 1918 22,000 had been called up, and the Civil War total was more than 48,000. A special effort was made to get General Staff officers, men who under the Tsar had had staff-college training, fast promotion, and a near monopoly of wartime high command. (Bonch, with his contacts, was invaluable here; the railway coach where he interviewed old comrades was known as "the general trap.") Officers asked in early 1918 to explain why they had agreed to serve a regime that rejected Faith, Tsar, and Fatherland might well have agreed with General Parsky, newly appointed commander of the Northern Screen. "You know," he told Bonch, "I am far from this socialism that your Bolsheviks preach. But I am ready to work honorably not only with them, but with anyone, even the Devil and his disciples, if only to save Russia from German slavery."[9] Many volunteered on the understanding that they would fight only the *external* enemy. This acted, however, as a bridge—a one-way bridge—to the service of the Soviet regime and to battles on the "internal" front.

Compulsory, rather than volunteer, officer service (introduced in July 1918) and the appearance of serious anti-Bolshevik forces, supported by the Allies, brought a new situation, with numerous betrayals of Soviet power. Besides Muraviev, the most important defector was Colonel N. N. Stogov; as Chief of the Main Staff he was in charge of *all* the Red Army's administrative services. Several army commanders and many junior officers changed sides in the early fighting; the most extraordinary case was the mass desertion at Kazan of the instructors and students of the General Staff Academy.

But overshadowing all this was the growth of the number of officers in Red service; as Trotsky kept telling a skeptical party, only a small proportion became active traitors. The Soviet state found other ways of controlling the officers. Evasion was made as difficult as possible. "The conditions are now being created," wrote Trotsky in August 1918, "whereby we can carry out a radical weeding-out of the officer corps: on the one hand concentration camps, and on the other combat in Eastern Army Group." Hostages were another primitive but effective lever. Trotsky ordered the arrest of defectors' families: "Let the turncoats realize that they are at the same time betraying their own families—their fathers, mothers, sisters, brothers, wives and children."[10] Violence was not usually necessary, given that the officers and their families had the simple need to exist in the new world of Soviet Russia. They had little chance to escape and no skills; the state was the supplier of rations and accommodation. And while a career in the Red Army must have seemed a bad dream in 1918, things would change when that army defeated all comers in 1919 and emerged in the spring of 1920 as the master of most of the old Empire.

Bonch, rather than Trotsky, initiated the recruitment of officers, but all of Trotsky's revolutionary prestige was needed to maintain the policy. Many revolutionary activists in the army detested the end of elected commanders and the use of Tsarist officers, and these activists were in a majority at a special army conference in late March 1918; Lenin's intervention was apparently required to force acceptance.[11] The arguments would continue in 1919, but Trotsky remained dominant.

The *komissar* was another major element: without what Trotsky called the "iron corset" the use of officers would have been impossible. Trotsky's centralization applied here as well; in April 1918 he issued formal regulations on commissars and created an All-Russian Bureau of Military Commissars. The effectiveness of the early commissars can be exaggerated. In January 1919 Stalin and Dzerzhinsky called for a purge of the bureau, "which supplies the military units with whippersnapper 'commissars' who are quite incapable of organizing satisfactory political work"; "the word 'commissar' has become a term of abuse." A Red brigade commander named Kotomin who defected in 1919 reported that only five per cent of commissars were "idealist Communists"; the rest included self-seeking workers and poor peasants "and the dregs of the other classes, mostly youngsters and failures, and, of course, almost a majority of Jews." Yet the commissars were essential. If there was often mutual loathing between commander and commissar, it was more common for a working relationship to be created. Many officers were only too glad to avoid sole responsibility; some officers and commissars built up good personal relations and tried to be kept together when transferred from front to front. Even Kotomin admitted that for all their careerism and spying on one another the commissars were "amazingly hard-working, supervising commanders and agitating among the men"; "The role of the commissars in the army is enormous. They maintain class antagonism among the mass of soldiers."[12]

This last role of the commissars followed another basic change in the Red Army during 1918: the volunteers of the early days were replaced by conscripted peasants. During the winter of 1917–1918 anyone trying to raise an army in Russia had had to use the volunteer principle. On the Don there was the anti-Bolshevik *Volunteer* Army; in Petrograd the essence of the January decree which set up the Red Army had been voluntary (and short) service. Opinions vary on the early "Red Army man" (the Soviets rejected as demeaning the term "soldier" [*soldat*]; *krasnoarmeets* was used for all those serving in the Red Army, or *Krasnaia armiia*). The army gave a living for the unemployed and attracted veterans with no other experience. Some party people looked on the volunteers as *déclassé*; Colonel Vatsetis described the majority as *shkurniki*, self-seekers. On the other hand, Stalin and Dzerzhinsky, complaining in 1919 of a conscript army that had just fallen apart at Perm, noted the "staunchness of the formations of the volunteer period." Whatever their faults, the early volunteers were important; they were the first to be thrown into battle in the summer, and they formed the Russian (non-Latvian) core of the army as it developed in the second half of 1918.[13]

Regardless of the quality of the volunteers, Bonch's million-man army was impossible under the volunteer system. Conscription was the only solution, and the Bolsheviks proved to have less principled opposition to mass conscription than they did to the use of officers. But they had to move carefully for lack of effective machinery and for fear of antagonizing the mass of the population. As a result, neither the April 1918 decree proclaiming Universal Military Training (*Vsevobuch*) nor the announcement of conscription on 29 May 1918 had much effect. The first real call-up (in June) was a local one reflecting the immediate crisis: workers and peasants born in 1893–1897 (five of the last Tsarist mobilization classes) were called up in fifty-one counties of the Volga-Urals area and in Moscow. The Volga-Urals call-up was unsuccessful—a reflection of local confusion and lukewarm support for Soviet power— but in Moscow things were better. Other local mobilizations were announced later in the summer, with an emphasis on the workers of the central provinces. A general mobilization followed in September, first of the class of 1898, then those of 1893–1897. Some call-ups provoked mutinies, some conscripts had to be sent home for lack of food and accommodation. By the end of 1918, however, the strength of the Red Army was probably about 700,000[14], which meant it was already larger than all the armies it would meet in 1919. In early October 1918 Lenin himself called for a three-million man army, and if this was not to be realized for a long time (until early 1920) the Reds had certainly made great strides since the spring.

Control of central Russia reduced the problem of equipping this growing army. The Tsarist army is frequently depicted as being short of everything, but the supply of equipment had improved greatly in 1916, and it was equipment for an army of 9,600,000, a force thirty times larger than the Red Army of mid-1918. The Soviet forces were able to live off the Tsarist arsenals of central Russia for much of the Civil War. The successful combining of officers, soldiers, and *matériel* testified to the energy of the Bolsheviks. It also showed the value of controlling enormous resources—including 60 million people. The inheritance of the central army apparatus made it possible to turn these resources into a regular mass Red Army in 1919.

The Volga Counterattack

At its peak Komuch, the Committee of Members of the Constituent

Assembly, controlled Samara and Ufa provinces, and large parts of Saratov, Simbirsk, Kazan, and Viatka. Twelve million people lived in this region. If any group should have been able to raise support here it was the one that dominated this new government in Samara, the Socialist-Revolutionary Party. The great majority of the local people were peasants; the SRs were the peasant party. They had won an absolute majority here during the Constituent Assembly elections. Unlike practically every other anti-Bolshevik government, then or later, Komuch had a radical agrarian policy; in June 1918 fixed grain prices were ended and a land law gave the peasants permanent use of the land. I. I. Maisky, the most prominent Menshevik in Komuch, later coined the term "Democratic Counter-Revolution" to describe the Samara government. By that time Maisky had gone over to the Reds; he meant the term as an insult. But "Democratic Counter-Revolution" does express both the unique features of Komuch and its potential. Unlike the counter-revolutionaries of 1919 and 1920, who were mostly army officers of conservative or reactionary views, Komuch claimed to oppose the Bolshevik government in the name of the people. And yet it failed more rapidly than did the conservatives.

One problem was that the leadership of Komuch was weak. Although the Committee eventually numbered over 100 people, it was led by little-known provincial SRs, of whom the most important were probably V. K. Volsky and P. D. Klimushkin. These leaders did little to translate policy into reality, and they seem to have occupied themselves in "diplomatic" relations with neighboring anti-Bolshevik governments. Few expressed much interest in the army, and those who did, such as V. I. Lebedev, spent their time leading front-line battalions rather than raising and training mass reinforcements.

Most important, Komuch proved unable to rally large-scale popular support. The 10,000 men who volunteered in May–June 1918 remained the fighting core of the People's Army; in late June Komuch announced conscription, but probably only 30,000 were successfully drafted, and these did not fight well.[15] This military weakness came partly from the universal difficulty of mobilizing peasants, partly from the war-weariness of 1918. In part, however, it came about because in the early summer of 1918 the Volga peasants saw no reason to fight the Moscow government. The Bolsheviks had let them take the landlords' estates; forced requisitioning of food, active attempts to incite class war in the villages, and Red Army conscription were all in the future. The fact is that neither side found the Volga peasants eager to fight; the Reds had as little success on their side of the river.

The problem for Komuch was that *it* had to rely so exclusively on the reluctant Volga peasantry. The Reds controlled the big industrial cities of central Russia. Komuch had nothing comparable on the Volga, and it had little success even in the towns it did control. The workers' attitude was at best one of *neitralitet*. The Menshevik CC rejected armed struggle against the "workers' government" in Moscow, and only against its wishes did a few Mensheviks, like Maisky, join Komuch.

Komuch was also unable to gain the support of educated society, and unlike the Bolsheviks it did not seriously attempt compulsion. The small middle class disliked the Samara government: Komuch was based on the socialist-dominated Constituent Assembly; it used the hated red flag (the "red rag"); its—unsuccessful—attempts to broaden its base with "worker conferences" or "peasant congresses" were seen as a return to "mob politics." For the propertied classes there was little to choose between Sovnarkom and Komuch. "When two dogs are fighting," remarked one local businessman, "a third shouldn't join in."[16] Counterrevolutionary army officers, meanwhile, were drawn not to Komuch but to the more conventional forces being raised by the regional government in Siberia.

There was little point in raising a large Komuch military force if leaders and equipment were lacking. Some of the People's Army conscripts had to be sent home for lack of equipment, and many of those who actually fought were armed with sticks. The Komuch territory contained the Simbirsk and Izhevsk rifle factories, and much artillery was captured at Kazan, but there was not enough time to mobilize these scattered resources. And time was a key factor. By August 1918 the Bolsheviks had been in power for ten months; Komuch, for its part, was under deadly counterattack before it was twelve weeks old. It had to build an army in the front line, and it failed. This military weakness meant that the few effective detachments had to be shuttled up and down the Volga, repelling one Red attack after another. The day after his capture of Kazan, Colonel Kappel was steaming away to plug gaps on the southern Komuch front. So the dreams of an advance upstream to Nizhnii Novgorod and Moscow were shattered a few miles west of Kazan, where the Reds dug in with superior artillery. The people of Kazan did not rally to the Komuch cause, and their city became not a spearhead but another beleaguered outpost.

And yet if Komuch seemed doomed to fail, consider what happened at Izhevsk. A few nights after Kappel took Kazan, Soviet power was overthrown in the arms-factory town of Izhevsk, which is 150 miles to the northeast. It was the largest workers' rebellion against Bolshevik rule, and the rebels soon expanded their control over the surrounding countryside. The Samara Komuch never paid much attention to distant Izhevsk, and the Reds were able to surround the rebels and, on 7 November, retake the town. Tens of thousands of refugees fled to the east, where many fought in Kolchak's armies. Was the rising the result of freak local conditions? Or had the economic failures and political heavy-handedness of the Bolsheviks shaken their support among the Russian working class? Did the rising foreshadow what would have happened had the People's Army succeeded in striking west? The answer to this tantalizing riddle was lost in the failure of Komuch and the triumphant counterattack of the Red Army.

The Reds had gradually accumulated forces for their Volga campaign. Later each Red army group would draw on local manpower, but this was less the case in 1918; the June call-up was at first quite unsuccessful in the east.[17] More important for this first campaign were forces from the central zone. Worker detachments were raised in Moscow and other big towns. Bolsheviks were drafted to Eastern Army Group and to the civilian administration of the Volga and the Urals—essential stiffening in regions at best ambivalent to Bolshevik power. Lenin made an important but little-known gamble at this point. On 10 August 1918, three days after the loss of Kazan, he instructed General Bonch-Bruevich to shift troops to the Volga from the skeleton divisions forming in the anti-German screens: "All battle-worthy units should go." Trotsky and Bonch apparently expressed doubts, but Lenin took the risk of believing the Germans' promise that they would not attack. He could not have known that 8 August had been Ludendorff's "Black Day of the German Army" in France, when it passed the limit of its resistance. But he knew that the Central Powers were hard pressed, and he knew too of their hostility to the Czechoslovaks.

The results of the gamble were immediate: the Supreme Military Council estimated that between 25 July and 18 August more than 30,000 men were transferred to Eastern Army Group, mostly from the screens. The flow was not smooth; the railways were in a poor state; there was intense rivalry between Bonch's Supreme Military Council—which still stressed the threat of the Central Powers in the west—and the Operations Department of the War Commissariat (*Operod*), which supervised the Volga. Still, Eastern Army Group grew and grew—from 53,000 on 21 June to 70,000 on 15 September, and to 103,000 on 7 October; between 15 September and 7 October artillery rose from 225 guns to 298, and machine guns from 1059 to 1627.[18] Among the units arriving in the east were the Latvian Riflemen, still the elite of the Red Army. And the Reds controlled the central resources of the navy as well as those of the army:

four Baltic Fleet destroyers arrived to end Czechoslovak control of the Volga River.

By August Eastern Army Group was starting to hold its own. On the left flank Third Army was successfully defending the north Urals. On the right Fourth Army (based on Saratov) was gradually advancing, and drawing the attention of Komuch down the river. In the center, threatening Simbirsk, was Tukhachevsky's First Army. The most important battle was fought around Kazan by Fifth Army. Colonel Slaven, the army commander, had previously led a Latvian regiment, and he was now using his Latvian units to put more and more pressure on the city's defenses. At the end of August Colonel Kappel made a desperate attempt to regain the initiative for the People's Army. He penetrated the Red lines and tried to take the giant Romanov Bridge, which carried the Moscow-Kazan Railway across the Volga near the county town of Sviiazhsk, twenty miles west of Kazan. With one blow he could cut off the main Red forces, deployed between Sviiazhsk and Kazan on both sides of the Volga. He could also threaten their high command, for Trotsky's headquarters train had been shunted into a siding near the bridge. On the morning of 28 August the War Commissar's staff awoke to find that the rail line to Moscow had been cut, and that they themselves were the main defense of the bridge approaches. It was a day of heavy fighting, but in the end the Romanov Bridge was saved, and with it the rear of Fifth Army. Kappel had commanded the entire Komuch mobile reserve, but this numbered only 2000, many of them raw conscripts, and the fifteen-mile approach march had exhausted and disoriented his columns. Eventually, with their ammunition running out, Kappel's men fell back.[19]

Fifth Army could now safely continue the attack on Kazan. The Baltic Fleet destroyers gave the Reds command of the river, the advancing Latvians seized the heights on the right bank overlooking Kazan, and Red troops on the left bank pressed closer to the city itself. Lenin instructed Trotsky to use his artillery: "In my opinion it is wrong to spare the city and delay things further, because merciless annihilation (*besposhchadnoe istreblenie*) is essential once Kazan is in an iron ring." Kazan was spared this, as the Red Army entered the town on the same day, 10 September; the exhausted Czechoslovaks and People's Army had pulled out. (Trotsky, too, had shown ruthlessness. During the Sviiazhsk battle one of the Red regiments panicked, commandeered a river steamer, and tried to flee. They were stopped by a steadier force, a field court martial was appointed by Trotsky, and on 29 August twenty men—one in ten—were shot. Among the victims was regimental commissar Panteleev, who had fled with his men.[20])

Some 100 miles farther south Tukhachevsky's First Army finally broke through to Simbirsk, which fell two days after Kazan. The thousand-yard-long railway bridge was captured by sending across an unmanned engine, followed by an armored train and an infantry brigade. Unfortunately the bridge was recaptured and the last span blown up; this was greatly to hamper Red supply east of the Volga in later months. Around Samara, meanwhile, the noose closed. Komuch dissolved itself, and on 7 October Samara fell to the Red Fourth Army. The giant bridge at Syzran was destroyed, and the remnants of the Komuch forces withdrew east along the Samara-Ufa-Cheliabinsk railway; most of the conscripts melted away. The morale of the Czechoslovaks, meanwhile, was also plummeting. "The Czech army," as one of its leaders characteristically put it, "is like a well-bred young girl who has been locked up in a brothel. She suffers there, and is contaminated."[21] The local Czechoslovak commander (Svec), broken by his men's unwillingness to fight, shot himself. The gesture had an impact; afterward the Czechoslovaks—aided by the Orenburg Cossacks—put up more effective resistance. But the last major battle of the Corps was fought before Ufa in November; in 1919 the anti-Bolshevik Russians would have to do their own fighting.

In the Volga campaign a regular Red Army was formed, and the moderate socialists were defeated. These two developments were linked: the Bolsheviks created effective forces, while the SRs of Komuch could not. The Soviet side began with big advantages: five times the population, a richer military inheritance, and a longer period for consolidation. But the fact remains that Komuch failed politically and militarily. Stephen Berk, the Western historian who has studied the Volga episode most closely, concluded that "not one important group in the Volga region gave Komuch its support."[22] And Komuch's forces were in the end not able even to hold the first-class natural barrier of the Volga.

Success on the Volga produced a reliable fighting commander in Colonel Vatsetis; on 6 September, with the Kazan attack well advanced, the commander of Eastern Army Group was made the first Main Commander-in-Chief (*Glavkom*) of the whole Red Army. (Defeat would have brought its own reward. On 30 August Lenin proposed that Trotsky follow the example of the French Revolution and shoot Vatsetis and other commanders if the Kazan operation met with delay.[23]) General Bonch-Bruevich, the senior "specialist" from March to August, had always been most concerned with the German front; now he was replaced by a fighting Civil War commander. (Bonch supposedly resigned for reasons of "ill health.")

The pattern for the Red Army was worked out on the Volga. Trotsky's regular army was proven. A command structure was forged that would lead the Red Army to victory. Throughout the summer various organizations had been vying for power; September saw the creation of a new central coordinating organ, the Revolutionary Military Council (RevMilCouncil) of the Republic (*RVSR*). Trotsky was chairman, Vatsetis a key member, and the council had control over both operations and army administration. Vatsetis was in direct charge of operations; in November his unified Field Staff (GHQ) began to function. Organizations that had proved their value in the east were extended to the whole army. The traditional army group (*front*) was introduced in other areas; by the start of 1919 there were Southern, Western, and Northern Army Groups, each with its own RevMilCouncil (consisting of a senior officer and several commissars). Each army group contained several armies, and each of these had its own RevMilCouncil. And everywhere regular units replaced improvised detachments; by the end of 1918 there were forty-five Red divisions, organized (in theory) on uniform lines. Even the Bolshevik Party was brought into this structure. The army's political structure was made separate from the civilian party organization and controlled by tiers of army Political Sections (*Politotdely*), the first of which had been set up in Eastern Army Group.

The Volga campaign stimulated the Red Army's development in a way that the early fighting in the Don and the Ukraine, and in the Eleven Days War (against the Central Powers), had not. By August, in his battles with Tukhachevsky's First Army, Colonel Kappel first sensed that he was fighting against a real army that would obey its commanders' orders. Trotsky summed up what had happened at the time Kazan was recaptured: "if the Czechoslovaks had not existed they would have had to be invented, for under peacetime conditions we should never have succeeded in forming, within a short time, a close-knit disciplined, heroic army."[24] The Red Army was not as close-knit, disciplined, or, indeed, heroic as Trotsky suggested, but it had been hardened by a summer's battles. The Volga Campaign, difficult though it was at times, was an inoculation—a relatively mild form of counter-revolution—which prepared the Reds for what was to come. Without it they might have perished, unprepared, in the much more lethal campaign of 1919.

6

SOVDEPIA: THE SOVIET ZONE,
October 1917–November 1918

We shall now proceed to construct the socialist order!

Lenin, 26 October 1917

Economic Revolution

The Bolsheviks' enemies gave the name "Sovdepia" to the area under the authority of the Soviets of Workers' and Peasants' Deputies. The comic-opera term was intended to mock, but actually it is a useful short way of describing the Soviet zone. Sovdepia was vast. A common misconception is that the Reds held on to only a small island of territory. They had, it is true, lost the Baltic provinces, Belorussia, Finland, the Ukraine, the Don, the Kuban, Transcaucasia, Siberia, the Urals, the arctic coast, and the middle Volga. But the thirty provinces that were still wholly or partly in Soviet hands stretched over nearly a million square miles and could have swallowed up *all* the warring countries of Europe. More people—some 60 million—lived in the Soviet zone than in any other state on the continent.[1] This wealth of land and people, more than anything else, explains the eventual victory of the Reds in the Civil War. But before that victory could be achieved the new masters of central Russia had to cope with the conflicting tasks of transforming and controlling Sovdepia.

Land reform and workers' control were crucial for the Bolsheviks' seizure of power and for their political survival in the following winter. The social revolution was partly inspired by the Bolsheviks and partly created by spontaneous mass activity but, combined with the economic

70

ruin of the World War, it created the gravest of problems for the new government. Food supply was the worst. Food shortages had brought down the Tsar—after the world war had disrupted production, transport, and trade. Revolution added to the chaos. Large estates that had produced a surplus for the market were replaced by small family farms. These farms were relatively inefficient and tended to produce food for their own consumption. The lack of factory-made consumer goods (due to a Tsarist concentration on war production, followed by revolutionary disorder) meant there was little to give the peasants in exchange for what they could bring to market. And things were made much worse by the loss of the main food-producing areas: in the early months the Ukraine and the north Caucasus, and later the Siberian and Volga provinces. From the summer of 1918 to the spring of 1920 Sovdepia was really the hungry north.

The Bolsheviks' approach to food supply, like other issues, was formed by vague preconceptions. They believed that all problems could be solved by the intervention of the state, a new type of state that harnessed the energies of the masses. They despised the legacy of the capitalist market economy, which had caused such hardship and had failed in 1917. From the start they stressed state-run trade, trade moreover that was carried out by barter rather than money. Measures were taken against the "bagmen," the small traders who carried on their backs what food they could. But given the lack of manufactured goods, the primitive machinery of administration and distribution, and the breakdown of transport—the result of both the economic crisis and of their own revolutionary program—little came from Bolshevik promises.

In the end, the only effective contribution that the new rulers could make to feeding the towns was to move state control a step further and take the food from the peasants without giving *anything* in exchange. This began on a local basis in the winter of 1917–1918 and became more prominent in the spring, as the last of the 1917 harvest was consumed. The blunt instruments for this were the ad hoc "food supply detachments," through which unemployed and hungry workers were urged to go out and feed themselves. The process developed with the Food Dictatorship, declared on 9 May 1918 (three weeks before the Czechoslovak uprising), which gave the state and food detachments control of the peasants' produce. The Committees of the Village Poor (*Kombedy*) were also meant to solve the food problem. Although they were founded on 11 June 1918 (just after the Czechoslovak uprising), they had more to do with the general food shortage than with the Civil War fighting. Their roots lay deep in Bolshevik ideology. There were (so

Lenin had long argued) intense class divisions within the villages. The cause of the food crisis was the rich peasant (*kulak*) grain hoarder; the savior of hungry Russia was to be the poor peasant (*bedniak*), who would take the grain from him. The Kombedy would also extend Bolshevik support from an urban minority to a huge rural proletariat. In fact, the Kombedy often kept the food for themselves, and they showed that basic Bolshevik assumptions were faulty. The October Revolution seems to have increased *cohesion* within the peasantry rather than set off class war. The village united against the outside world, and Bolshevik policy led to confrontation with the peasantry as a whole.[2] After months of turmoil the government would come to see the dangers of the experiment; in November and December 1918 the committees in central Sovdepia were disbanded and attention turned to yet another "layer," the "*middle* peasant" (*seredniak*).

The Bolshevik Revolution was supposed to be a workers' revolution, but it coincided with a disastrous decline of industry. Russian industry had from 1914 been dislocated by the conversion to war production and starved of imported fuel and raw materials. After that came the post-October demobilization of war industry, the panicky evacuation during the Eleven Days War, and finally the breakaway of the Empire's outlying regions. Other industrial problems were brought about by revolutionary labor unrest and Bolshevik policies. The new government had had great difficulty finding a way to run the factories. An elaborate structure of "workers' control"—the supervision of production by elected factory committees—was thought up in the winter of 1917–1918, only to come crashing down. (Lenin's posthumous verdict on workers' control was that it had been and "was bound to remain chaotic, splintered, primitive and incomplete";[3] a year before the Bolsheviks had the highest hopes for the workers' self-management, and this led them to ignore many of the practical obstacles to nationalization.) Once workers' control was abandoned, attention was hastily shifted to the more manageable trade unions as a means of controlling industry, but they too could have little effect.

The official nationalization of large factories, in the form of a Sovnarkom decree, took place only on 28 June 1918. Even in the spring, however, the central government had nationalized some plants, and since October 1917 many others had been taken over by local soviets and groups of workers; Lenin later called this the "Red Guard assault on capital." Many factory seizures were seen as defensive, preventing closure or "sabotage" by the employers, but in the winter of 1917–1918 the emotional slogan "Loot the looters!" had its greatest impact. Lenin,

72

in April 1918, did try to slow the pace, and even to attempt cooperation with some of the factory owners, but this came only after six months' delay and was itself a sign of how radical the earliest policies had been ("we have nationalized, confiscated, beaten down [the bourgeoisie], and put down [economic sabotage] more *than we have been able to count*"). Lenin's *basic* view even in April 1918 was clear: his unpublished "Basic Propositions" on economic policy included the complete nationalization of industry, trade, and banking.[4] In any event, Lenin's belated experiment of cooperation with the capitalists was notable for its failure and for the resistance it met in the party and among the workers.

Nationalization of banks and annulment of loans in the first months of the Revolution did nothing to restore financial stability and created powerful enemies among foreign lenders. Printing of banknotes furthered high inflation. Local soviets imposed punitive taxes and contributions on the "bourgeoisie" but failed to raise the real funds required; the central government imposed in October 1918 its own disastrous "extraordinary" tax, which produced little revenue and alienated many. With the crises of agriculture and industry, of trade and finance, there could be little chance for the economic centralization and planning on which Marxists had long rested their hopes. The Supreme Economic Council (*VSNKh*), founded in December 1917, did not fulfil its intended role. Its early leaders lacked administrative skills and devoted their attention to visionary schemes. They never had authority over such key commissariats as Food Supply and Finance, and even in what became the Council's main sphere of activity—industry—it was limited by local autonomy and by the military. Bolshevik intellectuals had argued that the concentration of the economy in the World War had made a jump to socialism, through a body like the VSNKh, relatively simple. "That would have been extremely pleasant," Lenin admitted in early 1919, "but it was not so in reality." Eighteen months earlier, Lenin himself had used precisely such arguments to justify the seizure of power.[5]

The nature of the Bolsheviks' radical economic policies is a matter of controversy. The name usually given to them, "War Communism," is wrong on several counts. It is an anachronism; the term " 'War' communism" was first used—in Lenin's notes—only in 1921. It suggests that the policy was a wartime stopgap. (It is often said that the policy was provoked by the supposed "outbreak" of the Civil War in the summer of 1918.)[6] My view is that while this fighting deepened an existing crisis, the economic policies later called War Communism—the food detachments, nationalization of industry, restrictions of trade—had been developing at the center and in the grass roots since the early winter of 1917–1918. There was no "normal" period followed by crisis; the crisis began with the start of the Bolsheviks' Civil War in October 1917. The fact that the policies did not all come into force immediately after October was not due to any early moderation, to any general belief in a mixed economy or in "state capitalism," but simply to the fact that it took the new government a certain amount of time to gain a measure of control over the country.

"War" Communism was essentially *the* economic policy of victorious Bolshevism. In January 1918 Lenin urged making peace with the Central powers.

> The reorganization of Russia on the basis of the dictatorship of the proletariat, and the nationalization of the banks and large scale industry, coupled with exchange of products in kind between the towns and the small-peasant consumers' societies is quite feasible economically, provided we are assured a few months in which to work in peace.

Lenin himself admitted in 1921 that the first goal had been "the break-up at a stroke of the old socio-economic system in order to replace it with a new one." Trotsky too recalled that the radical policy had *become* that of a besieged fortress; "It is necessary to acknowledge . . .," he admitted, "that in its original conception it pursued broader aims." Trotsky excused this "theoretical mistake" by the expectation of revolution in the West[7], but this was only one of the false assumptions of the Bolsheviks and their supporters; as important was an overconfidence in the ability of the workers to run their factories, of the poor peasants to dominate the villages, and of the state to administer industry and trade.

Was there an alternative? Roy Medvedev recently suggested that the New Economic Policy of 1921 could have been introduced in 1918: nationalization would have been limited, war industry effectively demobilized; the state grain monopoly replaced by free trade and a small tax "in kind."[8] Medvedev was right that the policy that took shape in early 1918 was *not* a prototype of the 1921 New Economic Policy (as is sometimes suggested), and correct that this 1918 policy was "fundamentally wrong." But he was incorrect himself to expect the Bolsheviks to have the advantage of hindsight, to think purely in terms of economic rationality and not to be militant revolutionaries. Lenin was in some ways more rational, but he was not the whole party.

The initial success of Bolshevik economic policy was less economic than political. "Loot the looters!" won popular backing for the Bolsheviks as the bosses and landowners were driven out; it did not matter at first that people were not immediately better off. Radical economic policies helped the Bolsheviks to take power and then to consolidate it in the winter of 1917–1918. As the months passed, however, even the political benefits came to look more dubious. "Workers' control" of the factories and the general dislocation of economic administration actually contributed to a decline in production; they led (with other factors) to a shrinking of the working class and the rise of anti-Bolshevik sentiment in the factories.

This urban unrest was also the result of food shortages, which in turn came partly from the rural disorder created by the agrarian revolution. Soviet attempts to replace private trade with a state-run barter foundered, angering both the peasants and the hungry urban consumers. Grain requisitioning, at first ad hoc and then more coordinated, helped create the crisis on the Volga, and made the peasants of the Ukraine, Siberia, and the north Caucasus more ready to break away. (Peasant dissatisfaction in these areas was probably not the main reason why the Reds lost them, but the loss of the main food-surplus producing regions increased the requisitioning pressure on the peasants who still remained in Sovdepia.) Rural disorder also made it harder to extend Soviet control to the countryside. Stalin, that student of popular feeling, summed up the general situation in early August 1918: "The front-line soldier (*frontovik*), the 'competent *muzhik*,' who in October fought for Soviet power has now turned against Soviet power (he hates with all his soul the grain monopoly, the fixed prices, the requisitions, and the measures against the bagmen [black-marketeers])."[9]

Medvedev believed that the economic mistakes of early 1918 led to the Civil War.[10]. It is more accurate to say that the Civil War began in October 1917, but if Civil War is taken to mean the new fighting in the summer of 1918, then what Medvedev says *is* certainly more true than saying that this fighting led to the economic mistakes.

The Dictatorship of the Proletariat

The Bolsheviks' plans for the state showed the same utopian streak as their economic program. Lenin is famous for his 1917 prediction in *State and Revolution* that after the revolution the state would immediately begin to wither away. In an article of early October 1917 entitled "Can the Bolsheviks Retain State Power?" he argued that the number of

75

people who voted for the Bolsheviks showed that "we already have a 'state apparatus' of *one million* people"; moreover, "we have a 'magic way' to enlarge our state apparatus *tenfold* at once, at one stroke," and this was "to draw the working people, to draw the poor, into the daily work of state administration." The reality was different. Lenin had discovered by the Eighth Party Congress in March 1919 that there was an acute lack of reliable and trained personnel: "If some day a future historian collects information on which groups administered Russia during these seventeen months . . .," he said, "nobody will believe that it was possible to do this with such a minute strength."[11]

How, then, *did* the Bolsheviks "retain state power"? Consolidating their grip on the thirty provinces they still held (in whole or in part) was one of their greatest challenges. Only six of these provinces had given the party an absolute majority in the Constituent Assembly elections, and in thirteen the SRs had taken over sixty percent of the vote. The economic catastrophe of 1918, the hunger of the towns, the crop seizures, and the Kombedy cannot have increased Bolshevik support. And Sovdepia was a vast and overwhelmingly rural country with poor communications; of the sixty million inhabitants perhaps fifty million lived in the countryside, mostly in villages remote even from the small county towns. Even for an experienced and unambitious government it would have been hard to govern properly; *this* regime wanted to do much more: to mobilize the people and transform society.

On the positive side, certain benefits came from the huge losses at Brest-Litovsk. Although only a fifth of the provinces left in Red hands after Brest were strongly Bolshevik (based on the Constituent Assembly election returns), this was a higher proportion than when Soviet power nominally extended all over Russia. The provinces where the party had done very badly were on the frayed edges of Sovdepia or—more often—under anti-Bolshevik or foreign control. The nationalities problem was also for the moment much reduced. Only in two of the surviving Sovdepia provinces (Kazan and Chernigov) had the nationalist parties won more than half the vote (and only part of each of those provinces was in Soviet hands). Sovdepia was now a land overwhelmingly dominated by Great Russians.

One key to Bolshevik success was the gradual development of more effective state institutions. Trotsky recalled the change of tone at the center after March 1918, when the government moved to the Moscow Kremlin from the chaos of its first headquarters, Petrograd's Smolny Institute. "Where are you, old chap, in the Smolny?" Lenin would ask a comrade who was still spouting mere propaganda formulas. "Absolute Smolny"; he added, "pull yourself together, we are no longer at the

Smolny, we have gone ahead since then." The central organ of Sovdepia remained the Council of People's Commissars (Sovnarkom), which Lenin covened in the Kremlin's Senate Building. T. H. Rigby has described both the efficiency of Sovnarkom as an institution and the remarkable way Lenin changed from professional revolutionary to effective chief executive. The other major central body was the All-Russian Central Executive Committee (VTsIK). Unlike Sovnarkom, there was a considerable minority of SRs and Mensheviks here; it was largely due to the political cunning of Yakov Sverdlov, the Bolshevik chairman, that power was concentrated in the Central ExCom's Presidium, hostile debate controlled, and the influence of rival factions minimized. After the expulsion of the Mensheviks and SRs in June-July 1918 the Central ExCom seldom met; Sverdlov ignored the parliamentary niceties and used the organization to rubber-stamp Sovnarkom's decisions.[12]

The importance of the *local* soviets cannot be exaggerated. (The Central ExCom was important partly because it provided a link with them.) Fundamental policy decisions might be made in Moscow, but implementation, as well as such day-to-day administrative control as existed, was in the hands of hundreds of local soviets. One major development of 1918 was the ending of the ultrademocratic internal structure of individual soviets; power shifted from the general meeting of deputies to smaller executive organs. It is often argued that something of great value died with direct democracy, but in fact the growth of the executive organs meant the soviets were making the necessary transition from revolutionary forums to administrative organizations.

A second and related development was the meshing of the soviets into an administrative network, with a reduction of local autonomy. One effect of the July 1918 constitution was to standardize the structure and relations of the soviets, and shortly afterward this trend was reinforced by a conference of the chairman of Provincial ExComs in Moscow. Power was concentrated more and more at the provincial tier, and especially in the province-level excoms; these became the government's islands in the peasant sea. The tiers below the province—at the county (*uezd*) and rural district (*volost'*) level—were relatively undeveloped. The tier above—the region (*oblast'*), containing several provinces—was useful in areas distant from the center but disappeared in early 1919.

One-party rule in these soviets was another feature of 1918. In mid-June the SRs and the Mensheviks were expelled from the Central ExCom and many local soviets. The Left SRs suffered the same fate in July. The SRs had been moving toward armed opposition, the Mensheviks were rallying support among disgruntled workers, but it was neither of these developments, nor even the Czechoslovak uprising that killed off a broadly based socialist coalition. This was really only the finale of a process that had begun with the October rising. From the beginning Lenin and many of his closest comrades had not wanted to share authority, and from the beginning the mainstream SRs and Mensheviks had rejected the Bolshevik seizure of power; then the closing of the Constituent Assembly and the Brest capitulation made collaboration impossible. The position of the Left SRs was different, but here again it was not the Civil War but Brest and Bolshevik food policy that led to the break. (Indeed, "proper" civil war, against the conservative Whites, would actually lead in the winter of 1918–1919 to more tolerance for the other parties.) The Bolsheviks were able to clear enemies out of the soviets because of the physical weakness of those enemies. The Left SRs attempted direct action in July 1918, but their Moscow rising had little support elsewhere; its main consequence was to destroy what Left SR party leadership existed. The mainstream SRs never created a base within Sovdepia, despite peasant discontent. The economic troubles of 1918 were most helpful to the Mensheviks, who agitated in the city soviets and set up rival Assemblies of Factory Representatives. These were not able to take real power, and there was a reluctance among the Mensheviks to oppose the "workers' government" by force. The Bolsheviks were fortunate, too, that the mutual hostility of their three socialist rivals—Mensheviks, SRs, and Left SRs— made it impossible for them to form a united front.

Despite Lenin's disillusioned comments of March 1919 about "minute strength," one of the great achievements of the Bolsheviks was their mobilization of proletarian forces. Uneducated workers and (to a lesser extent) peasants were brought into the administration of the state and the economy. This was true even after the end of the era of soviet mass meetings. But it would be wrong to conclude from this that a wholly new state machine was created. Another source of administrative strength was the personnel of the old regime. For example, when Stalin and Dzerzhinsky investigated "Soviet" institutions in the town of Viatka in January 1919, they found that 4467 of 4766 officials and employees had held the same positions in the Tsarist provincial administration: "to put it plainly, the old, Tsarist, Zemstvo institutions have been simply renamed Soviet ones." This might have been expected of Viatka, a peasant province on the northeast edge of Sovdepia, but even at the heart of the Soviet state the continuities were striking. Even in the offices of the central commissariats, some 50 percent of all officials and 90 percent of senior staff had been in the administration before October 1917. In 1923 Lenin was to complain that Soviet Russia needed "to reorganize our machinery of state, which is utterly useless, and which we took over in its entirety from the preceding epoch; during the past five years we did not, and could not, drastically reorganize it."

Another important new element came neither from the simple workers and peasants nor from the old regime. One pool of talent excluded from the civil service by the Imperial government had been the Jews; they now provided educated personnel for the Soviet administration. (Trotsky, himself a Jew, saw that this could create problems: "Without connection with the native population, peasant as well as proletarian . . . these [petty bourgeois Jewish] elements hastened to take over the official posts in the state, party and union apparatus." An exaggerated identification of Jewish officials with Soviet power was a feature of White propaganda.) Daniel Orlovsky has recently suggested the importance of a much broader group, what he calls the "lower middle strata" (and which Marxists called the petty bourgeoisie); he may well be right that the rise to power of this group was one of the most significant developments of the revolutionary years.[13]

Much has been written about the "bureaucratic degeneration" of the Soviet state as a result of its Tsarist legacy and the influx of non-proletarian elements. But a Soviet state structure had to be created covering a vast territory, and the new masters of Russia were inexperienced; given this, the mixture of old and new, of proletarian and non-proletarian, was an advantage to the new regime.

The Communist Party (the Bolsheviks' proper name after March 1918) was slowly becoming another pillar of authority. It *was* no larger in size. One indirect result of the October Revolution had been a drop in membership. Some party members were disillusioned with power, more left with demobilization and the urban collapse. By the middle of 1918 there was some improvement, but membership in early 1919 was still 350,000, roughly that of 1917. Party organization also became worse right after October 1917. Able party veterans turned their attention to running the state. Local party groups served simply as propaganda agencies. Links with the center were few, and there were only a handful of organizations in the rural districts.

But in May 1918—at a time of rivalry with the Left SRs and when control over local soviets was limited—the center made the first concerted attempt to bring discipline to local party organizations and make them strong points for the new regime. In August 1918 the party Secretariat began to develop its communications with the localities;

79

Sverdlov, having asserted control of the soviets, now turned his attention to the party. In particular, the Provincial Committee (*Gubkom*) was made the key local organ and the link with the center. It was most significant that the localities too saw the need for improved organization. Under the shock of the crisis, beleaguered local party leaders were themselves by the end of 1918 calling not for autonomy but for greater centralization, and more support from Moscow.[14] The party became more unified as 1918 progressed. Opportunities for debate were few. After the Seventh Congress (March) there passed twelve months with no national party meeting, and even the small Central Committee rarely met. Few illusions about "revolutionary war" survived the February debacle, and more radical economic policies satisfied "Left Communist" intellectuals. With limited popular support and with enemies ranging from anarchists to cossacks, even the most narrow-minded comrade could see this was not the time for spirited argument. The next large-scale debate would come only in the spring of 1920, after the main White armies had been broken.

Red Terror

The Bolsheviks had, beyond the state machinery and the party, another weapon: political terror. Red Terror was partly Bolshevik self-defense against the crisis of the Civil War and, immediately, of anti-Bolshevik terrorism. A state of Red Terror was announced on 2 September 1918. Three days earlier there had been attacks on Soviet leaders: an SR named Fania Kaplan fired several shots at Lenin outside a Moscow factory, gravely wounding him, and a young socialist officer killed the head of the Petrograd *Cheka* (political police). A month earlier, on 29 July, the Central ExCom had declared the "Socialist Fatherland in Danger" and called for "mass terror" against the bourgeoisie to protect the rear. Certainly the victories of the Czechoslovaks and the threat of landings in the north increased tension.

But the roots lay deeper than the events of the summer and autumn. Imperial repression of revolutionaries created both a tradition and a climate of revenge. People such as Dzerzhinsky, the head of the Cheka, had suffered greatly. Both Bolshevik veterans and the 1917 generation shared common assumptions: History justified their every act; "bourgeois" legality was to be despised; all who opposed them had the most evil intentions. Class conflict was the foundation of all their policies, and an extreme exposition of this were the famous public instructions by Dzerzhinsky's chief deputy:

> We are exterminating the bourgeoisie as a class. During the investigation, do not look for evidence that the accused acted in deed or word against Soviet power. The first questions that you ought to put are: To what class does he belong? What is his origin? What is his education or profession? And it is these questions that ought to determine the fate of the accused. In this lies the significance and essence of the Red Terror.

Terror also came from the logic of the October uprising. No less an authority than Trotsky wrote (in 1920) that "Red terror cannot, in principle, be distinguished from armed insurrection, of which it is a direct continuation."[15] The Bolsheviks seized power with limited support, and they tried to impose a maximalist economic program. From the start there was bound to be bitter social and political conflict ("civil war"), and to this radical regime, hanging by its fingertips, any measure was justified.

Repression of class enemies was welcomed by all levels of the ruling party (and even, before July 1918, by many Left SRs). Local leaders— who were most exposed to counterrevolution and popular hostility— enthusiastically created, after the middle of 1918, their own Chekas. How far attitudes could go was shown by the Cheka of Nolinsk County (Viatka Province), which publicly called for the execution of the British diplomat Lockhart after "the most refined tortures." This did earn a rebuke from the Bolshevik CC, but there is no doubt about sympathy for terror at the center of the party. Well before the Czechoslovak uprising Lenin urged the harshest measures. "Until we use terror against speculators—shooting them on the spot—nothing will happen," Lenin had said in *January* 1918. In June, after the killing of Volodarsky (a Central ExCom member) in Petrograd by the SRs, Lenin sharply criticized Zinoviev, the leader of the Petrograd organization; Lenin had heard that "the *workers* wanted to reply to the murder of Volodarsky by mass terror," but that the local party leaders had restrained them: "I protest most emphatically! We are compromising ourselves: we threaten mass terror . . . yet . . . we *obstruct* the revolutionary initiative of the masses, a quite correct one. This is im-pos-sible." On 9 August he sent two remarkable signals. One, to Nizhnii Novgorod, informed the local leader that he should "organize *immediately* mass terror, *shoot and deport the hundreds* of prostitutes who are making drunkards of the soldiers, as well as former officers, etc." The second, to the Penza ProvExCom, urged steps "to carry out merciless mass terror

81

against the kulaks, priests and white-guards; suspects are to be shut up in a concentration camp outside the town."[16]

The continuity of terror was embodied in the history of the main instrument of the terror. The Cheka (ChK: an acronym for "Extraordinary Commission for the Struggle with Counter-Revolution and Sabotage") was founded in December 1917—nine months before the attempt on Lenin. Like other Soviet institutions, the early Cheka was a ramshackle affair; no decree set it up, and the provincial soviets were slow to follow Petrograd and Moscow. But the institution existed, and from July 1918 the Cheka began a rapid development into an all-Bolshevik, widespread, and merciless organ of repression. Red Terror, as Lenin's comments above show, had two fronts: against conscious political enemies and against "non-political" popular opposition.

On the *political* side the Cheka reported uncovering 142 counterrevolutionary organizations in just twenty provinces in 1918, and facing 245 insurrections. The Cheka did strike against the Left—against Moscow's so-called Anarchists (in April 1918) and against the Left SR July uprising. Most early victims, however, especially of the Red Terror launched in September, were from the old elite, politically bankrupt since February 1917. Petrograd was the worst: the killing of 500 hostages was announced in early September, and the total may have been twice that. In Moscow the victims were fewer but included a number of Tsarist ministers.[17]

The extreme case was Nicholas II and his family, murdered at Ekaterinburg in the Urals on the night of 16 July 1918. Much has been written about this affair, which combines the deductive problems of a detective thriller with gory terror and the spectacle of the mighty fallen. It has been suggested that some of the family might have escaped, but none was ever seen again, and there exist eyewitness accounts, some medical and documentary evidence, and statements by leading Urals Bolsheviks and by Trotsky. In corroboration was the even more brutal massacre of the Empress' sister and five Romanov princes in nearby Alapaevsk on the following night; in this case the bodies were found, and there was good eyewitness evidence. More interesting is *why* the Romanovs died, and on whose orders. The kidnapping and murder of Grand Duke Mikhail (Nicholas's brother) at Perm in mid-June seems to have been the work of what today would be called a "death squad." The "official" Soviet version gave the initiative for the Ekaterinburg and Alapaevsk killings to the Urals Regional Soviet. The leading emigre authority, S. P. Melgunov, was also inclined toward this interpretation, which fits with the disorganized state of Sovdepia in 1918. Against this is Trotsky's version: "We decided it here," Sverdlov supposedly told him in Moscow; "Illich [Lenin] believed that we shouldn't leave the Whites a live banner to rally around."[18]

The other victims of the terror were the non-political popular opposition: private traders ("speculators"), peasants who resisted food requisitioning (lumped together as "kulaks"), and even hungry and protesting workers. Rural disorder was rife in 1918. *Pravda* reported that 4140 Soviet activists had been killed by July 1918, and 6350 in the period August-September;[19] the number of victims of the Soviet activists must have been even greater.

It is difficult to gauge the scale of internal repression against both political and popular enemies in 1918, but it was large relative to the previous history of Russia. Official figures of 6300 executions by the Cheka in twenty provinces must be an understatement (although they rightly put most deaths after June 1918, when the Civil War reached a new intensity). Many others were locked up in political prisons and concentration camps (often former monasteries).[20] Whatever the numbers, the Bolsheviks' readiness to use extreme methods against their enemies was an important element in their keeping control of central Russia—at a time when their political base was small and they had little to give the people. But Terror also made enemies and provided an issue on which a spectrum of opinion—including Allied governments, Western socialists, Russian anarchists, and White generals—could unite to condemn Moscow; Red Terror would be used to justify Allied intervention and White Terror. In the long term it continued a tradition of political repression. Red Terror bought short-term benefits at a terrible price.

By the summer of 1918 the pattern of Sovdepia had been set; no major economic change took place until 1921, and one-party rule still continues. This system was not a response to the military challenge of the White generals or the Allies—that would come only in 1919. The economic revolution and the political dictatorship came from within. They were part of a "civil war" that began with the seizure of power by Lenin and his comrades.

The Bolsheviks failed to create a genuine Workers' and Peasants' Republic, but they *did* hold on to the vast territory of north-central European Russia—Sovdepia—and this was what made 1918 the decisive year. The reasons for this success include the popularity of the original "Soviet" program and the Bolsheviks' ability to create political institutions. Also important was the weakness of the opposition. In the later part of 1918 small enemy armies had sweeping successes against (even weaker) local Bolshevik forces. But nowhere was there a coherent popular challenge to Soviet rule from within. The old elite had been shattered, the liberals had never struck deep roots, the socialists were poorly organized. As for the masses, the second (October 1917) revolution had coopted their potential leaders, especially from among the workers and the intelligentsia. For other workers, the natural reaction to the 1918 crisis was not to make some kind of third revolution, but simply to abandon the towns. In the villages, meanwhile, the peasants adapted to new times and were able—as they had before 1917—to take only a minimal interest in the political life of urban Russia. In this political wasteland the Bolsheviks could slowly consolidate their position.

7

THE COSSACK VENDÉE:
May–November 1918

Starogo mira—poslednii son / Molodost'—doblest'—Vandeia—Don. (The last dream of the old world / Youth—glory—the Vendée—the Don.)

Marina Tsvetaeva, *"Lebedinyi stan,"* March 1918

Don Revival

In the early summer of 1918 Sovdepia faced rebellion on the Volga and in Siberia, internal crises in the lands that remained to it, and tense relations with the Great Power coalitions. These developments, however, masked equally ominous developments in the cossack lands of southeastern European Russia. The Triumphal March of Soviet Power in the winter of 1917–1918 had broken the resistance of the Don and Kuban Cossacks. Kaledin, the Don ataman and figurehead of the counterrevolutionary movement, shot himself. Soviet control was set up in Novocherkassk (February 1918) and Ekaterinodar (March). The little-known Volunteer Army disappeared into the Kuban Steppe. Failure at Ekaterinodar (April), with the death of Kornilov, seemed to confirm the Volunteers' complete defeat. But the Soviet victory was short-lived. By the autumn of 1918 a powerful counterrevolutionary center had been founded in the southeast, comparable to the Vendée of the French Revolution. From the southeastern base of the Don and Kuban regions would come, in 1919, the greatest military threat to Soviet Russia.

The Soviet hold was first broken in the Don Region. Cossack unrest began in late March, only a month after the Soviet victory; by 6 May

85

anti-Soviet cossacks had recaptured their capital, Novocherkassk, and made it the center of a general rebellion. A bloody civil war raged across the Don steppe. Podtelkov, the subaltern chairman of the Don Sovnarkom, was caught on an expedition to the north and hanged; seventy-three Red cossacks with him were shot.

The overthrow of Soviet power on the Don had both general and specific explanations. The Bolshevik hold over most of Russia was weak; little was needed to break it. The extension of Bolshevik control to the southern periphery had been due less to a local revolution than to the detachments of Red Guards sent from the northern cities during the "railway war." The Red Guard advance was frequently marred by indiscipline or class hatred and, while initially successful, it created many potential enemies of Soviet power. The various cossack hosts scattered across the Russian Empire presented a special challenge to the new order. They were a privileged social group, certainly compared with the local non-cossack population (the *inogorodnye*), and they were unlikely to support Soviet power in the long term. Once they got to their home *stanitsas* (villages), the radicalized front veterans, essential for the winter overturn of the conservative leadership, were brought back under their elders' influence.

The Don Soviet Republic was affected by all these influences. It had little concrete support among the cossack part of the Don population in their scattered stanitsas. Some anti-Bolshevik cossack bands were still on the loose. Badly disciplined Red food-requisitioning groups and punitive detachments quickly turned other cossacks into active enemies. The Don rebels were also helped by outside forces. There were White survivors: Denikin's Volunteer Army in the south, and Colonel Drozdovsky's detachment that arrived after a long march from the old Rumanian front. Most important of all were the German troops who had just overrun the Ukraine and Donbas to the west, and who arrived in Rostov, the biggest city of the Don, on 8 May. The German advance discredited Soviet power, took its main urban base, and diverted its forces from the internal struggle. All of this helped make possible the successful start of an anti-Soviet rising.

Once the Soviet authorities had been driven from the main Don towns, the conservative Don Cossack government that was set up had a number of advantages. The political machinery was there to create an authority for the whole cossack population of the region, an alternative to Soviet power. A crude democratic tradition had existed in the cossacks' early history, and this had been developed in 1917. Even while most of the Don Region was still in Red hands, the representatives of the "liberated" stanitsas met in Novocherkassk at an emergency

"*Krug* (Assembly) for the Salvation of the Don" in May. A Great Krug of delegates from the various stanitsas met from late August to early October. The inogorodnye were hardly represented, but the cossacks had a focus for their struggle.

The Krug for Salvation elected as their new ataman General Petr Krasnov, and to him must be given much of the credit for Don Cossack success. The son of a cossack general, Krasnov was well known as the heroic commander of cossack divisions in the world war, and also as a writer (in emigration he would make a living as a popular novelist). During the October 1917 Revolution small detachments from his cavalry corps briefly threatened Petrograd, until he was captured by the Bolsheviks—and paroled. As ataman, Krasnov had the advantage of being a colorful and effective speaker, and a man who understood the minds of the rank-and-file cossacks. (He was, among other things, an excellent horseman.) He governed with an iron hand, giving the inogorodnye little say in affairs, but his popularity among the cossacks was great. He appealed to local cossack traditions and patriotism, adopting for his cossacks the grandiose and venerable name of the All-Great Don Host.

Krasnov was able to build on the inherent military advantages of the Don. The rapid spread of the rebellion was helped by the cossacks' unique military tradition and the existing mobilization machinery. No non-cossack area could have raised so many experienced fighting men so quickly. By the middle of June a Don Army was in the field with 40,000 men, 56 guns, and 179 machine guns.[1] It was important, too, that the Don Host Territory existed as an entity, an objective for liberation. After the bloodshed of the World War and the revolution, many cossacks were unenthusiastic about more fighting, especially outside their native stanitsas. But the vigorous leadership of Krasnov and his army commander, General S. V. Denisov, was able to get cossack troops to complete the takeover of the Don and create a buffer zone in neighboring provinces.

The overall military situation was favorable. The Reds, as well as only having limited local support, had very few mobile troops to spare for restoring Soviet power on the Don. What troops there were had been thrown into the Volga campaign, 600 miles northeast of Rostov. The Don Cossacks now had important allies, unlike in the winter of 1917–1918, when Kaledin was attacked from all sides. The southern approaches to the Don were covered by Denikin's Volunteer Army, fighting a second and victorious campaign in the Kuban Region. Even more valuable was the support of the Germans. Troops from Army Group "Kiew" guaranteed Novocherkassk by garrisoning Rostov, thirty miles away, and they blocked the main railway line from Sovdepia to the center of the Don. They also held Taganrog and the Donbas, the base of many of the previous winter's Red Guard bands. German aid to Krasnov included the supply of arms, some from captured Russian stocks. This was a strange turnabout, given three years of world war and the fact that General Alekseev had come to the Don in December 1917 in order to create a new Eastern Front for the Allies. Krasnov made a Faustian bargain, taking a German Orientation and going so far as to write friendly letters to the Kaiser. The bargain would ultimately—with the Allied victory—drive him from power, but in the short term it was an essential ingredient in his victory.

With these advantages the recapture of the Don Region was completed between May and early August 1918; the question then became one of what to do next. In early September the Great Krug approved the idea of advancing beyond the borders of the Don Region to occupy vital points on the approaches, mostly railway junctions in neighboring Voronezh and Saratov Provinces. By October Don Army was involved in heavy fighting in the direction of two large Soviet cities, north to Voronezh, and east to Tsaritsyn. The Reds' Ninth Army, between Voronezh and the Volga, was pushed back steadily north. On 23 November the Don Cossacks briefly took Liski from the Red Eighth Army. Liski, where two railway lines crossed the Don, was only fifty miles south of Voronezh, and it was 100 miles nearer Moscow than was Kazan.

The Red Verdun

The Don Cossack advance led to one of the most famous episodes of the whole Civil War, the siege of Tsaritsyn. The city of Tsaritsyn was 550 miles southeast of Moscow; it was 400 miles down the Volga from Samara, and the last major town on the river before Astrakhan. (The place became internationally famous twenty-four years later as Stalingrad—and is now called Volgograd.) Tsaritsyn was just a few miles beyond the eastern border of the Don Region, in Saratov Province. By the end of July the Don Cossack anti-Soviet rebellion had reached the middle Don River, about twenty or thirty miles west of Tsaritsyn. In August the first big attack began on Red Tsaritsyn itself. A cavalry group under the cossack General Mamontov approached the town, but by the middle of the following month had been driven back behind the Don. At the end of September a second, bigger, Don Cossack offensive was launched. Krasnov threw in his newly formed regiments, and by the middle of October Don Army had nearly surrounded the city and was fighting in the outskirts. In the end it was driven off with the help of superior Red artillery; by the end of October the cossacks had been pushed back to the Don. Bolshevik propaganda compared these battles to the French defense of Verdun in 1916. The importance of the "Red Verdun" did not rest only on its actual strategic value. Joseph Stalin was among the early leaders of the city's defense, and the battle was stressed by a generation of Soviet historians; Tsaritsyn was renamed in Stalin's honor in 1925. The battles around Tsaritsyn also brought out political conflicts within the Red camp: between the center and localist leaders; about Trotsky's idea of a regular army; and between Trotsky and Stalin.

In the early summer of 1918 the most important Red military forces in southern Russia were concentrated around Tsaritsyn. They included locally raised detachments and Red survivors from the Donbas and the Don Cossack Region. The commander of the Tsaritsyn garrison from late June was Kliment Voroshilov, a thirty-seven-year-old worker and veteran Bolshevik. Voroshilov had been one of the leaders of the workers' movement in the Donbas from the spring of 1917. He was to have a great career: for decades one of Stalin's closest allies, he survived as an old man to be USSR head of state (1953–1960). And then there was Stalin himself, the man who was to become, with Lenin, the most important Russian leader of the twentieth century. He was sent south in May 1918 to take charge of food supplies from the north Caucasus, but the course of the battles with the cossacks and the Volunteer Army meant that he got no farther south than Tsaritsyn. In mid-July, without authority from Moscow, he took over the military supervision of the Tsaritsyn area, working closely with Voroshilov.

What set off direct confrontation between Moscow and Tsaritsyn was the development of a mass Red Army. There was now a national command structure, based on the War Commissar (Trotsky). Former officers had a major role; Colonel Vatsetis, having taken Kazan, became Main Commander-in-Chief of the whole Red Army. His Eastern Army Group became the model for the Red front-commands. The breathing space after the recapture of Kazan (10 September) allowed Trotsky and the new "regular" General Headquarters (Stavka) to turn their attention to the other fronts. The Southern Army Group was one result of these changes, and command there, like that of the other army groups, was entrusted to a RevMilCouncil. But Moscow had combined the incompatible: on the one hand there were three Tsaritsyn leaders, Stalin, Voroshilov, and another Bolshevik (S. K. Minin); on the other a former Tsarist general named Sytin. The three "civilians" were preoccupied with Tsaritsyn and wanted all resources for their sector. The Tsaritsyn forces became Tenth Army in late September, but there were three other armies in the army group: Eighth and Ninth north of the Don, and Eleventh in the north Caucasus. Sytin's headquarters was 350 miles from Tsaritsyn, at Kozlov. And the attitude of the Tsaritsyn comrades towards the former officers was one of contempt and even hatred; Sytin himself had no revolutionary pedigree; he was a Tsarist general (and a classmate of Denikin's).

The volatile mixture exploded after only three weeks. Stalin, Voroshilov, and Minin remained at Tsaritsyn, and the new RevMilCouncil never worked together. When Stytin finally visited Tsaritsyn on 29 September, the meeting of the RevMilCouncil degenerated into argument. Two days later the civilian members reported that Sytin had been removed, and requested that Voroshilov replace him. This was intolerable to Trotsky and Vatsetis, and with Lenin's support Stalin was recalled to Moscow in October.

The assertion of central control during the "Tsaritsyn affair" was handled with some tact. People's Commissar Stalin was not disgraced; he remained at Tsaritsyn for some weeks until the end of the cossack siege; when he got back to Moscow he was put on Trotsky's RevMil-Council of the Republic, and later he was given further tasks in the field. Voroshilov was made commander of Tenth Army (at Tsaritsyn), and General Sytin was transferred to a staff post in Moscow in November. But Trotsky and Vatsetis had made their point. Sytin stayed, if briefly; Stalin left. Voroshilov was removed in December, and Sytin's replacements were, like him, former Tsarist officers. And it was an important practical victory for Trotsky's principles of centralism. No comparable challenge had been made in Eastern Army Group, and when a challenge did come in the south Trotsky was supported by Lenin, and presumably other Bolshevik leaders. Some of the Tenth Army people would figure in the "Military Opposition" to Trotsky at the Eighth Party Congress in the following spring, but Trotsky would win that victory too.

The conflict had had much to do with Stalin's attitudes. In 1918 he was in favor of a fully socialist army, dominated by the party. His idea of the new "officer" was the politically reliable and battle-proven former private. Stalin disliked Tsarist officers ("our military 'specialists' (bunglers! [sapozhniki])"),[2] and he showed very little tact in dealing with them. This was hardly unique to Stalin. Where Stalin was different, perhaps, was in his high-level opposition, his desire for his own personal authority, and his willfulness. A Central Committee member and People's Commissar, he refused to be part of the military system that Trotsky was trying to create. He appealed over Trotsky's head to Lenin; "I shall myself," he said, "without any formalities, dismiss those army commanders and commissars who are ruining things . . . and, of course, not having a paper from Trotsky is not going to stop me."

Stalin's attitude was understandable in the summer of 1918, when local leaders had to act on their own or go under. At that time Trotsky could claim no greater military expertise; Stalin had been "in the field" for a month before Trotsky's train began its famous journey to Kazan in early August 1918. But Stalin's willfulness was also evident in his actions in 1919–1920. Trotsky, on the other hand, was fighting hard to win the principle of using former officers, and he too was contemptuous of his opponents. He wrote to Lenin about "Party ignoramuses," and Stalin must have been one of the ignoramuses he had in mind.[3] Here the beginnings of the personal conflict between the two men became more obvious.

The irony of the Tsaritsyn affair was that Stalin and Voroshilov, the two men who opposed Trotsky's regular army, were to preside over an army more centralized, more regular, more powerful than anything Trotsky could have dreamed of in 1918. Voroshilov was head of the Red Army from 1925 to 1940, as People's Commissar and later with the rank of Marshal. As for Stalin, he was a Marshal, then a Generalissimo, hailed as a military genius, and from 1941 to 1945 Supreme Commander-in-Chief of the largest army the world has ever seen. Poachers do make the best gamekeepers.

The defense of Tsaritsyn was not the decisive battle of the Civil War, as Stalinist historians would have it, but neither was it, as Trotsky later suggested, relatively unimportant. Tsaritsyn had developed as an industrial town in the World War and in 1917 had been a radical revolutionary center. But it was the connection between Tsaritsyn and the Caucasus region that was vital. The rich lands north of the Caucasus Mountains were a major source of food, and south of the mountains there were the mineral resources, especially oil, of Azerbaidzhan. Politically the Caucasus was a potential base for counterrevolution; here were not only the national minorities but also the cossacks, and the kernel of the White Russian counterrevolutionary movement. Red armies were already fighting in the north Caucasus and had to be supported. Tsaritsyn was a gateway to the Caucasus. The main railway from Moscow to the Caucasus via Voronezh and Rostov was under

German control, but there was (in May–June 1918) an alternative indirect route southeast from Moscow to Tsaritsyn, and then southwest to the Kuban. Also crucially important was the great waterway of the Volga. For both of these routes Tsaritsyn was an essential link, and loss of the town would effectively cut the Caucasus off from Sovdepia. Tsaritsyn was also one of the natural anchors of the Soviet armies in the south, defending against an attack from the Don and the North Caucasus. In particular, the city blocked any link between the Don Cossack host west of the Volga and either the Ural or Orenburg hosts to the east. Likewise, it covered Saratov (200 miles upstream) from the south and prevented a link with the Komuch forces at Samara.

On the other hand, by the late summer Tsaritsyn had lost much of its significance. The city held out, but the vital railway line was cut northwest and southwest of it in July. And the loss of Tsaritsyn would not have been a direct threat to Moscow, which was 550 miles away. The cossacks attacking Tsaritsyn were moving east, *away* from the Soviet capital; they wanted protection for their borders, not a route to the north. A more direct threat to Moscow was the other prong of the Don advance, north towards Voronezh. (And this was one of the reasons why Trotsky was concerned about an overconcentration on Tsaritsyn.)

The successful defense was no miracle. The attacking forces were not the combined hordes of the counterrevolution, just the Don Cossacks. Denikin's Volunteer Army was moving in the opposite direction, south, deeper into the Kuban. (In May and September he rejected Krasnov's suggestion that he join the attack.) The defenders were hardly outnumbered. "We have," Trotsky noted in his October signal demanding Stalin's recall, "a colossal superiority of forces." Two-thirds of the Red forces facing the Don were concentrated at Tsaritsyn—40,000 men and 240 guns.[4] The Don Cossacks were meanwhile under considerable pressure from two other Red armies (Eighth and Ninth) advancing south. But the cossacks were able to blockade Tsaritsyn, even if they could not take it, and this meant doom for the Soviet armies farther south.

The Volunteer Army

Don Army fought alone on its northern and eastern borders, because Volunteer Army was 300 miles to the south, in the Kuban Region. The

First Kuban Campaign, the Ice March of February–May 1918, ended in failure and the death of General Kornilov. The Second Kuban Campaign was the making of Volunteer Army, now commanded by General Denikin. The fighting was bitter and merciless. It began at the end of June, after the Volunteers had regrouped on the Don; within three weeks they had taken Tikhoretskaia, the central rail junction of the Kuban, and indeed of the whole north Caucasus. On 18 August they captured Ekaterinodar, the capital of the "North Caucasus Soviet Republic" and the town where in April Kornilov had been killed and Volunteer Army nearly broken. The local Reds were forced to move their capital 200 miles southeast down the railway to Piatigorsk. Volunteer control was quickly extended through the north and west of the Kuban Region, and a series of bitter battles began to the east and south, into Stavropol Province and along the rail line to Piatigorsk. The last big effort of the Red armies in the north Caucasus was the recapture of Stavropol at the end of October, but on 18 November the White General Vrangel finally took the city back. As the World War ended the Red forces were trapped in a pocket in the center of the north Caucasus, and their complete destruction was only a few months away.

The advance of Volunteer Army was an extraordinary victory. Denikin began with only 9000 men, while total Red forces in the north Caucasus were something like 80,000–100,000 men.[5] The paper strength of the Soviet side hid serious weaknesses. The situation in the north Caucasus was very complex. Various areas—the Kuban Region, the coastal Black Sea Province, and Stavropol Province—were combined in early July into the North Caucasus Soviet Republic, with its center in the Kuban capital, Ekaterinodar; this unity, however, was largely a fiction. Much of the local population was hostile to Soviet power, and there were few urban centers to provide proletarian supporters. Worse still, the north Caucasus was isolated from the Soviet mainland.

In May 1918 the German advance and the Don uprising cut the direct rail link to central Russia, through Rostov. In July even the indirect rail link via Tsaritsyn was broken, thanks to the Don Cossack blockade. The Tsaritsyn forces were too busy fighting for their own survival to send reinforcements south. Meanwhile, the southeastern part of the north Caucasus, the Terek Region and Dagestan, were in great turmoil; insurgent Terek cossacks and fighting tribesmen occupied much of the countryside and cut the rail line leading southeast to the Caspian; for some months Soviet power here was restricted to a few towns. The area south of the Caucasus mountains was outside Soviet control, being claimed by various national governments; here there were also detachments of German, Turkish, and British troops.

The Reds had some good fighting troops. The most notable was the 30,000-strong force trapped in the Taman Peninsula (the extreme west of the Kuban) by the Volunteers' advance. In August–September the Taman Army carried out a 300-mile march around the White lines, an episode that formed the basis of Serafimovich's famous novel of 1924, *The Iron Flood*. The overall cohesion, training, and supply of the Soviet forces, however, was bad. Although the "Red Army of the North Caucasus" was renamed Eleventh Army in October and incorporated into Southern Army Group, this veil of regularity meant little. The various detachments were not well coordinated, and they were manned by a mixture of types, including refugees from the Ukraine and marooned survivors of the Tsarist Caucasus Army Group and Black Sea Fleet.

The overall commander at the time of the Volunteer attack in July was a Latvian Ensign named K. I. Kalnin, but he was unable to cope, and was replaced in August by Ivan Sorokin, a cossack subaltern. Sorokin was apparently one of the "revolutionary" commanders of whom Stalin and Voroshilov thought highly; in September they confirmed his appointment and general strategy without General Sytin's approval. Unfortunately Sorokin was neither militarily gifted nor politically obedient. He executed the commander of the Taman Army, apparently in an argument about strategy. Then, in October, he attempted a coup in Piatigorsk, shooting the Bolshevik leaders of the Central ExCom of the North Caucasus Soviet Republic. It was a murky affair reminiscent of Muraviev's Volga uprising three months earlier. Sorokin apparently feared his own dismissal; he was a Left SR and, according to Denikin, hated the Jews who led the Central ExCom.[6] No one supported him, and he was killed by loyal Red forces a week later; in any event, a very difficult military situation was made even worse.

The Volunteer Army, on the other hand, may have been outnumbered, but it had strong local support. The Kuban cossacks, who made up 45 percent of the population of the Kuban Region, were hostile to the local Soviet government, which they saw as the rule of the inogorodnye. Many cossack stanitsas rose in revolt against Soviet rule and helped the Volunteer advance. Operating behind Red lines with great effectiveness was the partisan band of Colonel Shkuro. The Red Army of the North Caucasus also had the misfortune to be fighting the most effective of the counterrevolutionary armies. The Volunteer Army was made up largely of officers and Kuban Cossacks, men who were military professionals, men who had elected to continue the struggle against Bolshevism. Hardened by the First Kuban Campaign, with their rear now protected by the Germans and Krasnov's Don Cossacks, they were able to cut through a much larger enemy force. Denikin's capture of the northwestern Kuban provided manpower for the rapid expansion of his army. By September 1918 the Volunteer Army had increased to 35,000–40,000 men in three infantry and three cavalry divisions, with a number of detached brigades.[7] They were now increasingly an army of conscripts rather than of more highly motivated "volunteers," but many of the conscripts were Kuban Cossacks, men with experience and a strong military tradition.

The Volunteers were still thought of by outsiders as "Alekseev's army." General M. V. Alekseev, the former Chief of Staff to Nicholas II, had moved to the Don at the end of 1917 to set up a center of resistance to Bolshevism and to Germany. But the victories of the Second Kuban Campaign were actually organized by the little-known General Denikin, who had taken over military command following Kornilov's death in April 1918. A rather stout officer of forty-six (fifteen years younger than Alekseev), with a shaven scalp and a beard and full moustache, Anton Ivanovich Denikin was an intelligent man and a gifted military commander. Denikin had proven himself in the World War as the courageous commander of the 4th ("Iron") Rifle Division. When the February 1917 revolution came, his flexibility and talents suggested him for rapid promotion; he was made Chief of Staff to the Supreme Commander-in-Chief (he had attended the General Staff Academy), and then Commander-in-Chief of two army groups in succession. Denikin never proved himself as a leader of very large armies; his 1919–1920 campaign ended in disaster. But he seems to have been well suited to the relatively small Second Kuban Campaign. The victories of June–August 1918 were ones for which he was directly responsible; this was also his last campaign as a front-line commander. (In September 1918 he looked back, obviously with regret, and remarked: "Earlier I *led* the army, now I *commanded* it.'"[8])

In the autumn of 1918 Denikin became not only the military commander of the Volunteer Army but also the unchallenged ruler of the territory captured by it. One reason for this was Kornilov's death in April, after which Denikin and Alekseev divided the military and political spheres between them. Then, on 8 October 1918, Alekseev too died—after a year of serious illness—and Denikin was left with sole control over both spheres. The deaths in battle of Generals Markov and Drozdovsky, two of the Volunteer Army's three original infantry-division commanders, also confirmed Denikin's "seniority" over the surviving Volunteer leaders. Denikin was catapulted into the political leadership of the counterrevolution more by accident than by his own initiative or that of political allies. He was not personally ambitious for power, he was not the instrument of internal or external interests, and he was a man whose personal politics were narrow but not reactionary.

Denikin laid the foundations of his administration and set out his political program during the autumn of 1918. Whatever his personal beliefs, his solution to the new Russian "Time of Troubles" (*Smuta*, the term he used in his memoirs) was military rule; he had emerged as a believer in the firm hand of authority while an army-group commander in 1917, and he maintained this position as the "Troubles" worsened. The Volunteer-Army administration was in essence a centralized military dictatorship, headed by the Commander-in-Chief (Denikin) himself. Denikin created a kind of "government," the Special Council set up in Ekaterinodar in late August 1918, but this dealt with only minor issues. Little attempt was made to create a wider base for the Volunteer regime, either at its center or in the newly captured areas.

Denikin's program, a program of conservative Russian nationalism, was brought out in speeches he made that autumn. One basic point was a claim to be "above" politics ("the tricolor flag of Russia the Great Power is surely higher than all party flags"). As for the Constituent Assembly, the backbone of the Komuch regime on the Volga, it "arose in the days of popular insanity, was half made up of anarchist elements, and does not have the slightest moral authority in the country at large." There would be no "predetermination" of politics, but likewise there would be no attempt at social reform ("the hard and painful days in which we live, when Russia is reduced to mere threads, are not the right time for solving social problems"). Local autonomy was promised, but alongside it was the famous slogan of "Russia One and Indivisible"— and the treatment of the minorities and the cossacks as merely part of the "Russian people." Finally, there could be no dependence on foreigners, an implied criticism of Krasnov and his German allies.[9]

Denikin's narrow "politics" were to be one of the reasons for his defeat in the winter of 1919–1920. But just as Denikin was well suited to command the 1918 north Caucasus campaign, so his political program was no great liability in the Kuban in the summer and autumn of 1918. The Volunteers were fighting a battle to capture a cossack area in revolt against Soviet power; in the joint life-or-death struggle with the Reds there was no need to worry about relations with the cossacks. Anyway, the Kuban had no Krasnov, no popular leader who could rival Denikin. (Krasnov's Don, for its part, was distant and—at this time—outside Denikin's zone of influence.) The Volunteer Army's leaders did not yet need to worry over much about a stable administration or social reform. There were few politicians to compete with, and the Volunteer movement rested on Kuban Cossacks and disgruntled officers rather than on Russian peasants or the ethnic minorities. What was needed in the short term was a nationalist program that would rally conservatives, and that Denikin had.

At various times in 1918 the Volunteer leaders were urged to send their army north toward Voronezh or Tsaritsyn rather than south to the Kuban. But probably the decision to move south was the right one. Although the Volunteers might have helped the Don Cossacks liberate their territory, they also made a contribution in the Kuban, protecting the long southern flank of the Don. Given that the Don Cossack rank and file were ready to free their "own" land but not to attack the "Russian" provinces to the north or the Kuban to the south, it was an intelligent division of labor for the Volunteers to undertake the Kuban campaign. The Volunteer Army's capture of the Kuban in July and August 1918 was one of the most important events of the Civil War, more important in retrospect than the battles on the Volga. The conservative officers of the White movement now had their "own" territorial base (assuming the subordination of the Kuban Cossacks), and from this base they would build their "state" and hold it for nearly two years, as the main threat to Bolshevik Russia.

In November 1918 Trotsky confessed to the Sixth Congress of Soviets about weaknesses in the south.

> Until recently the Southern front was, so to speak, our stepchild: our attitude towards it was almost one of letting things slide, the reason being, of course, that we had to concentrate our attention, forces and assets upon the Northern [sic] front. The English, French and Czechoslovaks were there, and the Americans and Japanese had already appeared on the Eastern horizon. [He added:] And we during the first year of the revolution became too easily used to disposing of the internal counterrevolution and our own bourgeoisie . . . by means of improvised workers' detachments. . . . Because of this we developed a contemptuous attitude towards the Southern front, a conviction that we should get rid of our enemies eventually, sooner or later.[10]

By the start of November 1918 the anti-Bolshevik forces had made great gains. They now controlled the Don and Kuban. The Red armies in the rump of the north Caucasus had been cut off; they would only survive a few more months. All the economic wealth of the Caucasus region was beyond the reach of the Reds. The Triumphal March of Soviet Power was reversed only for a few months on the Volga, but it was overturned more decisively in the cossack lands. Comparing the defeat of Komuch on the one hand, and the victory of the Don Cossacks and the Volunteer Army on the other, it is clear that the Reds' decision to concentrate

97

forces on the Volga was not the only factor. The southern counterrevolutionaries had a less attractive political program than Komuch, but they had much superior military assets in the form of the cossacks and the officers. They were farther, too, from revolutionary central Russia, and had a shorter front to defend. Perhaps most important, they had, in the form of the two cossack hosts, a large social group opposed to the revolution and one with its own sense of community.

Any account of the Civil War that stresses Allied intervention would be hard put to explain the difference between the Volga and the south. The Volga front had a link—although a very long one—with the Pacific, and operating on the Volga were Allied troops of a sort—the Czechoslovak Corps. The southern counterrevolutionaries were completely cut off and lacked the help of any sort of Allied troops. But before the World War Armistice, before the first tenuous contact was made with representatives of the Allied powers, and months before substantial Allied supplies arrived, the Don Cossacks and the Volunteer Army had established a southern Vendée some 500 miles deep and up to 300 miles wide.

8

SIBERIA AND THE URALS,
February–November 1918

The SR Party ... must before anything else guarantee that it will not be submerged in the counter-revolutionary tide as it was a year ago in the tide of Bolshevik anarchy.

Chernov Circular, October 1918

Having given me supreme power, the government thus recognized that in these final hours of the state's life only the armed forces, only the army, offer salvation; everything else must be subordinated to its interests and tasks.

Admiral Kolchak, 23 November 1918

The End of Soviet Power

Soviet power had been extended right across the Eurasian land mass during the "Triumphal March of Soviet Power" in the winter of 1917–1918. By midsummer 1918, however, both Siberia and the Urals had been lost; within nine months Siberia would serve as the base for a general offensive against Soviet power. The immediate cause of this drastic change was an outside force—the uprising of the Czechoslovak Corps at the end of May 1918. Why the Czechoslovak Corps was in Russia and why it rose in revolt have already been discussed. The Siberian soviets must take some responsibility, as they interfered with the Corps' movement east. In any event, when the rising began the Corps was positioned along the only east-west line of communications, the Trans-Siberian Railway.

The Corps' task was far from easy. There were only 40,000 Czechoslovaks, and they were split up into four groups: in the Volga region, at Vladivostok on the Pacific, and—in between—around Cheliabinsk in the southern Urals and around Novonikolaevsk (now Novosibirsk) in central Siberia. In terms of American geography the Volga group were 300 miles *east* of New York, the Vladivostok units were 1000 miles *west* of San Francisco; the Cheliabinsk group were in Pittsburgh and the Novonikolaevsk group in Salt Lake City. In early July the Volga and Cheliabinsk groups finally linked up and turned toward the north Urals and the regional capital of Ekaterinburg. One indirect consequence was the Bolsheviks' killing of the Imperial family in the besieged city on the 17th. Ekaterinburg was taken on 25 July, and the Reds pulled back to the west, abandoning all the Urals and Siberia. Three months after the uprising began, at the end of August 1918, the Czechoslovak leader Colonel Gajda broke through the last Red barrier in Transbaikalia and opened the railway from the Volga to the Pacific.

If the Czechoslovak outsiders were crucially important in Siberia and the Urals, the same cannot be said about Allied forces from Japan, Europe, and America. Some military planners wanted a new Japanese-manned eastern front in the Urals or even on the Volga, but this was strategic dreaming. On top of the immense logistical difficulties there was inter-Allied suspicion, especially between Japan and the United States. After much hesitation some Japanese and British marines came ashore in Vladivostok in April. Later in the year more Japanese, up to 70,000, were landed; the numbers were large, vast by the standards of the Allied intervention, and the Japanese were largely responsible for ending Soviet power on the thinly populated Pacific coast. But most of the Japanese forces stayed near Vladivostok; only a few were sent the 2000 miles to Lake Baikal (which was in turn still 2000 miles from the Urals). The Americans, pushed into action by a desire to "save" the Czechoslovaks, sent several thousand troops to Vladivostok in August, but their commander—having been warned that he would be "walking on eggs loaded with dynamite" avoided an active role.[1] The British were the first to send forces deep into Siberia, but only in mid-October did the 25th Middlesex Battalion (a second-line unit) arrive in Omsk, the Siberian capital, and it was not involved in combat.

Soviet power in Siberia, according to two of the most recent Western accounts, was not actually heading for internal collapse in the spring of 1918.[2] That may well be true. But what happened in the Urals and Siberia is not explained just by the intervention of outsiders. The Czechoslovaks had the striking effect they did because of the weakness of Soviet power. When he was most worried about a German attack at the start of 1918, Lenin had talked seriously about retreat with his government deep into Siberia, basing the regime on the iron of the Urals and the coal of Siberia's Kuznetsk Basin (550 miles east of the Urals); "From the borders of our Uralo-Kuznets Republic, we will spread out again and return to Moscow and Petersburg."[3] Just how much of a fantasy this was became clear when the Czechoslovaks swept through the region.

It has already been shown that the east was a poor base for Bolshevik power. As in European Russia, the great majority of the population worked on the land, but among the Siberian farmers there were few large landowners and relatively few who were desperately poor. There were not many workers and the intelligentsia was small. In the November 1917 Constituent Assembly elections the Bolsheviks received only 10 percent of the votes in Siberia and 20 percent in the Urals. Four or five months of Soviet rule reduced the party's base of support. One major factor was grain requisitioning; of 500,000 tons of grain collected in the six months after November 1917, four-fifths were collected in Siberia.[4] In addition there had been a ham-fisted expropriation of the widespread farmers' cooperatives. Meanwhile, the general economic chaos caused by war and revolution had not been solved, and this cost the Bolsheviks support in the Urals and the small Siberian cities.

Meanwhile, there was disorder in the Soviet ranks. Eastern Russia, with its vast size, small population, and primitive infrastructure, was hard for anyone to govern. Between central Russia and Siberia was the independent-minded Urals Region (oblast'), centered on Ekaterinburg. In Siberia the nominal center of Soviet power was Irkutsk, where the "Central ExCom of the Siberian Soviets" (Tsentrosibir) had its headquarters. Regional subcenters with more real power were at Omsk in Western Siberia and Khabarovsk in the Far East; they—and even smaller units such as the Amur Socialist Republic (centered on Blagoveshchensk)—frequently disagreed with Tsentrosibir's policies. The lack of coordination, especially in military matters, paralleled that of the south Russian "soviet republics" during the Austro-German invasion.

The Reds had had more armed men in the east than the Czechoslovaks and the Russian anti-Bolsheviks. The Red forces, however, were static and badly organized, and in May 1918 the best of them were away fighting a cossack uprising in Transbaikal. Outside the Urals there were few workers to form Red Guard detachments; a few "Internationalist" detachments existed, with Hungarian and other freed POWs, but nothing like the well-organized Latvian Riflemen, who were such a help for the Bolsheviks in central Russia. Even in the north Urals, where the Reds had significant resources of enthusiastic manpower, they were no match for the Czechoslovaks. The loss of that region in late July came partly from the inexperience, weakness, and lack of concentration of the Red Army, as Vatsetis, the new Eastern Army Group Commander-in-Chief, complained. Third Army, defending Ekaterinburg and the north Urals, had 16,000 men spread along a front of 600 miles without any reserves: "This would have been alright if our job had been to organize a border patrol to catch smugglers."[5]

Internal disorder was also a factor, especially in the aftermath of Muraviev's abortive July coup. Third Army had been created from the "North Urals-Siberia Army Group," but at first this was regularization in name only, and there were great problems finding a suitable commander. Trotsky wanted an experienced officer, General Nadezhny, the local Bolsheviks wanted a reliable comrade, the Latvian Ensign R. I. Berzin. The compromise appointment, General Bogoslovsky, served two days and defected to the Czechoslovaks with much of his staff, Ekaterinburg fell without a fight, and Berzin had to be brought back.

A final sign of the Reds' weakness was their inability to organize an effective underground in the East once they had been swept from power. A small underground Siberian regional conference of Bolsheviks was held in Tomsk in August 1918, but its call for a general armed uprising had little practical impact. The liberation of the Urals and Siberia would have to wait the development of a powerful Red Army in central Russia.

Czechoslovak initiative and Bolshevik weakness were the two most important general factors in the reopening of the Civil War in the east. Tomsk was the only major town where Soviet power fell without active interference by the Czechoslovak Corps. But a sustained movement needed *Russian* anti-Bolshevik forces; these began to surface immediately after the uprising and in 1919 would take full control of the movement. There was, it should be stressed, no popular upsurge against Soviet rule. In addition, the party that had the largest popular backing, the SRs, made little effective impact in the east. Their brief moment would come at the start of 1920; in 1918 their resources were concentrated on the Volga and the Komuch government.

The dominant active political forces were non-socialist. Among the civilians were the "regionalists" (*oblastniki*), the advocates of Siberian self-government (most Siberians were of Great Russian stock). Their first general conference was held only in December 1917, they had no

SIBERIA AND THE URALS

Constituent Assembly list, but they had considerable local appeal. On the right, too, were the junior officials who ran the day-to-day affairs of the Siberian government; many were Kadets (and on the right of that party). A number were all the more convinced counterrevolutionaries because they had fled from Soviet central Russia. These conservative civilians were the main force behind the Siberian and Urals provisional governments. The Provisional Siberian Government (PSG), based in Omsk, was the earlier and more important of these two authorities. It was originally formed on 23 June, and its most prominent figure was the veteran regionalist P. V. Vologodsky.

Cossack hosts played a major part in Siberia, as they did in South Russia. The Siberian Host was dispersed and small in numbers (170,000), but its headquarters was in Omsk. The Transbaikal Host— 1700 miles to the east—was the fourth largest in Russia, and here an anti-Soviet force took shape. Its active leader was a twenty-eight-year-old cossack subaltern named Grigory Semenov; in January 1918 he swooped in across the Manchurian border, and although he was driven off he distracted the Tsentrosibir forces during the Czechoslovak uprising.

Then there were the army officers. A secret inspection by the Volunteer Army in May 1918 (before the uprising) found that there was a loosely organized underground of nearly 8000 officers of various ranks in Siberia, over a third in Omsk. These had had no active cossack core to rally around, as had the Volunteers on the Don, but they quickly supported the Czechoslovaks. Once Soviet power had been restored the officers turned their attention to raising a regular Siberian Army. The army's leaders stressed, especially from the autumn, traditional discipline rather than "revolutionary consciousness." On the whole the civilians of the Provisional Siberian Government let the army run its own affairs; this was to have grave repercussions in the future.

Siberia seems to have been better territory than the Volga for the raising of troops. The new Siberian Army flew the green and white flag, symbol of the forests and snows of the region, and it won local support. A general mobilization was announced in late June 1918, with a stress on the eighteen- and nineteen-year-olds; these youngsters were thought to be politically more reliable than the veterans. By September the Siberian Army had 38,000 men with seventy field guns; by October it had been organized into five corps, deployed from the Urals to the Amur. The Siberians could build up their forces partly because they did little to help Komuch, which was then fighting for its life; but although this made the defeat of Komuch all the more certain it did mean that powerful forces were saved for a future campaign.[6]

The new Siberian Army fitted, nominally at least, into an alliance of anti-Bolshevik forces. When, in late September 1918, a body claiming overall authority was formed, the Provisional All-Russian Government, it appointed General V. G. Boldyrev as "Supreme Commander-in-Chief of All Russian Armed Forces." Boldyrev was an experienced officer of humble origins and relatively liberal views. He was in charge of the Siberian Army, the remains of the Komuch Army, the Ural and Orenburg Cossacks, and the Bashkir nomads. Boldyrev was also nominally in charge of the Czechoslovaks, but because they were by far the best trained and equipped they were the ultimate masters; the operational commander on the main front, facing Bolshevik European Russia, was the Czechoslovak General Syrovy.

The eastern armies were not able to carry out major offensive operations for some time after July–August 1918, but it was important that once Boldyrev took over he decided to build up the *right* flank of his forces facing Sovdepia. The main line of advance would be from Ekaterinburg in the northern Urals toward Perm, Viatka, and eventual contact with the Allied Arkhangelsk front. The commander of this Ekaterinburg front was Rudolf Gajda, the Czechoslovak leader who had just captured Transbaikal. The core of his forces from the end of 1918 would be the combat units of the new Siberian Army. But before that campaign the Siberian Army was to have an important political part to play.

The Directory and Kolchak

The end of Soviet power was only the first major political change in Siberia in 1918. The second was the November coup d'état and the military dictatorship of Admiral Kolchak. In the early summer of 1918 the new rulers of the vast region from the Volga to the Pacific faced the same problems of geography and communications as had their Soviet predecessors; there were even greater political differences. One center was the Committee of Members of the Constituent Assembly (Komuch), formed at Samara on the Volga on 8 June. The other, the Provisional Siberian Government, took shape in Omsk at the end of June. The PSG was far removed from Komuch, both geographically and politically. Samara was on the Volga; Omsk was 1100 miles by rail to the east, beyond the Urals in the west Siberian steppe. Komuch was dominated by the Socialist-Revolutionaries; the PSG was politically to the right. (There were other political administrations in the Far East—which until September 1918 had no physical link with western or central Siberia: the ephemeral leftist "Provisisional Government of Autonomous Siberia" and the conservative administration of General Khorvat in the Chinese-Eastern Railway zone of Manchuria. Although both groups claimed wide powers, the region would be brought—nominally—under the Omsk government in September.)

The conservative government in Siberia did not reflect a conservative population. The per capita base of the SRs was, if anything, greater in Siberia than the Volga-Urals area; for every twenty Constituent Assembly voters in Siberia, fifteen had voted for the SRs, one for the Kadets, and none for the regionalists (two would have voted for the Bolsheviks). The SRs also had a good base in the powerful agricultural cooperative movement. Given this situation, the Provisional Siberian Government was careful to contain its rivals to the Left, and it blocked the SR attempt to reopen the Siberian Regional Duma. (The Duma had been closed by the Bolsheviks in January 1918; it had been created by the SR-dominated All-Siberian Regional Congress.)

The rivalry between Samara and Omsk took several forms. Control over the territory of the Ekaterinburg-based "Urals Provisional Government" was disputed. (It became a kind of buffer zone, leaning more to the PSG than Komuch, and in November was abolished.) A customs war of sorts was fought between the two, with Siberia refusing to send grain and Komuch blocking the shipment of manufactured goods. There was rivalry in officer recruitment, with Omsk, because of its more conservative policies, poaching officers from the Volga government. Most important, there was no agreement on an overall government for the area liberated from Soviet control. Even if the two "governments" did not realize the folly of this situation, the Czechoslovaks, the Allied representatives, and even Komuch army leaders did, and they put pressure on both sides. The result was two meetings at the Urals town of Cheliabinsk which finally agreed—13 weeks after the Czechoslovak uprising—to call an "all-Russian" conference.

The State Conference (*Gosudarstvennoe Soveshchanie*) met in Ufa from 8 to 23 September 1918. Ufa was a province capital halfway between the Urals and the Volga. The conference met, too, roughly halfway in time between the start of the overthrow of Soviet power in the Volga-Urals-Siberia area (in May) and the establishment of Kolchak's military dictatorship (in November). The State Conference was the last attempt to form from below an all-Russian anti-Bolshevik authority. The 170 delegates represented not only Komuch and the PSG but also various smaller authorities and the political parties. On the left was a large

105

delegation from Komuch, and individuals from the Urals, from various Moslem groups, and from the Center-Left parties. On the right, in a minority, were the representatives from the PSG and seven cossack hosts. Various factors forced the two sides toward compromise. Most important were the military difficulties of the "front-line" government, Komuch, which lost Kazan and Simbirsk, north of Samara, on 10 and 12 September; Samara itself soon came under military pressure (and would fall on 7 October, two weeks after the conference closed). The PSG, for its part, was embarrassed by the kidnapping and murder of a leftist politician in Omsk by cossacks, and was worried about retaliation by the Czechoslovak forces (who were generally sympathetic to the SRs). A Center-Left group, the Union for the Regeneration of Russia, and local Allied representatives had an important mediating role.

The final result of the Ufa conference, the Provisional All-Russian Government (PA-RG), was a compromise. Komuch won recognition for the SR-dominated Constituent Assembly as the eventual basis of power. The Right won a three-month stay of execution, until January 1919, before this would happen; even then the Assembly would only have authority if it had a quorum of 250. Komuch lost its claim to be the legal all-Russian government, and in its place the embodiment of the PA-RG, temporarily at least, was to be a five-man Directory (*Direktoriia*); this included only two SRs, Avksentiev and Zenzinov; the other directors were Vologodsky, a regionalist and head of the Omsk PSG, the liberal General Boldyrev, and the left Kadet Vinogradov.

The Provisional All-Russian Government promised much but lasted for only eight weeks; it was formed on 23 September 1918 and overthrown by a rightist coup on 18 November. This failure was, in retrospect, of great significance for the anti-Bolshevik movement: the PA-RG was the last broadly based government to exist on Russian soil. Some of its weaknesses were personal and institutional. In its short life the coalition Directory never had much real power. It lacked the talented personnel of its French revolutionary namesake. It was never intended to be more than a temporary institution; it only established a fixed base in mid-October, and that was in Omsk. (Ekaterinburg, in the Urals, had been the original choice for the "capital," but it was too near the front.) Even then the Directory, until near the end of its existence, was based in railway coaches. The important thing about Omsk was that it had been the capital of the Provisional Siberian Government. Effective day-to-day administration was in the hands of a Council of Ministers, which was in turn dominated by veterans of the PSG—ten of fourteen members; the chairman, the Director Vologodsky, was a Siberian regionalist and the former head of the PSG.

Even more important were the political weaknesses of the PA-RG. The Directory would be overthrown from the right, but was also challenged from the left; it has been described aptly by Peter Fleming as "sandwiched like the Dormouse between the Mad Hatter and the March Hare." Komuch and the SRs had given up more at Ufa than had the Siberians. This brought out again the fatal splits in the SR Party. Many radical SRs wanted to avoid the coalition with the Center-Right that had tied the party's hands in 1917; they saw Ufa as a betrayal of the doctrine of *narodovlastie* (people's power), a doctrine that they identified with the Constituent Assembly—and themselves. The SR Central Committee, dominated by moderates such as Avksentiev, had approved the Ufa settlement; then three more members arrived at Samara, with the SR's theorist Viktor Chernov, and the balance shifted against the agreement. Chernov criticized the PA-RG in a circular; the Ufa settlement, he declared, was unsatisfactory, and "counterrevolutionary elements" were involved in the new government. The party's policy should be to rally the population around the Constituent Assembly; as a practical step an independent armed SR force was needed.[7]

The Right was equally unsatisfied. Just as new arrivals shifted the SR party to the left, so new arrivals shifted the Kadets to the right. The Right believed in a strong state and struggle with Bolshevism, both of which it alone could lead. It identified the 1918 Provisional All-Russian Government with Kerensky's 1917 Provisional Government, with the government that had led to internal catastrophe (the October Revolution) and national humiliation (Brest-Litovsk). The Left disliked the Directory because it only had two SRs; the Right disliked it because it *had* two SRs. For many, the SRs were no better—perhaps worse—than the Bolsheviks; all SRs were identified with the Chernovite Left, and Chernov's widely publicized circular confirmed their fears of a return to the *komitetshchina* (rule of the committees). And then there was the Constituent Assembly, in which the Right and Center had played almost no role; any move toward representative government on those terms would ban the Right from power.

The final political force was the most powerful in the east, the military. The Siberian Cossack leadership was a conservative force, and so were the young officers leading the Siberian Army. There was a vocal monarchist element among the Omsk garrison, and a number of *skandaly* took place, with drunken officers singing "God Save the Tsar." Even those of less extreme views wanted to avoid a repetition of the 1917 military disintegration, which would follow if the Chernovites came to power. And a resolution of the political crisis seemed all the more urgent when the Red Army began to make rapid progress in the area between the Volga and the southern Urals.

The Provisional All-Russian Government was overthrown on the night of 17 November 1918. With the approval of the Omsk garrison commander, a cossack detachment arrested those present at an SR meeting, including the two SR Directors, Avksentiev and Zenzinov. In response Director Vologodsky called an early-morning meeting of the PA-RG's Council of Ministers. There was little support for the Directory, and Admiral A. V. Kolchak, the War Minister, was chosen as head of state, the Supreme Ruler (*Verkhovnyi pravitel'*). The Right now had the military dictator it wanted, and Kolchak would lead the White movement in both Siberia and (nominally) all of Russia for the next fourteen months.

One of the oddities of the anti-Bolshevik movement is that it should have been led by an admiral without a fleet, head of a government in a town 3500 miles from the nearest port. Aleksandr Vasilevich Kolchak came to power partly by accident, but partly for logical reasons: he had been a very senior commander in the pre-Bolshevik armed forces, and he was available. The Imperial Russian forces had had a General Headquarters and seven field commands (five army groups and two fleets). Of those who filled these high posts only four were active anti-Bolsheviks—Generals Alekseev, Kornilov, Iudenich, and Admiral Kolchak. Kolchak commanded the Black Sea Fleet from August 1916 to June 1917. He was a hero of both the Japanese and the German wars and had been catapulted to high command at the age of forty-one. He established some links with Duma circles in the period of naval reform before the world war and developed these links in the summer of 1917. He made his name politically, however, by his refusal to make major concessions to the fleet committees after February 1917; in the end he threw his sword overboard and resigned in protest at increasing democratization.

Kolchak's availability was no small factor. Most prominent figures had been trapped in central Russia; Kolchak was on a special mission to the United States when the Bolsheviks took power. There then followed twelve months of waiting in Manchuria before he decided, according to his own account, to make his way to south Russia via the Trans-Siberian Railway. He reached Omsk in mid-October, and there General Boldyrev (who had only been a corps commander in the Tsarist army), asked him to become War and Navy Minister in the PA-RG's new Council of Ministers; Kolchak agreed, and entered the government officially on 4 November.

The Omsk coup was organized by local right-wing civilians and by middle-ranking officers and cossacks from the garrison. Kolchak may well have been a kind of "accidental" figure, whose arrival provided a figurehead for those who would have overthrown the Directory anyway. The admiral himself, on trial before a revolutionary court in January 1920, denied that he had been part of the conspiracy, although he did admit contacts with the plotters. General Boldyrev did not believe he was directly involved.[8] It was Boldyrev who arranged Kolchak's appointment as War Minister, and Boldyrev himself left power in protest at the coup.

The Allies are sometimes implicated, especially in Soviet propaganda. The senior British officer in Siberia, General Knox, was hostile to the Directory and friendly with Kolchak (indeed they arrived in Omsk on the same train). Boldyrev, in his memoirs (written in the USSR), said he had no doubt of British assistance for Kolchak. Certainly the French commander in Siberia, General Janin, believed that the British installed Kolchak: "The coup d'état was certainly carried out with the support of British military representatives." Janin, however, arrived four weeks after the coup and Knox, for what it is worth, wrote in his own copy of Janin's memoirs at this point, "Rot."[9]

There is no evidence of direct Allied involvement, and native hostility to the PA-RG was great enough to make it unnecessary. Kolchak had links with the Allies, but this may have been most important in convincing the *Russian* kingmakers that he could get outside support in the future. It is true that local Allied representatives did little to support the Directory. Knox apparently knew of the conspiracy but did not block it, British troops protected the Council of Ministers on 18 November to prevent a countercoup, and the French (including Janin—in Vladivostok) discouraged any pro-Directory action by the Czechoslovaks. But Allied policy at the highest level was against the coup. Certainly London had been impressed by the agreement reached at Ufa, and on 1 November the War Cabinet had decided to give the PA-RG de facto recognition.[10]

Kolchak did not create a whole new government; he simply took over the Council of Ministers. The coup was bloodless, and the arrested Directors were sent abroad. The coup did, however, mark a basic change in policy. The PA-RG's Declaration of 24 September (after the Ufa conference) had stressed its legitimate roots in the Constituent Assembly and at least paid lip service to social reform. Kolchak put forward *his* basic goals in a Manifesto of 18 November:

> Taking up the cross of this power in the exceptionally difficult conditions of civil war and the complete breakdown of state life I declare: I will not go

either on the road of reaction or on the fatal road of party politics. I set as my chief aim the creation of an efficient army, victory over the Bolsheviks, and the establishment of law and order, so that the people can choose for itself, without obstruction, the form of government which it desires and realize the great ideals of liberty which are now proclaimed all over the world.[11]

The coup met no effective resistance. The SRs, who had undermined the authority of the PA-RG, now were confronted by something much worse. An attempted meeting of the "Committee of Members of the Constituent Assembly" in Ekaterinburg was broken up by the army. The SR leaders were expelled to Ufa, and eventually some of them crossed into Soviet territory. This was the end of the Constituent Assembly, and of the SR Party as a serious political force.

"Mexico amidst the snow and ice"[12] was how General Boldyrev summed up the situation on the eve of the coup, with its intrigues and rebellious atamans. The important point about the Omsk events was not Kolchak's personal role—which was probably "accidental"— or the British role, which was at most secondary. What the coup showed was the continuing weakness of civilian politics in Russia. This came about partly because of the small intelligentsia and the lack of a tradition of public political participation but also because of the impossibility of cooperation; the Bolsheviks were not the only party that would not share power. The Right saw the SRs as little better than the Bolsheviks; the SRs saw the Right as counterrevolutionary. Mutual loathing came from an opposition of both basic principles and perceived experience. The main lesson both Left and Right learned from 1917 was the danger of compromise. It was not the correct lesson: the result of their policies this time around was the destruction of the SR Party and the isolation, sterility, and ultimate defeat of the Right.

The coup may have made no difference. If it had been avoided in November there would still have been problems. Both sides saw the Directory as temporary. Even if the five-headed Provisional All-Russian Government had survived into 1919 the final outcome might have been the same. Civil war would not have been avoided. Even Chernov bitterly opposed the "commissarocracy." The Bolsheviks, for their part, would have been no happier than the Right to accept the results of the 1917 Constituent Assembly elections. The Directory would probably have fought the Reds no more successfully than Kolchak did, although General Boldyrev would—as we will see—not have been any worse than Kolchak and his high command. SR propaganda in the armed forces would not have been compatible with the traditional officer corps. The survival of the Directory would also not necessarily have meant more Allied support. The Czechoslovak Corps was disintegrating before the Kolchak coup, and the collapse of Austria–Hungary meant the Czechoslovaks could now (in theory) go home. The survival of the Directory would also probably not have led to more effective government in Siberia, even if the Constituent Assembly vote gave the SRs a "right" to govern Siberia; they had failed in 1918 on the Volga.

November 1918 was a centrally important time for the Russian Civil War. The first year had ended. The Omsk coup meant a fundamental shift in the politics of the anti-Bolshevik movement. The era of the "Democratic Counter-Revolution" was over, and the White generals were in command; within two months General Denikin would have established a similar unity of command over the cossacks in the southeast. November also brought the Armistice. With this was achieved a central objective of the anti-Bolshevik movement, the defeat of the Central Powers and the liberation of Russian territory from enemy troops. Allied victory also opened direct routes to Russia through the Baltic and Black Seas. In 1918 the German invasion and the Czechoslovak uprising had shaken Bolshevik rule and undone much of the "Triumphal March of Soviet Power." The paradox was that the defeat of the Central Powers ended any need for the Allies to support anti-Bolshevik forces. As Churchill put it, "The snows of winter war had whitened five-sixths of Red Russia, but the springtime of Peace, for all others a blessing, was soon to melt it all again."[13]

II

1919: YEAR OF THE WHITES

I make my main goal the creation of a combat-ready army, victory over the Bolsheviks, and the establishment of law and order.

Admiral A. V. Kolchak, November 1918

9

THE REVOLUTION ON THE MARCH: SOVDEPIA AND THE OUTSIDE WORLD, November 1918–June 1919

In view of the situation, please issue an order to the commanders of the appropriate units so that they render all possible assistance to the provisional Soviet governments in Latvia, Estonia, the Ukraine and Lithuania, but, of course, only to the Soviet governments.

Lenin to Vatsetis, 29 November 1918

So everything depends on whether the Entente wants to come in actively against us or, for various reasons of internal and external policy, does not.

Vatsetis, 15 March 1919

The storm is rising. The flames of the proletarian revolution are spreading all over Europe, and it is invincible.

Komintern May Day Appeal, 1919

The Borderlands

Thursday, 7 November 1918, was the first anniversay of the Bolshevik Revolution, and there were great celebrations in Moscow. In the morning Lenin unveiled a statue of Marx and Engels in front of the Bolshoi Theater, and then led massed singing of the "Marseillaise" and ' the "Internationale" in Red Square. The 6th All-Russian Congress of Soviets had convened in the Bolshoi on the previous afternoon. "Germany has caught fire," Lenin told the delegates, "and Austria is burning out of control." On the afternoon of the 8th Lenin again addressed the congress; "we have never," he said, "been so near to international proletarian revolution as we are now"; the victorious Western allies would try to cut Red Russia off with a "Great Wall of China", but they would not succeed.[1]

Another watershed in the Civil War would occur ten days later and 1300 miles away, when Admiral Kolchak took power in Omsk. But it was the collapse of Germany that was in everyone's mind on the seventh; as the Soviet congress met a German delegation was making its way to Compiègne to sign an armistice with the western Allies. The defeat of the Central Powers opened grand opportunities for Soviet Russia and presented grave dangers. First, and most immediately, the German and Austrian garrisons began to pull out of the western and southern borderlands, giving Moscow access to what had been lost at Brest. Second, the crises in Berlin and Vienna brought nearer the final objective of the Bolshevik leaders: the conversion of the Russian Revolution into a great international movement. And third, after the Allied victory the troops of the *Antanta* were in theory freed for use against Soviet Russia; the opening of the Baltic and the Black Sea meant that they might operate much nearer Sovdepia's heart than in 1918.

In the late autumn of 1918 Soviet territory ended only 150 miles west of Petrograd; the Brest demarcation line arced 1000 miles south and southeast, from the Gulf of Finland to the Don Region. Although the Tsarist provinces on the "German-Austrian" side had been mainly non-Russian, Moscow made a major effort in the nine months after November 1918 to advance its authority across the line. The first action came in the north, in Estonia (Estliand Province). There were worker demonstrations in the main town, Reval (Tallin), as the German occupation regime crumbled, but no effective local Bolshevik organization existed. A Center-Left nationalist government quickly took effective power; it had a broadly popular program, and it could combine nationalism and social reform by dividing the estates of the German-speaking landlords. Soviet power had to depend on armed intervention from outside. By the end of November the new Red Seventh Army had crossed the demarcation line, taking Pskov and Narva, and a pro-Soviet government, the Estliand Toilers' Commune, was set up in Narva. By mid-December Red forces had covered 130 miles and were within a few miles of Reval.

The Estonian nationalists, however, were able to raise small but effective forces and to get outside support: anti-Bolshevik Russians, Finnish and Swedish volunteers, and a British flotilla. The advancing Red troops were mostly Russian, seemingly more invaders than liber-

116

ators. (A separate [Red] Estliand Army was set up in February 1919, but it was never very effective.) Soviet forces were demoralized and numerically weak, the best detachments had been sent to the Volga; much of what was available had to be kept northwest of Petrograd to cover the old capital against a possible attack from Finland. After a few small battles the invading Reds had to pull back to their starting point. After this Lake Chud (Lake Peipus) gave Estonia a natural eastern frontier and one, moreover, that was covered by Russian Whites. The Toilers' Commune, which never evoked much sympathy from the Estonian peasants, was wound up in June 1919. The nationalist victory in Estonia had vital strategic consequences: the rear of the Soviet forces operating farther south in the borderlands was threatened, and in 1919 Petrograd itself would twice come under attack from the direction of Estonia.

It is interesting that there was no offensive, political or military, against the Finns, the cousins of the Estonians. This was considered by the Red Northern Army Group, but rejected.[2] In reality the Reds did not even go so far as to set up a Finnish puppet government in Soviet territory. The Red Finns had been smashed in the Civil War of early 1918; the Finnish nationalists had consolidated real power in the form of an army and a government, and they did not just rely on German military occupation. Finland was a large country to attack. Possibly the Reds were also restrained by Finland's long history of autonomy and the 1917 Soviet recognition of independence. In any event, Finnish neutrality was, for Moscow, more useful than small victories.

South of Estonia, in Latvia (Lifliand and Kurliand provinces), the prospects for Soviet power were better. The radical Left had a strong tradition both in the countryside and the towns, and was still powerful in 1918. The ruined capital, Riga, was the scene of heated debate between the local Bolsheviks and the nationalists. The arrival of Red Army units on 3 January 1919 confirmed an existing turn to the left. The Latvian nationalists had had a more difficult frontier to defend than the Estonians, and the Reds possessed in the Latvian Riflemen a unique asset; the Riflemen were transferred from the internal Russian fronts and reorganized in early January into the "Army of Soviet Latvia." The Latvian Socialist Soviet Republic (SSR) was set up in Riga; its first All-Latvian Congress of Soviets was held in January in the presence of very senior Bolsheviks, Sverdlov and L. B. Kamenev. The small Latvian nationalist forces, meanwhile, were driven back to the Baltic port of Libava (Libau, now Liepaja).

But the Latvian SSR faced great economic problems after being a battle zone for five years, and its radical policies were no solution;

popular support was hard to mobilize. More important, operating against it were German forces raised from the garrisons and the local (ex-Tsarist) German-speaking minority. They existed partly as an Allied proxy, partly as an instrument of the new Berlin government, and partly for their own ends. Under General von der Goltz they expelled the Reds from Mitava (Mitau, now Jelgava), just southwest of Riga, and this made it possible for the town to become the capital of the Latvian nationalist government. Meanwhile, the Red failure on the Estonian front and the lack of coordination between the Reds' Seventh and Latvian armies allowed the victorious Estonians to cut from the north the main rail link between Riga and Soviet Russia. By this time the morale of the Latvian Riflemen, who had borne the brunt of a year's battles, was badly shaken, and Moscow had no replacements or reinforcements to send. Then Goltz's Germans retook Riga in May 1919, bringing effectively to an end the Latvian SSR (although a Soviet government-in-exile existed until January 1920).

The situation in what had been Tsarist Russia's western provinces (Kovno, Vilna, Grodno, Suvalki, Minsk, Volynia) was different from that in the Baltic. The largest groups were 1.5 million Lithuanians and 5 million Belorussians. They did not have much in common, besides being peasant nations with little national tradition; their languages were unrelated. The local towns had large Jewish, Polish, and Russian populations. And unlike the Baltic provinces, the belt of the western provinces was claimed (on strategic, historic, and political grounds) by both Russia and the reborn Poland. Lithuania was initially occupied by the German Eastern Command, *Oberost*, but the Lithuanian Bolsheviks also claimed power in Vilna (now Vilnius), before the Red Army reached the town in January 1919. The Lithuanian SSR, set up in December 1918, had little territory, little popular support, and an ineffective government. The Lithuanian nationalists, meanwhile, had established a base of their own farther west in Kovno (now Kaunas), under German protection. Belorussia was even more of an artificial creation. Minsk was taken by the Red Army on 10 December, and a Belorussian SSR was set up by Moscow two weeks later.

The Red attempt to get around the weaknesses of the two regions was to combine them in February 1919 as the Lithuanian-Belorussian SSR, or "Litbel"; this had little effect. In April the Poles, who had been able to assemble an effective army of their own, moved east to take Vilna from the Reds. Although the Lithuanians and the Poles would argue about their mutual border, the Poles in Vilna effectively screened Kovno and the Lithuanian nationalist government. Litbel itself was wound up in August 1919 when Minsk fell to the Poles; a Belorussian SSR would be reestablished in 1920.

Moscow did not give its military front in this region a high priority until 1920, although there was a long, if intermittent, confrontation with Poland. In November 1918 the Reds set up a Western Army, and in January Vatsetis told the Soviet leaders that it was advancing "to the former borders of Russia (*Rossiia*)," taking Grodno and Brest—i.e., all the disputed borderlands between Russia and Poland ("from the point of view of strategy it is desirable that disputed territories come into our hands prior to the resolution of the question by diplomacy or force of arms").[3] The first skirmishes with the Poles took place early in 1919. But, despite the presence of a large Polish army, major Red forces were not committed to the west throughout 1919. Moscow preferred giving up territory to the Poles rather than risk open war.

The extension of Soviet power across the demarcation line into the Ukraine was an even more difficult task than in the Baltic or the West, given the population and area of the Ukraine. There were 32 million Ukrainians, and they inhabited a region the size of France. The previous winter Red detachments had hardly driven the Ukrainian Rada out of Kiev before the local Soviet government was turned out itself by the Germans and Austrians. The Ukraine had been occupied by the Central Powers since before the middle of 1918, under the nominal rule of the Hetman, General Skoropadsky. In the nine months of its existence the Hetmanate had been able to develop neither a political base nor effective armed forces. The collapse of the Central Powers led to the reemergence of the Ukrainian leftist nationalists, the men of the 1917–1918 Rada, as the dominant force. Under Vinnichenko and Petliura they formed a Ukrainian Directory outside Kiev, and after a month, on 14 December 1918, they took the capital and recreated the Ukrainian People's Republic. Skoropadsky could offer little resistance and left for exile in Germany.

The UPR, however, only lasted for seven or eight weeks. Fighting among Ukrainians had done little to help their national cause, which already faced enormous problems. The UPR had little administrative machinery or army. Large regions were controlled by partisan chieftains, the atamans. Most important was the invasion from the north; Kiev fell to the Red Army on 5 February 1919. After that the Directory was forced back to smaller centers in the western part of the country. What army it had was crippled in battles in March–April 1919. In May the remnants were pushed west across the Zbruch River, into what had been Austria-Hungary; there they were immediately struck by a Polish offensive from the north and west. The last refuge of the Ukrainian nationalists was known as the "triangle of death."

The instrument for the sovietization of the Ukraine had begun to take shape in late November 1918, when Moscow formed a "Ukrainian Soviet Army"; in January it became the Ukrainian Army Group. The commander was Antonov-Ovseenko, the veteran revolutionary who had arrested the Provisional Government in October 1917 and led the campaign in the Ukraine in the winter of 1917–1918. The military capaign was decisive, but prolonged. It was the middle of winter, and Antonov was given few troops. German and Austrian occupation troops took some time to leave, and the Reds did not want to provoke them to resistance. Bolshevik forces did not start to move south any distance from the Brest demarcation line until early January. The middle Dnepr River, with the vital crossings at Kiev and Ekaterinoslav, was reached at the end of January and the beginning of February. Not until the end of April, five and a half months after the armistice, was all of southwest Russia—including the western zone (Volynia and Podolia), the Black Sea Coast, and the Crimea—brought under Red control.

The Ukrainian SSR was set up, first on the "Russian" border then in Kharkov, under the twenty-nine-year-old G. L. Piatakov (after whom the Ukrainians called the regime the "Pyatakovshchyna"). The leaders of the UkSSR had only limited support, certainly outside the major towns. The leadership of the "Communist Party (Bolsheviks) of the Ukraine" (KP(b)U), set up in exile in Moscow in July 1918, saw itself as a branch of the Russian CP; many of its leaders were not Ukrainian; Piatakov's successor, the veteran Marxist Rakovsky, was according to some sources Rumanian, to others Bulgarian, but he was certainly not a native Ukrainian. Like the Directory, the UkSSR had no real administrative machinery. The "Ukrainian" Bolsheviks decided, admittedly after fierce debate, not to share power with other radical groups, such as the Ukrainian Left SRs (Borotbisty). The new rulers thought Ukrainian agriculture, more capitalistic and large-scale than in the Great Russian provinces, was "riper" for socialism; they also feared the villages were more dominated by the better-off peasants. As a result they put forward radical socioeconomic policies and set up Committees of the Village Poor. Most important, they requisitioned grain, partly for the hungry Great Russian north. All of this alienated large sections of the Ukrainian peasantry.

The Soviet military position in the Ukraine was no firmer than its political position. Trotsky only made his first wartime visit to the region in May 1919; "the prevailing state of chaos, irresponsibility, laxity and separatism," he reported to the CC, "exceeds the most pessimistic expectations." (Even worse, Trotsky reported that there were, in effect, no "organizations" *other than* the military ones.)[4] Antonov could not control the local partisans, the "insurgent" (*povstancheskie*) forces, who made up much of his army group, and the Red high command could not control Antonov. Vatsetis would have been content with about half the Ukraine, with a line of defense on the Dnepr river (running southeast across the region). Behind this line consolidation of forces could take place and resources could be exploited for the greater good of the all-Russian war effort. Antonov and his detachments, however, were sucked across the river by their revolutionary élan, by the weakness of the Directory, and by the desire to liberate all corners of the country; they were influenced by the uprisings of local atamans and by partisan bands seizing control of large zones on the far side of the Dnepr. (Not content with the trans-Dnepr region, the Ukrainian Bolsheviks wanted to push into the Crimea and across the Dnestr into Rumanian-occupied Bessarabia.) The weakness of Antonov's position became clear in May when Major Grigoriev, the most important of his atamans, changed sides. Grigoriev took control of most of the southwest in the name of an anti-Bolshevik "Soviet" Ukraine. Red Army units defeated the "Grigorievshchina," but only after their rear areas had been badly disrupted. Griegoriev himself was killed by another famous ataman, Makhno, in late July.

Antonov's main shortcoming, however, was to give so little support to the Red armies in the neighboring Don Region. The final defeat of the Don Cossacks did not take place as expected in January–February 1919; instead, the White Volunteer Army counteroffensive took first the Donbas (in early May 1919) and then Kharkov and the whole left-bank (eastern) Ukraine (in late June). Antonov's diversions to the southwest and south may even have prevented the establishment of a link with revolutionary Hungary via the northwest Ukraine and Bukovina. Ukrainian Army Group was broken up in June, its formations transferred to the neighbouring "all-Russian" army groups. Antonov would never have another major front-line command. (Indeed, except for M. V. Frunze, he was the last non-officer commander of a major Red front.) On the other hand, Antonov's pell-mell invasion of the southern Ukraine did have the positive effect in February–March 1919 of driving out French forces that had landed at Odessa. Had the Red Army stopped on the Dnepr, the Ukrainian-nationalist Directory might have been able to reestablish its authority, and the French might have been tempted to stay and extend their influence in the southern Ukraine.

121

The borderlands campaign (like that of 1917–1918) showed the nationalists' weakness. They could mobilize neither mass support nor effective military forces. The Ukraine was completely overrun, and the Reds were only driven out by the victories of the Whites, who were Great Russian nationalists. The survival of nationalists in the Baltic and the western regions was due, at least initially, to outside forces—German stragglers, Allied vanguards, Russian Whites, and the new armies of the stronger central European states, such as Finland, Poland, and Rumania.

Also unsuccessful, at least in the short term, had been the advance of Soviet power into the western and southwestern borderlands. One reason for failure was that the scale of the task had been enormous. It was 250 miles west from the demarcation line to the Baltic coast, 350 south across the Ukraine to the Black Sea, and 450 southwest across the Ukraine to the farthest corner of pre-1914 Russia, Bessarabia. The population of the borderlands was 40–50 million and largely non-Russian. There was some support for Bolshevism among the workers, but the borderlands had few industrial towns; and only in Latvia was there some rural support.

The Bolsheviks were also shown the problems involved in trying to develop an effective nationalities policy. The central leadership had backed the notion of quasi-independent "republics" in the borderlands, but this had led to a dangerous loss of control. At the same time, another reason for the Bolsheviks' failure was their own narrow political outlook on the periphery; this in turn came from the dogmatism of local leaders, an underestimation of nationalist sentiments, and a reluctance to seek political allies. The *third* wave into the borderlands, in the winter of 1919–1920, would see a greater awareness of national feelings and a more serious attempt to find local allies.

But if flexibility was one lesson learned from the experience of the spring of 1919, another (both in the borderlands and "Russia") was the need for central control. The Eighth Party Congress met in Moscow in late March 1919 and confirmed that while separate republics might exist at "state" level, this by no means meant that the "RCP" (Russian Communist Party) was to be a federation of independent parties; "the existence is essential of a *single* centralized Communist party with a single CC leading all party work in all parts of the RSFSR"; the CCs of the Ukrainian, Latvian, and Lithuanian Communists had the rights only of Russian regional committees, and were wholly subordinate to the CC of the RCP. Two months later (1 June) this was extended to the state sphere when the (Moscow) Central ExCom decreed a centralization of basic activities; in the interests of defense, a "close unification" (*tesnoe ob"edinenie*) of armies and military commands, of economic

122

organizations, of transport, finance and labor was ordered.[5] The most immediate result was the end of the national armies, and their integration into the "central" Red Army.

There was a strategic paradox too. Moscow did not send enough troops to the borderlands to win victory, but what *was* sent badly hurt the other fronts. When the First World War suddenly ended, the Reds had few effective troops in the west; the bulk of the new Red Army had been sent to the Volga front. In December 1918 there were 193,000 combat troops in Eastern and Southern Army Groups and only 16,000 in Seventh Army (advancing on Estonia) and Western Army. On several occasions, in December 1918 and in February and June 1919, the Red high command wanted to make the western front one of the most important. Each time there were distractions. The "Perm Catastrophe" of December 1918 reopened the eastern front, and Kolchak's Ufa offensive of March 1919 activated it yet again. Throughout the spring of 1919 Moscow was concerned to complete the destruction of the Don Cossacks, and in May Denikin broke out to the north. In June smaller White operations threatened Petrograd. In any event, the Eastern, Southern, and Caspian-Caucasus Army Groups had 236,000 combatants in mid-February 1919, while the new Western Army Group had 81,000, and Ukrainian Army Group had 47,000. By June the number in the two western-borderlands groups had actually fallen.

And yet *some* Red forces had been committed to the borderlands. Moscow's response to the collapse of the Central Powers was what the historian Kakurin called a "grease-stain" strategy, spreading strength in all directions.[6] The reinforcements sent to the borderlands were relatively small, but they included the only central reserves that the infant Red Army had been able to accumulate; these reserves were not available for battles against the Whites and the cossacks in the east and the south. The Whites and cossacks survived, and eventually their attacks in turn forced the Reds to give up the borderlands; with this most of the winter's gains were lost.

The military and political decisions made by the Reds in the winter of 1918–1919 made sense, given their general objectives and the unknowns of the situation. The forward policy in the borderlands may even have gained Moscow space and time and prevented greater Allied intervention. But the use of the Red Army to spread revolution turned out to be a failure both in political and strategic terms. Moscow learned another lesson here, and in the next campaign (winter 1919–1920) it respected the independence of the Baltic states rather than risk diversion of forces. This put the Baltic nationalists, at least, among the victors of the Russian Civil War. But in 1919 the failure on the periphery of the

123

old Empire also doomed attempts to spread the revolution to other countries.

European Revolution

The Bolshevik leaders had always thought in terms of international revolution. They justified the seizure of power in peasant Russia as the trigger of revolution in the industrialized West. Up until the last months of 1918, however, the Bolsheviks could do little to influence events in the outside world. The capitalist regimes seemed stable enough. Russia was contained by a ring of enemy-occupied territory; the enemy, the Central Powers, was not to be offended. And Moscow had enough trouble controlling its *own* territory to worry about other countries. Then, quite unexpectedly, the international earthquake began. The German and Austro-Hungarian monarchies, defeated by the Western Allies, suddenly crumbled. Rioting and demonstrations broke out in central Europe. Socialist-led governments took power. New nation states formed on the territories of the eastern empires. Radical parties appeared which were inspired by the great leading role of the Russian Bolsheviks.

European revolution was not to be. Historians are apt to forget, however, that the Bolsheviks thought it likely. In that exciting November of 1918 Lenin told the Sixth Congress of Soviets: "we have never been so close to international proletarian revolution as we are now." Lenin was generally vague about timing, but he did once promise international revolution by September 1919. "The revolution in Hungary," Lenin told the Moscow Soviet in early April 1919, "gives conclusive proof that in western Europe the Soviet movement is growing and that its victory is not far away." "But it is necessary to hold out for four or five difficult months in order to defeat the enemy." The new Communist International was also optimistic. "Before a year has passed," its 1919 May Day appeal promised, "the whole of Europe will be Soviet."[7]

In Germany the Hohenzollern Empire was replaced in November 1918 by a republic. With the support of the army the reformist Social Democrats (whom Lenin regarded as his greatest enemies) were able to weather both the crisis winter and the Allies' Versailles *Diktat* of the following summer. The radical Left was weak, relative to the mass parties of the Center-Left and Center. Early militancy by the small

124

German Communist Party ended in the Berlin fiasco of January 1919, when Rosa Luxemburg and Karl Liebknecht were murdered. A Bavarian Soviet Republic was created in Munich in April but was overthrown by counterrevolutionary *Freikorps* on May Day.

The only regime comparable to Soviet Russia was in Hungary. There, events were molded by the bankruptcy of the old regime, social discontent, and nationalism. Faced with unacceptable territorial demands by (Allied-backed) neighbors, the postwar liberal government resigned at the end of March 1919, to be replaced by a Hungarian Soviet Republic. The Hungarian Revolution was strongly influenced by Bolshevism through the return of POWs revolutionized in Russia. The revolution's leader, Bela Kun, had been prominent as an "Internationalist" in Moscow and Siberia in 1918. Also, the apparent success of Bolshevik Russia gave the radical Left in Hungary a credibility they would otherwise have lacked. In the end the Hungarian Bolsheviks lost popular support by pushing their program too quickly, and they were unable to defend the wide territory they claimed. A combination of internal disintegration and Rumanian invasion broke the regime. At the beginning of August, after nineteen weeks in power, the Kun government fled to Austria.

Moscow had to watch, virtually powerless, as the German and Hungarian revolutions collapsed. It had no effective political levers in western and central Europe. Lenin had since 1914 been attacking the (Second) Socialist International for not opposing the imperialist war, but real organizational steps towards a replacement could only be taken after the German-Austrian defeat. Even then, four months passed before an international congress of left socialists met in Moscow (March 1919), and it was unrepresentative. The result was the foundation of a Third, Communist, International—the *Komintern*. In 1919, however, this was a shadow institution, an untrained and unorganized general staff without an international proletarian army to command. It had hardly more reality than the giant Tatlin tower designed to house it. Communications with the outside world were still poor, and left-wing parties sympathetic to Bolshevism were still small and unbloodied.

The military instrument was also unavailable; 1918–1919 was not 1944–1945. Plans for a giant Red Army were indeed made partly with the changing situation in the West in mind. In Germany the critical war situation had led, on 30 September 1918, to the Kaiser granting a responsible ministry. "A crisis is maturing already in Germany and throughout Central Europe," Trotsky told the Central ExCom three days later. "Perhaps tomorrow the working class of Germany will ask you for help and you will create not a million-strong army, you will create an army of two millions, since your task will have doubled, trebled." Lenin was more definite in an open letter he wrote to the Central ExCom on the same day. "We decided to have an army of one million men by the spring; we now [with the political crisis in Germany] need an army of three million men. We can have it. *And we shall have it.*"[8] It was quite impractical quickly to assemble an army of three million. A Red Army of this size was only ready by the end of 1919, and then only a fraction were combat troops. And for most of 1919 it was a primitive infantry army with a weak supply organization. The Red Army was able to mount rapid offensives in the Urals, western Siberia, and south Russia because of the open terrain and the ability to capture supplies and manpower on "Russian" territory and from "Russian" armies; it would have been far more difficult to move into central Europe.

Even if Soviet troops had been available, there were the problems of geography to overcome. It took until the spring of 1919 for Red detachments to reoccupy Belorussia and parts of Latvia and Lithuania, and even then it was 600 miles to Berlin. The expanse of territory in between was occupied by fiercely anti-Russian Poland, and by the summer of 1919 the Poles were actually rolling the frontier to the east. The distance to Vienna was as far as to Berlin, and here the way was blocked by Poland, Czechoslovakia, and Rumania. The conquest of the western Ukraine began to clear the route to revolutionary Hungary, but problems were soon encountered. The Red forces moving west were halted by the Rumanian border and the remnants of Petliura's Ukrainian nationalist forces; the Grigoriev mutiny (7 May) threw their rear into chaos. The only connection between Soviet Russia and Soviet Hungary was a dangerous seven-hour flight over the Carpathians. A captured German plane made the first trip in April 1919 from Vinnitsa (in the Ukraine) to Budapest; a later flight brought Szamuely, one of the Hungarian leaders, to Moscow in late May. But it was the most tenuous of links. The Hungarian Communists were on their own.

Various claims have been made for the salvation of Europe from the Bolshevik peril. Goltz's victory at Riga in May, the "Miracle of the Dvina," was said to be the first check to Moscow's expansion. The Ukrainians maintained that they blocked the way from the Red Ukraine to Red Hungary. The French were developing a *cordon sanitaire* of border states. In general all this is exaggerated, as Soviet resources were so meager and the task was so great. But if anyone deserves the credit it is probably the Russian counterrevolutionaries, fighting in the Don region and Siberia. It was they who preoccupied the Moscow leadership. The military position in the Donbas, the industrial region threatened by the Volunteer Army, was so bad that reinforcements were sent there rather than to the western Ukraine. The decision was made at the very top. The Hungarian Soviet Republic was a month old when Main Commander-in-Chief Vatsetis queried (on 21 April 1919) if an advance into the provinces of Galicia and Bukovina, formerly part of Austria-Hungary, was politically possible. Yes it was, Lenin replied, provided it was limited to establishing a secure rail link with Hungary and did not involve a wider occupation. But the establishment of this link was, to Lenin, only one of Ukrainian Army Group's two main tasks: "the first, the most important and most urgent, is to help the Donbas."[9]

Allied Intervention

The other side of Bolshevik international policy was Moscow's relations with the victorious Allies. In November 1918 Lenin told the 6th Congress of Soviets that

> our situation has never been so dangerous as it is now. The imperialists were busy among themselves. But now one of the groups has been wiped out by the group of the English, the French, and the Americans. They consider their main task to be to smother world Bolshevism, to smother its main center, the Russian Soviet Republic.

Even in retrospect (from May 1920) Trotsky recalled that the autumn of 1918, after Germany's defeat, had been "the most critical moment in our international situation." Vatsetis's secret high-level appreciations of December and January 1918–1919 stressed the danger of Allied troops arriving through the Baltic and the Black Sea: Allied Forces landed at Odessa or Sevastopol "will undoubtedly push to the north to occupy the Kiev-Donets-Basin line"; in late February he suggested that 150,000 to 200,000 Allied troops might soon be deployed in the Ukraine.[10]

There was actually a brief period in the winter of 1918–1919 when better relations between Soviet Russia and the victorious Allies had seemed possible. Some Allied leaders wanted a settlement, partly because no powerful anti-Bolshevik center had appeared and the Reds were moving into the borderlands. In January, in the opening weeks of the Paris Peace Conference, the Allies suggested that the various Russian governments meet at the Prinkipo Islands (near Istanbul). Moscow, meanwhile, had launched a peace offensive. In December the Soviets called for an "understanding," including the withdrawal of Allied troops, and an end to the blockade. "The Russian workers and

127

peasants" were "prepared to make all possible concessions, bearing in mind the real interests of their country, if in that way they can secure conditions which will allow them peacefully to develop their social program." Moscow gave hints of financial and even territorial concessions in February, when it accepted the Prinkipo invitation.[11]

Prinkipo came to nothing. The anti-Bolshevik governments refused to talk to their enemy, and they could hardly have accepted a ceasefire. Paris had never been enthusiastic. The other Allied leaders reluctantly adopted the harder French position. When Bullitt, a young American diplomat, brought fresh terms back from Moscow in March 1919 he was ignored. Military intervention would continue for a year. Trotsky's explanation was simple:

> We proposed peace to the Entente, and were again ready . . . to sign the most unfavorable terms. But Clemenceau, in whose imperialist rapacity the characteristics of petty-bourgeois obtuseness have kept their full strength . . . decided at all costs to decorate the Invalides with the scalps of the leaders of Soviet Russia.[12]

Reality was more complex, and various factors pushed the Allies toward continued intervention. One was commitment to the Russian anti-Bolsheviks. Lloyd George put the dilemma to Parliament in April 1919:

> Bolshevism threatened to impose, by force of arms, its domination on those populations that had revolted against it, and that were organized at our request. If we, as soon as they had served our purpose, and as soon as they had taken all the risks, had said, "Thank you; we are exceedingly obliged to you. You have served your purpose. We need you no longer. Now let the Bolsheviks cut your throats," we should have been mean—we should have been thoroughly unworthy indeed of any great land.[13]

The Red Terror of the previous autumn made abandonment of "the populations" even more difficult. Anti-Bolshevik leaders, meanwhile, did what they could to win over the Allies. A number of them met in Jassy, Rumania, in November 1918 to appeal for help. Later, diplomats and liberal and socialist politicians set up in Paris a Russian Political Conference, with a Russian Emigre Delegation to the Paris Peace Conference. (This was, however, not granted official status, and had little influence. Paris became the cockpit of argument between the "all-Russian" delegation and various minority representatives, which did nothing to raise Russian prestige in Allied eyes.)

The Allies, especially the French, were also influenced by Bolshevik revolutionary goals. Moscow was calling both for diplomatic normalization *and* world revolution. The Prinkipo conference was proposed on

23 January 1919. It coincided with a call (on the 24th) by Lenin and Trotsky for a new International; "The task of the proletariat now," they declared, "is to seize power immediately." The Soviet final concessions to Bullitt were made on 12 March; a week later the new Russian Communist Party program heralded the beginning of "the era of the world-wide proletarian Communist revolution":

> A necessary condition for this social revolution is the dictatorship of the proletariat. . . .
> Setting itself the task of making the proletariat capable of fulfilling its great historic mission, the international Communist party organizes the proletariat into an independent political party opposed to all the bourgeois parties . . . and explains to it the historical significance and the necessary conditions of the imminent social revolution.[14]

Finally, in explaining Allied policy, it is worth remembering that in the winter of 1918–1919 everything was new and unclear. The Allies had little information about conditions in the Russian interior, and they could not know how things would turn out. If the Bolsheviks had been German puppets, would they not now quickly collapse? Limited support for the anti-Bolsheviks cost little, and could do no obvious harm to Allied interests. By the late spring the Whites seemed to be doing well. Admiral Kolchak's offensive, which reached its peak in March–May 1919, was an important factor in confirming the Allied decision not to treat with Moscow and in gaining Kolchak de facto recognition as the main anti-Bolshevik government.

The Allies, then, would treat Bolshevism as an enemy. Their main new presence was on the Black Sea—opened by the Turkish defeat. The British concentrated on the southeast; there the Volunteer Army and the Cossacks had created "friendly" territory. The French faced greater problems in the southwest; no one controlled the Ukraine and the Crimea, and the Reds were moving south unopposed. The first French detachments reached the great port of Odessa on 18 December 1918, but their numbers were small. The town was, as Denikin later put it, a "political Babel." The (Ukrainian nationalist) Directory had just taken the city over (as Hetman Skoropadsky's authority broke up), but not even a fifth of the people were Ukrainian (the rest were Russian or Jewish). After a month of confusion the French began to negotiate with the Ukrainian nationalists, but in February 1919 Kiev fell to Soviet forces and the Directory became a shadow. By belatedly negotiating with the Ukrainian "separatists" (what Denikin called a "marriage in the graveyard") the French fell out with the "all-Russian" Whites, and relations were never to improve.[15]

129

Ataman Grigoriev, then fighting with the Reds, took Kherson (at the mouth of the Dnepr) from 1000 French and Greek troops in early March. The population of the southwest showed no desire to oppose the Bolsheviks, and the local French commander kept thinking of the thirteenth-century "Sicilian Vespers," when Norman occupiers were massacred.[16] The French decided to pull out (without consulting Denikin); Odessa, their main bridgehead, was abandoned on 6 April amidst scenes of terrible civilian panic. (The French did not leave—as is sometimes suggested—because of a naval mutiny; this came three weeks afterward.) The Crimea, where the Reds arrived in April, was no better. The few French and Greek troops could do nothing, and left after a brief local armistice. (The British navy used the brief Allied presence to evacuate the surviving members of the Russian Imperial family.) The French blocked Denikin's attempts to take control, and the Whites kept only a foothold in the east of the peninsula. The main French intervention ended at Odessa and the Crimea. Paris's policy shifted toward building up a cordon sanitaire, a barrier of border states against Bolshevism.

There *were* Allied leaders who had favored strong intervention. Winston Churchill (army minister in 1919) was the most outspoken on the British side; "After having defeated all the tigers & lions I don't like to be defeated by baboons." Marshal Foch in February and March 1919 put forward projects for great operations using Allied troops and those of the border states. These were not to be. The Bolsheviks made much of the role of the Western masses in halting intervention, but there is little evidence for this. More important were the higher priorities of the Allied governments: the German peace treaty, the new order in Central Europe, and the League of Nations. The wartime armies pressed for demobilization. The scarce regular troops were needed on the Rhine and in the colonies. And then there was the expense. "Has anyone reckoned up," asked Lloyd George, "what an Army of Occupation would cost in Russia?" Full-scale war was out of the question; "I would rather leave Russia Bolshevik until she sees her way out of it than see Britain bankrupt. And that is the surest road to Bolshevism in Britain."[17]

Twelve months after the Armistice the intervention was nearly over. The French did little in Russia after April 1919. In March the British had decided to pull out of north Russia and the Transcaucasus (except for the Black Sea port of Batum), and this was completed in the autumn. The last major act of the Versailles conference was to give limited recognition to Kolchak's Siberian government in June 1919, but Kolchak had no Allied fighting troops,and his supplies were soon cut off. In his November 1919 Guildhall speech Lloyd George would suggest a normalization of relations with Russia. In December the Allies met to officially replace the policy of intervention with one of quarantine, the cordon sanitaire. Well before this, in June 1919, Trotsky had concluded that Allied intervention was a chimera. Soviet Russia was experiencing the "ninth wave"—the last desperate effort—of the counterrevolution. No matter how bad things seemed, the international situation was immensely different from that of the previous year.

> German and Austro-Hungarian militarism has been smashed to pieces. French and English militarism still exists outwardly, but it is inwardly rotten and incapable of fighting. Neither America nor England, and still less France, is in a position to send a single corps to Russian territory for the struggle with Soviet power.[18]

In November 1918 Moscow's situation had seemed full of revolutionary promise. By June 1919 things were clearer. There had been no Soviet triumph. The borderlands had proved very hard to digest. The nationalist governments in Estonia, Latvia, and Lithuania survived. Poland was hostile and had successfully occupied much of Belorussia. The Ukraine was no asset; the eastern part was already captured by Denikin, and the western part was soon to follow. The road to central Europe was blocked. The chances of European-wide revolution were fast receding. Only Hungary had a left-socialist government, and there the revolution was embattled and already tiring. The only good development was that Allied intervention had not taken on the extreme form that had been feared.

The Russian Civil War was to be much more of an "internal" Russian affair than had seemed likely in November 1918. The Revolution would not explode into other parts of the world, nor would it have to fight the armies of the Antanta. The fate of the Bolshevik government would be decided within the territory of the old Russian Empire, in battle against Russian anti-Bolshevik armies in Siberia and South Russia.

131

10

KOLCHAK'S OFFENSIVE, November 1918–June 1919

The Supreme Ruler and Supreme Commander-in-Chief decrees: the active armies are to destroy the Reds operating east of the Viatka and Volga Rivers, cutting them off from the bridges across those rivers.

Kolchak Directive, 12 April 1919

Eastern Stalemate

To the Bolshevik high command the front in the east seemed, in November 1918, solid enough. Eastern Army Group was now commanded by Colonel S. S. Kamenev, who replaced Vatsetis when the latter was made Main Commander-in-Chief; Kamenev's armies continued their advance in all sectors until the very end of the year, and in the center and the south they kept the initiative until late in February 1919. Fourth and First Armies, in the southern part of the front, took Uralsk and Orenburg—both "capitals" of cossack hosts—in January; Orenburg also controlled the railway to Red Turkestan. In the center, Fifth Army moved forward along the Simbirsk-Cheliabinsk (Volga-Urals) railway; on 31 December it took Ufa, site of the 1918 State Conference. Farther north still, Second Army captured the anti-Bolshevik towns of Izhevsk and Votkinsk. Only at the north end of the front, in Third Army's sector, was progress at first slow and then reversed.

Why, after destroying *Komuch* and retaking the Volga region, did the

Reds not go on to decisive victory in the east? In late January 1919 Lenin, thinking seriously of a general ceasefire (through the Allies' Prinkipo conference), told Trotsky to take within a month as much territory as possible, including Cheliabinsk (in the Urals) and Omsk.[1] In fact, even Cheliabinsk would not be in Red hands for seven months. One major problem for the Reds was space. It was 250–350 miles from the November 1918 front line even to the Urals, and a total of 850 miles to Omsk, Kolchak's capital, so the retreating enemy could trade space for time. The Czechoslovaks were demoralized and the Russian anti-Bolshevik forces still weak, but they could concentrate just on the three railways leading to the Urals. The Red armies, meanwhile, lost momentum as they pushed farther and farther from their central-Russian base.

Eastern Army Group was also the victim of its own success. The Red high command assumed that the back of the Urals-Siberian counter-revolution had been broken. The eastern front had had first choice of men and equipment in the autumn 1918 crisis, but now other fronts seemed more important. The southeast had the Cossack-Volunteer Vendée, and in the west and southwest there were possibilities for revolution or intervention; now the east had to give up resources. Success also led to overambitious tasks, with the eastern armies being ordered to advance not only to the Urals but also, through the Orenburg and Ural Cossack regions, to Turkestan. Finally, complete victory was made impossible by the exhaustion of Eastern Army Group's troops. They had been in continuous action for months: first with the battles for the Volga region, then the long pursuit toward the Urals. The newly captured regions had to be consolidated. Winter made conditions much worse. The problems were brought into sharp focus by what the Reds called the "Perm Catastrophe." In December 1918 a White counterattack threw Third Army, the northern wing of the Red advance, 190 miles back from the Urals, and on 25 December the Whites captured Perm. This was a most serious loss; Perm was a province capital and a major industrial city. Dzerzhinsky and Stalin, sent to investigate, found that Third Army was exhausted and poorly organized, and that a great deal had to be done to tighten up both military and civil administration.

Fortunately the White drive stopped, and the Perm Catastrophe began to be seen by Moscow as a local setback. Third Army might have lost Perm, but five days later and 250 miles to the south, Fifth Army took Ufa, the gateway to the Urals; Uralsk and Orenberg fell a few weeks later. So Red troops continued towards the Urals in the center and south, and for two months the overall situation in the east still looked favorable. And yet the weaknesses that had appeared at Perm would create new problems once the Whites had rallied their forces.

Race to the Volga

Admiral Kolchak's spring attack, also called the "Ufa Offensive," was one of the five most dramatic anti-Bolshevik operations of the Civil War (the other four being the 1918 Volga campaign, Denikin's May–June 1919 advance from south Russia, his September–October 1919 advance, and the Polish 1920 attack). The main blow came in the center of the front on 4 March 1919; the attacking White force was Western Army under General Khanzhin, a veteran artilleryman; it advanced roughly parallel to the east-west railway from Cheliabinsk (in the Urals) to Simbirsk and Samara (on the Volga). Khanzhin's troops moved rapidly across the snowy steppe in sledges. Ufa was recaptured on 14 March, and by the end of April the White army had taken points within 75 miles of the Volga, at Chistopol (on the Kama River) and on the Ufa-Samara railway. Some 250 miles had been covered in eight weeks. The Whites had taken 115,000 square miles of territory (an area bigger than Britain) and a population of five million. Moscow was badly frightened, and in faraway Paris the Allies saw the White movement finally justifying itself. At the same time the other major White force, Gajda's Siberian Army, made on Khanzhin's right flank an advance of about ninety miles, a third of the way from Perm to Viatka.

Unfortunately for the Whites, Khanzhin was soon driven back. Two weeks were lost fighting around Ufa; then, in mid-April, came the spring thaw, the *rasputitsa*, which turned the roads to mud, and rivers and streams into serious obstacles. Khanzhin had pushed back the Red Fifth Army, but his flanks were threatened by Second and First Armies. Once the ground became firmer, on 28 April, the Reds began their counterattack. During May Western Army had to retreat far from the Volga; by the end of the month it was trying to defend a line 275 miles east of the Volga along the Belaia River. Ufa itself, on the Belaia, was threatened. On the night of 7 June Chapaev's 25th Rifle Division made a surprise crossing below the city, which fell to the Reds on the 9th with large amounts of supplies and grain. By mid-June the Whites had been pushed fifty miles east of the Belaia. At this time the northern bulge of Kolchak's front had been crushed in as well: at the beginning of June Gajda's Siberian Army had actually pushed farther west along the Perm-Viatka railway to the town of Glazov, but then the Reds drove it back to within fifty miles of Perm.

Several factors were behind the events of March–June 1919, a White defeat that would prove to be decisive. One was political failure.

134

Moscow's propaganda always spoke of the "Kolchakovshchina," the reign of Kolchak. This was exaggerated, but the Omsk regime was unapologetically that of a military dictator, and any judgment of the Omsk regime must begin with the dictator, the Supreme Ruler, himself. The British and French military advisers had quite different views of the man. General Knox reported (as late as December 1919) that despite Kolchak's defeat and personal failings "he was and is the best man in Siberia." General Janin, however, regarded him as an incompetent neurotic and reported to Paris that he was probably addicted to drugs. Kolchak's associates found him moody and indecisive. The Russian General Budberg, in charge of army supply, assessed Kolchak's complex personality:

> He is a big, sick child, a pure idealist, a faithful slave of duty and ideals and Russia; he is undoubtedly a neurotic, who is quick to lose control, extremely stormy, and unrestrained in showing his dissatisfaction and anger. . . . He is wholly consumed by the idea of serving Russia, of saving her from Red oppression, of restoring her in all her strength and inviolable territory; thanks to this idea he can be made to do anything; he has no personal interests, no personal ambition, and in this respect he is crystal pure. . . . He has no notion of the hard practicalities of life, and he lives by mirages and imposed ideas. He has no plans, system, or will of his own and in this respect he is soft wax from which his advisers and retainers can make what they want, knowing that it is enough to present something as needed for Russia and the cause to get the admiral's agreement.[2]

Whatever the faults of his personality, Kolchak's politics did not fit the stereotype of a black reactionary. His father was a military engineer; Kolchak himself was a young specialist from a technically advanced part of the armed forces. He was apparently not a monarchist, and his regime did not call for a restoration of Tsarism. He took the advice of a small "Council of the Supreme Ruler," staffed by men who were often of Kadet sympathies and remarkable youth. The Kadets—of the party's right wing—had more influence in Omsk than in any of the other White governments. Gins, one of Kolchak's main advisers, was thirty-two in 1919; Sukin, running foreign affairs, was twenty-eight; Mikhailov, in charge of finance, was twenty-four. His associates grumbled with some justification against this reliance on *Wunderkinder* (both in the administration and the army).

But Kolchak had already lost the support of the political Left. The November 1918 coup overthrew a government, the PA-RG, which claimed—through the Constituent Assembly and the Ufa Conference— national legitimacy. At the end of December 1918 there was an uprising in Omsk, inspired mainly by the Bolsheviks; in their fierce suppression of the rising the authorities flailed out against everyone on the left. Prominent SRs, including several Constituent Assembly delegates, were summarily executed; the episode showed again that Kolchak's officers hated the SRs as much as the Bolsheviks. Even without the December events, however, the SRs would not have cooperated with Kolchak, and so the largest party in Siberia and the Urals worked against the Supreme Ruler from the beginning. After the Omsk coup a number of former Komuch leaders, including Volsky, even crossed over to the Red side, encouraged by Moscow's gestures towards socialist pluralism. And in January 1920 the Siberian SRs would wreak a terrible personal revenge on the admiral himself.

Whoever its friends and enemies were, the Kolchakovshchina was not an effective dictatorship. At the central level Kolchak was unable to make the government work. Budberg sat through many top-level meetings; "The regime," he remarked, "was only form without content; the ministries can be compared to huge and imposing windmills, busily turning their sails, but with no millstones inside and with much of their machinery broken or missing." This came about partly because Siberia had been an administrative backwater of the Tsarist Empire, with few experienced government personnel. But the nature of the November coup had made things worse by permanently alienating one source of administrative talent, the pro-SR intelligentsia. Kolchak's civilian subordinates felt also that he concentrated too much on military affairs; one felt "the Admiral who was Supreme Commander-in-Chief swallowed up the Admiral who was Supreme Ruler, along with his Council of Ministers." To a large extent the government just became an organization for supporting the army.[3]

If Kolchak could not create a proper administration in Omsk, he had no chance of extending effective control over the vast territory of Siberia. Much of western Siberia (the front) had been under military administration even during the period of the PA-RG, and in mid-April 1919 military control was extended to all towns and the railway. And army rule was disastrously inefficient. The lack of administrative personnel, meanwhile, was even more important at the grass-roots level than at the center. Kolchak was fortunate that most Siberians were Great Russians; he lost much of the organized support of part of the important Bashkir minority (between Orenburg and the Urals) when, in February 1919, the Bashkir Corps changed sides, but this was a small problem compared to General Denikin's friction with the Ukrainians or General Iudenich's (in the Baltic) with the Estonians. Kolchak could not control the Orenburg and Ural cossacks, but unlike the southern Whites he was not faced with great cossack claims; Denikin had to make his first headquarters (Ekaterinodar) in the heart of one of the cossack hosts; Kolchak's problem was that geography *cut him off* from the main Orenburg and Ural Hosts. Overall, however, Kolchak still had the greatest trouble imposing his will over the vast territory that had been taken from Red control. A notorious area of weakness was the region east of Lake Baikal. There local atamans such as Semenov and Kalmykov were a law unto themselves and enjoyed the support of the Japanese. "Stenka Razin under a white sauce" is how General Budberg described them.[4] They choked the long supply line upon which the Siberian army and economy had to rely.

Kolchak's economic policy was ineffective. Galloping inflation was made worse by the disastrous abolition of "Kerenki" banknotes in April 1919. Kolchak, seeing himself only as a trustee, would not use the captured Imperial gold reserve. The few Siberian capitalists gave little help; donations came, one minister recalled, "like milk from a billy-goat." The military gave little thought to the long-term condition of the economy, and as a result Kolchak's only industrial region, the Urals, was in a bad way; as early as April 1919 the official in charge resigned in protest at chaotic military rule, lack of food supplies, and an absence of coherent support from Omsk.[5] The Allies provided no economic aid. Siberia's economic problems were beyond the ability of any regime to solve quickly. The World War had upset the whole Russian economy, and Civil War cut Siberia and the Urals off from their natural supplies and markets in central Russia. Consumer goods had to be brought in along the one rail link with the Pacific. And the war against the Bolsheviks, fought on a limited base of manpower and natural resources, demanded great economic sacrifices.

In his base area, Kolchak faced no conflict between dispossessed landlords and revolutionized land-hungry peasants; prerevolutionary Siberia had had no large gentry estates. (There was, however, some tension between the *starozhili* the "old" settlers, and the poorer immigrants of the past few decades, the *novoseli*.) Nevertheless, there was no effective land law, no confirmation of the Bolshevik decree on land. This was a greater weakness once the Kolchak forces reached the fringes of European Russia, where the land question was more important. In newly occupied regions such as Ufa Province the peasants had little reason to welcome Kolchak, especially when some of his commanders enforced the return of seized lands to their owners. Meanwhile, there was no reason for the peasants in the Soviet-controlled Volga provinces to rise in support of the White armies advancing toward them.

The lack of "propaganda by deed" was matched by the lack of any effective mobilization of support. As one of Kolchak's generals later lamented, "we not only did not give the *muzhik* [peasant] the bird in the hand, we were even afraid to promise him the bird in the bush."[6] Kolchak's propaganda organization, *Osved*, was organized too late; funds were eventually pumped into it, but it was ineffective and it was unpopular among the army high command.

The weaknesses, political and administrative, of the Kolchakovsh-china had two major effects on the spring campaign. First, it made the Whites less attractive to the peasants of the Volga-Kama basin who were the first objects of "liberation." And second, it made it more difficult for Kolchak to raise enthusiastic popular forces to serve in his army. Kolchak seized power in November 1918 and called the population "to union and to struggle with Bolshevism, to labor and to sacrifices."[7] One of his basic problems was that the response to that call was so weak, and the weak response came partly from the nature of the Kolchakovshchina. Active internal resistance to Kolchak's rule was not, however, a major cause of the failure of the Ufa offensive. The rear of Kolchak's armies was more stable than it would be later, and it was not necessary to pull troops out of the front line for battle with anti-White partisans. And it is not clear that the alternatives to military dicta-torship would have been any more effective. Would the pre-Kolchak "liberal" Omsk PA-RG have been able either to attract military leaders or to enforce conscription? It would in any event have been challenged by the Chernov-led SRs. Would such a government really have created more enthusiastic forces, or brought about risings behind the Bolshevik lines? This had not been the case for Komuch in 1918, and the Bolshevik hold was stronger by the late spring of 1919.

The other side of the political equation was the attraction of the Reds. Too much should not be made of the level of active Bolshevik support in the Urals and Siberia. These regions had voted overwhelmingly for the SRs in 1917. Dzerzhinsky's and Stalin's investigation of the December 1918 "Perm Catastrophe" brought out the problems of Soviet power throughout the eastern region. They found the Red civilian administra-tion feeble and unpopular. The "Extraordinary Tax" (of 2 November 1918) on the kulaks and middle peasants was especially hated. The local Chekas were often the sole representative of Soviet power. The Red Army had had to fight on two fronts, against the Whites and "against the elusive population in the rear who, under the direction of whiteguard agents, blew up railway tracks and created all sorts of difficulties"; "All the Party and Soviet institutions are unanimous in describing the 'solidly counterrevolutionary nature' of the population of Perm and Viatka Provinces."

What was true for Perm and Viatka was true for the whole eastern region. The Reds had major problems in early 1919 with peasant insurgents on the Volga fighting under the slogan "Long live the Bolsheviks, down with the Communists!" and with worker rebels at Votkinsk. Trotsky wrote to Stalin and Lenin in late March 1919 requesting an inspection team to help calm the area behind Eastern Army Group: "The movement had acquired a broad character. The middle peasants are both exasperated by the manifest malpractices of [Soviet] institutions and hoodwinked by counterrevolutionaries."[8]

It also does not appear that conscious Bolshevik agitation was very effective in the White rear. The Bolshevik CC set up a "Siberian Bureau" (Sibbiuro) to coordinate work behind Kolchak's lines, but this had little early impact, not least because of the great distances involved. In the first months the small Bolshevik underground stressed urban uprisings, and it was possible for White counterintelligence to destroy them. The most spectacular failure was the Omsk uprising of December 1918. The Bolsheviks' Siberian Regional Committee was broken up by the Whites in April 1919, and its leaders executed.

On the other hand, as we shall see later, the Soviet side made a major effort in the spring of 1919 to make good some of its political weaknesses. The Eighth Party Congress in March 1919 introduced important new policies; it did this at least partly under the pressure of Kolchak's Ufa offensive, which was then in its third week. There was a tightening up of party-state administration (and also of the army). At the same time the party line was changed to win as much support in the countryside as was possible in the situation. Previously the stress had been on class warfare in the villages, with support for the "poor peasant" minority, and attacks on the kulaks (prosperous peasants); now the stress was on winning over the "middle peasant," which in effect meant the great mass of the peasantry. Even before this, however, much of the Siberian population had had no great reason to dislike the Bolsheviks, partly because Bolshevik control had been so weak and short-lived. Meanwhile the Soviet program of mass self-government, social reform, and a total rejection of the old regime must have won support; in addition Moscow already ruled the bulk of the people of the Russian motherland. Given the weaknesses of the Kolchak regime, the Soviet idea had more and more appeal as time went by.

Rival Armies

Kolchak's armies were stopped and then pursued back toward the

Urals. This was largely due to the growing size and quality of the Soviet forces. But the initial Red defeats were a sign of problems in the Red Army, and these were only gradually overcome in the course of the campaign. The Soviet high command had had little knowledge of what was going on in Siberia, and it was surprised by Khanzhin's Ufa attack on 4 March 1919. Ten days before, Vatsetis had reported to Lenin that the local situation was improving and that the Urals were nearly within reach; given the danger of Allied intervention, he urged that the main stress of Soviet grand strategy still be put on the Ukrainian and Western Army Groups. On 24 February Trotsky made a most optimistic speech in Moscow to a meeting of Red Army cadets: "Summing up the position on our fronts it can be said that the situation is completely favorable." The commander of Eastern Army Group misread White intentions; Colonel Kamenev assumed a concentration in the north around Perm, rather than in the center before Ufa, and the poor initial deployment of the Red armies was one reason for Khanzhin's successes.[9]

The confusion in the Red eastern command continued during the battles with Kolchak. Kamenev did work out a counterattack plan, which was approved at a high-level meeting with Trotsky and Vatsetis in Simbirsk on 10 April; he began a counterattack with his two southern armies, now under the command of Mikhail Frunze. (Frunze was a veteran Bolshevik who had become involved in the army in the previous summer, and in 1925 he would replace Trotsky as Red Army chief; his 1919 "Southern Group" had originally been formed for the advance into Turkestan.) In the end, however, the planned sweep from the south was threatened by rapid White progress. Troops had to be thrown in front of the Whites, and Frunze's counterattack was launched earlier than planned and with more limited goals. But the White drive was stopped, and clearly Kamenev deserved much of the credit. On 3 July, after his armies had pushed Kolchak back to the Urals (and with disaster threatening on other fronts), he replaced Vatsetis as Red Army Main Commander-in-Chief. But this was only after he himself had been sacked, on 5 May, just as the shape of his victory was becoming clear. (According to Kamenev's memoirs, Vatsetis dismissed him for "non-execution of his orders and, in general, for lack of discipline".) He was, however, brought back by Lenin (presumably over Trotsky's objections) three weeks later, at the demand of the Eastern Army Group commissars.[10]

The various Red armies had begun the spring campaign in a disorganized state. The shortcomings had been brought out at the time of the "Perm Catastrophe." Dzerzhinsky and Stalin reported that Third Army's move in December 1918 from the Urals to beyond Perm was not even a proper retreat, but "an absolutely disorderly flight of an utterly routed and completely demoralized army." It was in a deplorable state. Commanders were unreliable; commissars inexperienced; soldiers confused, hungry and cold. Of 30,000 men, only a third remained; some had begun fighting on the White side. Fifth Army—shattered at Ufa in March 1919—was a center of the Military Opposition to Trotsky's centralizing policies with, as Vatsetis complained in mid-April, continuing splits between officers and commissars. Trotsky himself blamed the defeat of Fifth Army on the local commissars' "system of slackness, grumbling and criticism implanted from above."[11] These shortcomings in the Red Army were gradually dealt with, partly as a result of Trotsky's victory at the Eighth Party Congress.

On the other side of the battlefield, the lines of advance and timing of the White Siberian armies have been much criticized. Kolchak on 6 January 1919 did order a halt at Perm and a shift of the main axis of advance from the north to the center of his front. This was, however, sound strategy. To have tried to develop the December victory and chase the Red Third Army west along the Perm-Viatka railway line would have been senseless. If Arkhangelsk was the objective, then the nearest rail route meant an advance of 600 miles to Vologda, and another 250 north from Vologda to the Allied-White lines; even the rail-river route via Viatka, Kotlas, and the Northern Dvina was a distance of 600 miles. Any deep thrust on the Perm-Viatka line alone would have been threatened on its southern flank from the Soviet heartland. The northern region, moreover, was thin in people and supplies, and it was the middle of winter; the frozen port at Arkhangelsk would not open until May 1919, and it would be some time later that (unpredictable) supporting operations by the Allies could develop from there.

More important, in January 1919 Kolchak's front was most seriously threatened in the center—from the Ufa direction—where the Reds were approaching the Urals passes. The situation demanded as a first step a counterattack in this central area. Khanzhin was originally only given limited goals, but Kolchak's Stavka (GHQ) was right to develop his initial success and urge him early in April, as a second step, on to the Volga. It was necessary to take control of the region between the Urals and the Volga-Kama river system, whether Kolchak moved on Arkhangelsk, Saratov, or directly to Moscow; only with the center of the White front covered by the great rivers, with rail links from the Urals to the crossings at Samara, Simbirsk, Sarapul, and Perm, could a further advance be considered. And an advance to the Volga line would give the Whites manpower and food, take those things from the Reds, and cut the most important Soviet river communications line.

A more telling criticism of the White line of advance is that a weak area was allowed to appear on the southern flank. The Bashkir Corps changed sides in February 1919, and the Orenburg and Ural Cossack forces were badly organized after the fall of Uralsk and Orenburg in January—which made it possible for Frunze to burst the White bubble from the south in late April. And poor overall coordination made it difficult to shift troops from Siberian Army (around Perm) to Western Army. But the general conception of the attack was sound enough.

The timing of the offensive was more debatable; it came before the White army had been properly organized. Knox summed up the faults of Stepanov, Kolchak's Minister of War—in charge of the rear—and Lebedev, Kolchak's Chief of Staff, in charge of the front-line armies. "Stepanov thought he had ten years to beat the Bolsheviks. Lebedev wanted to do the job in ten minutes. Both were excellent fellows in their own way . . . but together they were enough to ruin any Empire." Knox was annoyed at Stepanov's plodding approach to the formation of new units in the rear, and in March bluntly told Kolchak as much: "People are so occupied by talk and paper schemes that decisions are indefinitely postponed. The plain truth is that we will have to fight this year for our lives and every hour is of value."[12] Stepanov concentrated his resources on raising five new infantry divisions in central Siberia, and these were still only skeleton formations when the Ufa offensive began. Lebedev, however, attacked before the army was formed and trained, and he soon found himself without reserves. Kolchak's most experienced formation, Kappel's Volga Corps, was still refitting in early March and trying to incorporate Red POWs; it was thrown into battle piecemeal at the beginning of May and defeated. But what else could the Whites have done? In theory they moved too *late*, rather than too early. Two full months passed between Kolchak's January directive and Khanzhin's offensive, and an earlier start might have brought Khanzhin to the Volga before the *rasputitsa*. But it was winter, and his troops had had to be redeployed and refitted after a long campaign.

The Whites might, on the other hand, have had a much more cautious policy, holding the Urals line and equipping their army behind it. This made sense in purely military terms; it is what Stepanov and Knox wanted. Kolchak might have waited to mount, with General Denikin's southern White armies, a coordinated late-summer offensive against Moscow. But Denikin's advance, which took him to Kharkov and Tsaritsyn at the end of June, could not have been predicted, and may only have occurred *because* Red troops had been moved from south Russia to fight Kolchak.

And there were basic political, psychological, and military factors pushing the Whites forward. Some of their leaders thought the Reds would simply fall apart if attacked—a not unreasonable assessment, given the pressures on Bolshevik Russia from several sides. Whatever Knox's local advice, Kolchak saw the political necessity of an offensive as a means of getting Allied aid and recognition. "Foreign policy was made by the army," one of Kolchak's advisers recalled. "On it depended both the scale and continuation of the Allies' help."[13] And underlying Kolchak's dilemma was the overall balance against him: the Red Army—with its big population base—was getting stronger all the time.

Kolchak's Ufa offensive was later described by Stalin and a generation of Soviet historians as part of the "First Campaign of the Entente." In fact there is no evidence that the Allies provoked the March 1919 offensive; the most important Allied representative in Siberia, General Knox, wanted Kolchak properly to prepare his forces before going over to the attack. The March offensive, Knox later reported to London, "was commenced without our previous knowledge"; the local British mission had to accept it as a fait accompli.[14] The attack, unlike the 1918 Volga campaign, was a purely Russian affair; the Czechoslovaks, in particular, had been withdrawn to the rear to guard part of the Trans-Siberian railway. There were no Allied troops involved in the fighting. (A handful of Allied battalion-strength detachments were stationed deep behind the lines in Siberian cities, and there was a large Japanese presence east of Lake Baikal.) General Janin, the head of the French military mission, tried to assume command of all forces in Siberia, but this was stiffly rejected by Kolchak on grounds of national pride.

On the other hand Allied, and especially British, logistic support for Kolchak was most important. Rural Siberia had neither munitions factories nor arms depots. The Urals would be the arsenal of the 1941 war, but in 1918–1919 the factories there were in turmoil and starved of food and fuel. Weapons and supplies could only come from outside, and thanks to the port of Vladivostok they began to flow to Kolchak six months before they began to flow to General Denikin in south Russia (via the Black Sea). Knox stressed the British contribution in a letter to Kolchak of June 1919: "Since about the middle of December [1918] every round of rifle ammunition fired on the front has been of British manufacture, conveyed to VLADIVOSTOK in British ships and delivered at

OMSK by British guards." "Britmiss" (the British military mission) reported the arrival between October 1918 and October 1919 of 79 ships with 97,000 tons of supplies. The bulk arrived in Omsk between March and June 1919. Supplies included 600,000 rifles, 346 million rounds of small-arms ammunition, 6831 machine guns, 192 field guns, and clothing and personal equipment for 200,500 men. Kolchak was sent infantry weapons (rifles, machine guns, ammunition) on a scale comparable to that sent to Denikin. (He was, however, sent much less [five times less] artillery, and few if any aircraft or tanks.) One Soviet source spoke of 600,000 rifles and 1000 machine guns from the U.S. in 1918–1919, 1700 machine guns and 400 field guns from the French, and 70,000 rifles, 100 machine guns, and 30 field guns from the Japanese.[15] Whatever the figures, the Allies, led by the British, sent to Kolchak arms and equipment roughly comparable to *total* Soviet production in 1919.

But the bulk of British supplies did not begin to arrive in Omsk until after the Ufa offensive had started. And there would be great problems throughout 1919 in ensuring the flow of weapons. There was hardly anywhere on the globe that was less accessible than Kolchak's battle-front. Vladivostok was far from the military depots of western Europe and North America. And even then it was a trip of four to six weeks from Vladivostok to Omsk via the single-track line of the Trans-Siberian, a route dependent on Japanese good will and vulnerable to the looting of local leaders such as Ataman Semenov.

The Kolchak army, officially called the "Russian (*Rossiiskaia*) Army," was large by White standards. Kolchak's commanders realized, however, that Siberia could not match the Reds in overall numbers and that *quality* could prove the key factor. Vatsetis later explained the initial success of the Ufa offensive by the Whites' better officers and better disciplined and standardized forces.[16] But the overall quality of Kolchak's army was never very good, and in particular was below that of Denikin's "Armed Forces of South Russia," which had the advantage of a larger pool of experienced and capable generals and colonels, and the officer-veterans of the "Ice March."

Kolchak's defeat is often explained by his admiral's ignorance of land warfare. On the other hand Kolchak had been a very capable and energetic admiral; he was a distinguished combat officer in both the Pacific and the Baltic, and had been selected for early and rapid promotion (he was only 45 in 1919). In any event, while Kolchak was nominally Supreme Commander-in-Chief, the day-to-day command army was in the hands of his chief of staff. But it is just here, in his choice of subordinates, that Kolchak is most easily criticized. The de facto commander of Kolchak's armies from November 1918 to June 1919 was General D. A. Lebedev; Lebedev was a thirty-six-year-old wartime colonel who, although a General Staff officer, was better at political conspiracy than high command. Kolchak installed Lebedev in place of the Directory's competent commander, General Boldyrev, and passed over a number of other qualified officers. Perhaps Kolchak preferred him to a more senior man who would have challenged his own authority; in any event the poorly thought out spring campaign showed Lebedev to have been a bad choice.

Other aspects of the army's command left much to be desired. The administrative staffs in the rear were too big, which made them ponderously inefficient and starved the active units of officers; Kolchak's "Stavka," the former headquarters building of the Tsarist Omsk Military District, was described as a "military anthill." In addition, the quality of Kolchak's officers was not high. There were 17,000 of them, but only 1000 had been pre-1915 cadre officers with training and experience in mobile warfare; the great mass were young *"prapory,"* wartime ensigns (*praporshchiki*). None of Kolchak's corps or division commanders had been prerevolutionary generals; the only "proper" general active in the fighting of March–June 1919 was Khanzhin.[17] Lebedev and Stepanov, commanders of the front and the rear, were former colonels in their thirties. "Lieutenant General" Gajda, Commander-in-Chief of the other main front-line force, Siberian Army, was twenty-seven and an NCO deserter from the Austro-Hungarian Army. Of the other best-known Kolchak commanders Sakharov was thirty-eight, Kappel was thirty-six, and Pepeliaev was twenty-six. So in terms of experience there was little to choose between White and Red armies.

Kolchak was never able to make use of what might have been a major asset, the cossack cavalry. Cossack brigades were attached to each White corps but made little impact before September 1919; there was nothing like the successes of the Don Cossacks or the Mamontov raid on Denikín's front. Kolchak's potential cossack strength was much less than Denikin's. The front-line Orenburg and Ural Hosts, with total populations (men, women, and children) of 574,000 and 235,000 respectively, were considerably smaller than those of the Don (1,457,000), the Kuban (1,339,000), and the Terek (255,000). In the steppe south of Omsk was the Siberian Host (114,000) but this was mobilized— incompletely— only in August 1919. The 58,000 Semirechie Cossacks were tied down in Central Asia. (The 258,000 Transbaikal cossacks and 96,000 Amur, Ussuri, and Irkutsk cossacks were in eastern Siberia; with leaders such as Semenov and Kalmykov they were more a liability than an asset.)

The quality of Kolchak's rank and file was not high. He avoided older world war veterans, from a fear that they had been radicalized by the revolution. Instead he called up the youngest "classes," nineteen and twenty-year-olds who had not been "infected." These men had to be trained (unlike the veterans conscripted by the Reds). The main French adviser thought they were puny, and drily compared them with Jules Verne's hero: "the population of Siberia, particularly in the east, is rarely the Michael Strogoff type." Wide use was also made of captured Red soldiers, who were most unreliable. The White army began to fall apart once the Volga advance was stalled. As it was pushed back across Ufa province there were large-scale desertions and even mutinies. By the time Western Army had retreated to the Belaia its strength had fallen from 62,000 to 15,000.[18]

In March 1919 Kolchak's armies were the largest anti-Bolshevik forces, with a paper front-line strength of 110,000 men. (Total strength— combatants and non-combatants—grew from 160,000 in November 1918 to 450,000 in June 1919.[19]) Siberia had been under White control and free of serious fighting since midsummer 1918; in contrast Denikin and the Don Cossacks were fighting for their lives right through the winter 1918–1919. On the other hand Kolchak's population base was small, relative to the size of his territory and the strength of the Reds. At its greatest extent the White zone in the east—including the Urals, Orenburg, Siberia, Kazakhstan, and the Far East—contained about 20 million people. In the crucial central zone between the Urals and Lake Baikal, where Kolchak had fullest control throughout 1918–1919 (Tobolsk, Tomsk, Enisei, and Irkutsk Provinces), the population was less than eight million.

The population of the Soviet-held zone, on the other hand, was 60 million. The total strength (combat and non-combat personnel) of the Red Army in January 1919, two months before the Kolchak offensive, was 788,000, with 120,000 in Eastern Army Group and 147,000 in the Iaroslavl, Ural, and Volga Military Districts behind it. The *combat* strength of Eastern Army Group in February 1919 was 84,000, and there were another 18,000 combat troops behind it in the three military districts. At this time the Reds had 372 guns and 1471 machine-guns in Eastern Army Group (plus 184 and 231 in the three districts), compared to Kolchak's 256 guns and 1235 machine-guns.[20]

Meanwhile, after Kolchak's Ufa offensive, the Reds began to channel resources to the east. Special theses of the Bolshevik CC in early April said that Kolchak's victories were creating "an extraordinarily threatening danger for the Soviet republic" and demanded maximum effort. Fortunately for Moscow the situation on the other fronts *appeared* good in April; the French had withdrawn from the Ukrainian ports and the

Don Cossacks were under siege; Trotsky could announce in April that Kolchak was "the last card of the counter-revolution." (At the start of May Vatsetis told Lenin that all reserves were being sent to Eastern Army Group.) By mid-May the total strength in Eastern Army Group was listed as 361,000, plus 195,000 in the Iaroslavl, Urals, and Volga districts. The Reds, then, had large reserves of manpower, Kolchak did not.[21]

In May 1919 one White officer visited Ufa, which stands on a hill above the Belaia River, and looked to the west.

> Beyond the Belaia spread to the horizon the limitless plain, the rich fruitful steppe; the lilac haze in the far distance enticed and excited—there were the home places so close to us, there was the goal, the Volga. And only the wall of the *internatsional*, which had impudently invaded our Motherland, divided us off from all that was closest and most dear.[22]

But it was not to be. Kolchak's Ufa offensive failed. After two months of success his armies found themselves back where they had started. They would never again threaten the Red heartland, and for the rest of their existence would be on the strategic defensive.

If the White armies *had* actually achieved the intermediate goal of getting back to the Volga (and they would probably have trapped large Soviet forces in the process), they would have had the benefit of a mile-wide river obstacle between themselves and any Red counter-attack, and they might have been ready for some kind of coordination with Denikin's armies in the south. On the other hand, even if Kolchak had got to Samara and Simbirsk on the Volga in May 1919 he would still have been 500 miles from Moscow, and the Ufa campaign showed the huge difficulties to be overcome. This chapter has been about those difficulties that emerged in the first months of Kolchak's regime. The basic reason for failure was that even the limited task involved was too difficult. By May the Whites had lost the initiative. The next chapter will be about why Kolchak's army was unable even to hold its ground, and why, by November 1919, it had been shattered beyond redemption.

11

OMSK AND ARKHANGELSK:
KOLCHAK, June–November 1919;
NORTH RUSSIA, November 1918–March 1920

Give us the Urals!

Red Army Slogan, 1919

I know you value the assistance of my Government. It is my wish to help you, but frankly at present you make help impossible.

General Knox to General Golovin, 27 September 1919

Kolchak Defeated, June–November 1919

The campaign in the east progressed much faster than Moscow could have hoped. "If before winter we do not take the Urals," Lenin told the commissars of Eastern Army Group, "I consider that the defeat of the revolution will be inevitable."[1] He wrote on 29 May 1919; less than two months later the Red Army broke through the Urals. By the start of winter the Reds were actually 400 miles beyond the mountain range, on the outskirts of Omsk.

On the left flank of Eastern Army Group, the Red Second and Third Armies, aided by the Volga Flotilla, got across the Kama River and recaptured Perm (1 July). Gajda's Siberian Army was now in full retreat to the Urals, and was unable to make a stand even there. Colonel Shorin's Red Second Army covered 200 miles in four weeks, and on 15 July took the most important Urals town, Ekaterinburg. On the right flank, Tukhachevsky's Red Fifth Army, which had crossed the Belaia River and taken Ufa at the start of June, pushed on to the east. Sixty miles from the Belaia it entered the central Urals and, thanks to skillful maneuvering and White demoralization, broke through the defenders to take first Zlatoust (13 July) and then Cheliabinsk (24 July). The Whites had to pull back to the first defendable line in the grassy steppe of western Siberia, the Tobol River. By the middle of August the Red Third and Fifth Armies had reached the Tobol, having in just ten weeks advanced 350 miles across the Urals from the Kama-Belaia line.

The loss of the Urals spelled the doom of Kolchak's forces. The Urals are not a particularly high range—they do not compare, for example, with the Caucasus Mountains—but the rough terrain and dense woods of the region were the most easily defended territory east of the Volga. This barrier was now in Red hands; Kolchak had been pushed back too far to threaten central Sovdepia. And the Whites had lost the factories and mines of the Urals which had been their only industrial base; to the east was only thinly settled, agricultural Siberia. Meanwhile the loss of the Cheliabinsk rail junction completed the isolation of the Ural and Orenburg cossacks, and of General Belov's Southern Army; the army, which had withdrawn in desperation down the Orenburg-Tashkent railway, was forced to surrender in September 1919, rather than face death in the desert.

Both sides were exhausted on the Tobol. The Reds were able to cross the river and push on in mid-August, but it would take them another two and a half months to break the next river line, the Ishim, 150 miles east of the Tobol. In early September the Whites made their last serious counterattack. In a series of battles the Reds were stopped and then forced back 100 miles to the Tobol. (At one stage Kolchak was optimistic enough to set up a "Moscow Army Group".) These gains came mainly from the raising of a large cavalry force from the Siberian Cossacks, but the Reds were able to recover, and by 4 November had counterattacked to take control of the two rail crossings over the Ishim. The Reds were now closing in on Omsk, Kolchak's capital, which was 150 miles east of the Ishim on the Irtysh River. The jump from the Tobol to the Ishim took two and a half months, the jump from the Ishim to the Irtysh— roughly the same distance—took less than two weeks. Part of the Red 27th Division raced the last sixty miles in one day, and on 14 November—four days short of the anniversary of the Kolchak coup—took Omsk without a fight.

The internal failure of the Kolchakovshchina was one underlying reason why the White regime collapsed so quickly. Kolchak made a number of political promises to the Allies in June 1919. He said that a date for a Constituent Assembly was to be fixed "at the moment when the Bolsheviks are definitely crushed." But such promises could have little weight, especially given his rejection of the original Assembly. The military held power both in the center and the localities, where promises to the Allies of local self-government through zemstvos and town councils meant little.[2] The National Zemstvo Congress summoned in September 1919 was too late. Kolchak would only begin to promise a wider government at the very end of the year, after his armies had been hopelessly smashed and his capital abandoned. Meanwhile the economy in White Siberia was laboring under the difficulties of early 1919 plus the loss of the only industrial area, the Urals.

The clearest symptom of Kolchak's weakness was the emergence of hostile partisan bands. The movement developed gradually from the autumn of 1918, originally in response to conscription. By July 1919 one senior officer noticed how the spread of red dots used to show uprisings on the staff maps was "beginning to look like advanced spotted fever."[3] The situation was worst in central Siberia, between Omsk and Lake Baikal; the partisans thrived in the thinly settled *taiga* to the north and south of the railway line, and even established "partisan republics." (One radical hamlet called itself "Red Petrograd.") Punitive expeditions only made things worse. Although the partisans did not seriously threaten the railway lines or the big towns until Kolchak's main front had disintegrated, they denied some resources, tied down forces, and hurt morale. The Bolsheviks had little directly to do with this growing popular unrest. Their political base in Siberia had been narrow, the few local Bolsheviks in the towns had great problems in establishing communications with the Soviet heartland, and Kolchak's "counter-intelligence" units were effective against them. In the towns the Whites would meet open opposition only after their armies had been smashed, and that opposition would be led not by Bolsheviks but by SRs. Bolshevik links with the partisans in the taiga were weak, and indeed once the Reds had recaptured the towns many partisans turned against *them*.

Kolchak's actual downfall between May and October 1919 came not so much from insurrection in the towns and villages of the rear as from the collapse of his military front. This came in part from the growing effectiveness of the Red Army. The Red path to military success was not without its twists and turns. Conflict over eastern strategy led to one of the great upheavals in the Red high command. Personal relations between Colonel Vatsetis, Red Army Main Commander-in-Chief, and

Colonel Kamenev, Eastern Army Group Commander-in-Chief, were bad; in May Vatsetis had removed Kamenev, only to have him reinstated under political pressure. In early June Vatsetis ordered the armies to shift over to the defensive in the east, holding the line of the Kama and Belaia Rivers, 60–100 miles *west* of the Urals, and moving troops to other fronts, where the situation was more threatening (this was the time of White offensives toward Kharkov and Petrograd). Trotsky evidently supported Vatsetis. But Colonel Kamenev, the Red Eastern Army Group commander, urged a continued advance on his own front, to the Urals; in mid-June the Bolshevik CC backed Kamenev's offensive strategy, and in early July Vatsetis suffered final defeat when he was dismissed as Main Commander-in-Chief and replaced—against Trotsky's wishes—by Kamenev. Even then, Eastern Army Group received few supplies and no men from the center; it had to give up units to the more threatened southern front. And the September battles between the Ishim and the Tobol caused anxiety in Moscow, as they coincided with Denikin's drive from the south. Lenin thought the Republic RevMilCouncil (RVSR) was letting things slip.

> On the Siberian front they have put some scoundrel called Olderogge and the old woman Pozern in charge, and "reassured themselves." An absolute disgrace! And now they are beginning to beat us! We will make the RVSR responsible for this, if *energetic* steps are not taken! To let victory slip out of our hands is a disgrace.[4]

In any event, as the narrative of operations has already made clear, the Reds outfought the Whites in the summer and autumn of 1919, especially in the capture of Zlatoust, Cheliabinsk, and Omsk. The Red Army was clearly getting better, and there were able officer-commanders such as Kamenev, Shorin, Tukhachevsky, and Eikhe. Frunze was in command from late July to early August, followed by V. A. Olderogge. (Lenin's "scoundrel" was a former Tsarist general; he stayed in command through a series of victories to January 1920. The "old woman" Pozern was a veteran Bolshevik.) In August the White General Budberg noted in his diary that "we are up against not the *sovdepy* and motley Red-Guard rabble of last year but a regular Red Army." A White leader who visited Tobolsk after it was briefly recaptured was impressed at reports of how well the Reds had behaved.[5]

The White Army, meanwhile, was no better led than in the Ufa offensive. It was White ineptitude that made the big July battle around Cheliabinsk so decisive. In July, after the failure of the Ufa offensive, the White front-line command had been changed. The defeated com-

151

manders from the spring, Khanzhin and the uncontrollable Gajda, were removed. The front command was unified under General Diterikhs, an experienced officer, as "Main Commander-in-Chief of the Eastern Army Group" ("Eastern" compared to Denikin and Iudenich). Diterikhs was a strongly religious man and railed against the "Antichrist-Bolsheviks," but his real control over events was limited, which became clear at Cheliabinsk. Sakharov, the young commander of the central Third Army (formerly Khanzhin's Western Army), proposed a complex maneuver to turn the tide. The advancing Reds would be allowed to debouch from the Urals passes onto the west Siberian plain at Cheliabinsk; they would then be encircled by strong White forces (including three of the new divisions that had been forming in central Siberia), and the Urals would be retaken. Diterikhs did not approve the plan; he wanted to withdraw from the Urals and make a stand on one of the big Siberian rivers. General Knox, head of the British mission, also felt that Sakharov's was a risky operation, designed only to secure American support. Kolchak, however, approved the plan and so did his Chief of Staff, General Lebedev (Lebedev, like Sakharov, was a young and inexperienced officer). The operation went ahead. As so often happened in these years, the trap failed to snap shut. It was one of the biggest battles of the Civil War, costing the Reds 15,000 casualities and the Whites at least 5,000. But in the end the Reds held firm, aided by local workers fed up with White misrule. Kolchak's new divisions, thrown into complex maneuvers before their training was completed, fell apart; with them the Whites lost their reserves and the ability to make a serious stand further east.[6]

There was another strategic failure in the White September offensive between the Tobol and the Ishim. The Reds were stopped and forced back 100 miles to the Tobol, but the White cavalry leader, a former police official named Ivanov-Rinov, left much to be desired. At the critical moment (mid-September) the deep thrust of his Steppe Group failed to take the vital Tobol railway bridge behind the Red Army, and he was dismissed. The greatest example of White ineptness, however, was the fall of Omsk. When the Ishim River line broke in early November, General Diterikhs decided that Omsk could not be held. The army was breaking up; the Irtysh would soon freeze, and then there would be no defensible line before the White capital. Kolchak at first accepted this, then changed his mind when General Sakharov said he could hold the town. Sakharov replaced Diterikhs, but one army had already been pulled back to central Siberia, and refused to return, and reserves that Sakharov called in from the rear would not fight. Then the Irtysh froze. Such was the confusion that a pair of understrength Red

152

regiments dashed forward to Omsk and caught the White garrison by surprise. (One unfortunate senior White general stopped en route to his Omsk office to reproach some soldiers who had failed to salute him; to his amazement he found himself a prisoner of the Red vanguard.) Omsk and 30,000 White soldiers stationed there were taken without a fight. All the shattered White field armies could do was flee to the east.

Even with the most experienced and gifted battle commanders the Whites would have had great military difficulties. Their army was very badly organized. It had been enlarged in the summer of 1919, but the overall quality was, if anything, worse than at the time of the spring offensive. The best units were destroyed on the Belaia-Kama line and in the Urals. As the retreat through the mountains developed the Kolchak army, designed to rebuild the traditional *"Rossiiskaia"* Army, became most like the revolutionized army of 1917. Gajda's Siberian Army was particularly badly affected by indiscipline, and it pulled back through Perm and Ekaterinburg almost without a fight. In June 1919 there were incidents of whole units changing sides and soldiers shooting their officers. Desertion grew throughout the army; soldiers went home as they withdrew through their native provinces. A mass of conscripts was finally sent to the front in October 1919, but in a completely disorganized fashion, and they melted away almost immediately.

Supply problems remained acute. There were as many as 800,000 "spoons," people dependent on army rations, but less than a tenth that number of fighting men. Many officers and soldiers had their families with them. When Siberian Army pulled back out of the Urals in July its numbers shrank from 350,000 "eaters" to 6000 "bayonets." The supply demands of units were met at the expense of the local population. Some regimental supply trains had 1000 carts: "These were not military units," one disgusted officer recalled, "but some kind of Tatar horde." When Allied supplies finally began to get through in quantity at the end of the spring, the Kolchak army proved unable to incorporate them. At the end of September, writing to Kolchak's new chief of staff, General Golovin, Knox could only despair: "At present all seems to me to be *absolute chaos, and worse chaos than anything I have seen in the past 12 months.* . . . It is my wish to help you, but frankly at present you make help impossible."[7]

The Allies, for their part, could do nothing to prevent the change from stalemate into precipitate retreat. The Allies had sent no front-line troops even in the winter of 1918–1919. In the spring and early summer of 1919 nothing changed; an Anglo-Russian Brigade, with British officers and Russian soldiers, began to form in Ekaterinburg in mid-1919, but it never got beyond the early stages. The Japanese troops were all in eastern Siberia, and the Czechoslovaks were still stationed in the rear protecting the railways. In the late summer the European Allies removed even the small garrisons they had stationed in Kolchak's rear and, more important, the British training mission.

Allied policy in Siberia had been both opportunistic and ill-informed. Kolchak was supported—at least in a limited way—as long as his armies were advancing or thought to be advancing. This in turn pushed Kolchak into militarily foolish attacks at Ufa, Glazov, Cheliabinsk, and the Tobol. Influenced by the March–April 1919 Ufa offensive, and after long discussion, the Allied leaders in Paris on 26 May announced that they were "disposed to assist the Government of Admiral Kolchak and his Associates with munitions, supplies and food, to establish themselves as the government of all Russia"; the qualification was that the Admiral was to follow a democratic policy and accept the loss of some border areas. Kolchak quickly replied, agreeing to the conditions.[8] Nothing came of this de facto recognition, mainly because from early May Kolchak's armies had actually no longer been advancing. By June–July they were rapidly retreating; by August they were 1100 miles from Moscow and were no longer an effective threat to central Russia. Kolchak was losing and was given up by the Allies; if supplies were to be sent to the White Russians, Denikin's now-victorious southern front seemed a much better bet.

Kolchak's final problem, as before, was that his forces were numerically and qualitatively weak. It was true that the Red Army as a whole was under greater strain in the summer and autumn of 1919 than it had been in the spring. On the other hand, the total size of the Red Army grew as 1919 progressed. The Reds had a much larger population base, and they increased this base when they took the Volga and the Urals. They were able to support themselves with local reinforcements. The Reds, for example, raised 60,000 men in Ufa Province in July 1919, and in mid-September the Volga Military District contained 360,000 men and the new Urals Military District 40,000.[9] Kolchak's potential population base—even on paper—was never more than a third that of the Soviets, and much of this was lost with the Urals.

After the defensive battles on the far side of the Urals White combat strength was down to 50,000 men. Numbers were built up after that; meanwhile the Reds sent whole divisions to the west, and kept troops in the Urals or Turkestan, and the Red-White numerical balance was closer than it had been before. But at the start of November 1919, as Omsk was about to fall, the two remaining Red armies (Third and Fifth) fighting Kolchak had six rifle divisions and nearly 100,000 men, 1211 machine guns and 304 guns. Against them were front-line White forces of about 55,000, and of much inferior quality. (The 30,000 men in the Omsk garrison were all untrained conscripts.[10])

Kolchak understood his own weaknesses. In an order of mid-July 1919, just before the Cheliabinsk battle, he summarized five causes of failure: (1) exhaustion after constant battles; (2) poor army supply; (3) weakness of officer-soldier links; (4) Bolshevik and SR propaganda; (5) weak White propaganda. But there was nothing he could do. On 4 November 1919, on the eve of an even greater defeat, Kolchak again analyzed the situation (in a speech). The army, he said, had had to retreat because it was outnumbered, and

> the essence of the problem was this: the enemy was able to reinforce his ranks with new forces more quickly than we could.
> How can this have happened?
> Our units which were formed from men called up in the area behind the front, from Bolshevik-minded elements, crossed over to the Red side; this experience bred distrust of the new reinforcements among both commanders and veterans. We sent reinforcements, but detachment commanders refused to dilute their units with these reinforcements.
> We had to reinforce with great selectiveness, while the enemy freely used local manpower which was favorable to him.

Clearly, political and military failures were closely connected. In mid-August 1919 General Budberg had summed up the more general problems in his diary.

> In the army disorganization; at the *Stavka* illiteracy and hare-brained schemes; in the Government moral decay, discord, and the dominance of the ambitious and egotistical; in the country uprisings and anarchy; in society panic, selfishness, graft and all kinds of loathsomeness; at the top thrive various scoundrels and adventurers. Where will we get to with such baggage![11]

North Russia, November 1918–March 1920

Throughout late 1918 and 1919 the Whites, the Allies, and the Reds thought—or worried—about a link between Kolchak's Siberians and the anti-Bolshevik forces in North Russia. But Kolchak was stopped and the northern front was stable; the lines established in 1918 on the Northern Dvina and the Murmansk-Petrograd and Arkhangelsk-Vologda railways changed little; there were none of the spectacular advances and retreats of the other fronts. In September–October 1919 the Allies withdrew, and in February–March 1920 the Red Army completed the conquest of the region.

The features of North Russia have already been mentioned. Geography and the climate limited campaigning and meant the north could not be a decisive front. The population of the northern provinces, Arkhangelsk, Olonets, and Vologda, was small and isolated, so neither side could raise large forces locally. Meanwhile, commitments to other fronts meant that no one had large numbers of troops in the north. The northern Whites had a territory of 250,000 square miles, rather more than France, but a population of only 600,000 people. The Allies, for their part, were lukewarm about direct intervention in Russia; they certainly did not want to send large forces to an area that was cut off by the frozen White Sea from November to May. The largest anti-Bolshevik operation, the August 1919 attack down the Northern Dvina, had only 3000 British troops and 1000 Whites. For the Reds the north was remote. The main Arkhangelsk front was 500 miles from Moscow and with poor railway connections. Even at the time of their final victory the local Red force, General Samoilo's Sixth Detached Army (HQ, Vologda), had only three divisions, 1st on the Murmansk front, and 18th and 54th on the Arkhangelsk front. Earlier, the Reds had repeatedly been forced to transfer troops to other fronts, especially during the May and October 1919 attacks on Petrograd. Even in late January 1920 Kamenev, the Red Main Commander-in-Chief, was not confident that the Whites could be destroyed before the spring thaw blocked all movement; the Soviet railways were in such a bad state that the necessary reinforcements might not get through.

Neither side could make progress across the vast expanses of forest and swamp, especially given the climate. Movement was channeled into a few routes: the two single-track railways, a few roads, and the Northern Dvina. These routes could be effectively defended with blockhouses. The long winters were extremely cold, and all movement was impossible in the *rasputitsa*, the spring thaw. The Reds did take the county town of Shenkursk from its Allied defenders at the end of January 1919; the attack took place in deep snow and 37 degrees of frost. But Red plans to take Arkhangelsk, before a possible general armistice, came to nothing; their poorly clothed reinforcements could not cope with the blizzards and extreme cold, and then in April–May movement ended with the rasputitsa. In the summer and autumn the Reds had too few troops to think about offensive operations. Geography also blocked the White link with Kolchak. The only potential railway route was indirect—via Vologda—and across 850 miles of Soviet territory. The combined river-rail route down the Northern Dvina to Kotlas and then to Viatka was better, but still 600 miles long. A few small long-range patrols from Siberia and North Russia did meet one another in the remote taiga but this meant nothing. The North Russian Allied commander had very little idea what was happening on Kolchak's front, and it even took two and a half months for Omsk to acknowledge Arkhangelsk's recognition of Kolchak as Supreme Ruler.

Politically, the Arkhangelsk-based "Provisional Government of the Northern Region" was little different from the other White authorities. The power of the socialists had been broken by the abortive military coup of September 1918, and a more conservative government took over. The veteran socialist, Chaikovsky, remained as figurehead, but in January 1919 he left for the high politics of the Paris Russian Political Conference. In the same month General E. K. Miller (a Russian, despite his name) arrived by ship to take up the post of Governor-General, and from that time on was effectively the local leader. Miller was in historical terms the least important of the White commanders, but on paper he was better qualified than Kornilov, Denikin, Diterikhs, or Vrangel; he had commanded a corps in the world war. (The credentials of the commanders on both sides of the lines were impressive. Samoilo, who led the Red Sixth Army from November 1918 to April 1920, was a near contemporary of Miller's, and they had served together several times during the thirty years of their pre-1917 careers.)

Red propaganda made much of the internment of suspects in prison camps, but the regime does not seem to have been notably severe, and certainly it did not have the problems of peasant insurgency on the scale faced by the Whites in south Russia and central Siberia. Even so, it lacked effective power throughout its vast region. "As far as internal policy is concerned," a senior general complained in July 1919, "nothing has been done; the zemstvos are inactive and there is no power in the localities. The remote villages do what they want. There are no instructions; there is no leadership." A basic problem for the northern Whites was their inability to fire active local support among the peasants. As Ironside, the British commander, noted in his diary, "They simply don't care and you can do nothing with a nation that doesn't care."[12]

The nature and size of the population meant North Russia could not defend itself. There were no cossacks and few officers to build the White army around, and no surge to the anti-Bolshevik colors; the "Anglo-French soup" that Trotsky had described in September 1918 was still not thickening with Russian volunteers. Miller, meanwhile, was an

157

administrator, not a charismatic leader like some of the southern generals. The nature of his army, however, was complex. On the one hand it suffered a number of serious mutinies. Several British officers were actually killed by Russian conscripts, the only such incident in the Intervention; it took place in July 1919 with the mutiny of a company of the Dyer Battalion, part of a joint force, the Slavo-British Legion, that Ironside was trying to raise. The Dyer Battalion incident and the other mutinies were important in convincing the British that there was no future in the north. On the other hand the Whites did raise a substantial force; they eventually had thirteen regiments and a total of about 50,000 men, divided between Murmansk and Arkhangelsk.[13] They mounted a successful attack in the autumn of 1919 and held their own for nearly six months after the Allied departure.

The British, as they prepared to withdraw, offered to evacuate the White leaders; for a variety of reasons, partly the success of the other White armies, few accepted. But in the end the fate of North Russia depended on those other fronts. By the winter of 1919–1920 Denikin's drive toward Moscow had been reversed. Kolchak's armies were destroyed, and the Supreme Ruler killed. Allied diplomacy was edging toward Soviet Russia. The Red Army began an offensive up the Northern Dvina in February 1920, and the White regiments could not hold them. There were White plans to make the difficult overland trek from Arkhangelsk to Murmansk, but in the last days the Whites degenerated into great confusion. Samoilo's Red troops entered Arkhangelsk on 21 February 1920, three days after Miller had boarded an icebreaker and escaped with several hundred of his followers. (Miller would later succeed Generals Vrangel and Kutepov as head of the emigre White movement; he disappeared in Paris—presumably kidnapped by Soviet agents—in 1937. His opponent's fate was as remarkable, given the normal fate of Tsarist "specialists" in the 1930s; Samoilo served on as a Soviet military lecturer, and survived the Purges to get back his general's rank [at 71] and write his memoirs.) The end on the other northern front was as bad. The local commander was unpopular, and in February 1920 there was a revolt at Murmansk. The main White forces were trapped 400 miles down the Murman Railway, near Lake Onega, and disintegrated; some were able to escape to Finland. The Reds only reached Murmansk three weeks later, on 13 March.

Arkhangelsk and Murmansk are mainly interesting for Allied intervention (the north was a strategic sideshow and differed little politically from the other White regions). Allied troops were actually fighting the Red Army here, and the local Allied commander had control over the

White military effort and over the Whites' links with the outside world. The Soviet propaganda images of Allied intervention was closest to reality in North Russia. In fact, though, the Allies did little. During the winter of 1918–1919 the new British commander at Arkhangelsk, General Ironside, limited himself to defense; his troops were already overextended, and as most were still French or American his hands were tied anyway, especially after the German surrender. In the following spring the Allies decided to withdraw. The decision was not simple to carry out, partly because the ports were frozen. For the British, who had major responsibility for the theater, there were also a moral commitment to the Whites, and a desire to use every means to hit the Reds (Churchill was particularly keen on this). The British General Staff, for its part, was concerned that any withdrawal be "carried out with as little loss of prestige as may be" and avoiding "a repetition of the pitiable exhibition recently afforded by the [French] *sauve-qui-peut* at Kherson and Odessa."[14] In May 1919 Ironside was ordered to launch a "preventative offensive" down the Northern Dvina toward Kotlas (and Kolchak). But it was not until early June that the "Russian Relief Force," two British brigades, took over from the weary troops that had wintered at Arkhangelsk. By then Kolchak's offensive had been reversed. In July the British decided to implement the withdrawal; the August attack down the river covered the evacuation of Arkhangelsk, which was completed on 27 September 1919. The British also attacked on the Murmansk front, and then on 12 October left Murmansk.

There was another international dimension. In May 1919 the British and Whites had launched an offensive down the Murmansk-Petrograd railway; at the end of the month they had gained a foothold on Lake Onega, but they never reached the biggest town in the region, Petrozavodsk. This was so despite the long Finnish border that flanked the Red positions, and even despite an unofficial invasion of southern Karelia by Finnish troops in April 1919. The Finns took the province town of Olonets and threatened Petrozavodsk (and with it the Petrograd-Murmansk railway) from the southwest. But the British and Whites would not cooperate with a former German ally that claimed "Russian" territory in eastern Karelia. In the end the Finns had to pull back when Red troops landed from Lake Ladoga behind them. Later on General Miller begged Kolchak to recognize the Helsinki government in order to get cooperation in the Baltic and on the Murmansk front, but recognition never came.

North Russia and western Siberia had much in common. Both were remote, sparsely settled areas. Both were too distant and too weak to threaten the survival of Soviet Russia. In both regions the Red armies were able to hold their own in the second half of 1919. The chief threat to Soviet power, when it came, would not be from the east or the north. Nor, despite Moscow's hopes and fears, would the decisive action be in the west or southwest. Of the ring of fronts it was the south that would be the most important.

12

THE ARMED FORCES OF SOUTH RUSSIA,
November 1918–September 1919

Incidentally. A feature of Denikin's army is its large number of officers and cossacks. It is this element which, having no mass strength behind it, is extremely well-suited to swift raids, to gambles, to desperate ventures, with the aim of sowing panic, with the aim of destruction for destruction's sake.

In the struggle with such an enemy what is needed is military discipline and military vigilance of the highest degree.

Lenin, "All out for the Fight against Denikin!", 9 July 1919

Volunteers and Cossacks

In the summer and autumn of 1918, behind the barrier of the Don Cossack Region, Denikin's Volunteer Army had retaken the Kuban Region from local Red forces. Then, at the end of 1918, the Whites prepared to complete their conquest of the whole north Caucasus. The Red forces in the area had been hastily organized into the Caspian-Caucasus Army Group. The main strength of the army group was Eleventh Army, which faced northwest towards the Kuban; it held a front running 200 miles into the steppe from the Caucasus foothills. In early January 1919 the Volunteer cavalry punched a hole through the Red lines and quickly took Sviatyi Krest (Holy Cross), cutting Caspian-Caucasus Army Group's supply line to the Soviet "mainland." Eleventh Army broke up in panic. The Whites dashed southeast, following the railway line down the north edge of the Caucasus Mountains and taking one Red town after another: Kislovodsk and Piatigorsk (capital of the North Caucasus Soviet Republic) fell on 20 January, and Vladikavkaz on 10 February. The capture of Groznyi (5 February), and Kizliar (6 February) allowed a link-up with the Terek Cossacks on the Caspian Sea; the Red Twelfth Army, facing the Caspian, was also overwhelmed. The north Caucasus was now completely out of Soviet hands. Less than a tenth of Red forces in the region were able to withdraw across steppe and desert towards Astrakhan. The Volunteers took 50,000 prisoners, 150 guns, and 350 machine guns. A whole Army Group, 150,000 men, had ceased to exist; it was the biggest single Red loss of the Civil War.[1]

Trotsky sent an outraged signal to Aleksandr Shliapnikov, the leading Bolshevik in the region, when he learned of the disintegration of Eleventh Army. "Why did you give no warning of this? How could this catastrophe happen so suddenly?" Shliapnikov, in reply, blamed the center's lack of support: "The cause of the catastrophe is the extremely belated and weak attention [given] to this front."[2] Isolation *was* certainly a factor. The Soviet Republic's military resources were limited. The north-south railways were held by Krasnov's Don Cossacks, and the sea route from Astrakhan was blocked by ice. The little material that reached the north Caucasus came by camel train from Astrakhan, along a badly organized 300-mile supply line across wild country. Astrakhan was 250 miles down the Volga from Tsaritsyn; Tsaritsyn, besieged by the cossacks, was 550 miles from Moscow.

Trotsky, in the faraway Soviet capital, gave his postmortem: "a swollen army, really a horde rather than an army, has clashed with Denikin's properly-organized troops and in a few weeks has been reduced to dust. For the illusion of *partizanstvo* [guerilla warfare] we have once more paid a high price."[3] Reorganization *had* been attempted at the end of 1918, when the independent Caspian-Caucasus Army Group and its two armies were set up, on the model of the Volga forces. Some attempt was made to improve unit organization and training. New leaders were brought in from the center; the army-group RevMil-Council was supervised by Shliapnikov, a most experienced Bolshevik organizer. But time and distance were against the Reds here too; even Shliapnikov was 300 miles from the main forces, with his army-group headquarters at Astrakhan. There were other factors as well. Despite the organizational and supply problems of the new army group, the Red high command had demanded that it join the general offensive against the Don Region; Eleventh Army was supposed to march 250 miles up the railway to Rostov (the Don capital). The attack was launched early in January but immediately stalled, and at almost the same moment the Volunteers counterattacked. The Caspian-Caucasus Army Group was

162

also riddled with disease (one report said that three-quarters of the army were suffering from typhus).

And "Denikin's properly-organized troops" had once again shown their mastery of the battlefield. At the start of the final battle they opposed a force of 150,000 Red troops with only 25,000 men and 75 guns.[4] Their supply position was, if anything, worse than that of the Reds; Allied support was still months away. For the Whites the hero of this campaign was General Petr Vrangel. His 1st Cavalry Division led the main breakthrough, and at the end of January 1919 Vrangel was made Commander-in-Chief of the "Caucasus Volunteer Army," the beginning of a remarkable rise that would end in March 1920 with him replacing General Denikin as head of the southern Whites.

The Volunteers' brilliant winter success contrasted with the defeats of their Don Cossack "allies." Ataman Krasnov's cossacks had, in the summer of 1918, cleared all Red forces out of the Don Region, and they even threatened non-cossack Red territory beyond their borders, especially Tsaritsyn; in November they made one final bound as far north as the Liski junction, fifty miles from Voronezh. But Don Army had limited forces, and the war-weary cossacks had to fight harder and harder to hold just their "own" territory.

For the Reds the southern front was no longer a stepchild. In late November 1918 the Bolshevik CC declared it the most important front, and Trotsky's train spent much of the winter there. The first Commander-in-Chief of Southern Army Group, General Sytin, had been challenged in the Tsaritsyn affair, and left under a cloud in November. Sytin's replacements at the Kozlov HQ, Colonel Slaven and (from late January 1919) General Gittis, had more power; their commissars were now obedient to the center. A major effort was made to improve discipline. In November Vatsetis complained about Eighth Army (deployed on the approaches to Voronezh): "Revolutionary soldiers run like cowards from tiny cossack detachments. Thousands of Red-Armymen give away important positions at the mere approach of a few hundred Krasnovites." The Bolshevik CC agreed: "Red Terror is now essential . . . in Southern Army Group not only against outright traitors and saboteurs but also against cowards, scoundrels, [and their] accomplices and concealers." (Vatsetis later felt that the remedy had gone too far, with 2000 death sentences in Eighth Army alone—of which 150 were carried out).[5] Most important, the Red Army had gradually been able to concentrate more forces against the Don. By mid-February 1919 Southern Army Group amounted to over a quarter of the active Red Army, with 117,000 men, 460 guns, and 2040 machine guns. The cossacks, for their part, were reaching their manpower limits, especially as they could not call up the inogorodnye peasants. Cossack strength was only 38,000, with 1658 guns and 491 machine guns. "The Don Cossack," as Krasnov put it, "was like the mythical warrior, struggling with the hundred-headed hydra. He cuts off one head, and two heads grow to replace it."[6]

The Don Army was also hurt by the concentration of its strength in the east, for a third attack on Tsaritsyn. The cossacks besieged the city in January 1919, but they were finally driven off. Meanwhile the gradual withdrawal of Austro-German troops from the Ukraine opened up a long front on the other, western, side of the Don Region, and many of the Red units transferred from Eastern Army Group were sent here. In January the Reds attacked the neglected cossack northwest front, and crushed it in. All Krasnov's achievements of the second half of 1918 seemed to be swept away. Bolshevik propaganda was unusually effective in this campaign, and in the depths of winter cossack morale began to break. Whole regiments surrendered to the Reds, other cossacks went home, and the army of the "Great Don Host" dropped from 50,000 in November 1918 to 15,000 in February 1919.[7] By early March the Reds had swept through 250 miles to take back most of the northern Don Region.

Volunteer Army successes and Don Cossack defeats changed the southern counterrevolution in a basic way. The Volunteers and the cossacks had a common enemy but they had, since June 1918, fought independent campaigns. This came partly from geography. It also came from fundamental political differences—despite similar conservative politics and similar leaders. (The major leaders had all been senior officers in the Imperial Russian Army; Ataman Krasnov and General Denikin had both commanded divisions in the world war.) Krasnov began with the notion of cossack power; he was the elected ataman and could get nowhere without rank and file cossack support. The Don Cossacks, moreover, numbered 1,500,000 men, women, and children in one territory, and their leaders had a sense of representing a special group. Krasnov hoped to use the local patriotisms of different parts of south Russia to build an ever wider movement. He laid particular hopes on the Ukrainians (under another general, Hetman Skoropadsky). The Volunteer Army, dominated by officer-refugees from central Russia, was held by Krasnov and his followers to be an army not of "the people", but of the rootless intelligentsia; Denisov, Commander-in-Chief of Don Army under Krasnov, cruelly described them as "traveling musicians."[8]

The Volunteer outlook was profoundly different. Krasnov's opinion of them was probably not far wrong:

What was the Great Don Host to a Volunteer Army officer? Don Region, Don Province, and nothing more. Cossacks made up the fourth regiment of cavalry divisions, the HQ cavalry detachment, they covered the supply train, provided the escorts, they were—in a disdainfully affectionate word—the *kazachki* [little cossacks].[9]

The Volunteers saw themselves as the embodiment of a unified Russian state—and saw the Don Cossacks as provincials infected with a bogus cossack nationalism. For Krasnov's intended allies, the "separatists," they had nothing but contempt. And to the Volunteer officer's Great Russian nationalist notion of "Russia One and Indivisible" could be added the professional soldier's belief in the unity of command. The Volunteers insisted on cossack subordination, and they had already imposed this on their Kuban Cossack allies at Ekaterinodar. The different "orientations" of 1918 worsened relations. The Volunteers had seen themselves as continuing Russia's World War against the Central Powers. The Don Cossacks, in contrast, had established close relations with "enemy" German troops in the Ukraine. The cossacks had little choice in the matter, and they protected the Volunteers from any attack from the north and gave them German-supplied arms. But the Volunteers saw them as traitors. According to Krasnov, Denikin was particularly insulting: "The Don Host is a prostitute, selling herself to whomever will pay." (General Denisov's retort can hardly have improved relations: "if the Don Host is a prostitute, then the Volunteer Army is a pimp living off her earnings."[10]

The struggle had to be decided one way or another; it was Denikin who won, and Krasnov who had to leave. A meeting between the Don and Volunteer leaders at Torgovaia on 8 January agreed to operational unity. The Don Army and the Volunteer Army became parts of the "Armed Forces of South Russia," with General Denikin as overall "Main Commander-in-Chief." Within six weeks Krasnov had been replaced as Ataman. Krasnov had been in an impossible position. The Don Army was falling apart after the January-February defeats. It had to have Volunteer help, on whatever terms Denikin offered. All the anti-Bolshevik forces looked to the Allies after their victory in November 1918, and Krasnov had hopelessly compromised himself. In July 1918 he had written to the Kaiser, comparing cossack courage to "that shown recently against the English by a people of Germanic stock, the Boers." However sensible that "orientation" was at the time, Krasnov had to write another letter, four months later, asking for massive aid from "the Allied powers, which we now and always have seen as our true allies."[11] (The Ataman later became an out and out Germanophile; he was hanged in Moscow in 1947 as a Nazi collaborator.) Krasnov also had enemies among the Don leadership, both from the liberals and from other factions within the military leadership. When a specially summoned Don *Krug* met in mid-February it dismissed some of Krasnov's closest subordinates, including Denisov, the Don Army Commander-in-Chief. On 15 February Krasnov himself resigned; the new Ataman was a rival of Krasnov and a friend of the Volunteer Army, General Bogaevsky.

The whole counterrevolutionary movement in the south was now directed from Denikin's headquarters in Ekaterinodar. This centralization of command was essential for fighting a great southern military campaign against Bolshevism. With Kolchak's victory in Omsk three months earlier the White movement had been made ideologically one; the Russian military elite, the believers in conservatism and centralism, were dominant in both Ekaterinodar and Omsk. In many ways—but not all—the Whites were stronger than ever before.

The Breakout

In late February 1919 Colonel Vatsetis reported to Lenin and Trotsky that victory seemed near:

> In the Southern Army Group area the resistance of the enemy has been smashed and the situation may be considered firm: it remains, not weakening our efforts, to exploit success and then achieve decisive results—the conquest of the Donets Basin, all the Don [Region] with Novocherkassk and Rostov, and the liberation of the north Caucasus.[12]

Had Vatsetis been right, the Civil War would have ended in the summer of 1919. As things turned out, the Reds not only failed to "achieve decisive results" but suffered smashing defeats; by July they had lost much territory and were on the defensive everywhere in the south.

As the magnitude of the Red defeat sank in, Lenin blamed everything on foreign intervention. "Now the foreign capitalists," he announced in July 1919, "are making a desperate effort to restore the yoke of capital through the attack of Denikin, whom they have supplied, even more than Kolchak, with officers, supplies, shells, tanks, etc., etc." The British military mission to South Russia would have agreed; it reported that the White recovery from the desperate situation of March 1919 "was due almost entirely to British assistance."[13] In reality, however, the level of outside involvement should not be exaggerated. The first Allied representatives to arrive at the Don and Volunteer headquarters seemed to promise that large Allied forces would arrive soon. Krasnov asked the French Balkan commander for three or four corps, 90,000–120,000 men. In fact, French involvement was confined to the southwest (in accordance with the December 1917 spheres-of-influence agreement) and ended in the humiliating withdrawal of April 1919. The British alone supported the Don Cossacks and the Volunteer Army, and they sent no army units to the battle front. (A British division guarded the Batum-Baku railway in the Transcaucasus, but this was far removed from the fighting.) Commitment of British ground troops, even just covering the AFSR supply ports at Taganrog and Novorossiisk, would have prevented the disastrous vacuum in the White rear in the autumn of 1919. Diplomatic and political intervention were slight, partly because the White "capital" was with Admiral Kolchak in Siberia; economic assistance was also minimal.

What *was* sent was "Denmiss," a British military mission to supply and train Denikin's armies. During the course of 1919, 198,000 rifles, 6200 machine guns, and 500,000,000 rounds of small arms ammunition were sent to Denikin's soldiers. Heavy equipment included 1121 artillery pieces (mostly 18 pr.—84mm—field guns) and over 1,900,000 shells. Even some sixty tanks (Mk V and Medium A) were sent to a "tankadrome" at Taganrog, and 168 aircraft were provided. (British fliers and tank crews were the only ones who fought; the only unit involved was No. 47 Squadron RAF.) Clothing supplies included 460,000 greatcoats and 645,000 pairs of boots. The Whites occupied an area without major munitions factories, so these supplies were tremendously important.

But Allied material was most important in the *later* stages of the Denikin campaign, the battles of the late summer of 1919 and the final advance toward Moscow. It took time for military supplies to come even from the Allies' Mediterranean depots; the first ship arrived in March 1919, and only fourteen had arrived by the end of May; twenty-one more arrived before September, and the final ten arrived by the middle of December.[14] It took time to move material to the front and instruct the Russians in its use. In the campaigns of February–June 1919, the effect of Allied aid was mainly psychological. The promise of Allied supplies was a great boost to White morale—photographs of tanks on flatcars featured in their propaganda. But the fighting in the first half of the year was done mainly by the Whites using their own resources.

More important as a general factor in explaining the Whites' early victories were the difficulties faced by their opponents. The Reds' problems came from the very success of their winter 1918–1919 campaign. For one thing, the Soviet armies were now a long way from their bases. Supply lines to the core Soviet territory were weakly developed; the railways were badly damaged. Furthermore, the Red advance had swept south into politically dangerous country, and the Don Region presented the greatest challenge. The collapse of Don Cossack units had allowed the Reds to make their great advances in February 1919. In March, however, many of the same cossacks rose in revolt around Veshenskaia on the upper Don, now deep in the rear of Southern Army Group; farther south cossacks not yet overrun by the Reds were more willing to join a revived Don Army. Bolshevik policy in the captured cossack lands had thrown petrol on a smoldering fire. At first the policy came from the top; on 24 January 1919 a circular from the Bolshevik CC's Organization Bureau called for "the most merciless war with all the cossack leaders by exterminating the lot of them (*putem pogolovnogo ikh istrebleniia*)" and for "merciless mass terror in relation to all cossacks involved, directly or indirectly, in the struggle with Soviet power." Cossacks found with arms were to be shot, and Red detachments were to occupy the *stanitsas*. Power on the Don was to be given to the non-cossack "inogorodnye." *Raskazachivanie*—"de-cossackization"—was the order of the day. Local Bolshevik militants abolished the name "cossack" and forbade cossack dress.

A more diplomatic policy was adopted in later months, at least by the highest Bolshevik leaders, with an attempt to split the cossacks between rich and poor. But this distinction was lost on the Red leaders on the spot, and even Trotsky in the heat of the battle with the Veshenskaia rebels could talk about cauterizing the boil "with a red-hot iron" and exterminating "the Cains." The Veshenskaia rebels had as many as 30,000 men in arms and tied down a Red "Expeditionary Force" of 15,000.[15]

The Reds also received little support from another large part of south Russia, the Ukraine. The Red Ukrainian Army Group absorbed supplies and gave little help against the AFSR. The Grigoriev anti-Bolshevik mutiny in early May brought chaos to the western Ukraine. Meanwhile, the right flank of Southern Army Group was operating in a part of the Ukraine that had been in uproar for months. The Reds attempted to use the peasant anarchist leader Makhno to cover the western side of the White bulge, but in late May White cavalry cut through Makhno's troops, who fled in disorder. Moscow declared Makhno himself a traitor to the revolution. So neither the Ukraine nor the Don proved favorable territory for the Red Army. Vatsetis concluded in late June, after his last attack had failed and then turned into a rapid retreat, that the only course was to withdraw into the "secure zone," that is, the northern, Great Russian, provinces.[16]

Another reason the Whites were able to gain the initiative was that the whole Red Army was overextended. In the spring of 1919 it fought battles against the border states in the west, against the Allies in the far north, in the Ukraine, and—especially—against Kolchak in the east. The decisive months on the southern front coincided with Kolchak's spring race towards the middle Volga, and at the time Kolchak seemed much more dangerous. Trotsky was one of those who underestimated the southern threat. In mid-April he announced that Denikin's army fought only because Kolchak was in the field: "The collapse of the Kolchakites will lead at once and inexorably to the complete collapse of Denikin's volunteers ('volunteers' under the lash)."[17] This was a difficult time for the Red Army in terms of replacements and munitions, but when either became available they were sent east rather south.

The Red Army was still less effective than its enemies. In May 1919 Vatsetis could claim that the southern Whites had a local numerical superiority of 3:2 (and better troops), while Trotsky's verdict in July was that "Denikin's success was wholly and entirely due to the superiority of larger over smaller numbers." In reality it was the Reds who had the larger numbers. In February 1919 the forces facing Denikin and the cossacks were officially given as 152,000 men, in May they were 228,000, and by the first half of June 259,000. The number of Red *combat* troops must have been at least 80,000, and their equipment included 1500–3000 machine guns and 400–550 artillery pieces. Compared with this, Denikin had on his "northern front" 45,000 men (Volunteers and Cossacks) in March and 50,000 in May. (Total AFSR strength was 64,000; the balance were in the north Caucasus.)[18]

One reason the larger Red Army was defeated by a smaller White one was that Trotsky's regularization, begun in the autumn of 1918, was still incomplete. The relationship between Ukrainian and Southern Army Groups did not begin to be sorted out until June 1919. The leadership of the southern Red armies, while an improvement over 1918, was inferior to that of the Whites. Gittis, the Commander-in-Chief, was a professional soldier but a fairly young (thirty-eight-year-old) colonel. Two of the rising stars of the Red military served as army commanders, Tukhachevsky (Eighth Army) and Egorov (Tenth), but both were still inexperienced. Skachko (Second Ukrainian Army), Voroshilov (Fourteenth), Kozhevnikov (Thirteenth), Khvesin (Eighth), and Kniagnitsky

(Ninth Army) were men of little command experience or ability, mostly former wartime subalterns or NCOs; most were removed after the defeats. One commander of Ninth Army, Vsevolodov, was a former general, but at the end of June 1919 *he* deserted to the Whites, driving across the front with his family. He had been in command since early June and chief of staff for eight months before that; his earlier activities may help to explain the spring failures of the Red offensive. Overall the cooperation of ex-officer "specialists," Bolshevik commissars, and peasant soldiers was not yet assured. The peasant-based mass Red Army that had developed in the winter of 1918–1919 had poor organization and shaky morale, and the Reds suffered high rates of desertion.

The quality of the White armies was still higher than that of the Reds. The Don Cossacks had very good cavalry, which they used constantly to outmaneuver the Red infantry. Even better as a fighting force was the Volunteer Army, and the immediate cause of the failure of the Red spring offensive was the arrival of Volunteer Army on the open west flank of Don Army in the Donbas. This had not been part of the original plan of Denikin's staff. In January 1919 it had decided that when Volunteer Army had cleared the north Caucasus it would march north*east* toward Tsaritsyn, where it might link up with Kolchak.[19] The worsening situation of the Don Cossacks, however, meant that the transfer had to be to the north*west*, into the Donbas. Denikin really had no choice; Red occupation of Rostov and the lower Don would have been an impossible threat to the rear and flank of any army moving from the north Caucasus to Tsaritsyn. (If Vatsetis's hoped-for early victory in the southeast is an interesting might-have-been, so is stiffer Don resistance, providing an effective cover for a Volunteer advance to Tsaritsyn.)

In any event, the Donbas was brilliantly defended by Volunteer troops under a general named V. Z. Mai-Maevsky. General Vrangel described his extraordinary appearance: a provincial comic actor— short, stout, red-faced with a big nose and little piggy eyes. Later in the year Mai developed into an alcoholic, unwilling to control undisciplined troops, but he was a general of great ability, courage, and experience, having commanded I Guards Corps during the world war. (He was 52 in 1919, five years older than Denikin.) He led the first division to be sent to help the Don Cossacks, at the start of 1919, and he fought one of the most brilliant campaigns of the Civil War. With only 3000–6000 men, he used the interior lines of communication and the dense rail net of the industrial Donbas to beat off a series of attacks by as many as from 10,000 to 30,000 Red troops. Volunteer forces built up, and in May General Mai-Maevsky became Commander-in-Chief of the whole Volunteer Army (under Denikin, who was Main Commander-in-Chief of the AFSR).

The fighting in the south can be divided into three Soviet offensives against the Donbas, in late March, mid-April, and mid-May. The first was stalled by the thaw of the Donets River, then disrupted by the superior White cavalry, and the later attacks were effectively blocked by the growing Volunteer Army. The last attack by Southern Army Group stalled in mid-May; Volunteer units then smashed through Second Ukrainian Army, thanks to the unsteadiness of Makhno's partisans and the confusion caused by the Grigoriev mutiny. The right flank of the next army, Thirteenth, was thrown open, and simultaneously it was attacked with stupefying effect by the first handful of British tanks. Thirteenth Army rolled back, taking the whole of Southern Army Group with it. Retreat only ended after the Whites had advanced 200 miles and gone beyond Kharkov, the main political and industrial center of the eastern Ukraine and one of the most important towns in Russia. On 4 June Trotsky had assured the city's population that "I think that Kharkov stands in no greater danger than Tver, Penza, Moscow or any other city of the Soviet Republic."[20] Three weeks later the Volunteer Army rode in triumph into Kharkov; all local Red efforts—the creation of a Kharkov "fortified region," the total mobilization of fifteen age groups, and the founding of an "Extraordinary Military-Revolutionary Tribunal"—could not prevent it.

While these gains were being made on the left of the AFSR front, the Don Army in the center, now commanded by General Sidorin, regained most of the lost Host Territory and pushed north beyond the upper Don, joining hands in early June with the Veshenskaia rebels. Meanwhile, the Red attacks on the Donbas had been coordinated in April with an attack from the other, eastern, end of the front. Colonel Egorov's Red Tenth Army attacked southwest along the railway line from Tsaritsyn to the Kuban. His cavalry commander, Dumenko, got within fifty miles of Rostov (from the south) and threatened the encirclement of the main White armies operating north of the Don. Denikin personally commanded the first counterattacks (the last time he would personally direct operations). Then General Vrangel, who had led the victorious winter campaign in the north Caucasus, took over control of the White counterattack. At the end of May Tenth Army was outflanked on the Manych River and driven back in disorder; Egorov himself was badly wounded. Both north of Rostov, on Sidorin's Don front, and east of it, on Vrangel's, the Reds' anti-cossack policies recoiled against them; "along the route," Vatsetis candidly reported, "the whole population rose in revolt."[21] Vrangel advanced to Tsaritsyn itself and tried to take it by storm with his cavalry in mid-June. He was beaten off, but once the Kuban-Tsaritsyn railway was repaired Vrangel could move up heavy equipment, including tanks. Tsaritsyn, the "Red Verdun" of 1918, fell on 30 June 1919, and with it were captured masses of Red military supplies.

"All Out for the Fight against Denikin!"

General Denikin traveled to Tsaritsyn to celebrate its capture. From that city, on 3 July 1919, he issued secret Order No. 08878, better known as the "Moscow Directive." The directive outlined—in less than a page— the projected future strategy of the Armed Forces of South Russia. The "ultimate goal" was "the occupation of the heart of Russia, Moscow." In pursuit of this goal the armies were given basic tasks. In essence their commanders were told to fan out and then advance along the railway lines that converged on the Soviet capital. Vrangel's Caucasus Army was to follow one rail line through the western Volga region to Nizhnyi Novgorod, where it would turn west along the Vladimir-Moscow line. Sidorin's Don Army was to advance on a wider front: partly along the Voronezh-Riazan-Moscow rail line, and partly along the parallel line to the west. Mai-Maevsky's Volunteers would take the next line to the west: Kursk-Orel-Tula-Moscow. These were all very considerable tasks. Mai and Sidorin would have to cover 350–400 miles to reach their objective, and Vrangel 750 miles. ("For this directive," Denikin had boasted, "I had to use the hundred-*verst* [small scale] map."[22]

In June the AFSR's front was bounded on the west by one of the great rivers of Russia, the Dnepr. Denikin evidently wanted to confine his advance to the east bank of the Dnepr, using the river as a first-class natural barrier to cover his flank. The Moscow Directive only envisaged taking the Dnepr bridgeheads. But the corps commander on the left flank, General Shkuro, had already, on his own initiative, crossed the river to seize the province town of Ekaterinoslav (now Dnepropetrovsk) on the west bank.[23] White troops were soon involved in rapid advances beyond the Dnepr into the western Ukraine. The White III Corps broke out of the Crimea and marched across the lower Dnepr and west along the Black Sea coast, taking Kherson and Nikolaev (18 August). Odessa itself fell on 23 August to a White landing (aided by the gunfire of the dreadnought *General Alekseev*). White detachments also advanced

172

rapidly up the east side of the Dnepr, taking Poltava on 29 July and Kiev, the Ukrainian capital, 200 miles to the northwest, on 23 August. (The extreme advance in this direction was Chernigov, taken on 12 October.)

Trotsky's train moved to the threatened part of the Ukraine (where he had been born, forty years before). On 9 August the Politburo ordered him to hold Odessa and Kiev "to the last drop of blood" ("the fate of the entire Revolution is in question").[24] Once again the Ukraine proved a very hard place to hold. Red forces were the poorly organized remnants of Antonov-Ovseenko's Ukrainian Army Group. Fourteenth Army, on the Dnepr, bore the brunt of the AFSR attack from the east. The new Red Twelfth Army faced west towards Petliura's Ukrainian People's Army and a potential Rumanian intervention from Bessarabia. The large area between these two enemies was full of insurgent peasant bands. In the end all the Red forces could do was get out as rapidly as possible. Iona Iakir, a young commander (and later a prominent victim of Stalin's military purge), made his name by extricating several divisions from the trap of the southern Ukraine and marching them 300 miles north.

The Ukrainian campaign has been described as a major distraction for the AFSR and a cause of its defeat. But although Denikin needed every man he could get, the best White units were kept in the center, and only 10,000–15,000 committed to the Ukraine.[25] It was also an inescapable fact of geography that the course of the Dnepr ran to the northwest, and the farther north Denikin went the more his western flank opened out. The Ukraine was potentially valuable for food and recruits, and Odessa and Kiev boosted White prestige. The Red armies thrown from the Ukraine could no longer threaten the deep rear of the AFSR (as the Red high command had indeed intended).

On the opposite (eastern) flank of the AFSR was Vrangel's Caucasus Army. Having taken Tsaritsyn, Vrangel pursued Soviet Tenth Army up the Volga. On 28 July his cavalry took Kamyshin, and by the beginning of August was within sixty miles of Saratov. Meanwhile, at the end of July, in the empty steppe on the other side of the Volga (near Lake Elton), detachments from Caucasus Army made contact with the Ural Cossacks. The southern and eastern White armies had finally joined hands. Vrangel later argued that he should have been given reinforcements to develop his attack and effect a real link with Kolchak; indeed, one of the main reproaches he threw at Denikin in the following winter was that, having subordinated himself to the Supreme Ruler (which he did on 12 June 1919), Denikin failed to save him.[26] On the other hand Kolchak's armies had been broken in May, two months earlier, and it was a 300-mile march up the Volga from Kamyshin to Samara, and another 400 miles east from Samara to the Urals, through which Eastern Army Group was pursuing Kolchak. Supply for a northern thrust would have been difficult. There was no railway along the west bank of the Volga, and the Reds had been able to evacuate most of the river shipping when Tsaritsyn fell. And the Reds were concentrating their main strength precisely in this direction.

Despite the Moscow Directive, the Whites did not immediately carry out a general offensive in the part of their front closest to Moscow, the center. Mai-Maevsky's Volunteer Army, the most powerful part of the AFSR, stood on a line north of Kharkov and made almost.no progress from early July until early September. This was partly because it had to regroup after the last long bound, and partly because of the counter-attacks by the Red Army. The Don Cossacks did mount a spectacular raid. Their commanders had realized the value of massed cavalry after the spring campaign, and they concentrated their cavalrymen under General Mamontov in the newly formed IV Don Cavalry Corps. Mamontov rode north from the northern tip of the Don Region on 10 August, and eight days later rode into the Soviet province town of Tambov, 125 miles behind the Red Army's lines. He then moved west to Kozlov, an important railway junction and headquarters of the Red Southern Army Group. Before breaking back through the Red lines in the middle of September he even briefly took Voronezh. It is sometimes argued that Mamontov should have continued north to Moscow, but it was 250 miles from Tambov to Moscow, and Mamontov only had 9000 men. He could only have had decisive success had the peasants risen in his support, but this did not happen. Mamontov's corps was badly disci-plined and engaged in looting, hardly the way to win over the peasants. Trotsky called Mamontov's corps "a comet with a filthy tail of robbery and rape."[27] (Ironically, Tambov Province was to be the seat of the great anti-Bolshevik Antonov Uprising, which began a year after Mamon-tov's raid.) The looting also hurt the Whites by demoralizing their best cavalry forces. By the time Mamontov broke out to the south again in mid-September many men had gone home with their loot; the corps was in no condition to give much help to the decisive operations which were about to begin.

By midsummer 1919 the Soviet republic had suffered unprecedented defeats. Between 24 June and 1 July the Whites captured Kharkov, Ekaterinoslav, and Tsaritsyn. Trotsky reported that Southern Army Group had lost 200 guns in the retreat. Lenin issued a circular on 9 July,

"All Out for the Fight against Denikin!" calling for a concentration on the war effort: the Soviet Republic, he said, "must be *a single armed camp*."[28] The Red high command was shaken up. Colonel Vatsetis had been Main Commander-in-Chief since September 1918. In February 1919 he had reported that in the south the enemy had been smashed; now, in late June, he had to tell Trotsky that things were grave: "the enemy . . . is directing his blow at the weakest place in our Republic, leading him to our Tula [arms] plant on the approaches to Moscow, and pushing our southern armies back into the hungry center." Vatsetis had suffered too many defeats, and there was even talk of treason. On 3 July the Bolshevik CC decided to replace Vatsetis with Colonel S. S. Kamenev, the rising star from among the "specialists," the officer who as Commander-in-Chief of Eastern Army Group had broken Kolchak's offensive. This was a hard blow for Trotsky, as he and Vatsetis had effectively dismissed Kamenev only two months before, after debates about strategy. Trotsky demonstratively left the CC meeting—slamming the door behind him and offering his resignation.[29]

The reply to Denikin's Moscow Directive was worked out by a new team at the Red Army's Serpukhov headquarters. Colonel Kamenev's general directive No. 1116 was issued on 23 July 1919.[30] The essence of the plan was that the main attack was to come at the *eastern* end of the front, from a "Striking Group" made up of Ninth and Tenth Armies and commanded by General Shorin. This attack began on 15 August, drove the Whites 140 miles down the Volga, and in early September nearly took Tsaritsyn. Once again, however, Vrangel's Caucasus Army outfought its enemy, aided by some British tanks, and the Reds were stopped just north of the city, with the loss of 18,000 prisoners. Mamontov's cavalry raid also helped to stall the attack, as Shorin had to divert troops to chase him. The secondary Red attack, in the center of the Red southern front and led by General Selivachev, had begun two weeks late, on 14 August. It made considerable progress on the boundary between the Volunteer and Don Armies; Kupiansk, 95 miles south of the starting line, was taken by the Reds after only ten days, on 25 August. (The London *Times* correspondent, ever ready to find Berlin's influence behind Moscow, described this as a "typically German manoeuvre.") Nevertheless, the White counterattacks nearly succeeded in trapping the Red salient, and Selivachev only narrowly escaped encirclement. The retreat began in early September; by the 15th Selivachev was back at his starting line, and his disorganized units were about to be swamped by the final White offensive. (General Selivachev died on 17 September, supposedly of typhus, but it is possible that his death was connected with his failure.)

Kamenev's plan for an attack southwest from the eastern (Volga) end of the front set off one of the great strategic debates of the Civil War. Vatsetis had in June 1919 proposed a more direct attack, massing strength not in the east, but in the center and the west: Fourteenth, Thirteenth, and Eighth Armies would advance *southeast* to Novocherkassk. Trotsky supported this plan, even after Vatsetis was sacked. An advance to the southeast, Trotsky and others argued, would be the shortest route to the enemy's vital regions, and one that would march through the industrial (and pro-Bolshevik) Donbas rather than the cossack Don Region. And as Kamenev's attack got bogged down more and more voices were raised against it. In early September—three weeks after Kamenev's planned attack began but before the full-scale White counteroffensive—Trotsky and the commissars of the Southern Army Group RevMilCouncil wrote to Kamenev urging a concentration in the center. Kamenev refused to do this, and the Politburo backed him up, expressing "amazement" at the counterproposal.[31]

The Kamenev plan did not achieve its objective, "the destruction of Denikin's forces." It was later criticized by supporters of both Trotsky and Stalin (both of whom eventually opposed it). On the other hand, it *was* at the time backed both by the General Staff "specialists" of the Red Army high command and by the supreme Bolshevik leadership, and had much to recommend it. An attack in the center would merely have confronted the main White advance, and Kamenev was not a believer in simply plugging holes. His strategy promised Red initiative, and moreover offered the possibility of destroying the enemy, not just of pushing him back; the capture of Rostov and Novocherkassk would cut off Denikin's armies in the Donbas and the Ukraine from their north Caucasus base.

Indeed, Kamenev's plan was not unlike the one he had used effectively against Kolchak's Western Army in April 1919. (Shorin, the Striking Group commander, had led Second Army in the east, and he brought his staff with him.) The open steppe of the Volga attack was favorable for a rapid advance—unlike the Donbas, which Mai-Maevsky had defended so tenaciously in the spring. A concentration in the east would engage a dangerous part of the enemy forces, Don Army, which was larger than Volunteer Army. In addition, the Red Striking Force's base area, the middle Volga, was one of great importance. New Red units were being raised on the Volga; experienced troops from Eastern Army Group were more easily transferred there than to the center and west of Southern Army Group, which was up to 400 miles farther away. Concentration in the middle Volga also blocked any White advance up the river to effect a link with Kolchak's Siberian armies. This was just what Vrangel was arguing for; in May the Reds had found documents suggesting such a link when they captured a high-ranking courier between Denikin and Kolchak (aboard a Caspian steamer).[32]

The suggestion that Kamenev's strategy was adopted simply as a means of getting at Trotsky is farfetched. After the Civil War even Vrangel wrote that the Red concentration at the eastern end of the front was sound strategy. Shorin had pushed the White front line 140 miles down the Volga, and had also taken a large part of the northern Don Region. On 5–6 September Red Tenth Army very nearly succeeded in storming Tsaritsyn itself. Ironically, at the very moment Trotsky and the Southern Army Group RevMilCouncil were calling for a change of plan, Vrangel had evacuated what he could from Tsaritsyn, and his headquarters train was waiting with steam up, ready to abandon the city.[33]

But the Red Army's attempt, over two and half months, to mount a counterattack on the southern front had failed. Thanks to the failure of the secondary attack, Selivachev's divisions, in the center of Southern Army Group, were now in disorder. Volunteer Army was poised to undertake a deep pursuit. Whether the Soviet republic could withstand this final shock would depend on its internal strength.

13

THE ARMED CAMP: SOVDEPIA,
November 1918–November 1919

The Soviet republic is besieged by the enemy. It must be a *single armed camp* not in words but in deeds.

> Lenin, "All out for the Fight against Denikin!"
> 9 July 1919

The Red Army

In 1919 there was no change in Trotsky's "regular" principles of army organization: centralization, command by appointed (not elected) ex-officers, supervision by appointed commissars, rigid discipline, conventional units, and general conscription. The issue, however, was only finally decided at the Eighth Party Congress (March 1919). Trotsky's critics were known as the Military "Opposition," but the fact is that they made up a large section, perhaps a majority, of the party elite in the army. Lenin had much in common with the critics. In November 1918 *Izvestiia* quoted him as saying that

> the old command staff was made up mainly of the spoiled and depraved darling sons of the capitalists who had nothing in common with the ordinary soldier. So now, in building a new army, we must take our commanders solely from among the people.

Even during Kolchak's spring 1919 offensive Lenin considered sacking the officer-specialists and giving a party man (Lashevich) the post of Main Commander-in-Chief. But Lenin came down on Trotsky's side at the congress, partly from his confidence in the War Commissar, and partly because of the way he saw the general situation. Few proletarians served in the army; "Iron discipline is needed here," Lenin told the "Opposition." "And if you say that this is an autocratic-feudal system and protest against saluting, then you will not get an army in which the middle peasant will fight."[1] What would have happened had Trotsky's opponents carried the day is a matter for speculation. It is true that they wanted a modification of the system rather than a complete turnabout. But a vote of no confidence in Trotsky, less cooperation from the officers, and concessions to the ever-present centrifugal forces might have fatally weakened the Red Army at a time of great danger.

The victory of regular principles did not mean that Trotsky kept total control, and four months later his authority was much diminished. The very important Bolshevik CC meeting of 3 July 1919 has already been mentioned. After catastrophic military defeats—the loss of Kharkov and Tsaritsyn—the Bolshevik CC shook up the high command system that had evolved under Trotsky's leadership. Colonel Vatsetis, Trotsky's chosen Main Commander-in-Chief, was replaced by a man Trotsky had argued with over strategy—Colonel S. S. Kamenev. The central Revolutionary Military Council of the Republic was purged. Trotsky and his deputy (Skliiansky) remained, but the new members were people the War Commissar had differed with in the past: S. S. Kamenev, Gusev, Smilga (head of the Political Administration), and Rykov (the new "dictator" of army supply). Stung by this rebuke, Trotsky walked out of a CC meeting and resigned from his army and party posts, but this was refused; Lenin gave him a "blank check" endorsing any order he cared to make. All the same, Trotsky's authority would never be what it had been before. Gusev later claimed that before the July shake-up "a planned, centralized, business-like military center did not exist" and that Trotsky's improvised methods had been "a system of organized panic."[2] This lays too much blame on Trotsky personally and ignores the difficult conditions of 1918, but the reorganization did strengthen the Red Army.

The Tsarist officers, brought into the army in the spring and summer of 1918, were given more power in 1919. This did not always seem to be a wise course. In June 1919 "specialists" nearly opened the gates of Petrograd to the Whites. The Commander-in-Chief of Ninth Army (in the south) defected. The Chief of the Field Staff, General Kostiaev, was arrested in mid-June, along with many General Staff officers, and even Vatsetis was imprisoned for a time. In the end, however, Vatsetis and Kostiaev were released, and the response to defeat and treachery was' not a Bolshevik commander, but the new regular command team of S. S. Kamenev and P. P. Lebedev. The new Main Commander-in-Chief,

Colonel Sergei Kamenev, was (at thirty-eight) eight years younger than Vatsetis but was otherwise a more "conventional" appointment. Kamenev was more typical of the Tsarist officer corps; he was a Great Russian, while Vatsetis was a Latvian; his origins were not as humble (Kamenev's father had been a senior military engineer). Despite "backwardness in the political sphere" (as his dossier put it), Kamenev prospered with the revolutions; he progressed from command of a regiment in February 1917 to senior staff posts. Luck had played a part in his key promotion to command of Eastern Army Group (in October 1918); General V. N. Egorev of the Western Screen declined the honor on medical grounds, and Kamenev happened to be his deputy. But Kamenev was distinguished by more than just an enormous military mustache; in the east he finished off the *Komuch* army, and stopped Kolchak; from July 1919 to the end of the Civil War and beyond, he led the whole Red Army to victory. General P. P. Lebedev, the new Chief of the Field Staff, helped Kamenev plan the victorious campaigns; during the World War the British attache had described "little Lebedev" as one of the most able officers in the army (and "a most ardent patriot").[3]

Former officers were called up in large numbers, and dominated command posts from battalion level upwards. The new development in 1919 was the large-scale training of more junior (company and platoon) commanders; special courses produced 2000 "Red Commanders" in 1918 and 11,000 in 1919 (and 25,000 in 1920). Although this was small compared to the output of Tsarist courses (220,000 wartime officers, *praporshchiki*), it did mean that by the end of 1920 half of the "command staff" were "Red Commanders." These command *kursy* also gave elite troops, the *kursanty*, who were taken from their lecture rooms to the battlefield in emergencies. In addition, some 215,000 Tsarist-army NCOs were called up during the Civil War, some—like the future Marshal Zhukov—became commanders; others provided the military backbone of the Red Army.[4]

Political control over the army was consolidated. By the autumn of 1919 there were about 120,000 party members in the forces, and a further 40,000 were added in the "Party Weeks" during the October crisis. Something like half of all party members were in the army, and about five to ten percent of Red Army men were party members. The Bureau of Military Commissars became in May the Political Administration (*PUR*); this organization not only maintained army morale and loyalty but also carried out political work in captured regions.[5]

Great effort went into raising "conscious" discipline through army newspapers, lectures, and concerts; the Order of the Red Banner was used to reward bravery. At the same time there was the threat of harsh repression. The army was supervised by the Cheka "Special Department" (OO); a succession of important figures led it, including, in the crisis autumn of 1919, Feliks Dzerzhinsky himself. "Cordon detachments" blocked desertion and retreat. Punishments were severe. In January 1919 Vatsetis complained to Lenin that in Eighth Army (fighting the Don Cossacks) no fewer than 2000 had been sentenced to death and 150 actually executed. Such "bloody discipline," he argued, would create only mechanical obedience and not a combat-ready army capable of showing initiative. Lenin and Trotsky, however, wanted iron discipline to hold the peasant conscripts, and a stern regime was kept. According to one senior Denikin officer, Red deserters were amazed at the looser discipline found in the White army.[6]

The greatest change in the Red Army was its rapid growth. The army's strength in October 1918 was about 430,000 men; the figure given by one official source of 3,000,000 men in October 1919 seems exaggerated, but numbers were probably approaching that at the end of 1919; there were certainly sixty-one rifle and twelve cavalry divisions then.[7] It is worth considering why the Red Army was built up to such a size. The huge armies of the Central Powers had gone home, the combined combat forces of the White armies never exceeded 250,000; the Red forces, meanwhile, put a great strain on Sovdepia's resources. Lenin, as we have already seen, had been the first to call for a three-million man army (in October 1918), and he linked this to the German revolution. By the start of 1919, however, the army was concentrated in the east and south, not in the west. Another explanation was given by the emigre historian Bernshtam, who argued that large garrisons were needed to control the Soviet population. This may have been a secondary factor, but there is little evidence of large-scale fighting in the interior of the Soviet zone. A more obvious justification for a big army was the need to be ready to defend Sovdepia against widely spread opponents. In June 1919, for example, the Red high command estimated "enemy" strength at 657,000; of these only 111,000 were placed in Denikin's armies (the main threat, in reality); a further 129,000 were reckoned to be with Kolchak, 39,000 in the far north, and no fewer than 378,000 on the western border, mostly Poles and Finns. Vatsetis had to think about campaigns, as he put it, "on all points of the compass", a potential front totaling 8000 versts (5300 miles) at a time when the disorganized railways could not move reserves from front to front.[8]

Quantity also solved problems of quality. Vatsetis told Lenin in January 1919 that all Red victories had come from local numerical superiority, and speaking later of a possible campaign against Allied troops in the Ukraine he recommended that "we must outnumber the enemy by a factor of two or three to one, because in terms of equipment the enemy has the hugest advantage." Also, a given *combat* strength demanded from the Red Army a much larger overall total. In June 1919 Vatsetis gave Red combat strength as 356,000, but the Army Groups (the "front-line" troops) actually contained a grand total of 899,000 (including commanders and non-combatant troops); furthermore, the Military Districts (in the interior of Sovdepia) added 538,000, and the paramilitary forces 111,000. So the total Red strength was really something like 1,500,000, and the ratio of combat troops to the total was less than 1:4. The reasons for such a ratio include lack of equipment, the painfully slow conversion of mobilized peasants into combat soldiers, duplication of support facilities in each of the scattered army groups, and the army's non-military tasks in the newly conquered areas. Finally, size came partly from the fact that the Red Army was a very leaky bucket, one that needed constant refilling. As many as 2,000,000 Red soldiers were "lost" in the course of 1919 due to illness, desertion (including draft-dodging), and—much less significant—battle casualties.[9]

At one time it was hoped to realize the socialist ideal of a militia army. A decree on Universal Military Training (*Vsevobuch*) was issued in April 1918, and this militia system was approved as late as March 1919. But by this time the militia had ceased to be a major factor. The military specialists were hostile, and they could show that *Vsevobuch* tied up commanders and equipment. In the difficult spring of 1919 functioning units of any kind took precedence over the militia ideal. Manpower for the regular Red Army was raised, for the most part, in more traditional ways. In September 1918 came the first general mobilization, of the "class" of 1898 (i.e., nineteen-year-olds), and the 1899 class followed on 1 March; Kolchak's offensive led to the early call-up of the 1900 class. Between late September 1918 and April 1919 the younger World War classes (1890–1897) were called back into service. This recall of veterans was something most of the White armies did not dare do, and it gave the Reds some manpower with a modicum of training. But the veterans were very reluctant to take up arms again, and in any event the local machinery for mobilization was still poor, and extraordinary methods had to be used to get additional (older) men. The special mobilization of workers, trade unionists, and Communist Party members gave backbone to the army, but the numbers available were small (tens, rather than hundreds, of thousands) and their mobilization hurt political and economic work. And in the countryside the attempted voluntary mobilization of 10–20 peasants from each rural district (*volost'*) produced far fewer than expected.

The battle with "deserters" became very important, as most of these were actually men who simply ignored the call-up. In May 1919 the machinery for dealing with them was revamped. The carrot included words of sympathy for the "middle peasant" and better support for soldiers' families, but the stick was equally important. Systematic "roundups" were introduced, and everywhere there was tighter discipline and widespread propaganda; as Trotsky put it, "It is necessary to create such a situation, such a feeling in the country, that a deserter cannot find a place to lay his head, like Cain, who committed a treacherous act against his brother." The results were impressive: nearly 1,426,000 "deserters" were returned to the army in July–December 1919, compared to 334,000 in February–June. The total was nearly the same as those called up by normal means.[10]

The creation of the mass army did not come from strict centralization. Gusev (one of the party's top military men) felt that one of the Red Army's distinguishing features was that two-thirds of it was formed or reformed near the front by the army groups themselves. The army groups controlled large territories, and while advancing they came upon fresh reserves of manpower and many POWs. "Front mobilizations" were estimated as 500,000 in 1919. It was in theory more efficient to train and organize reinforcements in the rear, but the eleven complete new divisions the Main Staff tried to raise in the winter of 1918–1919 were dispersed in penny packets as emergency reinforcements; it was only *after* the decisive battles of 1919 that a "Reserve Army of the Republic" in the Volga region really began to form proper units to reinforce the front.[11]

Units also did not take shape according to plan. A November 1918 regulation envisaged a giant standard rifle division of 58,000 men, but in practice even 10,000 was a rarity. There were typically three regiments in a division, and the average size of each regiment was 1200 men, growing to perhaps 2000 by the end of the war. Little attention, moreover, was paid to standardization. The Reds did not set out to create any elite troops, but a British defector-source indicated that the best were very good, while many others were exceptionally poor.[12]

The mass army needed equipment. The most important weapons were the .30 (7.62 mm) rifle (M1891) and the Maxim machine gun. The standard field gun was the 3 in (76.2 mm) Model 02; heavier artillery was seldom used in the mobile campaigns. Most of the Russian weapons that had survived the World War ended up in the Soviet zone. The total weapons acquired by the old regime were 11,000,000 rifles, 76,000 machine guns, and 17,000 field guns. About five or ten percent seem to have survived the world war and 1917 and to have stayed in the hands of the Soviet government; according to Vatsetis's estimate, the Red Army began 1919 with about 600,000 rifles, 8000 machine guns, and 1700 field guns. The inheritance was crucial, since Soviet war production was low. The following figures compare Tsarist production in 1916 with Soviet production in 1919:[13]

	1916	1919	Percentage
Rifles	1,321,000	460,055	35
Machine guns	11,072	6,256	57
SAA	1,482,000,000	340,060,000	23
Field guns	8,208	152	2
Shells	33,000,000	184,998	1

The 1928 official history of the Civil War admitted that Soviet production only became important in the second half of 1919; "up until that time we were kept going by the legacy of the old army." This showed the extreme value for eventual victory of Soviet control over the arms depots of central Russia.

Artillery production was negligible, but even rifle production in 1919 cannot have brought the total to more than a million (there must have been losses)—at a time when the army numbered nearly three million. But it was rifle *ammunition* that caused most worry. In early May 1919, as his eastern and southern fronts collapsed, Vatsetis reported to the Defense Council that the supply of small-arms ammunition (SAA) was heading for "catastrophe"; the army was shooting off 70–90 million rounds a month, and the main arsenal at Tula was producing only 20 million. In December 1919 Trotsky was to look back on this as *the* great crisis, when there was "the danger that we might perish from lack of cartridges, rifles, machine-guns, and artillery."[14] Fortunately production, especially of SAA, improved somewhat over the summer.

The Civil War was fought largely with nineteenth-century technology; the main exception was the machine gun. Mechanization was minimal, due to backwardness and the lack of fuel. The condition of roads limited the usefulness of the few armored cars, and the Tsarist army had had no *tanki*. The mobile weapons were the armored train—of which the Red Army had 59 by October 1919—and the *tachanka*, a cart carrying a machine gun. Horse-drawn carts, mostly taken from the peasants, provided the main transport. The Reds had only a few hundred airplanes, whose condition won the nickname "flying coffins." Naval forces were only a fraction of World War strength, largely due to the lack of coal and fuel oil; the Reds did, however, succeed in improvising many river gunboats, which were especially useful on the Volga, Kama, and Northern Dvina.

The first Red Army uniforms, identical for all levels from War Commissar to the humblest peasant infantryman, were designed at the end of 1918, after a competition organized by Trotsky. The distinctive winter cloth hat with its pointed top, folding ear flaps, and red-star badge was nicknamed the "hero's hat" (*bogatyrka*) from its strong resemblance to a medieval warrior's helmet. The new overcoat was officially called a *kaftan* and was based on the coat of the seventeenth-century Muscovite *streltsy*. (One wonders what the more foppish staff-officer veterans of the old army felt parading around like extras from "Khovanshchina.") These uniforms only gradually became available in quantity. Some units made up their own uniforms, others (toward the end of 1919) wore British battledress captured from White stores. But most common was Tsarist army issue, modified with red ribbons or Soviet insignia. In general there was a great lack of proper uniforms, underclothes, footwear, and overcoats, which is not surprising given the economic ruin and the need to clothe two or three million men.

The growing Red Army needed more and more food. The army ate much of what was procured by the civilian supply organs, but it had to take on itself a good deal of the work. Soldiers in the rear were supposed to be fed by an elaborate organization set up by the Food Supply and War commissariats, but the Tsarist tradition of the "regimental economy," by which units procured and even *grew* their own food, continued. The element of "self-supply" was even stronger in the fighting Army Groups. Transport and administrative weaknesses meant that they got little from the center, and in any event they were nearer the food-producing areas of south Russia, the Volga, and western Siberia. Far from being well-supplied, their task included shipping food *back* to the hungry interior of Sovdepia.[15]

Was it then a mistake to create a huge Red Army in 1919? It imposed a huge strain on a feeble economy, and yet it was still a poorly equipped force. On the other hand, the vital supply problem could only be solved by taking the rich territories of the enemy. "Proper bases in our own rear were spectral, birds in the bush," recalled the official history; "realism led us to bases in front of us, these were the birds in hand."[16] And manpower was the greatest advantage that came from the vast zone controlled by the Bolsheviks. It could be—and was—used to overwhelm better-led and better-equipped opponents.

War Economy

In 1919 Sovdepia's economic position differed little from that of the second half of 1918. The provinces that grew surplus food were in the battle zone or held by enemies; these same provinces held essential raw materials and fuel. Large-scale industry in the Soviet zone was in a state of decay, internal trade was at a low level, and there were no commercial links with the world outside.

In the summer and autumn of 1918 the countryside had been exasperated by crop seizures, the *kombedy*, and the Extraordinary Tax (and conscription). After November 1918 there were no major concessions to the peasants in the interlinked areas of food supply and general agrarian policy, but the rural population were treated more carefully. In the winter of 1918–1919 "socialist" farming was verbally encouraged, but there was no peasant response and collectivization was not forced in the core of the Soviet-held zone. (The few "State Farms" showed the *failure* of the food supply policy; these *sovkhozy* were formed by townspeople who realized that to eat they would have to grow their own food.) The real focus of 1919 became not the collective farm but the "middle peasant" (*seredniak*). Lenin admitted to the Eighth Party Congress (March 1919) that grave mistakes had been made. The enemy was the *kulak* (prosperous peasant); "But very often, owing to the inexperience of our Soviet officials and to the difficulty of the problem, the blows which were intended for the kulaks fell on the middle peasants. Here we have sinned very badly." In contrast to its policies of 1918, the party now revealed that the goal was *not* to mobilize the supposed "rural proletariat"—the poor peasant (*bedniak*)—against the kulak. Now, at the congress, it was said that most peasants were "middling" and had to be won over; when food, conscripts, and internal order were essential, at least lip service had to be paid to the peasant majority.[17] One important symbol of this was Kalinin, the "peasant-worker" who succeeded Sverdlov as head of state in early 1919; he would supposedly be aware of peasant feelings, and he spent much of his time on propaganda tours. Tokens and propaganda, the avoidance of collectivization and the worst mistakes of 1918, all helped the Red victory.

The range of real concessions, however, was limited by the food supply system. It was not thought desirable, on either practical or ideological grounds, to bring back private trade; in November 1918 this was completely nationalized. But the alternative to the market, "collective barter," still yielded little, and the government had to fall back on the Food Levy (*prodrazverstka*) law of January 1919; the law formalized the arrangements by which the peasants were—on a province-level basis—obliged to give up their surpluses. The first food crisis had been eased by the 1918 harvest, but supplies ran short again, and the absolute low point in food supplies to the towns was probably reached in the late winter of 1918–1919.

Gradually the collection apparatus became more effective. Officially 108 million *puds* (195,000 t.) of grain and fodder were obtained in 1918–1919, as opposed to 73 million in 1917–1918. This improvement has to be compared with 393 million in 1916–1917.[18] What made the situation "tolerable" was that most Russians lived in the countryside and that there were now fewer mouths to feed in the towns than in 1917. Furthermore, the requisitioning system had only a paper monopoly of trade; the black market and the ubiquitous "bagmen" may well have played a dominant part in the food supply "system." Meanwhile the Red Army was only a third the size of its Tsarist predecessor, and the front line units were to some extent able to supply themselves.

In industry too there was no basic change, but rather continued shrinkage and more stress on war production. The state-run economy should not be confused with the centralized and planned system that socialists had long talked about. Soviet war production concentrated resources on a few key factories, and simultaneously placed much reliance on the artisan production of small workshops (especially for clothing). Planning could not work in Sovdepia, with its new institutions, vast and ravaged territory, and poorly educated population. Kritsman, the historian of "War Communism," admitted that the whole system had no real center, only an "ersatz one," a "completely unsatisfactory" center, in the form of the Defense Council (Council of Workers' and Peasants' Defense—*SRKO*), Lenin's inner cabinet, set up in November 1918.[19] The so-called Supreme Economic Council (*VSNKh*) of early 1918 survived, but even its control over industry was challenged.

In November 1918 a special organ (*Chrezkomsnab*) was charged with war production, and this was further developed in July 1919 when control of all war production was given to one person; the elegantly named "Defense Council's Extraordinary Plenipotentiary for the Supply of the Red Army" (the *Chusosnabarm*) was the veteran Bolshevik Rykov. But even Rykov did not control food, which remained under the Food Supply Commissariat, and there were other strong and competing institutions in Moscow and the provinces. Rather than planning, one key concept was *udarnost'*, "shock production"—the concentration of scarce raw materials, fuel, and labor in a few key defense factories while starving the rest.

Despite all these shortcomings of their war economy, the Reds won the great campaigns of 1919. This was partly because the Whites were even worse off. The Whites' one local resource was an abundant food supply; they inherited few factories or military depots. They were dependent on Allied supplies that arrived late or were pilfered en route to the front. The Reds had the advantage of a vast territory (to which the Volga, the Urals, and western Siberia were added in 1919); this meant that even if resources were not used efficiently the overall amount was very large—compared with what the Whites could muster. The general system created by the economic revolution continued, but with more of a feeling for peasant sensitivities and more concentration on the military essentials. Great popular sacrifices were still demanded, but Red political control within Sovdepia, as we shall see, contained the protests and made the system workable.

The Workers' and Peasants' State

In 1918 the new Soviet state had benefited from considerable popular support, an inherited bureaucracy, a reasonably united ruling party, and the use of political terror; also crucial was the political weakness of its internal opponents. In 1919 Sovdepia faced a different challenge, but now had the additional advantage of a more developed administrative machine. At the top of the structure the processes evident since the middle of 1918 went on. Sovnarkom and its apparatus, especially the Defense Council, became more effective. Despite extravagant claims in the 1919 Communist program that "the Soviet state realizes . . . in an immeasurably wider form than ever before, local self-government, without any sort of authority imposed from above"; the fact was that Soviet democracy had atrophied.[20] No congress of soviets was held for thirteen months—from November 1918 to December 1919. The Central ExCom, the main "elected" organ of the Soviet congress, did not meet at all; power was concentrated in its Presidium. The decline in the importance of the Central ExCom was furthered by the death of Sverdlov in March 1919 and his replacement by the "peasant" figurehead Kalinin.

Across Sovdepia real power was concentrated in the local soviet excoms, and even further, within their presidiums. This came partly because so many local activists were drafted into the forces, and partly because debate had to be kept from getting out of hand. It was dangerous to tap mass support at a time when the state was making great demands for food and conscripts. This was shown when relatively free elections to a provincial congress of soviets at Tver (between

188

Moscow and Petrograd) produced as many "non-party" delegates as Bolsheviks and bitter open criticism of government policy; in the end arbitrary methods had to be used here and all over Sovdepia to ensure Bolshevik majorities at province and county congresses. Meanwhile the local agencies of central commissariats (ministries) referred questions back to "their" centers in Moscow, rather than leaving the decision to local soviets; this happened with the army, the economic agencies, the Cheka, and especially the Interior Commissariat (*NKVD*). And in districts just behind the front, in recently captured areas, and places where there were armed uprisings, even the managed local soviets did not provide the necessary authority. Supreme power was given to an appointed "revolutionary committee" (*revkom*) in which the Red Army played a large part.

The greatest check on "soviet" power, and yet an important factor in explaining the success of the Red home front, was the development of the Russian Communist Party. If 1918 saw the development of the modern Soviet state, 1919 can be called the first year of party power. It was only at the Eighth Party Congress (March 1919) that the central institutions were clearly defined: the inner Political Bureau (Lenin, L. B. Kamenev, Krestinsky, Stalin, and Trotsky); the Organizational Bureau; and the Secretariat. These developments had long-term implications— such as Stalin's rise through the Secretariat's apparatus—but their immediate importance was that they made the party's center more solid. The Politburo in particular became the linchpin of the political system, a body that made it possible to bind together (or bypass) the various state and party institutions.

A major effort was made to improve communications between this center and the national network of party organizations. At the Eighth Congress the extraordinary weaknesses of the party machine had been clearly shown. Only three out of the 36 provinces, it turned out, sent in regular reports to Moscow, and nearly half of the 219 counties had never bothered to report at all.[21] Now the demand for tighter coordination came, as it had at the end of 1918, from both the center and the grass roots, where local leaders welcomed the support that only Moscow could give.

Locally, full-time party officials held more and more real power; province party committees rarely met, and urgent decisions were left to a few members of the ProvCom bureau, the local equivalent of the politburo, which became the center of local power. The Eighth Congress spelled out the party's task to create groups (*fraktsii*) inside the soviets with the aim "of undivided political supremacy in the soviets and of actual supervision [*kontrol'*] over all their work." But state institutions were not to be replaced by party ones—a development seen as leading to "fatal" confusion. "The party strives to *direct* the work of the soviets, not to replace them," and under Russian conditions this proved a sound way of creating institutions of mass democracy *and* keeping tight control over them.[22]

Party size in March 1919—350,000—was not very different from that of late 1917, but the center felt that the Bolshevik monopoly of power had attracted a careerist element of "margarine Communists." The result in April 1919 was the first general purge which, coupled with the resignation of fainthearted comrades during mobilization, brought membership down to an extraordinarily low 150,000 by August 1919. Policy changed again in September at the height of the White offensive; as the CC *Bulletin* put it, "in such conditions our party's membership card clearly meant being a candidate for Denikin's gallows," and this was felt to be enough to deter the careerists. An additional 160,000 party members were recruited in various "Party Weeks" that autumn, and for the rest of the war the number increased.[23] Altogether, this complex (and unplanned) process did "temper the steel" of the party, providing a small but effective core for the popular movement, and at the same time it enhanced the role of the party veterans in Moscow and in the provincial towns.

Political terror was still an important part of the formula, despite the Sixth Soviet Congress' (November 1918) approval of an amnesty and a release of hostages, and despite the strong resentment of the Cheka by many senior Soviet leaders. In January 1919 the county Chekas were closed and the political police concentrated at the province level, but this was the only major change. Although the Cheka's right to sentence offenders was ended, this did not apply to areas under martial law. In mid-March the long-standing rivalry between the Interior Commissariat and the Cheka was resolved by making Dzerzhinsky head of both.

Terror was still directed against both the masses and conscious political enemies. An extreme case involving the former came during the great transport crisis of February 1919, with the threat to shoot peasant hostages if the railway lines were not cleared of snow. Bolshevik civilians and trade unionists were formed into "Special Duties Units" (ChON) in order to safeguard Soviet power during the April 1919 crisis. More important were the 100,000 men of the Cheka's "Internal Security Troops" (VOKhR); the corps of "Internal Security Troops" was created in May 1919 and combined several smaller organizations.

The number of people executed in the twenty central provinces in

1919 was officially put at 3500, only half the figure for 1918. Even if the figures for both years are understated, it *is* possible that the scale of executions in the central provinces was lower once the Soviet system was more firmly in control. However, the Cheka's activities in the reconquered periphery—in the Ukraine, the Baltic, the Urals, and Siberia—must have been much bloodier. Denikin's advancing troops uncovered large-scale atrocities, and their retreat must have been followed by others. (One British report said something about the author's own prejudices: "The evidence of wholesale executions . . . of the cold-blooded and refined tortures carried out by Chinese experts and of the revolting Sadiism [sic] of young Jewesses is irrefutable.") Large numbers of people were held prisoner; the official Soviet figures for 1919 were 7500 concentration camps and 21,700 prisons (respectively 17 and 46 percent greater than 1918), and there were also 4100 labor camps.[24]

The anti-Bolsheviks failed to build an effective underground within Sovdepia; there were incidents, but nothing on the scale of the 1918 Iaroslavl or Izhevsk risings. The biggest organization was probably that of the National Center, which had a Kadet orientation and British support. As Denikin's offensive developed the Moscow group apparently planned some kind of uprising, but in late August 1919 its head, Shchepkin, was arrested, and in September the Cheka rounded up hundreds of suspects; sixty-seven were executed. A second National Center group in Petrograd had vitally placed supporters (including the chief of staff of Seventh Army) but achieved no decisive results. The leftist underground was also effectively impotent. An anarchist bomb thrown into the Bolshevik's Moscow Committee headquarters in September 1919 killed the Moscow Party chief and eleven others, and wounded fifty-five (including Bukharin), but the incident was an isolated one.

The Cheka kept control. In the first seven months of 1919 it uncovered in central Russia some 270 counterrevolutionary organizations. This, on a monthly average, was three or four times the number uncovered in 1918. On the other hand ninety-nine "uprisings" were reported, which was fewer per month than in the previous year.[25] All these figures must be treated with great caution, but together they seem to suggest—at a time when the external White threat was at its greatest—a higher level of internal control.

As important as repression was the continuing inability of the anti-Bolshevik political groups to stimulate mass opposition. In 1919, as in 1918, the opposition lacked roots, had thin popular support, and suffered from poor organization. But an additional problem in 1919 was the polarization between the Bolsheviks and the White generals; there was now little middle ground. This made only a marginal difference to the Kadets and the Right—they would have had little popular support anyway. But for the SRs and Mensheviks the choice was more agonizing. The new SR line stressed the party's role as a "Third Force," but more and more the centrist socialists had to choose one extreme or the other. For many the Bolsheviks became clearly the lesser of the two evils. Particularly striking was the case of the socialist leaders of Komuch. Maisky, the most prominent Menshevik in Komuch, was stunned by Admiral Kolchak's coup and withdrew from politics, disinfecting his mind in the winter of 1918–1919 by reading Sherlock Holmes and Sienkiewicz; he then had the "pleasant and unexpected surprise, given to us by history" that the immediate transition to socialism *was* possible.[26]

The Bolsheviks exploited this situation. After the Kolchak coup and the end of the world war there was within the Soviet zone a political thaw of sorts. In November 1918 the restrictions placed on the Mensheviks in the early summer were lifted. Volsky, the SR chairman of Komuch, took refuge in Sovdepia and was (briefly) in February 1919 given some freedom for political activities. But the Bolsheviks never entertained thoughts of a genuine partnership. The legal Menshevik newspaper in Moscow was banned on the grounds that it called for the end of the Civil War, and in March the Cheka arrested a number of Menshevik leaders. The Left SRs were attacked after a big strike at Petrograd's Putilov Factory. Nowhere were the rival socialists allowed to build a base in the Soviets or to have continuous access to the press.

Central Russia—Sovdepia—with its great resources of manpower and its still considerable economic potential was the key to Bolshevik success in 1919. The nature of the Bolsheviks' grip on Sovdepia had changed: the Soviet program, a positive political appeal, was less decisive. The Whites had even less mass appeal, and the Reds were now sensitive to the middle peasant, but the Bolsheviks had little to give, and had to demand more and more. One "new" Bolshevik advantage in 1919 was the polarization between White and Red, caused by the very success of the White movement, which led to the Center and Center-Left moving towards the Bolsheviks. Perhaps the main difference between 1917–1918 and 1919, however, was that the Bolshevik government was more firmly established. The Bolsheviks had had time to consolidate the soviet structure and the party, and to get the Red Army and the Cheka past the infant stage. The state was no monolith, but it gave the Reds the power to enforce popular sacrifices and to build and supply a war-winning army. When faced by the greatest military threat of the Civil War—Denikin's Moscow offensive—Sovdepia would prove a firm base.

14

THE TURNING POINT,
September–November 1919

Lenin s Trotskim—nasha dvoika,/Vot poprobui-ka, pokroi-ka!/Nashei dvoiki nechem kryt'!/Gde zhe tvoia, Denikin, pryt'? [Lenin and Trotsky are our pair,/Just try them, just cover them!/Our pair can't be trumped!/What have you got, Denikin, that can match them?]

Red Army propaganda poem, 1919

Za Rossiiu i svobodu/Esli v boi zovut,/To, kornilovtsy, i v vodu/I v ogon' idut. [For Russia and freedom/If they call for battle,/The Kornilov men will go/Through fire and water.]

"March of the Kornilov Shock Regiment"

To Moscow!

It is not easy to say when in the Civil War Soviet rule was most threatened. The choice is probably between the Volga campaign in 1918 and General Denikin's offensive in 1919. In the late summer of 1918, during the battles for Kazan, the Bolsheviks had only a small, disorganized army and a primitive and unstable political base. It may be that the *relative* threat was greatest at that time, because by the autumn of 1919 Moscow had had another year to build up its Red Army and consolidate its internal structure.

On the other hand the main anti-Bolshevik force was much larger and better organized (in military terms) in late 1919. Soviet Russia, moreover, was now surrounded by a ring of active White fronts—in western Siberia, north Russia, the Baltic, and south Russia. This, then, was the time that anti-Bolshevik military potential reached its peak, and Soviet power was certainly gravely threatened once again. The crisis reached its peak at the end of October 1919.

Six weeks before, in the middle of September 1919, General Denikin's Armed Forces of South Russia (AFSR) renewed the great offensive that had begun with capture of the Donbas, Kharkov, and Tsaritsyn and had been formalized in his "Moscow Directive" of 3 July. The Whites had withstood the Soviet counterattacks of August and early September. Now they grasped the initiative and thrust north again.

Fundamental to the Moscow Directive, to the outlook of the individual White commanders, and probably to the logic of civil war, was continued advance right along the front. Vrangel's Caucasus Army on the Volga flank was the exception, but it did hold on to the northern approaches to Tsaritsyn. Sidorin's Don Army, on Vrangel's left, drove the Reds back throughout September and October; the cossacks only came to a halt at the beginning of November after they had covered a hundred miles, threatening the rear of Red Ninth and Tenth Armies and even the strategic Volga town of Saratov. Meanwhile, on the extreme western flank of the AFSR, the troops of General Dragomirov's Kiev District reached Chernigov on 12 October, squeezing the Red defenders against the Polish positions.

It was in the center of the AFSR front, between Sidorin and Dragomirov, that the main blow was struck. The line of advance was the railway running north from Kharkov through Kursk, Orel, and Tula to Moscow. The shaft aimed straight at the Red capital was still Mai-Maevsky's Volunteer Army; the spearhead was I Corps, with the veteran Kornilov, Markov, and Drozdovsky units from the Kuban campaigns, now transformed into divisions. The Whites benefited from the failure of the August counterattack by the Red "Selivachev Group," whose exhausted remains retreated north before them. The extent of the threat became clear when Volunteer armored trains captured the province town of Kursk by a coup de main on 20 September. Whole units were deserting to the Whites. The two Red rifle divisions in the direct path of the Kornilov Division were shattered. The 9th, which repeatedly ran away, is of interest because one of its battalion commissars was the young Nikita Khrushchev. The 55th actually ceased to exist due to casualties and desertion; its commander, Stankevich, was captured by the Whites and hanged (his remains were later given the rare honor—for a Tsarist Major-General—of burial in the Kremlin Wall).

On 14 October, having taken 8000 prisoners, the Kornilov Division captured Orel, a province capital with a population of 100,000. Only 120 miles north of Orel was Tula, the armory of the Red forces, and 120 miles north of Tula was Moscow. Mai-Maevsky sent a telegram of congratulations: *"Orel—Orlam"*, "The Eagles have taken Orel" (*orel* also means "eagle"). As Skoblin, the Kornilov commander, rode his gray stallion into the main square of Orel, a piece of Soviet "monumental propaganda" covered in red cloth was knocked over, in a cloud of lime dust. Could Red Square be far away? On 27 September Moscow Province had been put under martial law and a RevCom had been put in charge. Eleven days later the British Military Mission to Denikin reported that "in the face of resistance, judging from the progress hitherto made, Moscow might be reached within 2½ months." Bad weather might add three weeks to that, but if Bolshevik morale cracked the time could be much less. There remained, it was added, many factors to take into account, and the situation was one of great uncertainty.[1]

Petrograd

Denikin's Moscow offensive was not the only immediate threat to Soviet power that October. At the height of the fighting around Orel a White "Northwestern Army" unexpectedly advanced to the outskirts of Petrograd—the "cradle of the revolution."

The formation of a small White-Russian force, then called the "Northern Army," had begun under German protection at Pskov in October 1918. Germany soon collapsed, and the Red Army moved west, but the Whites were able to withdraw into the new independent state of Estonia. The eastern border of Estonia was a natural barrier (Lake Chud [Peipus] and the Narova River), behind which the Whites could regroup, and in May 1919 they crossed back into Soviet territory. They made rapid progress in the direction of Petrograd, pushing back in disorder the larger Red Seventh Army. The Red authorities were very alarmed. The evacuation of Petrograd's factories was ordered, and the local commander warned that he might have to give up the city and pull back seventy-five miles southeast to the Volkhov River. Petrograd was (briefly) declared the most important front. Stalin, sent to the city in May, later claimed credit for saving it, but the invading force numbered only 6000 (supported by a few thousand Estonians), and their object was not Petrograd but a base of operations outside Estonia.[2] This

196

limited White aim was achieved. Despite successful Red counterattacks in July and August, the White forces—renamed Northwestern Army— now had their own territory, a wedge 100 miles wide and sixty miles deep to the east of the Narova–Lake Chud line and inhabited by Great Russians rather than Estonians.

The first weakness of the Baltic Whites was their leadership. Great hopes were placed in General N. N. Iudenich, who was recognized by both Kolchak and the Allies as Main Commander-in-Chief of the Baltic theater. Iudenich was one of the few Russian heroes to emerge from the World War, a general who never lost a battle and the man who stormed the "impregnable" Turkish mountain fortress of Erzerum in 1916. But at fifty-seven he was nearly a generation older than Denikin or Kolchak. An American officer described him as "a man five foot two inches in height weighing about 280 pounds; body shaped like a coupe, with unnoticeable legs." Iudenich only took over direct control of Northwestern Army's operations in early October 1919. The earlier fighting was led by other men, most notably General A. P. Rodzianko; to Rodzianko, Iudenich was a "decrepit old man," lacking any energy and ignoring requests for support and information.[3] Iudenich was supposedly occupying himself with coordinating strategy, developing a political program, and negotiating Allied support, but in none of these areas did he have success.

Iudenich coined the slogan, "Against the Bolsheviks, without Politics," and like Kolchak and Denikin he was not prepared to embrace political and social reform.[4] There would be no popular upsurge in favor of the Whites in the rural counties they controlled, let alone in Petrograd. The army was a force unto itself. A Northwestern Government claiming authority over Petrograd, Pskov, and Novgorod provinces was set up in August 1919, but it was important only as the product of the crudest interference from outside; exasperated by the Russians' inability to work together, a British general had given them forty minutes to form a government.

White military resources were tiny. The western counties of Petrograd Province had a total population of only a few hundred thousand. There were no cossacks and few prosperous peasants, so the local levies were hardly enthusiastic. A major source of manpower were Red POWs and deserters, but these too were poor fighting material. At its height in October 1919 the Northwestern Army had only 14,400 men. Discipline was poor, especially in partisan units led by a deserter from the Red Army, Bulak-Balakhovich. For supplies the army had to rely for most of 1919 on what little the Estonians gave them (from Tsarist depots). The

197

first British equipment arrived only in August 1919, and then in small quantities. (In October the army had only forty-four guns.[5])

Had the Allies intended a serious and general anti-Soviet campaign, Petrograd Province would have been an ideal theater. The Baltic Sea provided a short line of communications, immediately to hand was the Imperial capital with all its moral significance and its great seaport, and the distance from Petrograd to Moscow was much shorter than that from Omsk, Ekaterinodar, or Arkhangelsk. But in 1919 the Allies for the most part concentrated their limited resources either where they had sent forces in 1918 (north Russia) or where they felt a commitment to pro-Allied forces (Siberia and south Russia). Iudenich himself was untainted by compromise with "the enemy" (he spent 1918 underground in Petrograd), but the nucleus of his army had been sponsored by the Germans; the Allies looked on Northwestern Army with mistrust rather than with any feeling of obligation. So while British warships blockaded Petrograd and even raided the Kronshtadt naval base, no Allied land units were sent to the Baltic. The supplies sent were late in arriving and small in quantity.

Northwestern Army's success depended on the small states that had broken away from the old Tsarist Empire in 1917–1918. Its line of supply ran through Estonia, and the White Russians were so few that to succeed they needed a joint advance with at least the Estonian and Finnish armies. Both Reds and Whites saw the potential value of Finnish intervention. The Finnish border was only twenty miles from Petrograd. The Finnish army had broken the Red Finns in mid-1918 and given Estonia vital help in the following winter. The first Soviet fears for Petrograd's safety in 1919 had come not from the White Russians in Estonia but from Finnish partisan operations between Lakes Ladoga and Onega in April–May. Iudenich and his staff were based in Finland in the first half of 1919, and their original plan had been to mount the main attack from Finnish Karelia. In June 1919 Red Army intelligence reckoned on Finnish forces numbering 100,000, including 25,000 directly facing Petrograd[6], and much of the Soviet manpower and artillery around the city had to be directed toward the Finnish border.

But in the end the Finns did not let White Russian units operate from their territory, and their army took no part in the fighting. Kolchak, the White Supreme Ruler, would not guarantee Finnish independence, and there certainly would have been disagreement about how far the Finnish frontier would run east into Karelia and north to the Barents Sea. But a more practical factor was that most Finns did not want to fight in Russia, and this was reflected in the political leadership of the country. Parliamentary government resumed in Helsinki (Helsingfors) in the spring of 1919, and in July General Mannerheim—an advocate of an active policy against the Soviets—was replaced as head of state. The Allies were not prepared to offer Finland material or diplomatic advantages in exchange for intervention. Meanwhile the Reds alternated peace offers and dire threats. (In a September *Pravda* article Trotsky threatened the Finnish bourgeoisie with "merciless extermination" if they attacked; in particular he gleefully promised to unleash the Asiatic hordes of the Bashkir cavalry with the slogan "To Helsingfors!")[7]

The Estonian Army under General Laidoner—another Tsarist officer—did take part in the White Russian operations in May–June and October 1919. But the independent Tallin regime did not commit major forces, despite the experience of the Red Army invasion in November 1918, and despite the setting up on Soviet territory of an alternative government, the Estliand Labor Commune and a Red "Estliand Army." Independent Estonia's army was small, the population were unenthusiastic about adventures in Russia, and so was the parliamentary government that was elected in April 1919. The supreme White authorities, Kolchak included, were even less willing to concede independence to Estonia than to Finland, and given this attitude the Allied leaders declined to give Tallin full recognition. The Estonians had more than the Bolsheviks to worry about. The German Freikorps and a rogue "West Russian Army" (under Colonel Bermondt-Avalov) threatened the neighboring Latvian nationalist government—especially in June and October 1919, the months of the White Petrograd offensives. This tied up Estonian army units 300 miles from the Petrograd front and doubled suspicions of the Whites; it also dominated Allied diplomatic activity and diverted British warships from the Petrograd area. The British, meanwhile, could provide little concrete aid to Estonia; when in August 1919 Moscow began to put out peace feelers the Allies had to let Tallin negotiate freely.

The final offensive of Northwestern Army began with a feint by its right-flank corps on 28 September 1919. The main blow—on the direct route to Petrograd—began on 12 October; by 21 October the Whites had marched right across Petrograd Province to enter the palace towns of Pavlovsk and Tsarskoe Selo. From their forward positions the Whites could see the great golden dome of St. Isaac's cathedral, only twenty miles away in the heart of Petrograd. Given all its shortcomings, Northwestern Army was remarkably successful. One explanation was that the Reds were caught by surprise. They were preoccupied with Denikin's great offensive and saw Northwestern Army as a spent force.

On 26 September the Bolshevik CC had ordered the transfer of the best units from the Petrograd area to Southern Army Group, and a week later *Pravda* published an article by Lenin praising the mobilization of workers *away* from Petrograd. A second explanation was that the quality of the local Red troops was low. Two months after the event a leading commissar explained "why we needed fully 250,000 men in order to get the upper hand over Iudenich's 15,000 White Guards": units were badly supplied, and they "start to *disintegrate* before they have finished their formation, and they produce a huge percentage (up to 70 per cent) of deserters." The Whites also had the peculiar advantage that Colonel Liundkvist, the chief of staff of the army defending Petrograd (Seventh), was sending them details of Petrograd's defenses and actually helped to work out their attack plan.[8]

In the end Iudenich's lunge failed. Trotsky is often given the credit. He arrived with his special train on 17 October. The mercurial Zinoviev, the Petrograd party chief, was—according to Trotsky—in a state of near collapse. Trotsky doubled the food ration and urged the mobilization of the whole population to turn the city into a "stone labyrinth." (Lenin's helpful proposal was "to mobilize another twenty thousand or so Petrograd workers plus about ten thousand 'bourgies,' set up machine-guns behind them, shoot several hundred, and assure a real mass assault on Iudenich.") Trotsky toured the Red units, and at one point actually got up on horseback to turn around panicking troops.[9] For his efforts he was awarded the "Order of the Red Banner," and the front-line town of Gatchina was renamed Trotsk—until Trotsky was disgraced in the 1920s. But also important were Colonel Gittis (Western Army Group Commander-in-Chief), who coordinated the defense, and General Nadezhny and Colonel Kharlamov, who commanded the main formations on the spot—Seventh Army and a special Striking Group.

Whoever was giving the orders, the battle for Petrograd was not one of a handful of Reds against the White hordes. Northwestern Army numbered only 14,400 men and 44 guns. By the time they got near Petrograd they were exhausted and desperately short of supplies. The Finns did not move. The Estonians only covered the coastal flank. The local British advisors had urged an attack (to make some use of the arms that had been sent), but the Royal Navy was diverted to Latvia and the six British-manned tanks were held back from the final assault. Red Petrograd, on the other hand, still had a population of 600,000. Iudenich might have had to fight his way street by street through the industrial suburbs, and he would certainly have been faced with the task of feeding the great city. And by 1 November Red Seventh Army (in Petrograd) and the neighboring Fifteenth Army (south of the White bulge) had no fewer than 73,000 men—a 5:1 advantage—and 581 guns.[10]

The Reds would in any event have had a great numerical advantage, but at a time of critical battles around Orel, desperately scarce reserves were moved from Tula (behind Southern Army Group) to Petrograd. "This reserve," recalled Main Commander-in-Chief Kamenev, "was called our 'Queen of Spades'—the last trump which was needed to take the game. The 'Queen of Spades' had cost . . . a great deal. The feeling of responsibility for this decision literally [sic] burned the brain." According to Kamenev, Lenin himself made this crucial strategic decision. Trotsky, in his memoirs, had a different account: by about 14 October Lenin had concluded that Petrograd could not be held, and only the insistence of Trotsky and others made him change his mind. In any event, the arrival of reinforcements was very important; according to Kamenev these units were free from the contamination of the "totally demoralized units of the old front," and with them it was possible to form a new front line able to take the offensive. The arrival of reinforcements was only possible because of a White blunder when a unit failed to cut the Moscow-Petrograd rail line.[11]

Superior numbers and better coordination turned the tables on the battlefield. Seventh Army's counterattack began on 21 October, and the Whites withdrew to avoid being cut off from their base. Another of Iudenich's disadvantages—compared to Denikin and Kolchak—was that his position had no depth. Three weeks after giving up Tsarskoe Selo his army had been thrown back to the barbed wire of the Estonian frontier. It was finally allowed through in the middle of November, but only after being disarmed by its erstwhile allies. The refugees suffered terribly that winter from hunger, cold, and disease; many slipped back into Soviet Russia. Iudenich resigned in November. Trotsky had favored "hot pursuit" into Estonia, "the kennel for the guards dogs of the counter-revolution," but this would not be necessary.[12] Northwestern Army ceased to exist. Soviet-Estonian negotiations in Tartu resulted first in an armistice (31 December 1919) and then a peace treaty (2 February 1920). This was an event of great significance—Moscow's first settlement with a border state. (Lithuania signed a peace treaty in July 1920, followed by Latvia in August and Finland in October.)

Red propaganda posters depicted Denikin, Kolchak, and Iudenich as three slobbering guard dogs of the Entente, all equally large and fierce. In reality the Iudenich army was a very small pooch indeed, and hardly the favorite of the Allies. It is just possible that it might have taken Petrograd. Given the threat from Denikin the Reds might not have reinforced the city. But to suggest, as Trotsky did, that "in Petrograd Iudenich will find huge industrial resources and manpower" or that "there are no serious obstacles between Petrograd and Moscow," is going too far. Iudenich would have been very hard-pressed just to hold Petrograd (and feed it). The October attack on Petrograd was to a large extent a diversion to take pressure off Denikin's front.[13] Significant Soviet reserves had to be shifted away from the critical southern front, and given the distance involved it was really a remarkable piece of White grand-strategic coordination. But it would not be enough.

The Red Counterattack

Petrograd was saved, but for more than a month—from mid-October until mid-November—fierce battles continued in the south; the success or failure of the Moscow Offensive hung in the balance. The Volunteer Army had taken Orel on 14 October, and seemed on a direct route to Moscow. Since late September Colonel Kamenev had been concentrating reserves northwest of Volunteer Army, and these were now thrown in; the new "Striking Group" included Red cossacks and some cavalry, but the iron core were the Latvian Rifle Division, leather-jacketed veterans. The unexpected appearance of the Latvians in the rear of the tired and overstretched Kornilov Division forced the evacuation of Orel. The town was occupied by Red troops, the Estonian and 13th Rifle Divisions, on 20 October. Neither side yet realized it, but the long Red retreat was over.

Volunteer Army had been halted at Orel by the appearance on its left flank of the Striking Group. What turned pause into precipitate retreat was the appearance on its right flank of Red cavalry. On 24 October Semen Budenny's Red Cavalry Corps recaptured Voronezh from General Shkuro. A more important prize than Orel, the city was a province capital, a railway junction, the key to the upper Don River crossings, and the link between Volunteer and Don Armies; its loss threatened Volunteer Army communications with Rostov. The next step was to tighten the grip around the neck of the Volunteers' salient. On 15 November, after ferocious delaying actions by General Shkuro, Budenny's horsemen rode out of a blizzard to take the vital little railway junction at Kastornoe, on the Voronezh-Kursk railway. One of the best-known paintings of the Civil War, by Avilov (1930), shows Red cavalrymen, sabers drawn, taking the surrender of the snow-covered marshalling yard, as the Whites throw down their arms. The loss of Kastornoe threatened the immediate encirclement of the whole Volunteer Army and forced abandonment of its forward positions. The Volunteers were able to retreat south out of the trap, but the grudging withdrawal from Orel became a desperate race south, and the retreat would not end until all the White armies had been pushed beyond Rostov and the Don River in the first week of 1920. The Moscow Offensive had been utterly defeated, and never again would White armies pose a serious threat to the Soviet heartland.

It was not skillful handling of the Red southern armies that beat Denikin. The basic Red strategy had been set in July 1919, when Colonel Kamenev became Main Commander-in-Chief: the main blow was supposed to come from the east; Shorin's Special Group (Ninth and Tenth Armies) would assemble near the Volga and march southwest across the Don Cossack region to the Sea of Azov, cutting off the Whites in the huge area north and west of the Don River. Kamenev told the Bolshevik leadership at the end of September that taking units from Shorin and shifting them 400 miles west to cover Moscow would mean passive defense and withdrawal to a line further north (from Saratov to Orel) until winter came; continuing Shorin's attack, on the other hand, would lead to decisive victory. Lenin publicly accepted this view in an article published on 4 October:

> Denikin's men count on causing panic in our ranks and making us think only of defense, only of this [Kursk-Orel] area. . . . Our forces have been deployed according to a carefully thought out and strictly executed plan. Our offensive against the enemy's main source of strength continues. The victories won in the last few days . . . show the successful advance of our troops [i.e. Shorin's armies] to the center of Cossackdom.

Red strategy had to be fundamentally changed at the last moment. This was done in the panic on 15 October, the day after Orel fell. The seven-man Politburo decided—without consulting Main Commander-in-Chief Kamenev—to give the Moscow-Tula area the highest priority; Shorin was to transfer troops there and go over to the defensive. Nothing like the successful counterattack that actually occurred a few weeks later was mentioned, however; instead it was noted that "preparations are to be. made during the course of the winter for a general offensive."[14]

Both Trotsky and Stalin later claimed credit for the successful counterattack, neither with much justification. Trotsky said "his" plan was finally adopted on 15 October, but this plan dated from earlier in the summer and reflected a different situation, before the worst of the Red retreat: it was an attack from Voronezh southeast across the Donbas. In reality Budenny's main blow was struck *west* through Voronezh toward the rear of Volunteer Army. Trotsky was also away from the southern front in the critical weeks (rallying Petrograd's defenders). His claim to have planned the counterattack before he left ("Everything was prepared; the concentration of units for the attack was almost completed") is not convincing. Indeed, it has been claimed that Stalin only agreed to become Southern Army Group commissar (from 3 October) if Trotsky did not interfere. Stalin, for his part, may have tightened up control over Southern Army Group in the same way that Trotsky did at Petrograd, and his assignment showed how highly he was valued; "The best," Lenin had urged, "the *most energetic* commissars must be sent to the south, not sleepyheads." But the assertion that Stalin worked out the counterattack plan is a myth developed in the 1920s and 1930s (and based in part on a misdated letter).[15]

Colonel A. I. Egorov, the Red field commander, was a leader of questionable talent; he certainly had little time to settle into the job, being made Commander-in-Chief of Southern Army Group only on 11 October. Egorov's main qualification was his political reliability. A Volga peasant's son, he had welcomed the February revolution so enthusiastically that his fellow officers drummed him out of his regiment. It is true that he first supported the SRs, but in July 1918 he joined the Bolshevik Party and was one of very few more senior officers to do so. (After the Civil War he made a great career in the Red Army—becoming Chief of the General Staff and one of the first five Marshals. He replaced the purged Marshal Tukhachevsky in 1937— before being shot himself.) His courage was unquestioned; he had been wounded five times in the World War and again in May 1919. But in 1919 he was poorly qualified. He was 36, had only commanded a battalion in the World War, and was not a General Staff officer. Egorov had led individual Soviet armies (Tenth, then Fourteenth) since December 1918, but Kamenev had little confidence in him. In September 1919 he had warned Trotsky against giving Egorov the (much smaller) Selivachev Group: "by his personal abilities he is hardly suited to such a difficult task as the command of two armies . . . in such a complicated situation."[16]

The details of the Red counterattack suggest improvisation rather than design. Kamenev and Egorov hoped to use the Latvian Division and the rest of the Striking Group for a *deep* flanking movement into the rear of the Volunteers; the loss of Orel and the poor quality of many of the other Red divisions meant that the Group was thrown only at the

The "Railway War." Red Guards (armed workers) and de-mobilised soldiers helped the Bolsheviks to take control of most of central Russia in the winter of 1917–1918.

Bolshevik leaders review a parade of workers in Red Square on the first anniversary of the Revolution, 7 November 1918. In the centre, Lenin. To Lenin's left: Ia. M. Sverdlov, head of state and organiser of the party, who died in 1919, L. B. Kamenev, close comrade, Trotsky's brother-in-law, and theoretician N. F. Preobrazhenskii (in peaked cap). Note the sunrise motif painted on the Kremlin wall.

Reviewing another Red Square parade, this time of soldiers of the Universal Military Training Scheme, 25 May 1919. To Lenin's right V. M. Zagorskii, party leader of Moscow, assassinated 1919. To Lenin's left: L. B. Kamenev, Tibor Szamuely, Hungarian Communist leader (with goggles), and I. T. Smilga, chief commissar of the Red Army (with pince-nez).

Lenin, Trotsky (left) and L. B. Kamenev at a rally for soldiers setting off for the Polish front, Moscow, 5 May 1920. On this occasion was taken the famous photograph from which Trotsky and Kamenev were removed by Stalin's censors.

The victors. Delegates to the 8th Congress of Soviets, Moscow, 5 May 1920. Sitting at Lenin's right hand, Stalin; behind Stalin, the trade-union leader M. P. Tomskii. Sitting to Lenin's left, M. I. Kalinin, the head of state. Sitting on the right (in boots), M. M. Lashevich. Sitting on floor (left), I. T. Smilga.

M. D. Bonch-Bruevich. Senior "specialist" in the Red Army, March-August 1918. A general in the Tsarist army, Bonch's brother was Lenin's private secretary.

I. I. Vatsetis. A former Tsarist colonel. Commander of the Latvian rifles, then of the whole Red Army.

S. S. Kamenev. As a colonel, commanded a regiment in the World War. Kamenev was commander of the East Army Group in 1918–1919 and then of the whole Red Army from July 1919 to 1924.

M. N. Tukhachevsky. A junior officer captured by the Germans in 1915, Tukhachevsky returned to Russia in 1917, aged 24. He became one of the most outstanding field commanders in the campaigns on the Eastern Front, in the North Caucasus, and in Poland.

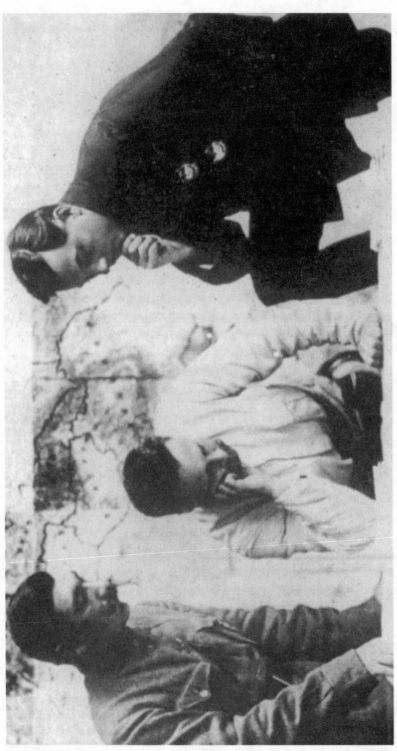

Planning the attack on the Crimea, 1920. Left to right. S. M. Budenny. M. V. Frunze, and K. E. Voroshilov. Budenny was commander of the 1st Cavalry Army, and Frunze and Voroshilov led the Red Army from 1925 to 1940.

Gen. M. V. Alekseev. Effectively commander of the Russian armies for much of the World War. Alekseev was a moving force behind the creation of the Volunteer Army, but he died of cancer in September 1918.

Gen. L. G. Kornilov (left) and Gen. A. M. Kaledin. The photograph is from the Moscow State Conference in 1917. Kaledin, Ataman of the Don Cossacks, shot himself when the Bolsheviks overran the Don in January 1918. Kornilov was killed by a Red shell outside Ekaterinodar in April 1918.

The high command of the Armed Forces of South Russia. Front left, Gen. Denikin, commander of the Volunteer Army, April to December 1918, and of the AFSR, December 1918 to March 1920. Directly behind Denikin, Gen. A. S. Lukomsky, his Minister of War, and Gen. A. M. Dragomirov. In doorway (behind Lukomsky), Gen. I. P. Romanovsky, Denikin's chief of staff, who was assassinated by an embittered White officer in April 1920. Note French adviser.

A. P. Kutepov. A colonel in the First World War, he commanded the spearhead I (Volunteer) Corps under Denikin and Vrangel from January 1919 to September 1920. Kutekov was kidnapped by the OGPU in Paris in 1930.

Gen. V. Z. Mai-Maevsky reviewing White troops. Denikin's best general, he commanded the Volunteer Army — within the Armed Forces of South Russia — from May to November 1919. Mai-Maevsky was dismissed after the failure of the Moscow campaign; he succumbed to alcoholism and died in November 1920.

Gen. P. N. Vrangel. The last of the major White leaders. A division commander in the World War, Vrangel was one of Denikin's most successful commanders and replaced him as the head of the Southern Whites in March 1920.

Cossack leaders, South Russia. Gen. G. A. Vdovenko, Terek Ataman, Gen. A. P. Bogaevsky, Don Ataman, Gen. A. P. Filimonov, Kuban Ataman (sitting; third, fourth, and fifth from the left). The Southern Whites had long-running difficulties with the independent-minded cossack leaders. In the winter of 1918–1919 they installed leaders who would work within the Armed Forces of South Russia.

Gen. Denikin reviews victorious White troops in Tsaritsyn in July 1919. The capture of Tsaritsyn was one of the high points of the campaign of the Armed Forces of South Russia. It was at this time that Denikin drafted his "Moscow Directive." Tsaritsyn, on the Volga, was later called Stalingrad and is now called Volopgrad.

White Cossacks in the Moscow campaign, 1919.

A White armoured train, south Russia. Armoured trains were among the most characteristic weapons on both sides in the Civil War.

Admiral A. V. Kolchak. Commander of the Black Sea Fleet in the World War. Kolchak was nominal "Supreme Ruler" of the White movement and led the Siberian Whites from November 1918 to January 1920. Arrested, tried, and shot.

V. O. Kappel. Probably the most able of the eastern White commanders. A wartime lieutenant-colonel, he led the briefly successful Volga campaign of 1918. Kappel was commander of a corps and then of an army under Kolchak. He died during the January 1920 "Ice March" in Siberia.

Gen. M. V. Khanzhin. One of the least-known White generals, but for a time he was one of Kolchak's most successful commanders. Khanzhin was a division commander in the World War. He commanded Kolchak's Western Army from January to June 1919 and led the "Ufa Offensive." Khanzhin emigrated to Manchuria, where he was arrested in 1945. He spent nine years in the GULAG and died in exile in Kazakhstan in 1961, aged 90.

D. A. Lebedev. A 35-year-old colonel, Lebedev was Kolchak's chief of staff and war minister from May to July 1919. His ineptitude contributed to the defeat of the Siberian White armies.

K. V. Sakharov. A colonel in the World War, he was commander of Kolchak's 3rd Army in July-November 1919, and of Eastern Army Group in November-December 1919, during the final collapse. He wrote important memoirs.

Gen. M. K. Diterikhs. Chief of staff of the Czechoslovak Corps, 1918–1919, Kilchak's chief of staff and war minister, July-November 1919, head of White Vladivostok government in 1922. In 1919 Diterikhs presided over the commission investigating the murder of the Imperial family.

General Iudenich and his staff, 1919. Iudenich was a highly successful commander against the Turks in the World War. Commander of the Northwestern Army versus Petrograd, February to November 1919.

Gen. E. K. Miller. Commander of the Army of the Northern Government, Arkhangel'sk, August 1919-February 1920. Miller was leader of the émigré movement in the 1930s. He was kidnapped by the NKVD in Paris in 1937 and executed secretly in Moscow in May 1939.

Evacuation of soldiers of Denikin's army aboard a British battleship, Novorossiisk, April 1920.

very tip of the White wedge, coupled with crude head-on attacks. Throughout, units were committed piecemeal. And Budenny's sudden appearance at Voronezh on the other side of the Volunteer wedge was as much chance as strategy. At the start of October his Cavalry Corps, located on the Don front 150 miles southeast of Voronezh, was ordered by Kamenev and Shorin to move even farther *away* from Voronezh to support Shorin's eastern offensive. It was only because Budenny disobeyed his orders and rode *northwest* in the hope of countering a new White cavalry breakthrough that he was, by mid-October, in place to strike the decisive blow via Voronezh and Kastornoe.[17]

White mistakes were as important as Red strategic planning. There was, however, no clear mistake in White grand strategy. It is true that by the late autumn of 1919 the Whites posed a serious threat from only one direction, the south, and that the Reds were able to concentrate their strength there. Iudenich was not even seen as a danger until early October (and was weak). The north Russian Whites were distant and insignificant. Most important, Kolchak's Siberian army was a spent force, despite its Tobol River offensive in September. But it is hard to call this a conscious mistake of Kolchak or Denikin, or the result of intra-White rivalry; it was just the way the war unfolded.

The west was perhaps different. In April 1920 the Polish Army would march to Kiev, occupying the western Ukraine and setting off full-scale war; six months earlier the Poles just watched and waited. There had been a gradual Polish movement to the east in the summer of 1919, but by October a representative from Moscow, Markhlevsky, was engaged in secret talks with Polish leaders. The Reds were sufficiently sure of the situation to move units from Western Army Group—facing the Poles— to the Denikin and Iudenich fronts. Denikin later (in 1937) wrote a pamphlet entitled *Who Saved Soviet Power from Destruction?* and laid the final blame on Warsaw. Denikin, himself, has to bear some responsibility, since his policy of "Russia, One and Indivisible" and his inflexibility on the question of the Polish-Russian border gave the Poles little reason to back him. On the other hand, *no* Russian government (including Lenin's) would have been willing to give up the territory Warsaw wanted. In any event, it is arguable whether a full-scale Polish offensive supporting Denikin was possible. It was 400 miles to Moscow, and influential Polish politicians opposed eastern adventures; even leaders like Marshal Pilsudski wanted only to gain territory, not to destroy the Soviet regime.

As regards Denikin's strategy in the south, two distinct and partly contradictory criticisms have been made: first, that he advanced in too many directions; and second, that he moved too quickly. The Moscow Directive of early July both set a daring objective *and* proposed an advance by widely spread armies. Baron Vrangel, Denikin's successor and one of his main critics, called the Moscow Directive "the death sentence of the South Russian armies" and stressed the dispersal of effort: "Striving for space, we endlessly stretched ourselves into a spider's web, and wanting to hold on to everything and to be *everywhere* strong we were everywhere weak." Denikin defended the spread and pace of his attack by saying that the normal laws of strategy did not apply to civil war. "We lengthened the front by hundreds of *versts* and became from this not weaker, but stronger." In south Russia the offensive took grain, military supplies, and manpower from the Reds and gave them to the Whites. At the time even Trotsky saw the situation much as Denikin did: on the Donets and in the Ukraine, "we left Denikin complete freedom of action, and gave him the chance to obtain a huge reservoir of new formations."[18]

Vrangel had a counterplan. In July he questioned the order to march his Caucasus Army north through the Volga region. Instead, the bulk of Caucasus Army, "a major cavalry mass of three or four corps," should be transferred to Kharkov, between Don Army and Volunteer Army. This concentration in the center of the AFSR front might just have brought Moscow's capture. (Denikin's response, according to Vrangel, was "Aha, you want to be first in Moscow.") Kakurin, the Soviet military historian, felt this to have been the best plan, and Lehovich, Denikin's biographer, saw it as the point where history might have been changed. Denikin himself, however, later claimed that he rejected Vrangel's plan because Tsaritsyn had to be held to protect Rostov, and it *is* hard to see how such a transfer could have been effected in the face of Shorin's August offensive.[19] In addition, shifting a large force 400 miles from Tsaritsyn to Kharkov would have been difficult.

Vrangel's July 1919 proposal shows that he at least could not fairly make the *other* main criticism of AFSR strategy—that Denikin moved too quickly; the involvement of Vrangel's cavalry would have led to an even more precipitate lunge. "To Moscow!" became the motto of the southern Whites from July, and the September–October advance on the Soviet capital ended in disaster. But in Moscow Denikin did find a goal, both symbolic and concrete, for his troops. Certainly this was what the army wanted; Denikin admitted that he had been optimistic in July, but so had the whole army leadership—"the Cassandras were silent." The rapid occupation of territory kept a larger enemy army off balance. "Our strength," Denikin recalled, "lay in the upsurge (*pod"em*) brought about by victory, in maneuver, and in the momentum of the advance."

206

Denikin made several important misjudgments. He did not realize how poorly consolidated his rear was, and he saw Soviet power as unpopular and unstable, ready to break under pressure. But had he (correctly) assumed effective Bolshevik consolidation he would have been even more justified in attacking, because time was not on his side; every passing week let the Reds shift more combat veterans from the Siberian front and raise fresh formations from their huge territory. The Moscow offensive failed, but that does not mean that another strategy would have succeeded. The Red Army historian Kakurin believed that Denikin's best chance would have been the earliest possible attack on Moscow.[20]

But given that he was embarking on a dangerous strategy, Denikin should have kept more control. The White advance into the central Ukraine began with Shkuro's insubordination in crossing the Dnepr. And the march north, according to Lukomsky, saw front-line units carried away by their success, "drawn north as if by a magnet." Denikin accepted the pleasant surprise but forfeited control. In the case of Sidorin's Don Army, the loss of control had fatal consequences. Denikin had since early September been trying to make Sidorin form a striking group on Don Army's left flank, next to the Volunteers, but he failed to overcome passive resistance at Don Army headquarters. Rapid cossack advances to the northeast in October and November pushed the Reds out of nearly all the Don Region. But this served no general strategic purpose, and it opened up a gap between Don and Volunteer Army. This was, then, perhaps Denikin's greatest military failing; as Egorov, the Red Commander-in-Chief, later put it, Denikin "reigned but did not rule."[21]

The AFSR had other military shortcomings. Replacement units were not as good as the veterans of 1918. Lukomsky, Denikin's war minister, recalled that a basic problem was the lack of a stable base where trained units could be formed; although the AFSR grew rapidly, many of the reinforcements were raised just behind the front line from unreliable conscripts and POWs. The British mission used the word "astonishing" to describe the contrast between new units formed from mobilized peasants and the elite Markov, Kornilov, and Drozdovsky regiments: "As infantry, the latter would have been hard to beat anywhere, whilst it would have been hard for any other infantry not to beat the former."[22] But even the elite units were being watered down.

The rear of the AFSR, however, was its real military Achilles heel. Even the best organized army, had it been in the AFSR's position, would have had trouble with its supplies. In October 1919 the leading

White units were 400 miles north of the nearest supply port (Taganrog), and 600 miles from their bases in the Kuban. The railways suffered from neglect and war damage, and the fleeing Reds had taken much of the rolling stock with them. But on top of this the AFSR supply organization, and the rear in general, were in a very poor state. Vrangel in December 1919 gave two reasons for White failure, faulty strategy and "the absolute disorder of our rear." The British Mission complained of "an entire absence of what we understand by good Q[uartermaster] work and administrative efficiency."[23]

Administrative inefficiency and poor supply lines made the advancing whites rely on *samosnabzhenie* (self-supply). The requisitioning of supplies from the local people often degenerated into looting, with extra booty being shipped to rear bases (further disrupting the railways). "Self-supply" was used to reward success, as Mai-Maevsky told Vrangel: "If you demand of officers and soldiers that they be ascetics, then they won't fight." ("Your Excellency, in such a case what would be difference between us and the Bolsheviks," asked Vrangel. "Well," came the reply, "the Bolsheviks *are* winning.") "Self-supply" led the Volunteer Army (known by its Russian abbreviation as *Dobrarmiia*) to be nicknamed "*Grab'armiia*" or "Looter Army" by its victims. In September Denikin wrote to Mai-Maevsky that he had learned from his supply officers of "this gloomy picture of grandiose looting and plunder, the bacchanalia of arbitrary rule, which reigns unchecked in the whole front-line zone."[24] Denikin, then, was aware of the problem, and its bad impact on public opinion and the troops themselves, but he could apparently do nothing about it.

Denikin was no fool, and he saw that the basic cause of failure was political rather than strategic. His strategy, his armies, *had* successfully taken most of southern Russia, over forty million people. But that, he saw later, had not been enough.

> Our liberation of vast regions was supposed to bring about a popular upsurge. . . . Would the people come over to us or would they, as in the past, remain inert and passive between two waves, between two mortally opposed camps?
>
> For a series of complicated reasons—some independent, some dependent on us—life gave an answer that was at first indecisive, and then negative.[25]

First of all, Denikin fought under the slogan of "Russia, one and indivisible," in a region that was Ukrainian in the west, cossack in the east. The cossacks were for the most part Great Russians, but there was still a tension between their desire for self-government and the centralist principles of the White leaders. The Kuban Host was the most difficult, as many were Ukrainian-speakers, and (unlike the Don and Terek Hosts) they could enjoy the luxury of politics in an area not directly threatened by the Reds and other hostile outsiders. The Kuban fought a tariff war against its neighbors and was slow in providing reinforcements for the main battlefront. The radical leaders of the Kuban *Rada* (legislature) attacked Denikin's military dictatorship, while the Great Russian press in the south vilified the Kuban politicians as *samostiyniki* ("separatists") and traitors. By early December 1919 things had reached a point where Denikin ordered a virtual coup against the Rada. Under the heavy hands of Generals Vrangel and Pokrovsky one of the most extreme Kuban "Mirabeaus" was hanged and others were exiled.

Although conflicts with the cossacks' leaders often preoccupied Denikin, these conflicts were not a major cause of his failure. Even the Kuban cossacks were on balance an asset, making up the mass of Caucasus Army at Tsaritsyn. There was much less trouble with the other cossack hosts, at least after Krasnov's fall in February 1919. It would be wrong, too, to say that Denikin brought problems upon himself by ignoring cossack rights. If anything, Denikin's problem was that so much of "his" main base territory, the Don and the Kuban, was administratively outside his control. Attempts to create a government uniting all anti-Bolshevik territories in the south were not implemented; what Denikin called the "Southern Authority" (*Vlast' iuga*) was a fiction. And reliance on the cossacks and acceptance of cossack autonomy meant alienation of the large non-cossack population. Nevertheless the cossacks were an essential part of the AFSR, which could not have existed without them.

The Ukraine, whose inhabitants eventually made up half of "Denikin's" population, was different; it gave the AFSR little of value. This was only partly because the Whites had such little time; there was also a basic antipathy between the White leaders and the Ukrainian nationalists. In any event, Denikin could not have "played the Ukrainian card." The Whites, whose main ideology was Russian nationalism, could never have come to terms with Ukrainian nationalists, *real* "samostiyniki," and furthermore Petliura had "betrayed the motherland" to the Germans in 1918. The nationalists, for their part, could hardly cooperate with a conservative movement that did not even see the "Little Russians" as a separate people.

In any event, the Ukraine was in too confused a state to offer help to anyone; there was no Ukrainian government, and no Ukrainian Army worth the name; the region had suffered years of revolution, occupation, reoccupation, anarchy, and banditry. Denikin and his governors general could no more mobilize the Ukrainian population than could Piatakov, Rakovsky, Antonov-Oseenko, and their Soviet organizers. And Petliura's nationalists themselves were no more successful in rallying the population in the winter of 1918–1919 (and again in May 1920).

The White pogroms against the Jews in the Ukraine must be mentioned here. The pogroms combined "normal" undisciplined looting with ideological antisemitism (which identified the Jews with Bolshevism). Jewish victims of murder, rape, and theft may have numbered in the hundreds of thousands,[26] but the AFSR was not the only perpetrator of pogroms; it only reached Jewish areas in the high summer of 1919. Also guilty were Petliura's armies, bandits, the local peasants, and even—on occasion—Red troops. The pogroms had no effect on the outcome of the Civil War, although they perhaps turned some public opinion in the West against the White cause. Although anti-Jewish outrages were not directly ordered by the White high command (any more than "normal" looting was), Denikin deserves criticism for not condemning them fully.

Other problems that blocked Denikin's hoped-for popular "upsurge" were common to the White movement as a whole. It is true that conditions were bad in the Soviet zone and that Denikin's area had the enormous advantage of being Russia's granary. But social and economic conditions were bad. Economic prosperity was hardly to be expected after three and a half years of world war and two of civil war, and in a region cut off from its industrial heartland. The Whites made little attempt to sort out the economic problems of the south or to encourage foreign trade. The Allies provided no economic aid. Inflation was high throughout 1919, which prevented stable wages and encouraged looting and bribe taking.

The greatest White failure was their alienation of the peasant majority. White army "self-supply" meant at best taking the peasants' property, at worst criminal looting. More important, Denikin's movement was identified with the *sharaban*, the landlord returning in his buggy (*char a banc*) in the trail of the White armies to take back the land he had lost to the peasants in 1917–1918. Denikin personally favored limited land reform, breaking up the large estates (while compensating their owners), but even his proposals got lost in government commissions. Denikin's advisers were conservative, and the local officials were more conservative still. In part this was because the White movement was essentially a movement of property owners and officers, but in mid-1920 Vrangel would show what could be done with more dynamic leadership. Only in January

210

1920 did Denikin advance the slogan "Land to the peasants and the laboring cossacks,"[27] and by then his armies had been driven back into the Kuban.

Not only did the Whites fail to provide concrete gains in the form of social reform and political representation, they even failed—like Kolchak's armies—to make promises. One of the major White weaknesses was a failure to match the scale and quality of Bolshevik propaganda. Denikin's Information Department (known as *Osvag*) was poorly organized, underfinanced, disliked by both Right and Left, and did little to try to reach the population, especially the peasantry.

Politically, too, the Whites had learned nothing from the Revolution. Peter Kenez, in his two-volume history of the southern Whites, made his central argument the idea that the Whites lost "above all because they failed to build those institutions which would have enabled them to administer the territories under their nominal rule."[28] Denikin's formal central government was the "Special Council" (*Osoboe soveshchenie*), a dozen conservative officials led (in the autumn of 1919) by General Lukomsky. The Special Council was inefficient, but it was not modified until the very end of 1919. The "cabinet of experts" that replaced it was little different. A "South Russian Government" set up in February 1920 had a wider—partly cossack—base and a more radical program, but it was ephemeral, and Denikin's toleration of it was more a gesture of despair than anything else (Denikin first publicly advocated a Constituent Assembly at about this time). Worse still, there was no effective local administration, institutions at the rural-district/county level that would have direct contact with the people.

Why the side that made the restoration of order a major plank should have presided over such chaos is a fundamental question—as it was in the case of Kolchak's regime. Denikin complained of a lack of trained and willing civilians to take on the work of administration: "I searched for people, but—I couldn't find any."[29] This came partly because the military dictatorship repelled the intelligentsia and partly from the generals' prejudices; Denikin would not work even with the moderate socialists of the Union for the Regeneration of Russia. He had to draw his support from the Kadet-oriented National Center and the more conservative Council for State Unity; only a tiny part of the south Russian population supported either group.

There *were* mitigating factors. The Whites had little time to set up a proper administration. Until May 1919 they controlled only the north Caucasus and part of the Don Region. Between May and July the AFSR offensive brought great gains, the Crimea, the lower Volga, and—perhaps most significant—the eastern Ukraine, but the Whites had only four to six months to consolidate their hold here. They had even less time in the central Ukraine, which was occupied between July and early September. As for provinces such as Kursk, Orel, and Chernigov in the north, they were in White hands for only a few weeks before the retreat began. And most of the captured provinces presented special difficulties. They had been run effectively by no one, not even the Soviets, for more than a year since the 1917 revolution. One reason why the Red Army had suffered such defeats earlier in 1919 was that it too could not control the region. There existed what Anishev, a Soviet historian of the 1920s, called a "dead zone," and the Red Army could only counterattack once it had retreated safely north of it.[30] In the late autumn Denikin was perched on the dead zone.

It has to be said that opposition to the White administration was not the work of the Bolsheviks. The Bolsheviks had little following on the Don, as a result of the earlier Soviet campaigns. The one major underground organization, at Rostov, was broken up in May 1919, and the Bolsheviks' *Donbiuro* had little success. Elsewhere the unexpected speed of the Red retreat left little time to think about creating an underground. The Ukrainian Bolsheviks set up a Trans-Front Bureau for operations behind White lines, but this had slight impact. White Counterintelligence was as effective as the Cheka in suppressing an organized enemy underground. (The Left SR contribution was a plot led by Irina Kakhovskaia, a friend of Mariia Spiridonova's, to assassinate Denikin, but nothing came of this.)

Even without Bolshevik help armed resistance groups formed in the countryside behind the White lines. How general this was is not clear, but the change of the inhabitants' mood was expressed in the Kornilov Division by a little rhyme: *"Vstrechali tsvetami, provozhaiut pulemetami"* ("They met us with flowers, they're seeing us off with machine guns").[31] The worst area was the southeastern Ukraine, and the key figure here was the anarchist Nestor Makhno. In the early summer of 1919 Makhno's peasant bands, then fighting with the Reds, had fallen apart and let General Mai-Maevsky break out; Makhno and some followers fled. Then, in the first days of October, Makhno suddenly raced back across the Dnepr to his home base at Gulai-Pole, from where he could raid Ekaterinoslav Province. He even briefly took the province capital, a sizable city (and he tried to put anarchist theory into practice there). This region was vitally important. Volunteer Army's supply lines passed through it, and it was near places vital to the whole AFSR—supply depots, ports, and even Denikin's new GHQ (at Taganrog). Denikin was able to drive Makhno off, but at the cost of committing his reserves and stripping units from the front line. Some

White veterans later maintained that it was the removal of half a dozen regiments from an already overstretched Volunteer Army that allowed the Reds to turn its open flanks at Orel and begin the successful counterattack.[32]

An unstable rear was not a problem unique to the Whites. The rear of the Red Army, with its gangs of deserters, has been called a "bubbling volcano."[33] Farther behind the lines, provinces like Smolensk, Kaluga, Tula, Riazan, Tambov and Saratov also had major problems. The Bolsheviks did not, to be sure, bring back the landlords, and they had had more time to consolidate their administration, but these provinces on the southern fringes of Sovdepia suffered heavy grain requisitioning from the hungry north. For all the Bolshevik wooing of the middle peasant, Tambov Province would be the scene of a major peasant uprising in 1920–1921. Everywhere outside the province capitals the institutions of the Bolshevik Party and the Soviet state were thinly spread. So it may be an oversimplification to say that White maladministration was *the* cause of White failure.

The great damage done by a few thousand of Makhno's partisans shows more than the Whites' failure to create a stable rear: it also shows how thinly stretched their armies were. Denikin estimated that he controlled 350,000 square miles of territory and a population of 42 million people.[34] This, however, was only at the very height of his success. Perhaps 8 million of these were in "White territory" for only a few weeks during the final offensive; no administration could have raised effective military forces quickly here. The same must be said of the 10–11 million (many of them Ukrainian) who were "liberated" between July and early September. Another 11 to 12 million people lived in the southeastern Ukraine and the Donbas, captured between May and July. Troops were raised here, but the territory had only been under White control for five months at the longest and it was in any event near the heart of Makhno's country.

The only area the Whites had held for more than five months, what might be called their real base, was the north Caucasus and part of the Don Region. But the first parts of this area had been captured only in the middle of 1918 at the earliest, and much of the rest had been a battle zone until February 1919. The total population of this base territory was only eight to nine million people, with the cossacks, the most valuable part, numbering only three million men, women, and children. By contrast, the core of Sovdepia, the heartland of European Russia, had a population of over 60 million, six times the AFSR base, and one that was mostly Great Russian. The Bolsheviks had had a relatively long time—

twenty months by October 1919—to consolidate their hold without serious "internal" warfare. It is true that in 1919 the Red heartland faced not just the AFSR, but military threats from several directions. But by the second half of 1919—as we have seen—none of these was any longer a serious danger.

The much smaller White population was reflected in the size of the armies. Denikin claimed a total strength of 97,000–99,000 combat troops at the start of November 1919. The flanking armies numbered 26,500–28,500, and the Don Army 50,000; Volunteer "Army," spearheading the drive on Moscow, had only 20,500 men (the equivalent of two "normal" understrength divisions). Volunteer Army's elite I Corps, was never more than 11,000–12,000 infantry and 500–1500 cavalry.[35] The vast breadth of the front meant that the Whites advanced not as a solid front but as mobile columns with great gaps between them. This showed the skill and flexibility of the White leaders; it also opened their front to counterattacks. The Red combat forces facing Denikin were numerically at least half again as strong as his. Official figures for *combatants* in the Red Southern and Southeastern Army Groups on 1 November were 127,000 infantry and 21,000 cavalry. In fact the *total* personnel (including non-combat troops) of these two army groups on 3 October were no fewer than 677,000, and behind the front were the Volga, Moscow, and Orel Military Districts with a further 575,000 men. (British figures suggest that Denikin's second-line forces were as many as 130,000, although according to the best Soviet authority, Kakurin, the figure in October 1919 was only 46,000.[36])

Denikin's armies may have been relatively well equipped. British supplies alone comprised 6177 machine guns and 1121 artillery pieces; the reported strength of the two Red army groups facing Denikin was 3974 machine guns and 864 artillery pieces.[37] In their officer-volunteers and cossacks the Whites had more experienced and better-trained fighters. But more important was the fact that in terms of manpower the Whites were greatly outnumbered, that they were trying to advance on a 700-mile front with 100,000 men, that their supply lines were increasingly overstretched, and that they were the attackers—with all the extra effort that required.

How close were the Whites to victory in October 1919? White victory probably depended on a Soviet internal collapse. The loss even for a few weeks of Petrograd—the Imperial capital and the "cradle of the revolution"—would have been a major blow to Red morale and a boost to the exhausted Whites. The capture of Tula, the next major town north of Orel, would have cost the Reds their main arsenal. Further defeats might have broken the confidence of the Bolsheviks in their "specialist" high command and might have encouraged the anti-Bolshevik underground. On the other hand, even at its furthest advance the Volunteer Army was not actually at the gates of Moscow; it was 240 miles from Orel to the Soviet capital—roughly the same distance as from the German border to Paris. Even the loss of Moscow need not have meant the end for the Reds, since they still would have possessed much of the Central Industrial Region, the middle Volga, and the Urals. The Whites had only been able to advance as far as they had by stretching their forces very thinly; they were far from their bases, and further advance would have been deeper into the food-short provinces in the middle of winter.

Seen in conventional military terms the White campaign faced great difficulties. Seen in political terms White prospects became even dimmer. The British mission told Denikin in February 1920 that "the procedure hitherto adopted would have led to complete shipwreck if you had reached Moscow, because you would have left behind you an occupied area which would not have been consolidated."[38]

III

1920: YEAR OF VICTORY

With the devil, but for Russia and against the Bolsheviks.

General P. N. Vrangel, 1920

15

THE END OF DENIKIN,
November 1919–March 1920;
THE CAUCASUS,
1918–1921

Proletarians to Horse!

Trotsky, September 1919

Soldatiki—k nam/Dobrovol 'tsy—po domam/Ofitseriki—po grobam. [Soldiers—
to us/Volunteers—to your homes/Officers—to your graves.]

Red Army leaflet

To all those who honourably accompanied me in the heavy struggle—a
low bow.
God grant victory to the Army and save Russia.

Denikin's Last Order, 4 April 1920

Retreat to the Don

"From the sublime to the ridiculous is only one step." What Napoleon
said about *his* Moscow campaign could apply equally to Denikin. In
October 1919 his armies raced—unstoppably it seemed—toward the
Red capital. At the end of the month they were checked, attacked from
both flanks. Then, between the middle of November and beginning of
January, in seven weeks, the Whites collapsed. They retreated in
disorder for 450 miles, not stopping until they had crossed the Don
River. By the start of April 1920 the cossack bases had been lost forever,
the AFSR liquidated, and Denikin himself deposed and exiled.

The same things that kept Denikin from Moscow in the autumn—numerical weakness, poor organization, lack of mass appeal—explain his inability to hold firm at the end of 1919. The price of "self-supply" was now paid; Vrangel reported that Volunteer Army retreated "through places where the population had learned to hate it." There were no organized reserves and no fortified fall-back positions. The railways were choked. By December Denikin had 42,700 sick and wounded—compared to a peak combat strength of 100,000. "Probably no army," the British mission reported, "has ever been so handicapped from a medical point of view."[1]

The speed of the retreat is also explained by the Red cavalry. The mobility and striking power of the cossack cavalry had helped in the early White victories. The Reds had been slow to respond; for the Bolsheviks cavalry was counterrevolutionary, for their officer "specialists" it was obsolete. The Mamontov Raid was the shock that changed Soviet attitudes. "The Red Army's principal misfortune is its shortage of cavalry," Trotsky announced in September 1919, and there followed his famous and bizarre slogan: 'Proletarians, to horse!" Large cavalry units were formed, though these were not factory workers on horseback (except for commissars and party organizers); most were Don and Kuban cossacks, or cavalry veterans of the World War. New cavalry units were raised in the rear, existing units were merged into a mobile war-winning mass. The most famous formation of the Red Army, First Cavalry Army (*Konarmiia*), was formed in mid-November, with 4th, 6th, and 11th Cavalry Divisions; by the beginning of 1920 it had 15,000 riders, 19 guns, 238 machine guns, and eight armored trains.[2]

Semen Budenny, commander of First Cavalry Army, came from a family of poor Don inogorodnye; he had been a Tsarist cavalryman since 1903, serving in the wars of 1904 and 1914, winning medals for gallantry and rising to the rank of sergeant-major (*vakhmistr*). From the spring of 1918 he led forces in the southeast—first a detachment, then a brigade, a division, a corps, and finally Konarmiia. The Cavalry Army was closely associated with Stalin, and its leaders—mostly of humble origin—would flourish while others perished. *Marshal* Budenny was buried with great ceremony in Red Square in 1970 (despite his fearful defeats in 1941); Marshal Timoshenko (commander of 6th Division) led the Red Army at the start of the Second World War; and Marshal Zhukov, Stalin's greatest soldier, began his career in Konarmiia as a young squadron commander.

Main Commander-in-Chief Kamenev described the happy situation: "The enemy's main trump, by the will of fate, passed to us." He was helped by Denikin's slowness to grasp the potential of massed cavalry.

Only after Budenny's success did a stunned Denikin try to concentrate northeast of Kharkov a big cavalry force—IV Don, II and III Kuban Corps. The conflict with the Kuban Rada hurt the morale of the Kuban units, and the Don Cossacks were outraged when their beloved General Mamontov was replaced by General Ulagai, who had led Kuban units under Vrangel. In any event, Ulagai's cavalry force was swept away in the Red advance before it could complete its assembly. In late December Ulagai reported the worst: "in general, we have no cavalry."[3]

The breakup of the White cavalry was matched by the breakup of the White high command. Early in December Denikin moved Vrangel from Caucasus Army to Volunteer Army, replacing the shattered Mai-Maevsky. But Vrangel, the daring cavalry leader, the conqueror of the North Caucasus and Tsaritsyn, failed. He inherited an army in full retreat, he squabbled with the Volunteer commanders, and he was ill with typhus. He did avert Budenny's attempts to cut him off from Don Army, but on 3 January he himself was replaced.

All along the front the AFSR was in retreat. Kiev fell on 16 December, Tsaritsyn on 3 January. Denikin hoped to make a stand with his main forces on the north side of the Don, building up a defensive zone around Rostov and Novocherkassk. He later argued that the AFSR was superior in manpower and equipment to the overstretched Red spearheads and could have stopped them—but what the Whites now lacked was spirit. As the remnants of Volunteer and Don Armies came together near the mouth of the Don the main desire of the White soldiers was to get through the neck of the bottle and put the river between themselves and the Red cavalry. "Nature favored her own sons," as one Don officer put it; the river froze, allowing the Whites across, and then thawed to block the Reds. Novocherkassk and Rostov, on the north bank, were taken by the Reds on 7 January. The Whites had saved themselves from encirclement, but they had lost everything captured in 1919.

The Destruction of the AFSR

From a strictly military point of view Denikin should not have suffered final defeat as quickly as he did. The Reds took ten days to prepare a Don crossing and when it came, on 17 January, they were driven off with heavy losses; Budenny's cavalry suffered most heavily. Then, in an abortive crossing of the Manych River in early February, First Cavalry Army lost most of its artillery. The Red command was in turmoil.

Colonel Shorin had back in August 1919 been charged with the main blow against the AFSR. When, after five months of battle, he finally reached his objective he was dismissed. (Budenny complained directly to Lenin about the way Shorin had used the Cavalry Army—"It is clearly a criminal matter"—but the decision to relieve Shorin had come a week earlier, after the first pause on the Don.)[4] In another incident Sergeant Dumenko, commander of the second largest Red cavalry force, was arrested and shot after a murky affair involving the killing of his corps commissar.

The main Red force was Caucasus Army Group (Shorin's old Southeastern Army Group plus First Cavalry and Eighth Armies). It is true that at the beginning of February the new Army Group comprised 215,000 men, as opposed to 60,000 Whites. But Red combat troops were only 48,000 infantry and 23,000 cavalry, men who had just completed a lightning winter campaign of up to 450 miles.[5] They too suffered from typhus. A vast gap of unstable territory separated them from the Soviet heartland. The Red forces were as exposed as they had been in the spring of 1919.

As for Denikin's armies, Kamenev had had to report to the Soviet Defense Council on 27 January that they

> are able to offer renewed strong resistance, making use of this breathing space to put themselves in order; squeezed by our armies into a limited front they are in the middle of their base where reinforcements can easily be raised, given the readiness of the population of the North Caucasus for a bitter battle where even women and children fight.[6]

In fact, Denikin was not able to take advantage of this situation. He did make unprecedented concessions to gain support. Bogaevsky, the Don Ataman, replaced the "Russsian" conservative Lukomsky as head of the Council of Ministers, itself a replacement for the discredited Special Council. When the Supreme Krug, an assembly of all the cossack hosts, met in January 1920, Denikin promised a Constituent Assembly and land reform. Sidorin, the Don Army Commander-in-Chief (and a cossack), was put in overall charge of the main front, including the Volunteers (now reduced to a corps). A separate Kuban Army was set up for the first time, under Shkuro. But all this was to no avail. Kuban Army fell apart, opening gaps in the White lines. The cossacks argued among themselves. The Russian officers felt that cossack "traitors" could not see beyond their own interests; they asked themselves, as Denikin put it, "What are we? Cannon fodder for the defense of the hated separatists?"[7]

The crumbling of the cossack rock on which Denikin's movement had been based was the greatest disaster, but it was not everything. In late January 1920 a new "Green" movement suddenly emerged in the deep rear of the White armies in Black Sea Province, where the beautiful wooded hills sheltered bands of White deserters. The Greens were led by the SRs and brought turmoil to the rapidly shrinking rear areas of the AFSR. Morale among the defenders of the Kuban was also damaged by the failure on the other White fronts. General Iudenich was interned in Estonia; in early February Kolchak was shot; the last Ukrainian foothold, Odessa, was lost on the same day; at the end of February Arkhangelsk fell. Allied support disappeared. Lloyd George made a speech in the London Guildhall on 8 November 1919, prefiguring an end to British support; in January the blockade was lifted, and in February the border states were called to make terms with Moscow.

The Reds had meanwhile weathered their command crisis. The new Commander-in-Chief of Caucasus Army Group from early February 1920 was Mikhail Tukhachevsky; he was only twenty-six and had been a mere lieutenant, but he had already had great success as commander of Fifth Army against Kolchak. A strong team of commissars was brought in, including Smilga, Gusev, and Ordzhonikidze.

Denikin hoped to exploit the Reds' difficulties by an attack to the north across the Don with Volunteer and III Don Corps; on 20 February Rostov was again in his hands. This was, as it turned out, the last success of the AFSR. Had the attack been mounted just a little earlier the tables might have been turned, as Kamenev himself later admitted.[8] The Reds, however, had struck first, on 14 February. After the failure of its head-on attack on the Don, First Cavalry Army was moved east around the White flank. Now it pushed in, opening the White rear with a drive southwest along the Tsaritsyn-Ekaterinodar railway into the heart of the Kuban. Denikin sent his own cavalry to cut off the Red spearhead. A forced march by II and IV Don Corps over the deserted steppe in temperatures of −15 degrees Fahrenheit froze men and horses to death. Less than half arrived, and in a confused series of battles around Egorlykskaia the White cavalry, Denikin's last mobile reserve, was defeated.

Denikin had to pull back, first from Rostov, then from the whole Don river line. The key junctions at Bataisk and Tikhoretskaia fell on 1 and 9 March. The last line of defense was the Kuban River, but by now the Whites were incapable of serious resistance. Ekaterinodar was abandoned on 17 March. Denikin's staff lost control. His troops simply marched, blocked by refugees and harried by the Greens, toward the appararent salvation of the sea. One White officer looked at the crowds of soldiers, cossacks and refugees, the strings of loaded carts, Kalmyk families driving herds of cattle and sheep: "The Exodus of the Russian people reminded me of Biblical times."[9]

Safety, temporary at least, lay 150 miles across the Black Sea in the Crimea. General Slashchev had fought a successful defense there against the Reds, thanks to his own abilities and the easily defended Perekop Isthmus, but he was helped by the fact that Moscow did not consider the Crimea a first priority. This was to prove a costly mistake for the Soviet side. The British provided ships to carry White forces from Novorossiisk in the Kuban to the Crimean ports, but there was not room or time to take everyone. (They also landed a battalion of the Royal Scots Fusiliers to cover the withdrawal.) Novorossiisk was an anthill of demoralized troops and refugees. British stores were thrown into the sea. Cossacks shot their horses. Some 34,000 were taken off by 27 March 1920, including 19,300 from Volunteer Corps and 11,850 from Don Army. (Don Army was considerably larger, which suggests Denikin's men were put first in line.) The Reds captured 22,000 Whites in the town. Other White troops retreated south down the coast. Some were picked up by White ships at Tuapse and taken to the Crimea, others slipped into Georgia. The end for 60,000, however, came in late April when they surrendered at Sochi.[10]

Denikin was among the last to leave Novorossiisk, but his leadership did not survive the Kuban debacle. At the start of January, just before Rostov fell, there was talk of a "generals' revolution," in which Vrangel tried with little success to organize the senior commanders against their Commander-in-Chief. Denikin struck back: on 21 February Vrangel, Lukomsky, and a number of other White leaders in the Crimea were dismissed from the army and went into exile. By the end of March the AFSR had failed, and the search for scapegoats led to attacks on Denikin's chief of staff (and closest friend), General Romanovsky (who was to be assassinated—probably by a disgruntled officer—in April). Denikin's will to command was broken when Kutepov, the Volunteer Corps commander, demanded that Denikin's Stavka not embark before the army; for Denikin this was the worst personal blow he had suffered, and he resolved to resign once he "had drunk to the bottom the bitter cup of the Novorossiisk evacuation."[11] But there was still affection for Denikin, and a Council of War in the Crimea in April had great difficulty choosing a successor. The problem was partly repugnance at "electing" a commander, partly the apparently hopeless task of continuing the Civil War. In the end Vrangel emerged as the leading

224

candidate, and Denikin was prevailed upon to "appoint" his rival as successor.

Anton Denikin was in some ways a humble figure who had been thrown up by history, and he had no strong ambition to rule. "My program," he said, "consists of restoring Russia and then raising cabbage." An excellent young division commander in the World War, he failed to give the soldiers of the counterrevolution the firm operational and political control that might have given them victory. Less of a narrow conservative than many of the men around him, he failed to force through flexible policies that might have won public support. Denikin was before all else a Russian nationalist. That explains his self-defeating policies and his ignoring of social issues. It also explains those remarkable strengths his movement had. It was part of Denikin's tragedy that he lost what he most believed in. Exile followed resignation; in April 1920 he left for Constantinople in a British destroyer. He would never see his country again. Six years later he described his leavetaking:

> When we put to sea it was already night. Only bright lights scattered in the thick darkness marked the coast of the receding Russian land. They grow dimmer and vanish.
> *Rossiia*, my Motherland . . .[12]

The Caucasus, 1917–1920

The fighting in the Don and the Kuban in 1918–1920 had been bounded to the south by the Caucasus Mountains, which stretched 930 miles between the Black and Caspian Seas and included peaks over 18,000 feet high. Pro-Soviet forces dominated the lowland parts of the Terek and Dagestan Regions until early 1919, pro-Denikin Terek Cossacks until early 1920, then the Reds again. None of these fully extended their power into the remote mountain valleys; even after the final Red victory there was a Moslem rising (September 1920). The *gortsy* ("mountain people") were divided into many small ethnic groups, mostly poor and backward. Their relations with one another, and with the lowland Russians, were complex. Fighting began with the October Revolution and continued for three years. The region's fate was decided elsewhere, but the Reds found a local political base by supporting warlike and land-hungry tribes (especially the Chechen and Ingush) against the Terek Cossacks. The Reds eventually formed two "autonomous" republics here, the Mountain and Dagestan ASSRs.

More important was the region *beyond* the mountains, the Transcaucasus. There were few roads through the high passes and the only railway ran along the Caspian coast. In May 1918, after a brief experiment in federation, three states appeared: Azerbaidzhan, on the Caspian; Georgia, on the Black Sea; and Armenia, sandwiched between Azerbaidzhan, Georgia, and Turkey. The Transcaucasus was one of the few places to miss the first "Triumphal March of Soviet Power"; the exception was the Caspian oil town of Baku, run by Bolsheviks from April 1918. (The Baku Commune was overthrown in July; its leaders, the famous "26 Commissars," were shot by anti-Bolshevik Russians.) Foreign intervention was important, but the new states were independent of Russia. By the end of 1918 the Reds had no contact with the region, given White control of the north Caucasus and the Caspian; Denikin, meanwhile, was preoccupied with the Moscow campaign. But victory in the Kuban (March 1920) opened the Red Army's road to the Transcaucasus. Azerbaidzhan passed to Soviet control in April 1920, Armenia in November, and Georgia in February 1921.

The Russian Civil War was a war of liberation for some minority peoples; in the 1920 treaties Moscow accepted the independence of the Estonians, Latvians, and Lithuanians. The Georgians, Armenians, and Azerbaidzhanis, however, were incorporated into Soviet Russia. One factor working against the Transcaucasian peoples was size: there were 2,000,000 Georgians, 1,800,000 Azerbaidzhanis, and 1,600,000 Armenians. Azerbaidzhan and Georgia were each about 30,000 square miles in area, while the "Russian" core of Armenia was about half that size. An area of 30,000 square miles is not *that* small; it was twice the size of Estonia and comparable to modern Austria. But it was very little compared to the Soviet Russia of 1920. National consciousness was also limited. The Transcaucasus, it is true, had only been part of the Empire for about 120 years and had very different languages and cultures from that of Great Russia; only about five percent of the population, moreover, were Great Russians. But modern nationalism was restricted to a small intelligentsia. Some 80 percent of the population were rural, mostly poor peasants. The minorities had not even seized their independence in 1917; it came about with the collapse of the Empire. Although the republics had several years' grace (much more than the Ukraine) and there was one dominant political faction within each (the nationalist Musavat and Dashnak parties in Azerbaidzhan and Armenia, and the Mensheviks in Georgia), they did not create successful state

226

structures. The nationalist governments of Azerbaidzhan and Armenia undertook little social reform, and Marxist Georgia's reforms made her only marginally stronger. Their armies were all weak; there were no cossacks, no foreign-trained force, and little military aid from outside. Within each of the three states there were also large ethnic sub-minorities.

The three small Transcaucasian states might have survived had they cooperated, but they were as different from one another as from the Russians, and had a long history of bitter feuds. The Armenians and Georgians were Christians, but traditionally hostile to one another. Both were deeply suspicious of the Moslem Tatars (Azerbaidzhanis); it was this—coupled with the Turkish advance of 1918—that broke up the Transcaucasus Democratic Federative Republic after only two months. But even separate statehood could not sort out areas of mixed population—where no ethnic frontier could be drawn. Each state squabbled with the others; most striking was the Azerbaidzhan-Armenia border war, which tied up the Azerbaidzhan forces in 1920 at the moment the Red Army took Baku.

Some or all of the republics might have survived with outside backing, but no outsiders had lasting influence. The Germans protected Georgia, but only in 1918. Turkey invaded the region in 1918, supporting Moslem Azerbaidzhan. But in 1919–1921 Turkey was shattered by defeat and lacked a common border with Azerbaidzhan, and neither Georgia nor Armenia would use their traditional enemy to counterbalance Russia. The Armenians, in particular, made great territorial claims against Turkey, leading to a successful Turkish invasion in late 1920, which in turn precipitated the Red takeover. Nationalist Turkey and Soviet Russia, both victims of the Allied peacemakers, worked together; the Treaty of Moscow (16 March 1921) formalized Russia's hold over the Transcaucasus at the cost of confirming the loss to Turkey of most of the territory (to the west of Armenia) ceded at Brest-Litovsk. The Allies did little, despite great efforts by Transcaucasian diplomats at the Paris Peace Conference. The British had landed a small force from Persia in 1918, and in 1919 a British division garrisoned the Batum-Baku (Black Sea-Caspian) railway. Whatever the region's economic and strategic potential, the British lacked the strength and will to hold the Transcaucasus (despite Soviet accusations—and Denikin's sense of British duplicity). (The British theater commander, at least, was unimpressed by the region's value: "I cannot see that the world would lose much if the whole of the country cut each other's throats. They are certainly not worth the life of one British soldier.")[13] Italy and the United States considered—but rejected—mandates. The Allies even recognized the

227

three republics de facto (January 1920), but this had no real impact. The Transcaucasus governments were meanwhile unwilling to throw in their lot with the White Russians, whom they knew opposed their independence. Georgia had a prolonged conflict with Denikin over part of the Black Sea coast; she also gave aid to the Greens and, with Azerbaidzhan, to the anti-Denikin *gortsy* (tribesmen).

In the end it was the attitude of Moscow that was decisive. For the Bolsheviks Transcaucasian independence was a sham; in general they had contempt for "bourgeois nationalism," and these states in particular were seen as the creatures of imperialism. Some leading Bolsheviks had a special interest in the region, including the Georgians Ordzhonikidze and Dzhugashvili-Stalin (Stalin called his homeland "the kept woman of the Entente").[14] And any Russian government would have wanted the mineral wealth of the region; Baku had been the center of the world's largest oil field, and the whole of the Transcaucasus, not just Azerbaidzhan, was needed to defend Baku against foreign attack.

Indeed, the Reds began to move into the Transcaucasus as soon as Denikin's defeat made it physically possible. On 22 March 1920, in the last stages of the Kuban battle, Colonel Kamenev ordered occupation of "the whole of the former Baku Province" (i.e., eastern Azerbaidzhan).[15] A Caucasus Bureau (*Kavkazkoe Biuro* or *Kavbiuro*) of the Bolshevik CC had been set up behind the Red Army in April 1920, led by Ordzhonikidze. Several divisions of Eleventh Army were massed on the Caspian rail line. This, confusion in Azerbaidzhan's nationalist Musavat government, and an uprising in Baku led to the surrender of power to a Bolshevik RevCom. The RevCom "requested Soviet military assistance" —which was already on the way. The first armored trains reached Baku on 28 April 1920, and an Azerbaidzhan Socialist Soviet Republic was declared.

The Reds paused after the Azerbaidzhan coup; on 7 May 1920 a treaty promising non-intervention was signed with Georgia. The general situation was unfavorable. Moscow was trying to come to terms with London, and there were still British troops in the Georgian Black Sea port of Batum. In March 1920 Colonel Kamenev had urged caution, given the state of the Red Army—and then came the Polish War (April 1920), followed by Vrangel's attack out of the Crimea (June).[16] Once the Polish and Vrangel campaigns had stabilized, however, the pressure was renewed. The Turks invaded southern Armenia in September 1920; in the crisis the Dashnak government surrendered power to a Bolshevik "RevCom of Armenia," which had been organized in Azerbaidzhan and which arrived with Soviet troops. The Armenian SSR was set up in November 1920.

Georgia survived Armenia by three months, and the Soviet takeover was a confused affair. The Menshevik government in Tiflis had been stable, had been recognized by major western states, and had the support of foreign socialists. Turkey's position was still unclear. Soviet Russia, meanwhile, faced economic and political problems, and the Red Army was being demobilized. Sovietization, when it came, had much to do with the fait accompli of Ordzhonikidze's *Kavbiuro*. The Moscow CC approved the action only after it had begun, and apparently neither Trotsky or Main Commander-in-Chief Kamenev had had advance warning.[17] A RevCom of Georgia was set up in February 1921; it declared a Georgian SSR and called in Red Army support. In violation of the May 1920 treaty, Gekker's Red Eleventh Army advanced from western Azerbaidzhan (with some support from Ninth Army moving down the Black Sea coast). The Red Army met more opposition in Georgia than elsewhere in the Transcaucasus—there was a week-long battle for Tiflis—but resistance was still limited.

The takeovers of all three republics by Soviet Russia were not without internal support. Social revolution had its appeal; most of the population was poor, and economic hardship had been increased by war, revolution, and separation from Russian supplies and markets. In Azerbaidzhan a working-class movement and a Bolshevik underground had survived the 1918 Baku Commune; Georgia also had a radical Left. Armenia had no significant underground, but the Bolsheviks represented the protection of Russian power against Turkey. The Bolsheviks had also learned from their mistakes. Nominally separate Communist Parties were set up in 1920 in Azerbaidzhan (February), Georgia (May), and Armenia (July), and even national independence could be granted (in the form of the three "soviet republics"). But there was no sign of a strong local desire for union with the Russian proletariat. Attempts in Georgia and Armenia (in May 1920) to seize power by internal uprising alone failed. Even after the invasions the Soviet grip was weak. Two major anti-Soviet revolts broke out in Azerbaidzhan in 1920, and Ordzhonikidze reported in June that the whole Eleventh Army was needed to keep control;[18] the Armenian capital was retaken by the Dashnaks in February–April 1921 (and in 1924 there would be a great rising in Georgia). The threat, potential or actual, of the victorious Red Army was a vital element in maintaining the Soviet hold on the region.

16

STORM OVER ASIA:
SIBERIA, November 1919–1922;
CENTRAL ASIA, 1918–1920

Within a year one of two things will have happened; either the Constituent Assembly will have met in Moscow or I shall be dead.

Admiral Kolchak, Spring 1919

Kolchak Destroyed

Kolchak's armies were broken at the same time as Denikin's, although their retreat had begun earlier. Omsk, the Supreme Ruler's capital, fell on 14 November 1919 (as the AFSR pulled back from Orel). By March 1920 (as Denikin was making his last stand in the Kuban) the Red Army had advanced another 1500 miles, taking all of central Siberia as far as Lake Baikal.

The Whites might have made a better showing. I. N. Smirnov's SibRevCom and the Bolshevik CC's *Sibbiuro* were hard put to regain some control over the vast captured territory of central Siberia. Older-ogge's Eastern Army Group headquarters was dispersed (finally in January 1920). A number of Red divisions were sent back to European Russia. Third Army became a "Labor Army," committed to the economic reconstruction of the Urals. Only the five divisions of Fifth Army (commanded by Major Eikhe in place of Tukhachevsky) continued beyond Omsk. They started 1900 miles from Moscow, with only a badly damaged supply line back to the Bolshevik heartland, and they were to cover the same distance again in midwinter.

The White armies, however, were in a terrible state. Never very effective, lacking a fighting core, their will had been broken. Tens of thousands of POWs and much of Kolchak's stores were taken at Omsk. As more and more of Siberia was occupied by the Reds, so most of Kolchak's remaining peasant conscripts slipped away home. What was left of the armies was riddled by typhus. The frozen railway was choked with trains, and partisans moved in from north and south. The White command was in spectacular disorder. General Diterikhs had resigned as Main Commander-in-Chief over defending Omsk. General Sakharov then lost the city, and was overthrown in turn (early December) by rival leaders. The conspirators installed the most able White commander, Kappel—who had nearly trapped Trotsky at Sviiazhsk in 1918—but it was too late.

The great rivers of Siberia were now frozen and presented no obstacle to the Red advance. The White Second and Third Armies were unable to make a planned defense of the Ob (400 miles east of Omsk); Novoniko-laevsk (now Novosibirsk) fell on 14 December 1919, and First Army, reforming behind the Ob at Tomsk, simply disintegrated through mass desertion. Some 450 miles east of the Ob, at Krasnoiarsk on the Enisei River, things were even worse, and military defeat was followed by urban revolt. In early January 1920, the city was seized by anti-Kolchak forces—including SRs, the garrison, and its commander. The main White armies' path of retreat along the railway was blocked, and they were too weak and disorganized to fight their way through. Three days later, on 7 January, the Red Fifth Army and partisans reached the city; 200 guns were captured, and 60,000 prisoners (bringing to 100,000 the number taken in the Red pursuit).[1]

Only a few Whites, under General Kappel, escaped, abandoning their trains and road transport and taking to small sledges. The five-week retreat from Krasnoiarsk to Lake Baikal, through the Siberian wilderness was called the Ice March. Kappel himself was struck by frostbite and pneumonia while leading his survivors along a frozen river in 40 degrees of frost; he died on 26 January.

Krasnoiarsk was a sympton of Kolchak's catastrophic political weakness. His civil administration had never been strong, but after the loss of Omsk he had hardly any state at all. Kolchak made changes in his government personnel and promised a "State Assembly," but these were just signs of desperation. The ministers moved to Irkutsk, but lacked authority. Kolchak had not remained with his armies, but neither had he moved east with his government, where he might at least have secured control of Irkutsk. (One thing that greatly slowed him down was the thirty-six heavily laden freight cars carrying the gold and silver of the Imperial reserve—originally captured at Kazan.) Instead, the political collapse continued further east. The power vacuum made it possible for the socialist opposition to reappear for the first time since mid-1918. Even before the Krasnoiarsk disaster an anti-Kolchak "Political Center" had begun to seize power around Irkutsk; the town was completely in its hands by 4 January. At first the Mensheviks and SRs were dominant, because of their roots in the region and the earlier destruction of the Bolshevik underground. They hoped to create their own state in Siberia, and even to get the cooperation of Kolchak's commanders. The Political Center might have let Kolchak pass through Irkutsk to the east unharmed, until some of their supporters were massacred as hostages by pro-Kolchak forces.

Admiral Kolchak's own fate was determined by his foolishly cutting himself off from both his army and his government. But the action and inaction of foreigners were also important here. The Czechoslovak Corps, withdrawn from the front in late 1918 and assigned to patrol the railway west of Irkutsk, now had life-or-death control over who passed along it to safety. The Czechoslovaks had never liked Kolchak's regime; they were sympathetic to the Irkutsk socialists; and they did not want the Political Center to block their own escape route. The result was that the Czechoslovaks first trapped Kolchak's trains for two weeks west of Irkutsk, and then, on 15 January, handed him over to the Political Center. "It seems," Churchill sadly recalled, "that for a while these legionaries forsook the stage of History on which they had hitherto acted and mingled with the ragged and demoralized Siberian audience."[2] The British and French representatives did little to save the man they had supported for so long.

Six days after Kolchak was handed over, the Political Center was replaced by the Bolshevik-dominated Irkutsk Military-Revolutionary Committee. The admiral was interrogated, secretly, by a Bolshevik lawyer, a Menshevik, and two SRs, between 21 January and 6 February 1920. He spoke candidly and with dignity. It was planned to try him in Moscow, but the Red Army was still far away; the White army, now under General Voitsekhovsky, was on the highway between it and Irkutsk. The night before the White troops arrived, on 6–7 February, Kolchak and his prime minister were shot, and their bodies thrown through the ice of a frozen river.

Lenin had ordered that Kolchak not be killed, probably because he did not want to stiffen the White resistance on other fronts; after the execution he tried to keep the news secret. In any event, of the leaders of the all-Russian White movement only Admiral Kolchak was caught and executed. He was the "Supreme Ruler" of the White movement for 14 months, but he was not its most important or capable leader. "His fate," one minister recalled, "was to wear on his honest head not the Cap of Monomakh but a crown of thorns" (the Cap was the Tsarist crown).[3] In the end he died a victim of the chaos that had dominated so much of his regime.

Voitsekhovsky's troops passed Irkutsk without entering it and then crossed the ice of Lake Baikal to eastern Siberia. The Czechoslovaks, for their part, arranged an armistice with the Reds; in exchange for Kolchak's gold reserve they were allowed to withdraw without hindrance. On 5 March 1920 the Red Army reached Irkutsk and completed the capture of central Siberia.

The Reds created a military and administrative bridgehead on the far side of Lake Baikal, but Soviet power was not victorious throughout the Russian Far East until thirty-two months after Kolchak's death. Lenin told Trotsky in February 1920 that

> everyone in Siberia should carry out the slogan: 'not a step farther east, all-out efforts for the rapid movement of troops and locomotives to the west, to Russia'. We would be idiots if we were to allow ourselves to be distracted by a stupid advance into the depths of Siberia, permitting Denikin to revive and the Poles to strike.[4]

A special problem was the Japanese Army's presence in Transbaikal Region and farther east. Early in 1920 the Bolshevik Smirnov set up a government, the Far Eastern Republic (FER), with nominal control over all the territory from Lake Baikal to the Pacific. This had originally been proposed by the SR-Menshevik Political Center, although their proposal envisaged real independence; in fact the new republic was closely supervised by the *Dalbiuro* (Far Eastern Bureau) of the Bolshevik CC, and its role was to act as a buffer. The FER had the value of being an "acceptable" government; the outside world would deal with the FER when it would not deal with Soviet Russia. The "People's Revolutionary Army" of the FER was composed of Red Army units, commanded by Major Eikhe (formerly of Red Fifth Army), and controlled by the new "Assistant Main Commander-in-Chief for Siberia," General Shorin.

At first not only the independence but the territory of the FER was a fiction; the bulk of even Transbaikal Region was still controlled by Ataman Semenov in Chita, and the "Chita Cork" blocked any advance along the railway to the Pacific. Semenov had been a thorn in Kolchak's side in 1918–1919, but in his last weeks the admiral had made him overall commander of White Siberia (mainly because Semenov alone seemed to have the strength to rescue him). There was a parallel in time and situation with General Vrangel, who shortly afterward succeeded General Denikin; Vrangel had the Crimea as a base, Semenov Transbaikal. There the resemblance ended. Unlike Vrangel, Semenov lacked the resources and skill to counterattack or even make a stand; a Red attempt to take Chita in the spring of 1920 was beaten off, but Semenov could not hold out for very long. The natural barrier of Lake Baikal had been broken by the Reds. Transbaikal was sparsely settled and backward, and the population were thoroughly alienated by the demands of Semenov's lieutenants and of the Transbaikal and Ussuri cossack forces. The refugee survivors from Kolchak's army, the "Kappel Men," disliked Semenov and had no desire to fight for him or Transbaikal. And Transbaikal was isolated, with no support in the three other east Siberian regions: Iakutsk Region was remote and empty, Amur Region was controlled by pro-Soviet partisans, and Primorskaia Region was run from Vladivostok by a leftist zemstvo government.

The decisive element was the Japanese withdrawal from Transbaikal, which was followed by an attack by the FER army and the partisans. Chita fell on 22 October 1920, popping the cork. Semenov was able to fly out of his capital; the survivors of his forces had to fight their way to the Manchurian border. In November 1920, the moment when Vrangel's Crimean army was making the final White departure from European Russia, Transbaikal passed to the control of the FER, and with it most of eastern Siberia.

With the loss of Transbaikal one of Semenov's lieutenants, Baron Ungern-Sternberg, took a small force south into Outer Mongolia; nominally part of China, this region had a large area and a tiny nomadic population. After prolonged fighting Urga (now Ulan-Bator) was taken in February 1921. Ungern-Sternberg, an unbalanced Baltic nobleman, was already notorious for his atrocities in Transbaikal, and his regime in Urga was bloody. He intended to use Mongolia as a base for war against Soviet Russia, but he was overthrown in the summer of 1921 by an Expeditionary Force from the Red Fifth Army; Ungern himself was captured and executed. A pro-Soviet government was set up, which became the Mongolian People's Republic. This was the one area beyond the 1914 Imperial borders to which Soviet power was spread; it happened also to be among the most backward and remote places on earth.

Most White survivors of the Transbaikal defeat went southeast across Manchuria to the Pacific. There followed eighteen months of three-sided confrontation between them, the Far Eastern Republic, and the crucial Japanese garrison. The surviving White zone, the southern part of Primorskaia Region, had an area about that of Norway, but its population was only 200,000–300,000. The leftist government that had taken power in Vladivostok in January 1920 was overthrown in May 1921 by the Right, supported by the Kappel veterans. The politics of the region were a shambles. The last "Ruler," from June 1922, was General Diterikhs, one of Kolchak's commanders; Diterikhs was notable for giving his state and army medieval titles (he even summoned a *Zemskii Sobor*). In the winter of 1921–1922, encouraged by successful operations against Red partisans, the Whites made their last offensive; they marched on Khabarovsk, hoping to spark off an uprising across Soviet Russia. But the FER army, now commanded by the Red veteran Bliukher, recaptured the town in February 1922.

One factor above all dominated the situation: Japan. The Japanese Army remained in Siberia after the departure of the last Americans and Czechoslovaks (in April and November 1920). Tokyo declared that a military presence was needed to prevent chaos and cited the killing by Red partisans of several hundred Japanese at Nikolaevsk (near the mouth of the Amur) in the spring of 1920. In early April 1920 the Japanese Army took effective control of Primorskaia Region, driving the Bolsheviks underground (and in one infamous incident handing over Lazo, a member of the Dalbiuro, to the Whites, who burned him alive). The Japanese garrison alone kept the Whites in power, and its withdrawal in October 1922 meant the end of the White foothold. The last Whites withdrew to Korea and Manchuria. Emigration was hard for all the Whites, but those in the Far East would suffer the most bitter conditions. Soviet troops under Uborevich entered Vladivostok on 25 October 1922; in November the puppet Far Eastern Republic was absorbed by the RSFSR. Two years after the fighting had ended in Europe the last part of "Russian" territory was cleared of counter-revolutionary and foreign forces.

Central Asia, 1918–1920

Kolchak's defeat in late 1919 opened the way not only to eastern Siberia but also to Central Asia. This region covered 1,500,000 square miles (over a third of the area of the United States, but much of it was empty steppe or desert and the total population was only 14,000,000. In the north (Kazakhstan) about 20 percent were Russian, while in the south (Turkestan) it was only five to ten percent; the great majority were Moslems (most of them Turkic-speaking): Kazakhs, Uzbeks, Kirgiz,

Turkmens, and Tadzhiks. Central Asia was the closest thing to a Tsarist colony (and the last regions had been conquered as late as the 1890s). Despite this, and despite the 2000 miles between the core of the region and Petrograd, Central Asia shared in the Triumphal March of Soviet Power—thanks to the efforts of Russian soldiers and workers living there. Most remarkable was Turkestan; Tashkent, the capital of the region, declared for Soviet power in 1917 only a few days after Petrograd, and in April 1918 it became the center of a Soviet Republic.

The Turkestan Soviet Republic was at the heart of the Civil War in Central Asia. For two years, from October 1917 to September 1919, it was cut off from the Soviet "mainland." The most dangerous counterrevolutionary center, the Orenburg Cossack Host, was far from Tashkent, 1200 miles to the northwest, but it controlled the "Orenburg Cork," the region of the south Urals through which the Tashkent-Samara-Moscow railway ran. The town of Orenburg was captured by the Reds in January 1919, but a planned "Tashkent Operation" had to be canceled when Kolchak launched his spring 1919 offensive. Troops from the central Red Army held on to Orenburg (through a long siege), but the cossacks blocked the railway line south of the town, and in the summer they pushed Tashkent's forces as far south as the Aral Sea. (Civil War in Turkestan, even in 1919, was a "railway war"; the "fronts" numbered only a few thousand on each side, mostly Russians.) Final Red victory became possible with Kolchak's defeat. North of Orenburg the Reds had been building up their forces, now called Turkestan Army Group; their commander was M. V. Frunze, a Bolshevik who had grown up in a Turkestan settler family. Kolchak's Southern Army was finally crushed between Frunze's First Army and the Tashkent forces; in mid-September 1919 the two Red groups joined hands on the railway, 300 miles from Orenburg and 900 from Tashkent.

Turkestan Army Group then devoted the winter of 1919–1920 to destroying the remnants of the Orenburg and Ural cossack armies in the wild country between the southern Urals and the Caspian (a few survivors of the Ural Cossak Host eventually reached Persia, after an 800-mile trek across the Transcaspian desert). Successes on this front, together with the main advance along the Trans-Siberian, assured Soviet dominance in the vast but thinly populated steppe region (modern Kazakhstan) between Siberia and Turkestan. A vast Kirgiz Autonomous SSR was set up in August 1920, with its capital at Orenburg; in addition to the lands of the Kazakh nomads (then known as the Kirgiz), the new ASSR incorporated the former lands of the Ural and Orenburg cossacks. (The Kirgiz ASSR should not be confused with the modern Kirgiz SSR, which is in southeast Central Asia.)

In late 1918 and early 1919 the most active front had been along the Turkestan's other railway, which ran west from Tashkent to the Caspian port of Krasnovodsk. The enemy here were, curiously enough, anti-Bolshevik Russian railway workers; their Transcaspian government was set up after an uprising in Askhabad—800 miles west of Tashkent —in July 1918 (this government's closest parallel was Izhevsk). Transcaspia benefited from the support of the British, who—worried about German-Turkish penetration—sent detachments overland from Persia in August 1918. But with the British withdrawal in the spring of 1919 the Transcaspian Government was gradually forced back toward the Caspian. The Reds were able to concentrate here once the Orenburg cork had been popped, and the front was liquidated with the capture of Krasnovodsk in February 1920. Then the only non-Soviet centers in western Turkestan were the feudal Moslem states of Bukhara and Khiva, Tsarist protectorates made independent by the revolution. A combination of the Red Army and revolt by Moslem reformers toppled the feudal rulers, Khiva's in February 1920, and Bukhara's in September.

Tashkent had had another, smaller, front, to the northeast in Semirechie; the main town, Vernyi (Alma-Ata), was 500 miles from Tashkent, and Soviet power was threatened by the small Semirechie Cossack Host. The remains of Kolchak's southern armies withdrew here, after a 350-mile desert march, when their Siberian line of retreat was cut in late 1919. In the following spring Soviet forces took the region; the White survivors fled over the border to China, where 12,000 were interned in terrible conditions. Dutov, the Orenburg ataman and one of the first to rise against Soviet power in 1917–1918, was killed there in February 1921.

Central Asia had a different history from other regions on the eastern periphery. In the Transcaucasus, nationalists were strong enough in early 1918 to form their own governments, independent of Soviet Russia. Siberia and the north Caucasus were swept up in the first wave of Soviet power, but the first was lost to Moscow in the summer of 1918 and the second in the winter of 1918–1919. In contrast, the Turkestan Soviet Republic was never defeated (although the northern steppe and Transcaspia were lost).

The survival of Soviet power in Turkestan is another testament to the popularity of the Soviet revolution and the weakness of other forces. The situation *was* confused. There had been few Bolsheviks in Turkestan in 1917, and many of the Tashkent government's leaders were SRs. The Moslems were excluded from power and exploited economically.

The Bolshevik War Commissar, Osipov, tried in January 1919 to seize power, and actually killed many of the senior leaders of Soviet Turkestan. The Tashkent Army was run by committees and was desperately short of weapons. But all the same, its base in the Great Russian minority gave Soviet power the towns, the railways, the telegraph, and what modern weapons there were. Tashkent had the peculiar advantage, too, of its "Internationalist" troops, Austro-German POWs; there had been 155,000 of these in Turkestan at the start of 1917; most were trapped in the region and many joined the Soviet forces.

Later, the complete victory of Soviet power was assured by the breaking of the blockade and the support of the central Russian government. A general from Frunze's staff, Novitskii, led the conquest of the outlying parts of Turkestan in 1920. Moscow also limited abuses against the natives by sending south special organs of the Moscow regime, the *Turkkomissiia* (Turkestan Commission) of the Central ExCom and later the party's *Turkbiuro*. In 1919 Moslems were given more of a role in state and party, thanks to Moscow's influence. The center kept overall control, but more than a semblance of power was given to progressive natives. Kirgizia and Turkestan emerged from the fighting as autonomous republics (ASSRs) and Khiva and Bukhara were given unique status—at first—as the Khorezm and Bukhara People's Soviet Republics.

The Tashkent government was lucky that—unlike the Bolsheviks of Siberia or the north Caucasus in 1918—it did not have to face serious military opposition. Russian anti-Bolshevik forces, including cossacks, were both weak and far from Tashkent. Denikin tried to organize a "Turkestan Army" in Transcaspia in early 1919, but with little effect. Kolchak made little attempt to win over the Kazakhs (Kirgiz). Foreign involvement was limited to small British detachments in Transcaspia, but they left in the spring of 1919. Despite Britain's long interest in the "Great Game" and the "forward defense" of Persia and India, it did not intervene in strength. Russian Central Asia was very remote; the British Empire's forces were already overstretched, and the feelings of the "all-Russian" White government had to be considered.

A more basic factor in keeping "Russian" control over Turkestan and other parts of Central Asia was the political impotence of the Moslem majority. There was an attempt to form an all-Moslem government at Kokand (southeast of Tashkent) early in 1918, but this was ruthlessly crushed by (Great Russian) Red troops from Tashkent. Another ephemeral pan-Turkic government, set up in Orenburg by intellectuals of the Alash-Orda party, was suppressed at about the same time. In any event, the Moslem population was fragmented. Nearly all the Kazakhs were nomads. In Turkestan the population was scattered among separate oases. Terrible famine wore the population down even further. The great bulk of the Moslem population were alien to modern politics. Pan-Turkism was a meaningless concept for most, and Islam, although a way of life as much as a religion, did not form the basis of political movement; indeed, there were splits between reformist and conservative Moslems. Some of the Moslem reformers were won over—at least temporarily—to Soviet power. Moslem armed resistance was unsuccessful. The most serious fighting for the Tashkent government was not against the Moslems but against Russian cossacks or—in Transcaspia—Russian railway workers. Bukhara and Khiva had only primitive armies and made no attempt to form a united front with Russian anti-Bolshevik forces. The greatest Moslem challenge came from guerrilla bands, known to the Russians as the *Basmachi* (Plunderers), but these operated only on the fringes of settled territory, never threatening the Russian centers of power, and they frequently fought among themselves.

Russian Bolshevism was, on one important level, an internationalist movement, and in 1919–1920 the Bolsheviks began to talk more and more about revolution in the colonial world. In June 1920 a pro-Soviet regional government was set up at Resht in northwestern Persia. In July (as the Red Army raced across Poland) the Komintern announced a "Congress of Peoples of the East," which met in Baku in September and seemed to embody the prospect of eastern revolution. But despite all this activity, revolution in Asia—in the short term—proved even more illusory than revolution in Europe. This came, in part, from the situation in the Asian countries. The mass of the Asian population had been relatively little touched by modern politics. Communism had no organizational links, and the European empires were strong enough to contain unrest. The Baku Congress was unrepresentative and brought to the surface the difficulties of a Bolshevik partnership with Asian nationalists. Moscow became more and more aware of these difficulties by 1921, and perhaps that is why it was prepared to make concessions in Asia to ensure peace in Europe; in particular, the 1921 Anglo-Soviet Trade Agreement included a rejection of agitation against the British Empire. The failure came too because in the Civil War period there was little the Bolsheviks could do to influence events in Asia. The Red Army did not even get to the western Manchurian border until the end of 1920. Southwest Asia was little better. When the Baku Congress met, the host territory—Azerbaidzhan—was the one part of the Transcaucasus in Soviet hands, and the Red Army was needed to hold it down

239

against Musavat nationalists. Armenia and Georgia would be taken only with the help of Soviet troops.

It was Turkestan, however, that had seemed the best potential area. Stalin, for example, wrote in February 1919 (following the capture of Orenburg) that "Turkestan . . . is a bridge connecting socialist Russia with the oppressed countries of the East"; "the consolidation of Soviet power in Turkestan may exert the greatest revolutionizing influence on the entire East." Trotsky was even more excited. In August 1919, after the Red Army broke through the Urals, he urged the Bolshevik CC to begin long-term preparations for "a military thrust against India"; "The road to India may prove at the given moment to be more readily passable and shorter than the road to Soviet Hungary." In late September, when Frunze opened the rail line to Tashkent, Trotsky asked the CC to be allowed to concentrate resources "for a possible offensive by us from Turkestan southwards."[5]

But Turkestan also showed most clearly the problems behind Soviet revolutionary rhetoric. Although Delhi was—as the crow flies—no farther from Tashkent than was Orenburg, it was still 1200 miles away over some of the most rugged and inaccessible country in the world. Moscow in fact had the greatest difficulty reaching and controlling Turkestan itself. For one thing, it had to be placed low in Moscow's priorities, especially in 1919. "In my opinion," Lenin grumbled in December, "Frunze is asking too much. We must first finish taking the Ukraine, and Turkestan can wait and make the best of it."[6] When he had broken the blockade of Turkestan Frunze had first to finish off the Orenburg and Ural Cossacks, and he did not arrive in Tashkent for four months. Even in 1920 preoccupations with the European fronts and the bad state of the single-track railway across the steppe and desert from Orenburg meant that very few Red units could be sent to Turkestan; Frunze's divisions moved not into the struggle with colonialism but back to Europe to the Polish and Vrangel fronts.

Soviet power in Central Asia, and especially in Turkestan, also faced serious political problems. The demands of the native intelligentsia were crushed, at the start of Soviet rule, with their "government" at Kokand (and with a massacre of Moslems). A near-contemporary Soviet source admitted that "Turkestan's 'Left Communism' . . . in reality meant the rapacious *feudal* exploitation of the wide mass of the native population by Russian Red Guards, settlers and bureaucrats."[7] For nearly two years the Tashkent regime relied on the small Russian minority; this monopoly of power—along with policies favoring Russian farmers, economic demands on the mass of the population, decrees which offended conservative Moslem sensibilities—gave Bolshevism a weak base. The Kokand massacre was followed by an eruption of the Basmachi "front" in the Fergana Valley, southeast of Tashkent. When Moscow forced a change of line on the Tashkent government there were new problems. The Moslem reformist elite who were coopted into the Bolshevik Party in 1919–1920 were enthusiasts for a union of all Turkic peoples and eventually many either defected or had to be removed. Ultimately Great Russian domination continued—there were no Moslems in the Turkkomissiia or the Turkbiuro. The struggle with the Basmachi actually increased after the Soviet conquest of Bukhara, and continued at a high level until 1922.

Events in Turkestan—as well as in Transcaucasia and eastern Siberia—showed that Moscow had enough difficulty regaining control of the Tsarist eastern territories, without trying to set all Asia alight. Trotsky, at least, had by June 1920 given up his dreams about a "thrust against India,": "All information, about the state of Khiva, Persia, Bukhara, and Afghanistan, testifies to the fact that a Soviet revolution in these countries would at the present moment cause us the greatest difficulties." Until the Soviet economy had recovered the threat of Asian revolution could at best be used as a diplomatic tool against Britain: "a Soviet expedition in the east may prove to be no less dangerous than war in the west."[8]

17

CONSOLIDATING THE STATE: THE SOVIET ZONE, November 1919–November 1920

If we are serious about a planned economy, centrally directed, then labor must be distributed, shifted and ordered in the same way that soldiers are.

Trotsky, March 1920

Soviet autonomy is the most real, the most concrete form of the union of the border regions with central Russia.

Stalin, October 1920

The Army and the Economy

Soviet internal policies were partly dictated by the need to keep a huge Red Army. The victorious campaigns of the winter of 1919–1920 and the battles of the following summer against the Poles and General Vrangel were fought by a Red Army that had changed little in quality and organization since 1918–1919. The one qualitative change, the Red cavalry, has already been mentioned. In the winter of 1919–1920 there was talk of modifying the commissar system and starting a proper "socialist" militia system, but nothing came of this. The most striking development, as in 1918–1919, was numerical growth. In the autumn of 1919 Red Army strength had been about 2,500,000 men. By the end of 1920 it was 5,300,000—in fifty-five rifle and twenty-three cavalry divisions. Moscow's army actually *doubled* in size in the year after its decisive victories over the Whites at Orel and Omsk.[1]

The explanation for this continued growth lay partly with the

242

demands of the final campaigns: the destruction of Denikin's armies up to March 1920; the war with Poland after April (and with it the threat of renewed Allied intervention), and the final battles with Vrangel in the Crimea. The existence of Soviet Russia was no longer under immediate threat, but these campaigns were probably fought more intensely than those of 1919. And another factor was that the huge territory which had been taken in the winter of 1919–1920: the Ukraine, the north Caucasus, Turkestan, and western and central Siberia had to be garrisoned. And, as in 1919, a vast manpower reserve was necessary to create a smaller fighting force. (It was not possible to arm the huge number of new conscripts; in an average month of 1920 the army increased by 200,000 men, and yet monthly rifle production was only 35,000.[2] Whatever its justification, however, the big Red Army of 1920 was a great economic burden.

In the Soviet economy there were now a number of positive factors. Potential resources increased with the Red advance. During the summer of 1919 the Red Army took the industrial and mining districts of the Urals; in the winter of 1919–1920 it popped the Orenburg cork, opening the way to the cotton of Central Asia; it also recaptured the mining-industrial towns of the eastern Ukraine and the Donbas, and the grain-producing lands of western Siberia, the north Caucasus, and the Ukraine. The invasion of Azerbaidzhan in April 1920 gave Soviet Russia the Baku oilfields. In addition, the machinery of state was more consolidated, allowing stronger control of industry and transport, and promising greater procurements in Soviet power's third harvest.

But on the negative side, the newly captured zones were primarily a *potential* asset; the factories and mines there were in poor condition, and the countryside was in chaos. The whole Soviet transport system was in an especially bad state (and its repair was seen as a vital task); little fuel, raw material, or food could be moved into the hungry and cold heartland of the "old" Sovdepia during 1920. In that central Russian core, factories and transport were more run down than ever before, and most of what *was* produced went to the Red Army. Overall conditions in the towns were dreadful.

Soviet economic policies were not fundamentally different from those of the previous year, or indeed from those that had been introduced in the winter of 1917–1918. There was nothing to give the peasants in exchange for grain; although the "Workers' and Peasants' " government continued to stress the importance of the middle peasant, forced procurement—the *razverstka*—remained the essence of Soviet food policy. In February–March 1920 Trotsky did propose to the CC a peasant "tax in kind"—regulating the demands made on the peasants—but this was rejected. (The limited nature of the proposal did not justify Trotsky's later claim to have anticipated the New Economic Policy of 1921.) In November 1920 "sowing committees" were introduced to compel the peasants to plant more crops. (Forced procurements killed the peasants' incentive to produce a surplus; the government responded not by restoring incentives but by increasing administrative controls; Maurice Dobb aptly called this the *reductio ad absurdum*.[3])

There was no loosening of state control of industry and, indeed, in late November 1920 the nationalization of even the smallest enterprises was decreed, a step that had been ruled out in the 1919 party program. Another feature of 1920 was the evolution towards a moneyless economy. Financially orthodox attempts to maintain the value of Soviet currency having failed in 1918 and 1919, the printing press was now hailed as "that machine-gun of the Commissariat of Finance which poured fire into the rear of the bourgeois system."[4] As inflation destroyed the value of the currency payment was increasingly made in kind (in the cities a major effort was made to introduce communal kitchens).

In 1917–1918 the panacea for industry had been the spontaneous activity of the masses; by 1920 the panacea had become the state. Bukharin even produced, in May 1920, a major theoretical justification of this, *The Economics of the Transition Period*: economic "equilibrium" could only be created from the ruin of civil war by the coercion of the proletarian state; "the greater the extent of this 'extra-economic' power . . . the less will be the 'costs' of the transition period . . . the *shorter* will be this transition period."[5] In the course of 1919 Lenin, Trotsky, and many others of the Bolshevik elite had become used to "military"-type solutions; the model for the control of transport and industry became the Red Army, the most successful institution in Soviet Russia. A symbol of what was happening was the transfer of Trotsky's main attention from the Red Army to the economy.

The state was especially concerned with the mobilization of labor. At the beginning of 1920 Trotsky tried to fulfill simple but crucial economic tasks such as clearing railway lines or gathering fuel (timber or peat) by transforming some of his victorious armies into "Labor Armies." Opinions vary about the experiment's success, but it ended quite soon when it became clear that the fighting was not over. Rather more important was the application of military methods to the civilian economy. Labor conscription was developed on the basis of theses put forward by Trotsky in December 1919 and supported by Lenin and Bukharin; a system of "Universal Labor Mobilization" was applied

244

to workers and peasants. The trade unions, meanwhile, were to be brought further under state control and made into bodies for the mobilization of the working class. Parallel with this, and in the interest of efficiency, "one-man management" increasingly replaced more democratic collective forms.

Economic policy and the Civil War were not as closely connected as is sometimes suggested. It has already been argued that the Bolsheviks' radical economic policies—from 1917–1918—were only indirectly caused by Civil War and that the term "War Communism" is misleading (see chapter 6). E. H. Carr, on the other hand, believed that the influence of the Civil War was decisive: "So long as the war lasted, hand-to-mouth policies were inevitable; the end of the war dictated a review of these policies." This was only partly true.

Soviet economic policy *was* to change radically in 1921. Under the "New Economic Policy" forced requisitioning of foodstuffs was replaced in March 1921 by fixed payments (the "tax in kind"), and after a few months the peasants—now almost a favored class—were allowed to sell their surplus privately. In the early 1920s many of the smaller factories were denationalized. But it must be stressed that "the end of war" first seemed to have come in the early spring of *1920* and actually occurred in November 1920. Neither occasion led to a fundamental reexamination of policy. The Marxist leadership's ideology still led to a favoring of nationalized industry and an avoidance of the market. The early spring of 1920 brought the militarization of labor (and Trotsky, at least, regarded this as a *long-term* solution to the problems of industry). November 1920, and the clear victory, brought the sowing committees and the nationalization of small enterprises. (In connection with the November 1920 tightening up, Alec Nove said that Lenin "seems to have gone right off the rails."[6]) After November came December; after December January; after January February; after February March—and only then was it openly announced that there would be changes in *some* Bolshevik economic policies.

What *would* bring change in 1921 was not only the end of the Civil War but also the obvious problems of the existing policy, and the growth of active internal resistance. Best known was the uprising at the Kronshtadt naval base in March 1921, which was itself partly triggered by big strikes in nearby Petrograd. And peasant unrest was increasingly serious. The Antonov Movement that broke out in the autumn of 1920 in Tambov Province, southeast of Moscow, was just the best-known example; there were widespread disturbances in other areas, especially the Volga and western Siberia. The White defeat partly explains why this happened; it ended mass fears of a restoration, and it made the population question demands for continued sacrifice. The disturbances were also, however, partly a response to the increasing squeeze by the Soviet state. The peasants were influenced by the growing "efficiency" of the Soviet state in food procurement, a pressure that reached its height in the winter of 1920–1921.[7] The focus of unrest was on those surplus-producing provinces on the immediate fringes of central Sovdepia which had been most pressed to deliver food to the hungry north and to the army in 1918, 1919, and 1920.

There was significant internal unrest in 1920. Strikes were common in the towns, and there was trouble in the countryside. But mass internal discontent became a really serious factor only *after* the defeat of the Poles and Vrangel. Things might have turned out differently for the Soviet cause if Sovdepia had had to face the kind of internal unrest which crippled the Whites. Indeed, by 1920, with only the weak army of Vrangel in the field, it was only such unrest that could have threatened Bolshevik rule.

Politics

The continued burden of the Red Army and of economic communism was bearable because political control was stronger than ever before. Time was a factor here; the revolutionary government was twenty-four months old by November 1919. The most striking change in 1920 was the growth of the Bolshevik Party's power, both in absolute terms and in relation to the soviets. The full-time party officials increased in strength, independence, and organization. Organization and numbers meant that the party was for the first time having real influence in the countryside. Membership reached 600,000 at the Ninth Party Congress (March 1920), a fourfold rise since the summer of the previous year. The Communist Youth League (the *Komsomol*) grew even more rapidly, from 96,000 in September 1919 to 482,000 in October 1920.[8]

The party leadership remained close-knit, and while the fighting lasted there was no danger that divisions in the Red camp would give hope to the Whites. By contrast, the winter of 1920–1921 would see such intense debate that in March 1921 the 10th Congress banned all factions within the party (and despite this ban, intraparty debate bubbled away during the 1920s). In 1920 the Civil War still kept the lid on, partly because of the common cause against the Whites and partly because of the physical involvement of party leaders in the fighting. The first hints

246

of major argument came with the defeat of Kolchak and Denikin in the spring of 1920. Two factions criticized what was happening within the party: the "Democratic Centralists" attacked the way "democracy" had atrophied, and the "Workers Opposition" now stressed the need for class purity. But at the outset these criticisms were muted, and they never questioned the party's monopoly of power. A louder argument only broke out after the November 1920 victory; at issue was the role of the trade unions in the economy. Trotsky, Bukharin, and others called for continued strict state control, and the Workers' Opposition wanted autonomous workers' organizations (led by working-class Bolsheviks). But the "oppositions," although vocal, were small, localized, and easily contained by the Leninist leadership; this showed how far things had gone since the Brest debate of early 1918.

Outside the party a more complex approach to political control was evident. In the center there was some normalization with the abolition of RevComs in January 1920. But the soviets had a very small non-Bolshevik opposition element and were controlled in the localities by the party, especially the ProvComs. The party's ProvComs had become, in effect, the executive-administrative organs, and to help keep contact with the masses the regime in the winter of 1919–1920 developed a system of "non-party conferences." Meanwhile some attempt was made to check abuse by a new centralized organ of control, the "Workers' and Peasants' Inspection" (*Rabkrin*).

The population of the Soviet zone increased from about 85 million in the summer of 1919 to 140 million by the autumn of 1920, an increase of 65 percent (and the *area* to be administered increased by a much larger percentage). It was a large task to incorporate the newly captured regions, but the system of RevComs was extended to them, and the RevComs were then gradually replaced by "conventional" soviets.

The apparatus of Red Terror continued. At the Seventh Soviet Congress (December 1919) Lenin defended the record of the Cheka, after a direct attack by the Menshevik leader Martov. Trotsky even found time to rebut the charges of German socialist critics in a long defense of Red Terror entitled *Terrorism and Communism*. The death penalty was abolished in January 1920, but there were apparently hurried executions to beat this deadline, and in fact death-penalty powers were restored, with the wide use of martial law during the Soviet-Polish War. The year 1920 probably saw some of the worst terror, with the occupation of central Siberia and, especially, with the recapture of the Crimea in November 1920.[9]

The state and the Cheka helped to contain popular unrest caused by economic hardship, and also held in check the "political" critics of the regime. Moderate critics were contained by the carrot-and-stick policies developed in 1919. The remnants of "legal" opposition, a few SRs and Mensheviks, were allowed some participation in certain soviets, in part to impress foreign public opinion. The White underground was no more effective in 1920 than in the previous year. In August the Supreme Revolutionary Tribunal tried the case of the "Tactical Center," formed in early 1919 to link the right-wing Council of Public Men, the Kadet-oriented National Center, and leftist Union for the Regeneration of Russia. The external White threat was much reduced and the Red Army was at the gates of Warsaw, so the death penalties passed on four leaders (including the historian Melgunov) were commuted to ten years.

One remarkable development for the Soviet state in 1920 was the growing weight of the minority peoples. In the summer of 1919 less than a quarter of the population of the Soviet-controlled zone—north-central Russia, the Volga, and the Urals—were not Great Russians. The minorities were small, scattered, backward, and disorganized; the largest cohesive minority were probably the 700,000 Bashkirs. By the autumn of 1920 very nearly *half* the population were non-Russian, and there were now 30 million Ukrainians, as well as the peoples of Turkestan and Azerbaidzhan.

After their short-lived advances into the borderlands in the winters of 1917–1918 and 1918–1919 the Bolsheviks had learned important lessons and gained valuable advantages. Ambiguity remained about the paper independence or autonomy of various regions, and even about the separate existence of local Communist Parties. But more effort was made to secure local allies, and several important pronouncements in the winter of 1919–1920 emphasized local feelings, especially in the Ukraine. "Keep this firmly in mind": Trotsky told the Red Army in late November 1919, *"Your task is not to conquer the Ukraine but to liberate it."* An alliance was formed in the Ukraine with the non-Marxist "Borotbist" party, a link like that with the Russian Left SRs in 1917–1918. Stalin, in his capacity as head of the People's Commissariat for Nationalities (*Narkomnats*), summed up in October 1920 the basic policy of "Soviet autonomy," which was to vary with the size and development of peoples. "Soviet autonomy," Stalin wrote, "is the most real, the most concrete form of the union of the border regions with central Russia." Native intellectuals were now to be wooed, given the lack of local Bolsheviks; Stalin said the native intellectuals could be used just as former officers were used in the Red Army (an interesting parallel, given his Tsaritsyn experiences). Speaking for Moscow Stalin generally attacked "the haste, often becoming coarse tactlessness, displayed by certain comrades in the matter of sovietizing the border regions." Such "cavalry raids," he declared, continuing his military metaphor, were to be condemned.[10]

Already by the end of the Civil War in November 1920 a complex system of administration had been set up: there were three "Socialist Soviet Republics," the Ukrainian, Belorussian, and Azerbaidzhan SSRs (with the Armenian and Georgian SSRs soon to follow). Quasi-independence was also given to the "People's Soviet Republics" for Bukhara and Khorezm (Khiva), and even the "Far Eastern Republic." Lesser powers were given to five "Autonomous Soviet Socialist Republics," the Bashkir, Gorskaia (Mountain), Kirgiz, Tatar, and Turkestan ASSRs, and to the Chuvash, Kalmyk, Mari, and Votiak Autonomous Regions (and similar institutions for the Karelian Finns and the Volga Germans). Autonomy and independence were hardly all they appeared to be, and the relations of the national regions with the Russian Republic (the RSFSR) would only be made clearer with the creation of the Union of Soviet Socialist Republics in late 1922. But at least the system showed flexibility. Probably even more important than greater "tactfulness" was the fact that the military forces available to the Reds were much larger, and this time were unified on an all-Soviet basis. Party forces were much larger too, and more under Moscow's control than they had been the year before.

Neither the success of Bolshevik nationalities policy nor the depth of the Moscow regime's popular base in the borderlands should be exaggerated. But Soviet social policies won some mass support, and political promises won over part of the small national intelligentsia. The minority regions were irrevocably brought into the Soviet system, and the system—still in its early stages—survived the stress of the Poles and Vrangel, both of whom especially threatened the key minority area, the Ukraine.

By the end of the winter of 1919–1920 the main military threat to the Soviet state had been defeated on the battlefields of south Russia and western Siberia. An internal system had been created which allowed general control of Soviet territory, and which provided the essential backing when the Red war effort was resumed in the late spring. The most important point about the internal state of Sovdepia in 1920 was this: despite the strain of the Civil War there was not enough internal discontent to give any hope to the remnants of the White armies.

249

18

THE POLISH CAMPAIGN,
April–October 1920

But our enemies and yours deceive you when they say that the Russian Soviet Government wishes to plant communism in Polish soil with the bayonets of the Russian Red Army.

Central ExCom Address to the Polish People, 2 February 1920

In the West the fate of the world revolution is being decided. Over the corpse of White Poland lies the road to world conflagration. On bayonets we will bring happiness and peace to laboring humanity.

Order of RevMilCouncil, Western Army Group, 2 July 1920

War for the Borderlands

In the spring of 1920 the Civil War seemed almost over. Then, on 25 April 1920, the Polish Army advanced across the plains of the western Ukraine. It marched 150 miles in two weeks, took Kiev on 6 May, and threw bridgeheads across the Dnepr. With this began the most dramatic campaign of the Civil War.

Of the peoples of Eastern Europe the Poles had been the most ready to benefit from the downfall of the three eastern empires in 1917–1918. In November 1918 they declared in "Russian" Warsaw a reborn Poland, assembled from the lands seized by Russians, Austrians, and Prussians in the eighteenth-century Partitions. The key to the Moscow-Warsaw relationship, however, was not the new Poland's right to exist, but control of the borderlands. Ethnic Poland and ethnic Great Russia had no common frontier. Between them lay a belt of territory, stretching from the Baltic to the Black Sea and 300 miles deep; other peoples, the Baltic nations (Lithuanians, Latvians, Estonians), the Belorussians, and the Ukrainians, occupied blocks of territory, and scattered throughout were Jewish settlements. Before the First Partition of Poland (1772) the Lithuanian and Belorussian regions and much of the Ukraine had been ruled by Poland; once national independence was restored many Poles were eager to regain "their" lost lands. Particularly influential here was Jozef Pilsudski; a fierce-looking character with a walrus mustache and heavy eyebrows, he had been the best-known leader of both nationalist and socialist movements, and was now Polish head of state and commander-in-chief. Pilsudski was a native of the east and believed that the only way the border peoples could retain their identity was through a great federation—under Polish supervision.

The Russian Empire had collapsed, but the Bolsheviks too wanted to spread their influence into the borderlands. Conflict was inevitable and began with the collapse of Germany. The Poles had the better part of the engagements (small in scale) in 1919 and early 1920, because the Red armies were fighting for their lives in the south and east. Vilna was taken by the Poles in April 1919, and Minsk, the center of Belorussia, in August; in January 1920 the strategic town of Dvinsk was seized, and on 5 March so was Mozyr (between Minsk and Kiev). The march on Kiev, when it came in April 1920, was directly related to what had been happening in the previous year. Pilsudski had two objectives: bringing the Ukraine into a border federation, and preempting an attempt by the Red Army—now victorious over internal enemies—to take back the borderlands. Under a treaty signed with Petliura four days before the Polish invasion, Pilsudski promised to support a Ukrainian regime in Kiev, in exchange for a recognition that eastern Galicia, formerly part of Austria-Hungary, was Polish rather than Ukrainian. (This worsened the already bad relations between the "Austrian" and "Russian" Ukrainians.)

The complete success of the Kiev operation depended on the Ukrainians, as the Polish Army was too weak to hold the Ukraine on its own. But in 1920 Ukrainian nationalists proved no more able to create a state than they had been previously. As a spoiling attack, too, Pilsudski's operation was unsuccessful. The Red Twelfth and Fourteenth Armies retreated so rapidly that they could not be trapped and destroyed. The Bolsheviks were certainly preparing an offensive against the borderlands, but the Kiev operation was counterproductive. It left Polish forces in a dangerously exposed position, and allowed Moscow to claim all the propaganda benefits—domestic and foreign—of responding to Polish aggression.

The verdict of the Bolshevik CC was that "the Polish bourgeoisie . . . staked their fate on a card." There was some truth in this, and as the military campaign developed in July it looked more and more as though the Polish gamble had failed. The Red Southwestern Army Group was commanded by Egorov, the Bolshevik colonel thrown in against Denikin in October 1919. In May 1920 Egorov had to give up Kiev, but he was soon ready for a devastating counterattack. Before Pilsudski moved, Southwestern Army Group had been preparing for a deep drive of its own, across the southern borderlands to Brest (at least), and it had already been assigned the main shock force of the whole Red Army, Budenny's First Cavalry Army.[1] Budenny's six divisions were still riding toward their starting point when the Poles struck, but on 30 May they were in place. The Reds broke through the Polish lines north and south of Kiev, forcing the Poles to flee. On 12 June, five weeks after the Reds had abandoned the city, Kiev changed hands for the sixteenth—and last—time in the Civil War. Poor coordination of the Red wings allowed the enemy garrison to escape, but the effectiveness of the Red Cavalry was shown. It gave the Soviets a psychological advantage and let them turn the Polish flanks. The Poles (given World War experience) had ignored cavalry, and they would be at a serious disadvantage until they could fully develop cavalry units of their own.

The main Red offensive came, however, not from Egorov in the Ukraine but from Western Army Group in Belorussia. The 1920 campaign was fought in distinct northern and southern battle zones; the Reds had divided their forces into Western Army Group in Belorussia and Southwestern Army Group in the Ukraine, with the Pripet Marshes between them. At least since March 1920—following the loss of Mozyr—the Red high command had been working on plans for a summer offensive to be launched from Belorussia.[2] The Poles had made their attack in the Ukraine first, however, and Western Army Group was forced into a premature offensive to relieve the pressure there. Western Army Group was commanded by Tukhachevsky; he was only twenty-seven, but his brilliant Soviet career had included command of First and Fifth Armies in the east, and of Caucasus Army Group in the battles that finished off Denikin. Tukhachevsky's first attack, on the Berezina River on 14 May, failed; his forces were poorly coordinated and understrength. Seven weeks of hectic reinforcement were followed by a decisive second offensive on 4 July. Tukhachevsky now had four armies (Sixteenth, Third, Fifteenth, and Fourth) and a large mobile force, III Cavalry Corps (under Gai). With Gai's horsemen repeatedly turning their northern flank, the Poles were chased 400 miles back to the Vistula River. The breakneck chase, lasting six weeks, was the most remarkable feature of the whole campaign and Tukhachevksy's greatest triumph. His armies took Minsk on 11 July, Vilna on the 14th, Grodno on the 19th, and Brest-Litovsk on 1 August.

The Polish march on Kiev had been repulsed, and for good measure the Reds had taken most of the borderland districts that the Poles had occupied in 1919 and early 1920. Pilsudski's attempt to take the borderlands and to head off the Red Army had failed miserably. But already the campaign was going beyond the borderlands, and beyond the original intentions of the two sides. The fate of Poland itself and—some would argue—of Western Europe now hung in the balance.

The Battle of the Vistula

By the high summer of 1920 the implications of these confused marchland battles was being considered in Warsaw, in the Allied capitals, and in Moscow. In Poland Pilsudski's position remained firm, despite military failure and personal and ideological friction. But the federal idea was now dead, and in July Warsaw accepted the Allies' proposal for their eastern border. This had been drafted in December 1919, and made, roughly, the longitude of the Bug River the frontier. The Bug was an appropriate ethnic and historical dividing line—to the west was territory inhabited mainly by Poles, to the east the non-Polish borderlands. The proposed frontier was 180 miles west of Minsk and 280 miles west of Kiev. (The Allies did not set the line so far west in order to help Soviet Russia; they still thought of a great Russia that would emerge as an ally after the collapse of the Bolsheviks.)

The Allies, for their part, also hoped to use the Bug line to limit the Soviet counteroffensive. This was the essence of a note sent to Moscow on 12 July over the signature of the British Foreign Secretary; history knows the Bug frontier as the "Curzon Line." Pilsudski's Kiev offensive had come as a surprise to the most senior Allied leaders, none of whom wanted to continue armed intervention. The main element of Allied policy had become the strengthening of the border states, creating a cordon sanitaire, and by the end of 1919 the border states were no longer encouraged to undertake offensive enterprises. The British wanted to restore trade with Russia, and in the spring of 1920 had begun high-level negotiations. As the Red Army shifted over to the offensive the British and French did send to Warsaw an Inter-Allied mission, the best-known member of which was General Weygand

(Marshal Foch's chief of staff), but this was hardly the general staff of renewed intervention. The mission was a symbolic substitute for material aid that the Allies were unable or unwilling to supply, and one of its main tasks was to moderate Polish policy by getting rid of the firebrand Pilsudski.[3]

The view from Moscow was the most important, because the Bolsheviks alone had a choice of policy. They could content themselves with the Belorussian-Ukrainian borderlands or they could cross the Curzon line and extend the conflict west into Poland "proper." On 17 July the Politburo made the fateful decision to reject the Allied note; the advancing armies were told to reach and cross the Curzon Line as soon as possible. The enthusiasm with which the Bolsheviks took on a great new military commitment is remarkable, given all the strains that it put on their economically devastated country. Of the senior leaders only Rykov, the economic coordinator, seems to have been against broadening the war, and even he changed his mind.[4]

The Bolsheviks had their reasons. The destruction of "White Poland" would advance the cause of a general European revolution, which was a major objective of the Soviet regime. The Bolsheviks were perennial optimists about the closeness of international revolution, and it was widely believed in Moscow that the Polish proletariat was on the brink of overthrowing its ruling class. Even more important was Germany, which seemed to need only a spark from outside to explode into revolt; the Kapp Putsch of March 1920 was compared to the 1917 Kornilov affair—the last spasm of the old order. The invasion of Poland was equated with world revolution; in the meeting hall of the Second Congress of the Komintern the delegates watched the steady advance to the west of the red flags that represented Moscow's armies.

If they saw the European masses as ripe for revolution the Bolsheviks also saw themselves surrounded by cunning and rapacious imperialist governments; this was another factor pushing the Red Army forward. In early May 1920 Trotsky secretly advised the Party leadership to tell all provincial Party organizations "that never before has the military danger to the Soviet Republic been as great as it is now." Stalin wrote in *Pravda* in late May that the Polish attack was part of an Entente campaign (*pokhod*). (This was the article that established the Soviet "line" of the "three Entente campaigns"—spring 1919, autumn 1919, and summer 1920.) Lenin and other Bolshevik leaders now took the same view. Western talk of trade, they felt, masked continuing conspiracy; as for mediation, the Allies had arranged a de facto armistice with General Vrangel, but in June 1920 *he* had broken out of the Crimea to threaten south Russia. Stopping at the Curzon Line would not prevent the inevitable imperialist attack; crossing the Curzon Line and destroying the puppet bourgeois government in Warsaw would end Poland's use as an Allied base. As Colonel Kamenev later put it, "a wood that hasn't been completely chopped down will soon grow back."[5]

Granted that the Polish beast would be pursued into his lair, there remained the question of how fast to move. Tukhachevsky had this choice towards the end of July, at about the level of the Curzon Line. His divisions had marched 200 miles; a pause would let them regroup and reinforce themselves, and would allow Egorov's Southwestern Army Group to catch up and cover the left flank. A pause, however, would also let the Poles catch their breath and raise new forces; it might even give time for Allied support to arrive. In the end the decision was made to race on to Warsaw and a quick victory. The military decisions were mirrored by diplomatic and political activity. The peace terms presented by the Soviets in mid-August would have cut the Polish Army down to 50,000 men (from 740,000) with any extra arms going to a workers' militia (i.e., a Red Guard); these terms were meant to be unacceptable to the existing Polish government. Meanwhile on 30 July an embryonic socialist administration (or puppet government), the "Provisional Polish Revolutionary Committee," or PolRevCom, was installed 100 miles east of Warsaw at Bialystok. Everything now depended on the bayonets of Tukhachevsky's men.

By the second week of August Tukhachevsky had reached the Vistula and Wieprz Rivers, on a front running southeast 200 miles from the East Prussian border. On the right, III Cavalry Corps (Gai) and Fourth Army had turned the Polish flank and were *west* of Warsaw; the leading troopers were about to cut the Warsaw-Danzig rail link. In the center Fifteenth, Third, and Sixteenth Armies threatened the middle Vistula and Warsaw itself. On the left, however, there were only a few weak detachments, which were not yet supported by Egorov's Southwestern Army Group.

The great confusing battle before the Vistula River was fought out in the third week of August. The Poles under General Sikorski beat off the main Red attack north of Warsaw. The fortified line before the Polish capital itself withstood a secondary attack. Meanwhile, between 6 and 12 August, Pilsudski drastically and secretly reorganized his troops and formed five of his twenty divisions into a striking force southeast of Warsaw. On the 16th the trap sprang shut; the striking force burst through Tukhachevsky's weak left flank and drove north across his lines of communication toward the East Prussian border. Tukhachevsky, caught by surprise and threatened with encirclement, had no choice but to order an abrupt withdrawal. Fifteenth, Third and Sixteenth Armies fought their way out, but the troops farthest west could not. Three divisions of Fourth Army were savaged and forced into East Prussian internment, followed by III Cavalry Corps.

The loss of Gai's *Kavkorpus* was a serious blow, as it was cavalry that had given the Reds their early advantage. Tukhachevsky's whole army group was thrown off balance as the retreat continued. The Republic RevMilCouncil tried to assemble its own "striking group," but the Polish momentum was too great. Western Army Group attempted to stand on the Neman River, 150 miles east of the Vistula, but now it was the Poles' turn to outflank. The Battle of the Neman was lost by the Reds at the close of September, and Poles advanced to Minsk (15 October) and the Berezina; the Poles were nearly back where they had started in July.

Meanwhile, Egorov's Southwestern Army Group, once it had recaptured the "Soviet" Ukraine, had not made such dramatic progress as Tukhachevsky. First Cavalry Army was ground down in battles at the start of August and failed to take what became its main objective, the west Ukrainian city of Lvov. The Poles had succeeded in raising large units of horsemen, and at Komarow, on 31 August one of the last great cavalry charges in European history took place. First Cavalry Army escaped from this trap, but its cutting edge was blunted. The Poles pursued, and by October they were back within fifty miles of their April positions.

Peace talks had begun in mid-August when a Polish delegation arrived in Soviet-held Minsk. At that time it seemed that the victorious Soviets would dictate the terms of peace, but then came the battle of the Vistula. After that neither side was prepared to talk seriously until the smoke had cleared enough to reveal the true outlines of the situation. By late August the Bolshevik leadership could see that things were bad. Trotsky returned from a tour of the Vrangel front to argue for peace. Further Red defeats and the unlikelihood of a new turnabout before winter made this the dominant line. The Poles, however, now had no need to negotiate, and talks resumed only on 21 September (this time on neutral ground, in Riga). Ioffe spoke for the Soviets, and on 12 October was able to secure an armistice (converted into a peace treaty in March 1921).

The Riga settlement gave clear victory to neither side. The Bolsheviks did not achieve their limited goal of annexing the Belorussian-Ukrainian borderlands, their intermediate goal of destroying "White"

Poland, or their ultimate goal of breaking through to "revolutionary" Germany. Pilsudski failed to achieve *his* ultimate goal of an eastern federation, and he ended up with less territory than in April 1920. But looking at the period 1919–1920 as a whole, and bearing in mind that Poland would probably have had to fight for her eastern territories anyway, Warsaw did not come out badly. The Poles had effected a partition of the borderlands with their giant neighbor. In the end four to five million Ukrainians remained in Poland, compared to 30 million in Soviet Russia (many east of the 1772 frontier), and a million Belorussians, compared to four million. In the long term the October 1920 settlement contained the seeds of the tragedy of 1939 and 1944–1945 and more, but in the short term it seemed to guarantee Poland's eastern frontier.

Causes and Implications

The Polish high command deserves much of the credit for the victory; it conceived the Vistula counterattack and the daring and complex movement that preceded it. Pilsudski's rivals stressed the advice of Weygand or even the intervention of the Black Madonna of Czestochowa, but Weygand was ignored and the "Miracle of the Vistula" had a solid enough basis. In the Polish Army the Reds faced their largest and most effective enemy. Polish units may have been "so many children born of the same mother, but conceived of different fathers," but the Polish veterans of the Tsarist, German, Austro-Hungarian, and French armies brought military professionalism. The Poles had twenty months to consolidate their forces before the decisive campaign, and they had the advantage of a French training mission of 5000 officers (among them Charles de Gaulle). More important still was the *size* of the Polish army: Polish strength of 740,000 in August 1920 should be compared to the largest White force, Denikin's, which at its peak had only 100,000 combat troops. The effectiveness of the Poles was reflected in the scale of fighting—and of casualties. Red Army casualties were given as 131,000 in 1919 and 300,100 in 1920; Polish casualties in 1920 were 202,000. Trotsky publicly branded the Polish Army "a *szlachta* [gentry] army, an army of slaves, held by force, steeped in priests' lies and bourgeois deceit"; privately he warned the CC that "we have operating against us for the first time a regular army led by good technicians."[6]

The Reds made military mistakes. Egorov's Southwestern Army

Group failed to support Tukhachevsky's Western Army Group. At the critical moment Egorov's First Cavalry Army was actually moving *away* from Tukhachevsky and beseiging Lvov—200 miles southeast of Warsaw; it was through Tukhachevsky's open southern flank that Pilsudski was able to pour his striking force. Stalin was Southwestern Army Group's main commissar, and Trotsky (and later others) laid the blame on him: "He wanted, at whatever cost, to enter Lvov at the same time that Smilga [Western Army Group's commissar] and Tukhachevsky entered Warsaw. People have such ambitions!" When the danger to Tukhachevsky was revealed, Stalin and Egorov pushed on, "for surely it was more important that they themselves captured Lvov than that they should help 'others' to take Warsaw?"

It is true that Stalin behaved high-handedly. On 13 August, Colonel Kamenev instructed him to transfer his right wing, Twelfth Army and First Cavalry Army, to Tukhachevsky; Stalin refused. For this he was recalled and apparently censured, and it was the last act of his checkered front-line career. But the real blame lies elsewhere. By 13 August First Cavalry Army was already locked into an attack on Lvov, and 150 miles from where it would have needed to be to influence the Polish counteroffensive that began three days later. The fatal decision had been made on 23 July, when Main Commander-in-Chief Kamenev ordered Southwestern Army Group to thrust not northwest towards Brest, but southwest toward Lvov.[7] This made strategic sense; it would split the Poles, pushing their southern forces towards the Carpathians. But enemy resistance made it impossible for the Reds quickly to achieve this goal.

The second and more important Red strategic mistake was Western Army Group's rush across the Curzon Line toward the Vistula. Tukhachevsky wrongly believed that he could effect a decisive victory on his own. He underestimated the Poles and exaggerated his early victories; divisions that he reported smashed were actually able to retreat intact. He misapplied the lessons of the uninterrupted Civil War offensives that had kept the armies of Kolchak and Denikin off balance and broken their spirit. The magic formula did not work against a resolute enemy ("a regular army led by good technicians") that grew stronger as it retreated on its home base and did not give up manpower and supplies to the attacker.

There was an even more basic reason why a country of 125 million and an army of 4,600,000 could not prevail over a country of 27 million and an army of 750,000: Soviet Russia was something of a colossus with feet of clay. Most of the 4,600,000 "Red Army men" were poorly trained, poorly equipped conscripts sitting in internal garrisons. Mobilization and training were primitive. It was not just the Polish front that needed troops; the Red high command had to garrison the vast (and troubled) territories captured in the winter of 1919–1920 and those areas exposed to foreign intervention. There was fighting in Siberia, Turkestan, Azerbaidzhan, and—most important—the Crimea; on 19 August, when Tukhachevsky was on the brink of success, the Politburo made General Vrangel's White Crimea the main front. More important still, the Soviet economy could not stand the strain. In September, on S. S. Kamenev's advice, Lenin wanted to fight on through the winter if the Poles kept the Baranovichi-Rovno lateral railway. Then came the Neman defeat, and even Lenin had had enough; "ought we," he asked Klara Zetkin, "unless absolutely and literally compelled, to have exposed the Russian people to the terror and suffering of another winter of war? No, the thought of the agonies of another winter war were unbearable. We had to make peace."[8]

A particular problem was that the Red Army could not project its power very far. The terrible state of transport and distractions in other areas meant that the Polish front had to rely on its own resources. Lenin's best advice in August was to conscript the Belorussian peasantry, "even if they arrive in bast sandals and their birthday suits." Tukhachevsky's breakneck pace made things even worse. Red engineers did valiant work on the railways destroyed by the retreating Poles, but reinforcements had to detrain as far as 100 miles from the front. Tukhachevsky began with 108,000 combatants in June but was down to 40,000 by the time he got to the Vistula.[9] The huge paper superiority of the Red Army was thus converted into numerical inferiority before Warsaw. There were also command problems. By August Tukhachevsky's headquarters in Minsk was 300 miles from his armies on the Vistula, while Egorov and Stalin in Kharkov were 550 miles from the cavalry at Lvov; both army-group headquarters were 400 miles from the Field Staff in Moscow. The technical side of communications was poor, especially across the borderlands, and it was very hard for the Red commanders to assess the situation and monitor the movements even of their own forces.

The Reds also made political miscalculations about the Poles' "ripeness" for revolution. Poland was different from those "minority" territories of the Russian empire which Moscow was able to reannex in 1919–1920. Poland had a large territory (including parts of Germany and Austria-Hungary). Its population included 19 million ethnic Poles, a much larger number than that of most other minorities. The level of education and national consciousness was high. Austrian Poland had had home rule for decades, Russian Poland had been free of Tsarist administrators since its capture by the Central Powers in 1915. In 1918–1919 independent Poland created a parliamentary regime more advanced than anything seen in Russia. Red propaganda might call their enemies the "Pans" or the "Szlachta," stressing the gentry tradition, but the basis of Polish nationalism was much more solid than that.

Socialist parties as a whole won only nine percent of the vote in Poland's January 1919 elections, and in any event most of the socialist leaders supported the government's eastern policies. Three-quarters of Poles lived in the countryside, and the government courted their support with land reform, including a radical law passed at the height of the Soviet invasion. And a particular feature of Poles in both town and coutryside was the influence of the Catholic Church and a popular nationalism (and Russophobia). The small illegal "Communist Workers' Party of Poland" rejected the very idea of national independence and supported agararian cooperatives rather than individual peasant farms. The PolRevCom in Bialystok also had a collectivist land policy and it had, too, a notorious leader in Dzerzhinsky (a Pole, but also head of the Cheka). So a common sense of national struggle created a cohesive Poland and, wedded to a strong "traditional" army, the Poles were a most formidable enemy.

The Polish case seems so different that Norman Davies has maintained that the campaigns between Poland and Soviet Russia were not part of either the Russian Civil War or foreign intervention. Certainly there was a strong element of nationalism on both sides. Trotsky had to suspend ex-officers on the editorial board of the army journal for remarks about the "innate jesuitry of the Polacks."[10] But the Polish campaigns *were* part of the general Civil War. The Russian Civil War was concerned with national self-determination as well as social revolution. Poland (most of it) had been part of the Russian Empire for 130 years. If Tukhachevsky had taken Warsaw, if a "Polish Socialist Soviet Republic" had become a sister to the RSFSR, Soviet historians would call this another victory of the "Soviet" people over bourgeois nationalism. And the Belorussian-Ukrainian borderlands, which the fighting was initially all about, were certainly part of the Civil War.

Ultimate responsibility for the mistakes of the Polish campaign lay with the Bolshevik leadership. They probably did not, in the spring of 1920, plan the destruction of the existing order in Poland (at least not more than anywhere else), but this aim came to the fore after Pilsudski's attack and the first easy successes of Egorov and Tukhachevsky. The Bolshevik leaders then overestimated their own strength and the level

260

of revolutionary feeling. Trotsky blamed the supreme leadership for pursuing the Polish campaign, even after the Vistula defeat:

> Yes, Lenin was a genius, was full of human genius. But he was not a mechanical reckoner who made no mistakes. He made many fewer than anyone else in his position would have done. But he did make mistakes and very grave mistakes, in accord with the gigantic scale of all his work.

(The private Trotsky may have had reservations, but the *public* Trotsky declared otherwise: "We are striving towards the West, towards the European proletariat, which knows that we can meet it only over the corpse of White-Guard Poland, in a free and independent Workers' and Peasants' Poland."[11]

The Red Army took a great risk. Colonel Kamenev had given the Bolshevik leaders a warning in July:

> But even if we cross this line [the Curzon Line] and smash Poland we will still be in an extremely difficult strategic position, as the front will have been greatly extended in a situation where there are no reserves and our enemies will need only a small concentration of fresh forces at the right point to shake the whole front, just as we did during the battle with Denikin.[12]

The White commanders had been hypnotized by the church bells of Moscow and the towers of the Kremlin, and threw everything into headlong offensives. In 1920 Tukhachevsky and his political masters thought only of the distant steeples of Warsaw and behind them, in the smog of the western horizon, the factory chimneys of industrial Germany. For these mirages the Reds, like the Whites before them, made a desperate gamble, and like them they were thrown back in humiliating defeat.

19

THE CRIMEAN ULCER,
April–November 1920

Forward against the enemy!
Down with the last breeding ground of the counter-revolution and long
live our victorious Worker-Peasant Republic!

M. V. Frunze, Order to Southern Army Group, 25 October 1920

Vrangel

The last White army was formed in the Crimea in April 1920, from the
survivors of Denikin's Kuban forces. The White resurgence might have
been impossible without General Petr Nikolaevich Vrangel, the leader
who replaced Denikin. At forty-two he was younger than Kornilov,
Denikin, or Kolchak, and a generation younger than Alekseev or
Iudenich. He was closest to the stereotype of a White leader, coming
from an aristocratic (although not wealthy) family, and he looked the
part. In contrast to the round-faced, short Denikin, he was a very tall
man with a striking face, and cut a dashing figure in a dark grey
Circassian coat and a Kuban *papakha* (sheepskin hat). The "Black
Baron" was a favourite of Soviet cartoonists.

The political Vrangel was more complex than the caricature. He had
not been one of the first to take up arms against the Bolsheviks. He had
not been a Bykhov prisoner, and he only arrived in the Kuban in the
late summer of 1918, having spent the terrible time of the "Ice March"
with his family at the Crimean resort of Ialta. He at first took little part
in the political side of the AFSR, but he became linked with the more
conservative forces, and finally emerged as their champion against the

262

"liberal" Denikin. But Vrangel showed himself to be much more flexible—or cynical—than his predecessor. The Denikin government was a naked military dictatorship. Denikin stressed the notion of "Russia, One and Indivisible," he failed to create a functioning civil administration or do anything about land reform. Vrangel saw that Denikin had failed for political as well as military reasons, and he said much about the need "to make leftist policies with rightist hands."[1] Vrangel was no less a military dictator than Denikin or Kolchak—he took the title *pravitel'* (ruler)—but he was able to attract some influential politicians to his "Government of South Russia." A. V. Krivoshein, a Tsarist elder statesman in the Stolypin mold, was his main domestic advisor, and the well-known rightist Kadet P. B. Struve his foreign minister. Vrangel devoted much attention to working out laws on local government. He also pushed through a land law—to coincide with his June 1920 breakout from the Crimea; this would have distributed the large estates among the peasants, with compensation for the owners. Probably more important was his stress on order in the rear, especially in connection with food requisitioning. Finally, Vrangel had no inhibitions about finding allies. Acting in the spirit of "With the Devil, but for Russia and against the Bolsheviks,"[2] he tried to win the support of elements whom Denikin had treated with contempt, including the Ukrainians, the Georgians, and Makhno's peasant anarchists.

In all this Vrangel had the advantage over Denikin of a politically stable (if small) base. The steppe of the north Tauride (the region north of the Crimean peninsula) was rich agricultural land, and its capture in June meant that Vrangel had no food supply problems, and could even hope to export grain. The land law was helped by the relatively calm agrarian history of Tauride Province. Moslem Tatars made up a quarter of the Crimean population, but they were not active politically. There were no concentrations of factory workers, and the Bolshevik underground was confined to a few partisans working in the mountains of the southern Crimea. So, unlike Denikin, Vrangel was never threatened by the disintegration of his rear.

Vrangel was primarily, however, a soldier, and a good one. Despite his appearance he came to the military life late. Vrangel was educated as a mining engineer, he was the son of an insurance company director, and he was twenty-six before finally deciding on a military career. But after that his progress was rapid. He served in the army's elite Cavalry Guards, and took the General Staff course. He fought in the wars of 1904 and 1914. Success in the field led him on the eve of the February Revolution to command of a cavalry brigade and the rank of major-general—at the remarkable age of 39. But it was the Civil War that brought out his talents. It is true that some of his strategic proposals to Denikin were inconsistent and that he failed to rally the Volunteer Army in December 1919. Earlier, however, he had been one of Denikin's two most successful generals (with Mai-Maevsky), leading the conquest of the north Caucasus in the winter of 1918–1919 and capturing Tsaritsyn in the following summer.

Behind Vrangel were several tens of thousands of survivors from the Armed Forces of South Russia. The saga of the Volunteer Army continued in the Crimea; its elite units remained in existence as I Corps, under its last commander in the Kuban, General Kutepov. There was also a considerable force of refugee Don Cossacks. With men he was able to mobilize in the Crimea, Vrangel had by June 1920 some 30,000–35,000 front-line soldiers. Vrangel had seen the indiscipline of Denikin's forces as a major cause of the 1919 failure, and he was concerned to improve the behavior and image of his troops. One important symbolic change was the adoption of the name "Russian Army"; Vrangel felt that the term "Volunteer" had been discredited. Vrangel's Russian Army impressed the Reds as being better equipped, especially with aircraft and motor vehicles, than its predecessor. (Much had been lost in the Kuban, and Allied supplies dried up in 1920, so this may have come from shorter supply lines, a small White army, and the mastering of equipment ordered earlier for Denikin.)

Vrangel's army had geography on its side. The Crimean peninsula is very nearly an island (with about the same area as Sicily). The Perekop isthmus is only five miles wide at its narrowest point. The Reds had no Black Sea fleet; the surviving Tsarist ships were in White hands (which—with the threat of the Allied fleets—also meant the Reds had to garrison the long coast east and west of the Crimea). Even between June and October 1920, when Vrangel held the north Tauride on the "mainland" above Perekop, he benefited from the strong natural line of the Dnepr River to the west and north. In addition the Vrangel front was fairly remote from the Bolshevik heartland (500 miles from Moscow), and the territory on which the Reds had to base themselves was one of the strongholds of the "bandits" of the Green movement.

Meanwhile, the Bolsheviks had other, bigger problems. "The party must understand," a CC circular complained in July 1920, "that Vrangel has succeeded in his first steps only because the party did not pay enough attention to the Crimean ulcer and did not cut it out with a single and decisive stroke." But this inattention was logical enough. In the first months of 1920 the Red Army was concentrated 400 miles to the east, against Denikin's main armies and the social base of the AFSR, the Kuban. When Denikin was beaten, the Red high command *did* intend to liquidate the Crimean pocket before sorting out the Polish borderlands. But Pilsudski's April 1920 attack drew Red units far to the west, and the remnants of Denikin's armies did not seem as much of a threat. In any event the desire for normalized relations with Britain led to the acceptance (on 5 May) of a de facto ceasefire. So only a weak army, Thirteenth, was left at Perekop, and its planned attack was called off.[3]

Vrangel's attacks, first into the north Tauride, then into the Kuban, changed the situation. On 19 August, the Bolshevik Politburo itself had to stress the danger of the situation. "The Vrangel front," it resolved, "is to be recognized as the main one." But then there were the desperate battles against the Polish counterattack. The Poles were a much more effective distraction of the Red Army for Vrangel than Kolchak, Iudenich, or Miller had been for Denikin. As late as 12 October Main Commander-in-Chief Kamenev emphasized the problem: "simultaneous battle with Poland and Vrangel has not given us success; what is needed is a decisive massing of men and material against one of these enemies, and it should be against Vrangel, in view of the general situation."[4] This became possible only at the end of November.

On balance, however, Vrangel's various advantages were outweighed by his disadvantages. Trotsky called him "Vrangel the Last-Born." A Soviet poster of 1920 summed up the situation: a giant Red cavalry-man rides forwards with ten tiny white figures—from Nicholas II to Pilsudski—skewered on his lance; the caption reads, "Now it's Vrangel's turn!" Vrangel only accepted the post of Main Commander-in-Chief after getting his colleagues to sign a kind of waiver stating that his role was to extricate the army rather than to win victory. European Russia comprised fifty provinces; Vrangel at the height of his success only controlled one of them, the Tauride. The population of the Crimea and the north Tauride was only about three million, including soldiers and refugees. (If Denikin had more problems controlling his armies than did Vrangel, that was mainly because he controlled 350,000 square miles of territory to Vrangel's 25,000.) By 1920 the Bolsheviks held not only the Sovdepia heartland but nearly the whole of the old Empire. The "Russian Army" had only 30,000–35,000 effectives, at a time when the Red Army had a paper strength of 5,000,000.[5] Against such odds Vrangel needed more than his new medal dedicated to St. Nicholas the Wonder-Worker.

For all his "leftist policies with rightist hands," Vrangel was also never able to broaden his appeal to get that "upsurge" within Sovdepia that had eluded Denikin. Vrangel's program had perhaps more popular appeal than the conservative nationalism of Denikin, but this made little difference to the population either in White territory or on the other side of the front line. The "Vrangelevschina" was still a military dictatorship, and one that could promise little to improve the life of the population. In particular, the land reform could not compare to Soviet policy, and it was too complex to give quick results or a propaganda weapon.

Vrangel was not bedeviled as Denikin had been by constitutional arguments with the cossack politicians, but this was mainly because those politicians no longer had a strong base. Indeed, one of Vrangel's main problems was that he no longer controlled the cossack "vendée," which alone could provide a mass base for a movement with a program like that of the Russian Whites. In August Vrangel sent a seaborne expedition to the Kuban, but this was defeated. The Don, the Kuban, and the Terek remained under Soviet control throughout 1920. It is not clear whether this was because of a more conciliatory Bolshevik policy, a more effective occupation force, or simply the beatings the cossacks had taken in earlier years, but Vrangel was deprived of his greatest potential source of strength.

This time the Reds also kept control of the Ukraine. The situation was far from perfect. In October 1920 Frunze (the new Commander-in-Chief of Southern Army Group) wrote to Lenin from Kharkov, the Ukrainian capital, about the dangers around him: "I feel that I and the army-group headquarters are surrounded by hostile elements." Trotsky had no illusions; "Soviet power in the Ukraine," he told the Politburo in November 1920, "has held out thus far (and held out feebly) mainly thanks to the authority of Moscow, the Great-Russian Communists and the Russian Red Army."[6] Nevertheless, the Ukrainian nationalists were no more an organized force than they had been in earlier years. Rakovsky's Ukrainian Socialist Soviet Republic kept control of its capital, Kharkov, and much of the central and eastern Ukraine. The skeleton of Soviet power existed, various leftist parties were merged with the Moscow-controlled Ukrainian Communists—the KP(b)U— and the All-Ukrainian Cheka kept vigilant watch. The Red Army was much larger, and there was now no separate Red Ukrainian Army to confuse things. Even Makhno, who had been causing much trouble behind the Red lines in the Ukraine, refused to cooperate in a common struggle alongside the Whites against the "commissarocracy." He hanged the representatives Vrangel sent to him, arranged a truce with the Reds in September, and sent a brigade-strength "Insurgent (Povstancheskaia) Army" against the Crimea.

Soviet propagandists spared no effort to portray the Whites as foreign puppets. Trotsky called the Crimea a "French fortress" commanded by "a hired German-Russian General, Baron Vrangel." A generation of Soviet historians put Vrangel in the "Third Entente Campaign." Vrangel himself was not worried about his "orientation": *With anybody at all— but for Russia—that is my slogan.*" At one point he proposed joint Polish, Ukrainian, and Russian operations, all under the command of a "Main Commander-in-Chief of the Western Anti-Bolshevik Front," who would be a French general; Denikin would never have considered that.[7] But in the end Vrangel received less foreign help than Denikin, Kolchak, or even Iudenich.

Britain had been the great backer of the Whites. But by the late autumn of 1919 the flow of arms had begun to dry up, and then the winter of military disasters in Siberia and the Kuban seemed to prove that the Whites had no future. The British now wanted to normalize relations with Moscow, and they tried to interpose themselves between Reds and Whites. In April 1920 Moscow was asked to spare the White survivors in the Crimea, while Vrangel was warned against adventures ("if you attack . . . His Majesty's Government will be unable to concern themselves any further with the fate of your army").[8] When Vrangel did launch his June attack, after two months' breathing space spent preparing his forces, the British withdrew all support. What aid there was came from France. The French had been hostile to Vrangel's predecessor, Denikin, and did nothing to help the AFSR, but in their desire to support the cordon sanitaire of border states, especially Poland and Rumania, they valued any force that distracted the Reds. They went as far as according Vrangel de facto recognition in August. But the French made excessive economic demands and sent very little equipment.

Vrangel had the advantage of the Soviet–Polish War, but effective cooperation with Warsaw was limited by geography and politics. In the autumn Vrangel gave priority to an attack to the northwest to link up with the Poles, who by this time had stopped the Reds on the Vistula and were rolling them back into Belorussia and the Ukraine. But the Poles only wanted the borderlands, not the destruction of the Soviet regime. Vrangel's scheme for a link up on the Dnepr at Cherkassy (halfway between Kiev and Ekaterinoslav) was a mirage, designed to keep the Poles fighting, to keep his cause credible with the French, and to cover his own Kuban failure. Vrangel tried to form—with the help of the ubiquitous SR conspirator Boris Savinkov—a "Third Russian Army" from Russian refugees in Polish-occupied territory (First and Second Armies were in the north Tauride); this ephemeral force, however, was capable of no more than border raids. In any event, the Vrangel front and the Polish front were never less than 250 miles apart.

The Campaign

In the first two months of Vrangel's rule the front line was stable. Then, early in June 1920, the genie popped out of the bottle. The veterans of the Kornilov, Markov, and Drozdovsky Regiments drove the Reds back from Perekop and pushed on to the north, reaching the lower Dnepr within a week. Meanwhile General Slaschev landed on the coast of the Sea of Azov and forced the Reds back. In a week Vrangel had seized control of the north Tauride (doubling his territory) and captured 8000 prisoners, thirty guns, and two armored trains.

Eideman's Thirteenth Red Army, kept inactive by a lack of troops and the London-Moscow negotiations, was now stung into action. At the end of June the Reds' I Cavalry Corps, led by a miner named Zhloba, was ordered to attack from the open eastern approaches to the north Tauride, riding into the rear of Vrangel's armies, and cutting them off from the Crimea. Zhloba was not Budenny; he himself was encircled, and in an area of German settlements (with picturesque names like Lindenau and Heidelberg), the cavalry corps was practically wiped out. The Whites captured 3000 horses, which made up for some of those shot on the quayside at the Novorossiisk. The first Red offensive against Vrangel had turned into one of the last great White victories.

Ensign Uborevich took over Thirteenth Army, and attacked again in August, this time from the west. Supported by artillery emplaced on the high west bank of the Dnepr, Red troops—especially the Latvian Division—made bridgeheads across the river. Most of these were wiped out, but the most important was not, at Kakhovka, fifty miles north of Perekop. It now posed a constant threat to Vrangel's line of communications. The repeated battles around Kakhovka were fierce, probably the closest the Civil War came to world war trench fighting.

Vrangel was able to hold the initiative until late in the autumn. White troops got as far north as the big Dnepr town of Aleksandrovsk (now Zaporozhe), as far east as the port of Mariupol (now Zhdanov), and even threatened the Donbas. Vrangel's most spectacular operation was a landing on 8 August by 4500 men in the Kuban. White partisans had replaced the Greens in the Kuban hills, and if they could join hands with the attackers and take Ekaterinodar the cossack vendée would be re-created. As it happened, the Whites had to reembark after less than three weeks. Vrangel thought their commander, General Ulagai, moved too sluggishly, but perhaps the Kuban was too well garrisoned or the cossacks had had enough fighting. Vrangel's last move was the "Trans-Dnepr" operation, prepared for over a month and launched by General

Kutepov's First Army on 6 October. Originally meant to keep the Poles and French interested in the fight, it ended up as a desperate spoiling attack to damage the Reds before their reinforcements could arrive. The Whites got across the Dnepr, but they were badly outnumbered and within a week had to pull back. The initiative now passed to the Reds.

An armistice between Soviet Russia and Poland was signed on 12 October 1920, but even before that the Red high command had given the highest priority to the Crimean attack. (It had been reckoned that even if the Polish war continued over the winter Vrangel would have to be finished off to free troops for the west.) A new Southern Army Group had been set up in September to coordinate the battle with Vrangel. The honor of commanding the last offensive of the Civil War was given to Mikhail Frunze, the veteran Bolshevik activist turned military commander; Frunze had helped stop Kolchak in 1919 and for the last year had commanded Turkestan Army Group. Nevertheless, there were repeated delays. "It turns out," Lenin grumbled, "that *all* the calculations of the Main Commander-in-Chief [Kamenev] are not worth a damn and *are changed weekly*, like those of an ignoramus! Extremely dangerous vacillations!" Trotsky suggested in *Izvestiia* on 17 October that Vrangel might well survive through the winter.[9]

The problem was that a *partial* Red success would only allow Vrangel to pull back from the north Tauride into his Crimean fortress. For decisive results, to trap Vrangel north of Perekop, the Reds needed the shock force of Budenny's First Cavalry Army. Kamenev ordered Budenny to the Vrangel front on 23 September, but despite Kamenev and Frunze's urgings his progress over the three hundred miles from the Polish front to Vrangel's front was slow; the Cavalry Army had been battered at Lvov and Zamosc in August and some of its units were demoralized (and carried out pogroms en route). By the end of October, however, everything was ready. Trotsky and Colonel Kamenev came down to Frunze's headquarters at Kharkov to supervise operations. Five Red armies formed an arc around the north Tauride: First Cavalry, Sixth, and Second Cavalry on the Dnepr, Fourth and Thirteenth between the river and the Sea of Azov, altogether 133,000 men—against 37,000 Whites.[10] Frunze's greatest worry was that the Whites would retreat prematurely into the Crimea; Vrangel had seen the danger, but he wanted to secure the grain harvest. His armies were still in the north Tauride when, on 28 October, Southern Army Group launched its final attack.

The decisive victory Frunze expected was not immediately achieved. Budenny's First Cavalry Army swept southeast seventy-five miles from Kakhovka towards the rail line linking Vrangel to the Crimea, but the other Red armies advanced more slowly. The Whites lost 100 guns, seven armored trains, and 20,000 prisoners, nearly 60 per cent of their army—but the veteran units, including I Corps (the old Volunteer Army) and the Don Cossacks, won the race back into the Crimea. "I am amazed at the enormous energy of the enemy's resistance," Frunze reported to Kamenev. "There is no doubt that he fought more fiercely and stubbornly than any other army could have."[11]

White units now manned the Turkish Wall, at the top of the Perekop Isthmus. It was an easily defended line, even if its defenses had been neglected. But the infantry of the Red Sixth Army turned the White flank by a surprise attack across the shallow Sivash Salt Sea—thanks to the cold weather and favourable winds—on the night of 7 November (the Revolution's third anniversary). The following night the Whites fell back several miles down the isthmus to the Iushun line, which was stormed in turn by the Latvian Division and Bliukher's 51st Division (from Siberia) on 11 November. (Makhno joined these operations, but his part should not be exaggerated; "The Insurgent [Army]," Frunze told Kamenev, "did not play an important part and avoided missions involving the risk of serious losses.") Forty-five miles to the east Fourth Army was able to fight its way across the narrows at Chongar. The Red commanders had been ordered to ignore casualties, and these battles were intense; Frunze estimated total casualties at 10,000.[12]

At the moment of these decisive battles, on 11 November, Frunze sent a wireless signal offering the Whites surrender terms. They were generous (much to Lenin's annoyance); the Whites, to the highest level, were offered pardon for war crimes and the right of emigration if they surrendered immediately. But neither the terms nor the Red onslaught trapped Vrangel; his last achievement was the evacuation of most of his army. He was helped by Red ignorance of what was happening in the Crimea and by a crucial pause of Sixth Army on 12 November. Since April evacuation had seemed a possibility, and the White operation worked much better than in the Kuban in the previous spring. Denikin had had only one overcrowded port, Novorossiisk; Vrangel had Sevastopol, Kerch, Feodosiia, Ialta, and Evpatoriia. Vrangel embarked from Sevastopol on 14 November aboard the cruiser *General Kornilov*, and the last port was cleared on the 16th. It was a much bigger operation than at Novorossiisk; the extraordinary total of 146,000 people were taken off, twice what Vrangel had expected.[13] (This compares with 340,000 Allied troops evacuated from Dunkirk in 1940.) The weather smiled on the Whites. The Black Sea was calm, which meant even small ships could make the 350-mile crossing to Constantinople.

The Crimea had been the last refuge of counterrevolutionary Russia in

1919–1920. Despite the scale of the evacuation, many supporters of the White cause were left behind, under the tender mercies of Bela Kun's Crimean RevCom. In December Lenin said that 300,000 bourgeois were captured in the Crimea, but that they could be assimilated. (On the other hand he had earlier insisted that they "be dealt with mercilessly" if they did not surrender.) The emigre press spoke of the "liberated" Crimea as the "all-Russian graveyard" and their estimates of executions— impossible to verify—were in the tens of thousands.[14]

The more fortunate White soldiers were the ones who were able to escape abroad. Constantinople (whose traditional Slavonic name was "Tsargrad") had been *the* war aim of the Russian nationalists in the great struggle of 1914–1917 that brought down the Imperial regime; it was an irony that the city was the first stage of exile for the remnants of Russian nationalism. General Lukomsky was struck by the scene:

> In those November days, when the streets of Constantinople were filled with a mass of Russian officers and soldiers, and the Bosporus was covered by ships under Russian flags . . . and when the cheers of Russian soldiers for their commanders . . . could be heard from the Bosporus and in the evenings Russian Orthodox evening prayers resounded around the waters of the Bosporus, it seemed that the ancient Russian dream had come true, and Tsargrad had become a Russian town.[15]

But the long-term fate was grim. The survivors of Vrangel's army suffered first internment camps, then statelessness, and a difficult life of exile. Vrangel himself stayed on as White leader, leader without a country, until his death in Brussels in 1928.

Vrangel had remarkable success, given the size of his forces. He kept the pressure on Soviet Russia for another year. There is a parallel between Napoleon's "Spanish Ulcer" and the Red Army's Crimean one; both tied up forces that could have been used with success, perhaps decisive success, on other fronts. Vrangel's main achievement was to preserve the French cordon sanitaire and to give Poland generous eastern frontiers. But there could have been no victory for Vrangel and his army. The Civil War was certainly lost with the armies of Denikin and Kolchak and in 1919, and probably even before that. By mid-1920 Soviet power had been further consolidated and the Red Army had grown. The cossack regions were gone. Vrangel himself called his campaign an epilogue, the "epilogue of the Russian tragedy."[16]

CONCLUSION

Why the Reds Won

Sunday, 7 November 1920, was the third anniversary of the October Revolution. The evening before, Lenin had spoken to a large meeting in Moscow's Bolshoi Theater. "Today," he said, "we can celebrate our victory." Had the Bolsheviks been told on the night of the Petrograd rising "that, three years later what is would be, that we would have this victory of ours, nobody, not even the most incurable optimist would have believed it." (Lenin's memory failed him here; in October 1917 many Bolsheviks had expected victory not just in Russia but across all of Europe, and in a very short period.) *Pravda*, on the 7th, had banner headlines:

> For three years the Republic of Soviets has lived and fought, holding in its hands both the hammer and the rifle.
> For three years, hungry and cold, in fierce struggle, the worker has gone from victory to victory.
> He has waited for the time when his last enemies have perished, when the shackles on the hands of his foreign brothers have been broken.
> Forward again! No shrugging of the mighty shoulders. The hour of world victory is near.

That night the Red forces began the main attack on Vrangel's army at Perekop. A week later, on the 15th, Frunze sent a jubilant signal from the Crimea: "Today our units entered Sevastopol. With powerful blows the Red regiments have finally crushed the south Russian counter-revolution. The tortured country now has the chance to begin to heal the wounds inflicted by the imperialist and civil wars."[1] There was a parade of army cadets in Red Square on the 16th, but no great celebration. Soviet Russia's economic problems were nearing their winter crisis, and this was no time for relaxation. Nevertheless, the last large, organized, anti-Bolshevik force had been driven from Soviet soil. The terrible struggle was over. Soviet power, established three years earlier, was secure. Bolshevism had won.

Was Red victory based on the political and economic policies of the Soviet government? Without doubt the Bolsheviks' early promises were a basic reason why they were able to seize and consolidate power in 1917–1918; their program of Soviet power, peace, land reform, and workers' control was widely popular. But those promises could not be kept. Economic life suffered greatly in the aftermath of the Revolution and the World War. Factories closed, towns starved. The Bolsheviks faced in 1918 a big challenge even within the working class. Urban conditions remained dreadful throughout the Civil War, as Aleksandra Kollontai pointed out in March 1921: "To our shame, in the heart of the republic, in Moscow itself, working people are still living in filthy, overcrowded and unhygienic quarters, one visit to which makes one think that there has been no revolution at all."

Nor were peasants, the great majority of the population, satisfied. Once the gentry's land had been taken there was nothing else to offer them. And given the movement from the towns, the small size of the nobility, and the large amount of land that had been rented prior to 1917, the peasants had access to little more land than they had before. Instead the state had to take the peasants' produce for the towns and their sons for the Red Army. It has been argued that Bolshevik agrarian and food-supply policies had a worse effect than did Civil War fighting, since it was the provinces in the Soviet rear that suffered the worst decline in farm production. A frank (and secret) Soviet report of conditions in 1921 in Tambov, a typical rural province, made clear the dissatisfaction of the peasants: "what sort of Workers' and Peasants' regime is it that we have [?]" they were asking themselves, "the regime in fact is that of the workers, over the peasants."[2]

Nor were the Bolsheviks able to create the kind of mass democracy that they had promised in 1917. The same Tambov report showed great weaknesses even after three years of continuous Soviet rule, and spoke of the "Military-Administrative character of the Soviet Regime"; "the peasantry, in their majority, have become accustomed to regarding the Soviet regime as something extraneous to themselves, something that issues only commands". "Our party," it concluded, "has put down no firm roots in the countryside." By December 1919 Lenin had seen that power had to come first, mass support second: "The proletariat must first overthrow the bourgeoisie and win *for itself* state power, and then use that state power, that is, the dictatorship of the proletariat, as an instrument of its class for the purpose of winning the sympathy of the majority of the working people."[3]

Lenin once said that the underlying reason for "such an historical miracle," why a "weak, exhausted and backward country was able to defeat the most powerful countries in the world" was "centralization, discipline, and unparalleled self-sacrifice."[4] But if Bolshevik success was not explained solely by popular policies it was also not explained solely by some remarkable political efficiency, going back to the Leninist tradition of the elite vanguard party. Economic and military steps were not carried out across Soviet Russia under strict control from Moscow. The Civil War will be much better understood once objective regional studies have been written, but even now it is clear that given the size of "Sovdepia" and the low quality of communications there could be no all-powerful economic and political center; and a great deal of the success of the armies depended on their own efforts as they advanced into the food-rich periphery; the Polish campaign of 1920 was the exception that proved the rule.

The Soviet victory, then, must be seen as a mixture of several elements. The popularity of the Bolsheviks' economic programs was limited after the winter of 1917–1918, and they had not created a real mass democracy. (Indeed, one of the strengths of the Soviet regime was that it often knew better than to pursue unrealistic policies when they did not work.) Nor was the Soviet state highly efficient. Nevertheless, the popularity of Bolshevik programs and the effectiveness of their administration was acceptable—relative to that of their opponents. The effect of Red Terror is harder to assess. Even some Bolshevik leaders felt that terror was counterproductive, but on balance it must be seen as an additional factor leading to victory. It contained the worst effects of the dangerous economic policies and prevented a successful "internal" revolt. Red Terror ensured that no one, as Lenin feared they might, thought the Bolsheviks "old women."

The Bolsheviks kept control of the Red heartland throughout the Civil War, with the result that they outnumbered their opponents. The core territory of Sovdepia was the largest chunk of the population of the old empire, it was mostly Great Russian in nationality, it contained most of the war industry, most establishments and stores of the old army and navy. Gaining and keeping control of this heartland in 1917–1918 was the decisive achievement of the Civil War. Moscow was the symbol of the heartland. Lebedev, one of the SR leaders of the little Komuch-Czechoslovak force that took Kazan in 1918, dreamed of a further advance on Moscow: "all her resources of people, of war, of finance would now be in our hands." "In Moscow we would get masses of troops, there we would get the whole brain of our country, all her soul, all that is talented in Russia."[5]

In fact it was the Bolsheviks who held the Aladdin's cave throughout the Civil War, and their enemies could only dream of its treasures—

after Lebedev Kolchak, and after Kolchak Denikin. Moscow too was the center of communications which enabled the embattled Reds to defeat their isolated enemies one by one. ("The ancient capital," as Churchill put it, "lay at the center of a web of railroads . . . and in the midst a spider! Vain hope to crush the spider by the advance of lines of encircling flies!"[6] The Reds fought from this base in the winter after their revolution, and in the campaigns of 1918 and 1919. By the time of the 1920 campaign the Reds had an overwhelming numerical superiority. All that could have destroyed them was internal decay, and they were able to avoid the most serious internal crises until after their victory on the battlefront. The main campaigns were conventional military ones, and that is where their reserves of manpower gave them an enormous advantage.

They also controlled a vast territory and could give up ground without being seriously threatened. When Lenin in April 1920 listed four conditions facilitating victory, one of them was "the possibility of holding out during a comparatively long civil war, partly thanks to the gigantic size of the country and to the bad means of communication" (the other factors were the Bolshevik peace policy, imperialist disunity, and peasant revolution). Trotsky made the same point: "if we are alive today as an independent revolutionary country . . . this is due to our expanses."[7]

Red strategy probably should not be made too much of as a cause of victory. The Polish campaign was the most complex in military terms, but Pilsudski said he would not contradict those who described it as "a kind of children's scuffle, a mere brawl, unworthy to be considered in the light of the high theories of the military art." "We defeated our enemies," Trotsky admitted, "but it cost us the greatest losses. We took too long over every battle, every war, every campaign."[8] On the whole the Reds simply responded to one attack after another. Their one great adventure, the advance to the west and the southwest in the winter of 1918–1919, possibly prevented the defeat of the Don Cossacks and certainly exposed the Soviet zone to attacks from the east and southeast. One vital decision of mid-1919, to pursue Kolchak beyond the Urals, was largely made *despite* the opinion of Main Commander-in-Chief Vatsetis. The planned southern offensive of the late summer of 1919, with the main blow coming down the Volga and through the Don Host Territory, made strategic sense, but proved impossible to execute. In the destruction of Denikin in the winter of 1919–1920 the Reds overlooked the importance of the Crimea, Vrangel's future base. The final strategic counteroffensive against Poland in the summer of 1920 was clearly pushed too far. This patchy record was only partly due to the short-

275

comings of the Soviet high command; the size of the country and the disruption of the railway system also made it extremely difficult to follow a more "polished" strategy.

Nevertheless, the form that the Red victory took was a military one. However much the Russian struggle may have depicted—and in fact was—a war between classes, it was fought out by armies. Ultimately, Soviet victory owed much to the raising of a mass army commanded by former officers, equipped from Imperial stocks, and manned by peasant conscripts. The acceptance of military reorganization in 1918, under the pressure of the Volga campaign, prepared the Reds for the greater onslaught. Even then, they only won because their forces were so much larger than those of their enemies. Of course, it was terribly important that the Reds were fighting for a cause and had a big propaganda apparatus, but the Whites themselves showed that a remarkable military effort could be created in Russia without an attractivce ideology—beyond the supposed restoration of order.

It must never be forgotten that for the Bolshevik leaders the international dimension was extremely important. "We have always known," Lenin said in his third anniversary speech on 6 November 1920, that "until the revolution takes place in all states . . . our victory will be only half a victory, or perhaps less." E. H. Carr argued that "World revolution . . . was in fact imposed on the regime, not so much by doctrinal orthodoxy, as by the desperate plight of the civil war"; "World revolution" was for Carr the diplomatic counterpart of economic "war communism"; both came not from doctrine but from the war emergency. The parallel is clever, but the analysis is wrong in both cases. The stress on world revolution in 1919–1920 had little to do with the Civil War; the causes were Bolshevik utopianism and central European turmoil.

World revolution became subordinate to other strands of Soviet policy in the 1920s. This was not because the war emergency had ended, but because events had proved it to be just a dream. The basic assumptions had been wrong: Europe was not on the brink of revolution in 1919. Only in backward Russia could radicals take control. Neither the Komintern nor the Red Army gave Moscow a means of forcing the pace. The revolution could spread only by example, and the Soviet example was—on balance—negative. Karl Kautsky, the leading spokesman of western European Marxist orthodoxy, condemned the "Stenka Razin socialism," "barrack socialism," the "Tartar socialism" of Moscow; "Bolshevism has, up to the present, triumphed in Russia, but Socialism has already suffered a defeat."[9]. In other countries moderate leaders and mass opinion were alienated by political repression, terror, and economic chaos; and they were shocked by the Civil War. The Bolsheviks dreamed of turning world war into civil war; in the end only Russia suffered this fate.

Foreign policy was a crucial factor in the Red victory, but not in the way the Bolsheviks originally intended. The greatest single stroke, the event that more than anything else kept the Bolsheviks in power, was the separate peace that unfolded between 25 October 1917 and 3 March 1918. This was in many ways, as the Bolshevik Left realized, a rejection of full-blooded internationalist principles. It also had the negative effect of leading to anti-Bolshevik intervention by the Allies and deepening the economic crisis. But it did allow consolidation of the Bolshevik heartland in 1918, and that made victory possible in 1919 and 1920. After 1918 internationalism had the secondary benefit of maintaining Russian morale by putting forward the myth of the imminent European revolution.

Lenin's role in the Red victory was not as universal as Soviet historians now maintain. As Trotsky pointed out, he took little consistent part in military decision-making at an operational level; he never visited the front and very seldom consulted the high command. Stalin's estimate of 1946 seems about right: "In the Civil War Lenin urged us, then young comrades from the CC, 'Study military affairs thoroughly'. As far as he was concerned, he told us openly, it was too late to study military affairs."[10] Nor was Lenin's *political* judgment an unalloyed success. He was profoundly wrong about issues that were most basic to his beliefs. He was wrong about the ability of the masses to run the state and the economy, his basic economic policies were untenable (some of them were tested almost to the point of destruction in the winter of 1920–1921), and he was wrong about the likelihood of European revolution. On the other hand his leadership during the October Revolution and the Brest negotiations was of central importance, and he also established a personal control over the party and the state which prevented (after March 1918) internal instability. He was sometimes prepared, too, to back off when he met obstacles—as in the use of the regular army and in some aspects of peasant policy.

The historian looking at Trotsky's Civil War career must beware of two myths. The first is the Soviet view dominant ever since his disgrace in the late 1920s that he played no beneficial role in the Civil War. ("History," Comrade Stalin in fact pointed out, "shows that . . . Kolchak and Denikin were beaten by our troops *in spite* of Trotsky's plans.") The second might be called the "Trotskyist" myth that exaggerates his importance. The truth lies in between the two, but given the state of

Western historiography it is perhaps the second myth that deserves the most attention. Trotsky was, of course, the second best-known Soviet leader. But his career in 1917–1920 was marked by spectacular failures. He made major mistakes in foreign policy in early 1918 and in economic policy in 1920. Even his career in the Red Army had the bitterness of the summer of 1919. Trotsky's vital step was to support the creation of a regular army against much party opposition. He also played an important agitational role, his famous headquarters train covered 65,000 miles, and all this was something that Lenin, as their comrade Lunacharsky pointed out, could not have done.[11] The fighting men needed a figurehead to rally around, and Trotsky played his part effectively.

At the same time the other important leaders of the Civil War should not be lost sight of. Sverdlov, who died in early 1919, helped organize the state and the party, and Rykov, disgraced in the 1930s, was the man in charge of the war economy. Smilga, another future oppositionist, was the chief political organizer of the Red Army. Something should be said for Stalin, too, who had a most active career in the Civil War; if he had been killed in 1920 he would certainly be remembered as one of the great activists of the war. And outside the party probably no one was as important as two former Tsarist colonels, Vatsetis and Kamenev.

Why the Bolsheviks' Enemies Lost

The Bolsheviks' victory was also made possible by the weakness of their enemies. The parties of the Right had never commanded many followers, and the center-right Kadet party was hardly in a better state. The educated minority who opposed the revolution became more and more aware of their isolation as time went by. Gorn, an official active in the Baltic, was probably typical:

> It would be a mistake to think that Bolshevism was an alien element in Russia. Multi-million illiterate Russia nurtured it, she bore it and belched it forth from inside herself. The Russian intelligentsia was the thinnest film on the surface of the Russian *muzhik* [peasant] ocean.

G. K. Gins wrote something similar after the disaster of the Siberian Whites:

> Our culture was a frail boat in the midst of a raging sea but we, the representatives of the intelligentsia, argued among ourselves on the boat and

did not notice the elemental force coming at us. The ocean swallowed the boat, and us with it.[12]

Paradoxically, the moderate agrarian socialists who tried to swim in the "muzhik ocean" also drowned. This was partly a failure of will and organization, but it also came from a kind of peasant passivity, a passivity that was a key to the outcome of the Civil War. The secret Soviet Tambov report is useful here too. Even the kulaks, it noted,

> the most cultured, the most politically developed stratum ... do not, in general, show any capacity for raising their sights to thinking in terms of the state as a whole; their economic [mental outlook] has not carried them ... very far beyond the outskirts of their villages or rural districts ... without the guidance of the parties of the industrial bourgeoisie this movement can lead only to anarchical rioting and to bandit destruction.[13]

The SRs were never able to mobilize peasant support, to defend the Constituent Assembly, to oppose the "commissarocracy," or to counter the pressure of the White generals.

Given the weakness of the anti-Bolshevik civilians, it is not surprising that the soldiers took over. They alone had effective force. "*Kto palku vzial, tot i kapral*," "He who has the stick is the corporal," summed up the power relationships in anti-Bolshevik Russia.[14]

The Whites are sometimes said to have lost because petty rivalries blocked a common military strategy. It is true that their attacks were not coordinated, but this could not have been avoided. The difficulties of communication were immense. The four White fronts—south Russia, western Siberia, north Russia, the Baltic—were all far distant from one another; the two main fronts, Denikin's and Kolchak's, were separated by a 10,500-mile voyage around the Middle East and Asia, and then a 4000-mile rail trip across Siberia. The fate of General Grishin-Almazov, captured and executed while trying to take the "short" route to Omsk across the Caspian Sea, showed the danger. Denikin and Kolchak never met one another and could not have done so during the Civil War. The various White armies simply launched their attacks as soon as they were ready. There were sound reasons for this. With each month the Red army became larger. The Allies would only give support if there were successful White advances. Civil War armies did better on the offensive. The one serious mistake of grand strategy was the failure of the Siberian and South Russian armies to link up—either in the summer of 1918 or the summer of 1919, and at the time there seemed good reasons for advancing in other directions. The failure of the Poles to march in 1919 was also critical, although this was outside White control.

The anti-Bolshevik democrats had a popular program but few military resources. The White generals and colonels had better armies but made few promises to the population of their base territories and of the large captured regions. This was partly because the Whites' social foundation was the property-owning minority (the *tsenzovoe* society). But it also came from their very dislike of politics. The White leaders were narrow conservative nationalists. Sakharov, one of Kolchak's generals, summed up the White outlook in his 1919 appeal to the Urals population: "Our party is Holy Russia, our class is the whole Russian people." The Whites ignored parties and classes; they thought, moreover, in terms not of revolution or even of civil war, but of the *likholet'e* or *smuta* (time of troubles); the great smuta dated from the early 1600s. Denikin entitled his massive memoirs *Sketches of the Russian Time of Troubles*. One anti-Bolshevik cossack politican, defending demands for autonomy against the disapproval of the White generals, had to insist, "This is not a smuta but a popular movement."[15] But the Whites were even afraid of a popular movement.

The Whites feared the people; paradoxically, they counted on some vague popular upsurge to bring them victory. Sakharov again, talking about the late autumn of 1919, was typical. If the rear would give his poorly equipped army some support he would pursue the Reds back beyond the Urals.

> And then the road to Moscow would be clear, then the whole people would come over to us and stand openly under the Admiral's banner. The Bolsheviks and the other socialist filth would be destroyed—from the roots up—by the burning rage of the popular masses.

But the Whites, unlike the Reds, made little effort to mobilize the population in a political way, and their social and political program was not one that bred spontaneous popular support. Sakharov proudly wrote that "the White movement was in essence the first manifestation of *fascism*" (he was writing in Munich, nine months after Mussolini's March on Rome).[16] But this was distorted hindsight; the Whites lacked the mobilization skills and relatively wide social base of the Italian or German radical Right.

Linked to narrow political horizons was another vital drawback of White rule: arbitrary conduct by White authorities and a general lack of order. The source of this was the crude nature of White "politics" and the lack of vital resources: civilian administrators, an enthusiastic population, and time. The Whites also failed properly to organize their armies. This may seem odd, given that the movement was dominated by military officers. But they actually lacked properly trained military specialists, especially in Siberia. The cossacks gave them a major advantage in south Russia, but the cossacks were jealous of their own autonomy and fought best within their "host territories." The Whites had only a small base of manpower and material compared to Sovdepia. And, as was the case with general administration, they had less time than the Reds to organize their forces.

The Whites, as Great Russian nationalists, were also opposed to any concessions to the minorities. They have no tolerance for "the sweet poisonous dreams of complete independence" (Denikin's words) of people such as the Ukrainians, the Belorussians, the Baltic and Transcaucasian minorities. Denikin was right when he said that his officers, Russian nationalists, would not have fought for the "Federated Republic."[17] Although the Whites were prepared to accept some form of independence for Poland and possibility for Finland, they could not agree to all the territorial claims of the Warsaw and Helsinki governments. Polish action on the western border in 1919 might have made possible the capture of Moscow, while Finnish support would certainly have made Red Petrograd indefensible.

The Whites had little chance of winning. Certainly by 1920 Vrangel could only have won if there had been a catastrophic internal collapse on the Soviet side. But even Kolchak and Denikin faced, from the winter of 1918–1919, a struggle against great odds. The Bolsheviks had had a year to consolidate their position, they controlled most of the military resources of old Russia, they had more popular support, and their forces outnumbered those of the Whites by ten to one.

The "Russian" Civil War was a three-cornered struggle. Russian revolutionaries fought Russian counterrevolutionaries, but the national minorities resisted both. The Civil War was about what would become of all the peoples of the Empire. (And it was an internal affair; the only fighting outside the old Empire was the 1920 Lvov campaign—in what had been Austrian Galicia—and the 1921 Mongolian expedition.) Those regions that broke away were among the "winners" of the Civil War. They succeeded for various reasons. Finland and Poland won their *own* independence. Bessarabia, five Belorussian-Ukrainian provinces, and Kars Province had the pull of neighbouring states (Rumania, Poland, and Turkey). Estonia, Latvia, and Lithuania were helped by German and Allied forces. All benefited from the Red Army's preoccupation with other fronts. But more than 80 percent of the former subjects of the Tsar became citizens of the Soviet federation. Half of these people were not Great Russians. The multinational Russian Empire, the famous "prison of peoples," did *not* break up, a remarkable development in an age of nationalism.

Demographic, geographical, and cultural factors were involved. The Great Russians outnumbered each individual minority by fifteen to one or more (except in the case of the Ukrainians). Alliances that might have countered this—the Transcaucasian Federation, the cossacks and their southeastern allies, the Poles with the Ukrainians and Belorussians, Pan-Turkism—remained only theoretical projects. The central provinces, the Sovdepia heartland, were Russian-dominated. Even in the minority areas Russians often controlled the towns and transport. The trained military leaders were Russian, and the nature of Tsarism predetermined the minorities' weakness, just as it predetermined the weakness of Russian political parties. The Petersburg-centered Romanov autocracy had allowed little political or national activity. Even in areas where the minorities came to see themselves as distinct nations—and 1917 was a great awakener—they lacked the experience and the time to create an effective administration.

Bolshevik Moscow's social revolution attracted the intelligentsia, workers, and peasants of the outlying regions. Bolshevik national policy, too, seemed better than the "Russia, One and Indivisible" of the Whites, for whom cooperation with the "separatists" was ruled out from the start. It is hard to understand Richard Pipes's view that the Bolsheviks were "the least qualified of all the Russian parties (save for those of the extreme right) to solve the national problem." The cossack politician who spoke of "Trotsky's dreams of a Sovdepia, one, great, and indivisible" was making a crude oversimplification.[18] Bolshevik policy rejected Russian chauvinism, and the most enthusiastic "internationalists" were reined in; the Bolsheviks granted self-government, however imperfect, to a number of peoples, and to the Ukraine, Belorussia, and other regions they even granted a form of independence. Moscow allowed wide cultural autonomy and encouraged a national awakening that would cause problems for itself in the 1920s. And it combined this with the maintenance of centralized institutions such as the party and the army and with the unifying idea of social revolution. This was just the right—possibly the *only*—formula for holding multinational "Russia" together.

It was important that the Russian Bolsheviks had strong motives for holding the Empire together. Their leaders saw the nationalists as just a form of bourgeois rule. Their *spetsy* military commanders had simpler nationalist motives. For both, the defeat of "Russian" counterrevolutionaries and Allied intervention demanded an advance into the borderlands. And there were broad continuities. Denikin put it as follows:

> The state link of Russia with her borderlands was preordained by history, economics, markets, the railway system, the need for defendable frontiers, the psychology of Russian society, and the whole totality of the cultural-economic development of *both* sides and of *mutual* interests. The link would be restored, sooner or later, voluntarily—by treaty—or through compulsion—economic (tariff) war or an army offensive. And that would have been done by *any* Russia—"Red," "Pink," "White," or "Black"—which did not want to suffocate inside the limits of those artifical boundaries which the World War and internal chaos had confined her to.[19]

The link was something that the newly conscious, newly organized minorities could not tear apart.

Defeated with the Whites was foreign intervention. Bolshevik Civil War propaganda stressed Allied intervention, and later Soviet historians, following Stalin, reduced the Civil War to three "Entente Campaigns." An imperialist conspiracy fitted in with the Bolshevik world outlook; a foreign threat mobilized nationalist feeling; and the "Entente cannibals" (Stalin's phrase) gave a reason why the Civil War lasted so long. But Lenin had predicted on the eve of October 1917 that the Allies would not be a serious problem: "a combination of English, Japanese, and American imperialism against us is extremely difficult to realize, and is not at all dangerous to us, if only because of Russia's geographical position";[20] there is much to be said for this analysis.

Contrary to what is often thought, the most important "intervention" was not by the Allies but by the Central Powers. Up until November 1918 they held much of western and southern Russia. The "fourteen-power" anti-Bolshevik Allied alliance that was featured in Soviet propaganda was a myth. The Americans were cool about intervention; the Japanese stayed on the Pacific coast. The French gave up an active role after the spring of 1919 Odessa shambles and concentrated on a *cordon sanitaire* of the border states. (Even then, neither the French nor the British did much to help the border state of Poland in 1920.) Few Allied troops were sent; none fought in the main battles. The western Allies neither created the Czechoslovak Corps nor planned its uprising. The Czechoslovaks did clear a rallying area, but they were few in number and fought only for six months. Their success was a symptom not of Allied manipulation but of Soviet impotence and unpopularity. It is true that Allied munitions and supplies made possible the furthest White advance, but this material only arrived in quantity in the summer of 1919; Kolchak's spring offensive and Denikin's conquest of a south Russian base area came earlier. Even the Allied blockade had little effect. Bolshevik Russia's foreign trade possibilities were limited anyway (especially after the renunciation of foreign debts), and for most of 1919 Whites or nationalists held the major ports (Petrograd was the exception, but it had already become an economic wasteland).

Intervention was not a disaster for the Allies, if only because they committed so few resources to it. True, it did not defeat the Central Powers, save the anti-Bolsheviks, or deflect a Soviet onslaught on Central Europe (something the Red Army was hardly up to). The Reds *were* distracted from some of the border regions. Some White leaders resented the intrusions of the "dress-circle *internatsional*"[21], but Allied support was a major part of White propaganda. There is little evidence that intervention *helped* the Bolsheviks by making their cause a nationalist one. And if intervention lengthened the Russian crisis it did not create dictatorship and terror; they had deep enough roots in the soil of Imperial Russia.

The outcome of the Civil War has much to do with Russian history. Tsarist Russia contained elements of both backwardness and modernity. Russia's peculiar state-sponsored modernization meant that there was a considerable working class (although small in per capita terms) and only a small middle class. The victory of extreme radicals during the Civil War had much to do with the very strength of the autocracy before 1917. Until less than ten years before the start of the world war there had been no legal political parties. The Tsarist state had never tolerated rival forces in the form of political parties or the national minorities, or even in the form of the army or the church. As a result there were no strong forces on hand to take over the country when the autocracy disappeared in February 1917.

The Bolsheviks were able to take over, in the October 1917 Revolution and the "Triumphal March of Soviet Power," because they followed the popular movement. The workers and Tsarist soldiers, with their particular discontents, helped carry the Bolsheviks to power—and then economic collapse and demobilization largely ended their political role. The Right was still shattered by the impact of the world war, the fall of the autocracy, and the impact of social revolution. After that there was no one to challenge the "dictatorship of the proletariat." The reason the country did not just slide into anarchy with the October Revolution was, ironically, because of the state tradition that had been created under the autocracy. Modernization had progressed far enough to give a railway network that enabled the center to regain control of the

284

periphery, and meanwhile the Bolsheviks were able and willing to make use of much of the apolitical debris of the Tsarist state, including the army officer-corps and the civil service.

The Cost

Lev Kritsman began his classic history of the Soviet Civil War economy with a photograph of a nine-year-old in a sailor suit, and a dedication that began, "To the memory of little Iurii, to the memory of my only child, to the memory of the countless children who were victims of the intervention of world capital." The events of 1917–1920 were a great tragedy to countless Russian families.

Any attempt to count the Civil War dead makes depressing work, and does not even result in a reliable figure. The best recent estimate for the *armies* was probably that of the demographer Urlanis: 800,000 dead on both sides in 1917–1922:

	Killed in Action	Died from Wounds	Died from Disease	Total
Red	125,000		300,000	
White/Polish	175,000		150,000	
Total	300,000	50,000	450,000	800,000

Urlanis's reliance on official figures for Red Army deaths means that his estimates are probably on the low side. Few records, for example, can have survived the destruction of 150,000-strong Caspian-Caucasus Army Group in early 1919. Also, his detailed figures give the number of casualties in the big Kolchak and Denikin campaigns of 1919 as only two-fifths of those for 1920, and considerably less than for 1921. Perhaps the figures just represent better medical services and statistics; higher losses in 1919 were simply not reported. Another recent estimate, by Poliakov, suggested many more deaths among Red troops: 632,000 from battle and 581,000 from disease.[22]

Urlanis's figure of 175,000 enemy troops killed in action is conjectural. He suggested that 50,000 died in south Russia in 1918–1920, and 38,000 Poles (higher than the official Polish figure). This leaves 87,000; presumably Urlanis thought they were killed in Kolchak's armies and on the minor fronts. Fragmentary White data suggests that the south Russian figure is too low. The Kornilov Division alone claimed to have lost

285

13,700 killed (June 1917–November 1920), and a similar scale of losses could be expected at least in the Markov and Drozdovsky units, and in Don Army. Poliakov's rough calculations produced a figure of 1,287,000 for deaths from battle and disease in the enemy armies.[23]

The armies probably suffered more from microbes than battle; in this, as in much else, the Russian Civil War was a throwback to earlier centuries. Urlanis estimated that typhus and typhoid alone claimed the lives of 81,000 Red soldiers in 1918–1920. Hard figures of 15,000 deaths among White POWs at one garrison town in Siberia in December 1919–March 1920 support a contemporary estimate of 50,000 typhus deaths in Kolchak's armies; figures for 46,000 ill in Denikin's armies, nearly a fifth of paper strength, have already been mentioned.[24]

It is even more difficult to number the victims of "internal fighting" and of Red and White Terror. The following are four estimates of those who died at the hands of the Soviet government:[25]

	Executed	Comments
Latsis (1921)	12,733	1917–1920, Cheka only
Chamberlin (1935)	50,000	"Civil War"
Leggett (1981)	140,000	Dec 1917–Feb 1922
Conquest (1971)	200,000	1917–1923; as many as 400,000 died in prison or killed in suppression of anti-Soviet revolts.

Latsis's figures seem too low, and Conquest's too high, but one can only guess. The figures for White Terror are even more difficult. The Bolshevik underground was broken up in the White cities, there were operations against peasant partisans in Siberia, and pogroms in the west-central Ukraine; the victims must have numbered in the tens of thousands.

For what it is worth, *if* the estimates of both Conquest and Urlanis are right, then three times as many "class enemies" were killed in internal fighting as on the "regular" battlefront. In any event, the demographer "Maksudov" compared the surviving male and female population and—assuming that famine and disease affected both sexes more or less equally—concluded that extra male losses indicated 2 million deaths from Civil War action.[26]

Turning to the *general* losses resulting from the Civil War, it is important not to forget those who fled Russia as a result of the Revolution and Civil War. The demographers Lorimer and Volkov estimated these as about two million, more than Russian combat deaths in the World War; an unofficial Soviet source, Maksudov, suggested a figure of 3.5 million.[27] Given that many of the emigres came from the educated elite, the damage to economic and cultural life was even higher than the figures suggest.

Finally there is the question of the total human cost. This is bound up less with Red troops fighting White troops or Cheka executions; what killed most were the dreadful epidemics. The offical statistics show 890,000 deaths from typhus and typhoid in 1919, and 1,044,000 in 1920 (compared to 63,000 in 1917). In addition to that there was dysentery, cholera, and the *Ispanka*, the Spanish influenza pandemic of 1918–1919. The effects of hunger were tremendous. One source estimated that three million or more deaths could have come from higher child mortality. (Another indication of the scale of the Russian tragedy were the seven million *bezprizornye*, homeless children.[28])

Lorimer's study estimated deaths for the period 1914–1926 by comparing census figures and taking into account changes in territory and in the birth rate. The result was a figure of 16 million, which Lorimer divided between two million military deaths and 14 million civilian. Lorimer did not give a Civil War figure, but subtracting 1.7 killed in the World War and about five million who died in the 1921–1922 famine would leave nine to ten million deaths resulting directly or indirectly from the revolution. Urlanis, without giving any calculations, estimated losses from disease, hunger, and the fighting as 8 million, or 4 percent of the population (although it is not clear if this included 1921–1922). An earlier Soviet demographer, Volkov, reckoned population loss in 1918–1921 as just over seven million, and a similar estimate was recently made by Maksudov.[29]

Lenin was wrong in September 1917 when he compared a possible civil war with Kerensky's June offensive: "No 'rivers of blood' in an internal civil war can even compare with those *seas* of blood which the Russian imperialists have shed since 19 June." (Lenin gave a figure of 500,000 Russians killed that June; actual losses in *May–November* 1917 were 22,500.)[30] But Lenin was wrong even if the *whole* World War is included. There were seven to ten million Russian victims, four times those the country lost in the World War, and they were mostly civilians. The Civil War unleashed by Lenin's revolution was the greatest national catastrophe Europe had yet seen.

The economic impact of war and revolution was recently summed up by Silvana Malle, using Soviet data published in 1923. The total value of the output of finished products in 1921 was only 16 percent of that in 1912; for semifinished products the figure was 12 percent. For particular sectors, 1921 output compared to 1912 was (finished/unfinished products): mining, 29%/27%; oil, 36%/–; metals, 10%/4%; chemicals, 21%/33%; food, 10%/18%; cotton, 7%/5%; and wool 34%/16%. Losses were particularly high in the central region (Sovdepia), which had been cut off from fuel and raw materials. Nove produced similar figures (in million tons):

Year	Coal	Steel	Rail freight	Grain harvest
1913	29.0	4.3	132.4	80.1
1921	8.9	0.2	39.4	37.6

In addition, the production of cotton fabric dropped from 2582 million meters to 105 million.[31]

It is very difficult to work out how much of this was caused by Civil War and how much by the World War. On the one hand *direct* damage from enemy action to Soviet industry varied. The Donbas, the Ukraine, and the Urals suffered very heavily, while the big industrial concentrations around Moscow and Petrograd were never occupied. In any event Kritsman, the historian of the Civil War economy, estimated that national income in 1920 was only 40 percent of 1913; agriculture fell by 1.5 times, transport by 5 times, industry 5.5 times: "Such a fall of the productive forces . . . of a huge society of a hundred million people . . . is unexampled in the history of mankind."[32]

In the seven decades since October 1917 Soviet Russia has suffered from authoritarian and even totalitarian politics, outbursts of terror, and a morbid distrust of neighbors. Was all this another cost of the Civil War? There are various explanations of the way Soviet Russia has developed. One concerns politics, and especially Leninist ideology: Soviet developments can be traced back to the principles of Bolshevism, and to Lenin's "What Is to Be Done?" with its concepts apparently so compatible with Stalinism. A broader version of this is that any form of socialism claiming absolute control over society is bound to lead to "totalitarian" excesses. A second explanation makes Soviet developments the result of Russian history. The low level of economic development and education, the relatively primitive society, and even the "political culture" of Tsarism were legacies that the new rulers of Russia had to inherit. (The Menshevik interpretation links this to the "premature" October Revolution, the Trotskyist interpretation to its isolation.) A more complex version would tie together the economic and political and argue that the task of overcoming economic backwardness—with the need for popular sacrifice—is bound to demand an authoritarian state. There is also the view that neither the history nor the political traditions of Bolshevism were crucial; the explanation lies in the detailed political history of the 1920s and the political skills and diseased personality of Joseph Stalin.

The view that the Civil War was a basic cause of later Soviet developments is an interpretation less commonly met, although the war is often brought in as a secondary factor. Historians such as Sheila Fitzpatrick, R. W. Davies, Moshe Lewin, and Roger Pethybridge have argued that the administrative methods learned in the Civil War were revived in the late 1920s, with the forced collectivization of the peasants and the elimination of unorthodox Communists. Stalin's famous slogan of the 1930s was a throwback to the *Sturm und Drang* of the Civil War era: "There is no fortress Bolsheviks cannot storm." An alternative and related (if somewhat contradictory) interpretation bringing in the Civil War is Trotsky's view that the working class was destroyed in the Civil War and that this opened the way for the takeover of power by the "bureaucracy."

Certainly later events can be linked to the Civil War. It is, however, going too far to say that without the Civil War things would have developed differently. The crucial point is whether the "Revolution" and the "Civil War" were two distinct things. They were not. In the first place, many developments that might seem to come from the Civil War were really indirect, inevitable, and delayed consequences of the Bolshevik seizure of power. The Bolsheviks were great partisans of class conflict, and of class conflict pursued to the death. It is utopian to think that after the seizure of power one's opponents will simply lie back and think of the inevitability of human progress. The Bolsheviks were less afraid of civil war than they should have been. When Soviet power was so weak and thinly based, when the Bolshevik Party and class in whose name it ruled were so small, it is hard to see how the enemies of Bolshevism could not have had considerable success. The most dramatic example of this was the Czechoslovak Corps' whirlwind conquest of all the Urals and Siberia.

The political and economic system advocated by the Bolshevik leadership and many of their urban enthusiasts in 1917, the "pre-Civil War" program, was one that was basically unstable and utopian, and could not *fail* to be replaced by something else. In particular the general popular sovereignty of the "commune state" was incompatible with the divided interests of town and country, and with the inevitable consequences of the maximalist program. But even without looking at this aspect, it is hard see how any version of socialism could have flourished given the realities of Russian society and the overoptimism of the socialist-minded part of the intelligentsia.

The Civil War did not lead to Stalinism; rather, *both* the Civil War and Stalinism were likely consequences of the seizure of power. The October Revolution, the Civil War, the Red victory, and the later development of Stalinism can all be seen as a result of Russian historical development, notably the persistance of the Tsarist autocracy, its smothering of forces that might have provided an alternative to a maximalist government, the peculiarly unbalanced nature of Russian economic development, and the slow evolution of nationalism among the peasant masses of the minority peoples. The costs of the Civil War in human lives were vast. Given the nature of Russian society and given the ideology of the party that took power, Civil War was implicit in the October Revolution. The costs of the Civil War were the costs of the Revolution.

Maps

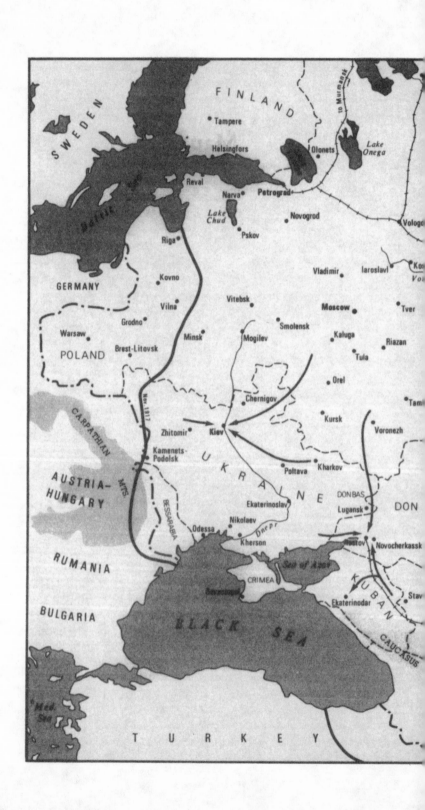

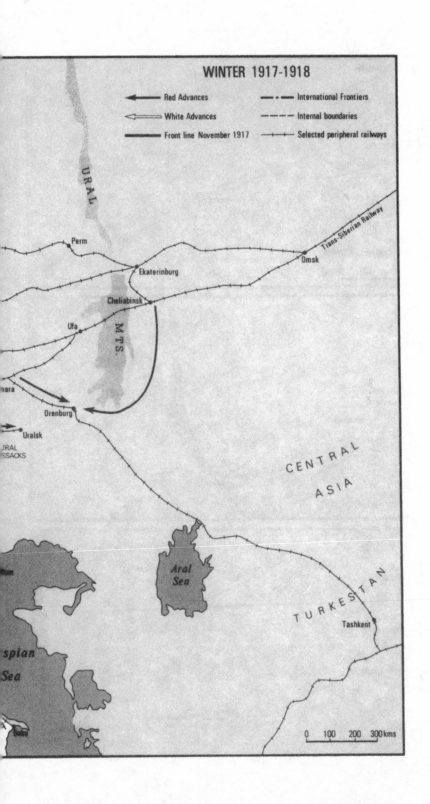

WINTER 1917-1918

Red Advances
White Advances
Front line November 1917
International Frontiers
Internal boundaries
Selected peripheral railways

URAL

Perm

Ekaterinburg

Omsk

Trans-Siberian Railway

Cheliabinsk

Ufa

M T S.

hara

Drenburg

Uralsk

JRAL
SSACKS

CENTRAL

ASIA

Aral
Sea

TURKESTAN

Tashkent

spian
Sea

Sea

0   100   200   300 kms

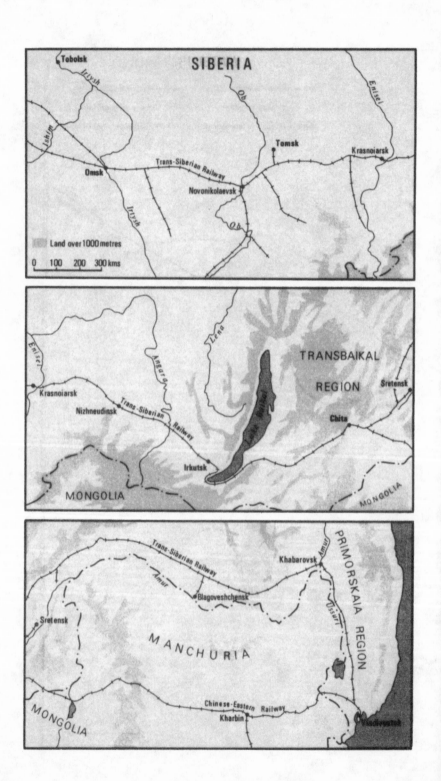

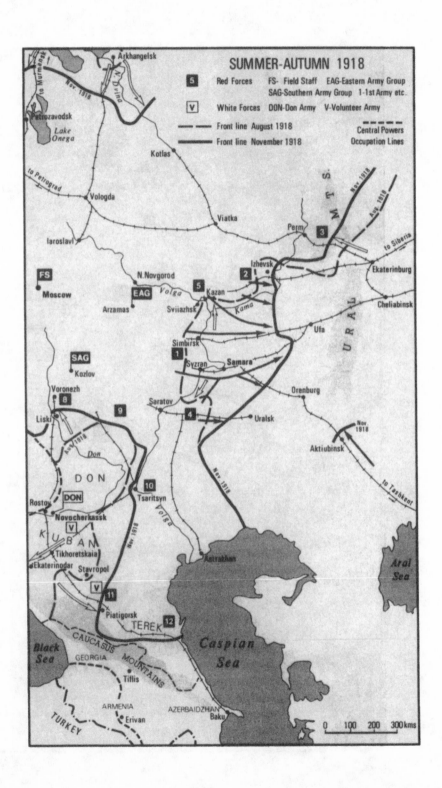

SUMMER-AUTUMN 1918

5	Red Forces	FS- Field Staff	EAG-Eastern Army Group
			SAG-Southern Army Group 1-1st Army etc.
V	White Forces	DON-Don Army	V-Volunteer Army

- - - Front line August 1918

—— Front line November 1918

Central Powers
Occupation Lines

to Murmansk

Arkhangelsk

N. Dvina

Nov. 1918

to Petrograd

Petrozavodsk

Lake
Onega

Kotlas

Vologda

Viatka

Iaroslavl

Perm 3

Nov. 1918

Aug. 1918

to Siberia

Ekaterinburg

N.Novgorod

Izhevsk 2

FS

Moscow

EAG

Volga

5

Kazan

Kama

Cheliabinsk

U R A L M T S.

Arzamas

Sviiazhsk

Ufa

Simbirsk 1

SAG

Kozlov

Syzran

Samara

Orenburg

Voronezh

8

Saratov

Uralsk

Nov.
1918

Liski

Aug. 1918

Don

4

Nov. 1918

Aktiubinsk

to Tashkent

9

D O N

DON

Rostov

Novocherkassk

V

K U B A N

Tikhoretskaia

Ekaterinodar Stavropol

10

Tsaritsyn

Volga

Nov. 1918

Astrakhan

Aral
Sea

V

11

Piatigorsk

TEREK 12

CAUCASUS

Black
Sea

GEORGIA

MOUNTAINS

Tiflis

Caspian
Sea

TURKEY

ARMENIA

Erivan

AZERBAIDZHAN

Baku

0 100 200 300kms

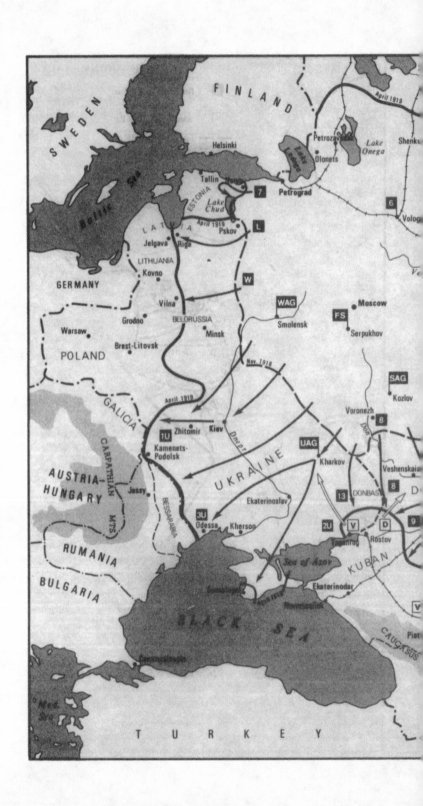

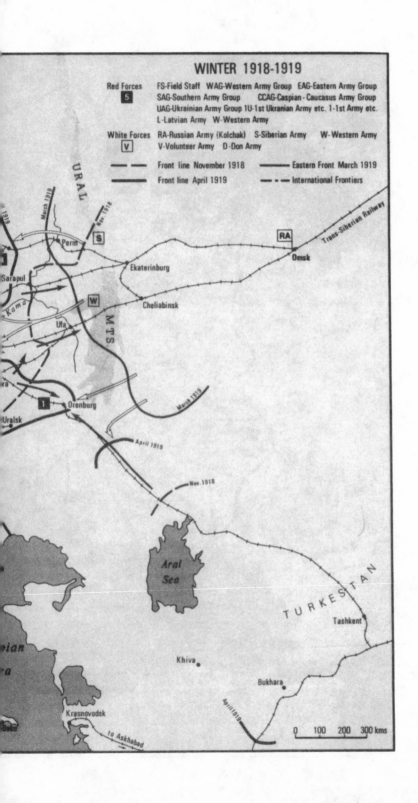

WINTER 1918-1919

Red Forces
S
FS-Field Staff WAG-Western Army Group EAG-Eastern Army Group
SAG-Southern Army Group   CCAG-Caspian-Caucasus Army Group
UAG-Ukrainian Army Group 1U-1st Ukranian Army etc. 1-1st Army etc.
L-Latvian Army W-Western Army

White Forces
V
RA-Russian Army (Kolchak)   S-Siberian Army   W-Western Army
V-Volunteer Army   D-Don Army

— — — Front line November 1918   ———— Eastern Front March 1919
———— Front line April 1919   — · — International Frontiers

URAL

March 1919

Nov 1918

S Perm

RA Omsk

Trans-Siberian Railway

Ekaterinburg

Sarapul

Kama

W

Cheliabinsk

Ufa

M T S

1 Orenburg

March 1919

Uralsk

April 1919

Nov. 1918

Aral Sea

TURKESTAN

Tashkent

Khiva

Bukhara

April 1919

Krasnovodsk

to Askhabad

0   100   200   300 kms

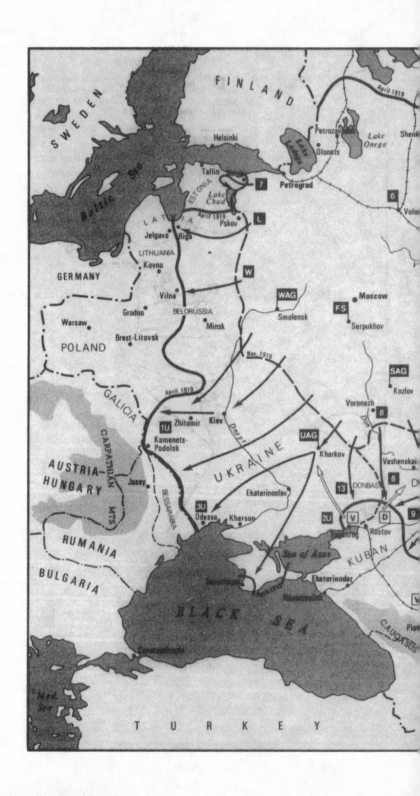

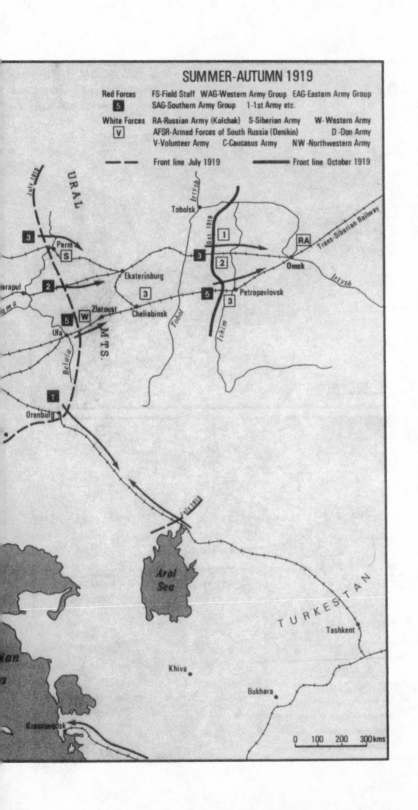

SUMMER-AUTUMN 1919

Red Forces FS-Field Staff WAG-Western Army Group EAG-Eastern Army Group
5   SAG-Southern Army Group   1-1st Army etc.

White Forces RA-Russian Army (Kolchak) S-Siberian Army W-Western Army
V   AFSR-Armed Forces of South Russia (Denikin)   D-Don Army
              V-Volunteer Army C-Caucasus Army NW-Northwestern Army

— — — Front line July 1919   ▬▬▬ Front line October 1919

URAL

July 1919

Tobolsk

Oct. 1919

Irtysh

RA

Trans-Siberian Railway

Perm
S

3

Ekaterinburg

Omsk

Irtysh

Sarapul

2

3

1

2

3

Cheliabinsk

Tobol

Petropavlovsk

5

3

Zlatoust
W

5

Tishim

Ufa

M T S.

Kama

Belaia

Orenburg

1

July 1919

Aral
Sea

TURKESTAN

Tashkent

Khiva

Bukhara

Krasnovodsk

0   100   200   300 kms

S.E. RUSSIA 1920-1921

1C - 1st Cavalry Army   1 - 1st Army etc.

———— Front line January 1920

UKRAINE · Kharkov · DON

Dnepr · N.TAURIDE · Rostov · 8 · 9 · Don · Volga

13 · Jan. 1920 · Perekop · Sea of Azov · Egorlykskaia · 1C · 10

Sevastopol · CRIMEA · KUBAN · Tikhoretskaia · Jan. 1920 · 11

Novorossisk · Ekaterinodar · TEREK · Caspian Sea

Black Sea · BLACK SEA PROVINCE · 9 · CAUCASUS 1920 · DAGESTAN

GEORGIA · MOUNTAINS · AZERBAIDZHAN · Baku

Batum · Tiflis · 1921

TURKEY · Turkish Army · ARMENIA · Erivan

0 100 200 300 kms

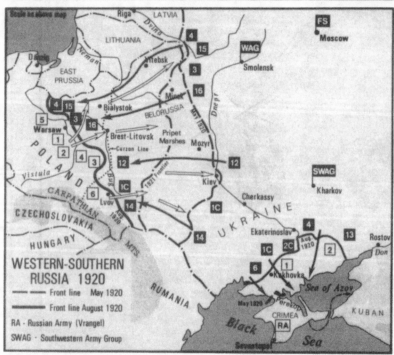

Scale as above map · Riga · LATVIA · FS · Moscow

Dvina · 4 · 15 · WAG

Danzig · LITHUANIA · Vitebsk · 3 · Smolensk

EAST PRUSSIA · Neman · Minsk · 16 · Dnepr

4 · 15 · Bialystok · BELORUSSIA · JULY 1920

5 · 3 · 16 · Brest-Litovsk · Pripet Marshes · Mozyr · 12

Warsaw · 1 · Curzon Line · 12

2 · 4 · 3 · 12 · 1921 Frontier · Kiev

POLAND · Vistula · 6 · 1C · Cherkassy · 1C

CARPATHIAN · Lvov · 14 · UKRAINE

CZECHOSLOVAKIA · 14 · Ekaterinoslav · 4 · SWAG · Kharkov

HUNGARY · MTS. · 1C · 2C · Aug 1920 · 2 · 13 · Rostov · Don

WESTERN-SOUTHERN RUSSIA 1920 · RUMANIA · 6 · 1 · Kakhovka

——— Front line   May 1920 · May 1920 · Perekop · Sea of Azov

———— Front line August 1920 · CRIMEA · RA · KUBAN

RA - Russian Army (Vrangel) · Black Sea · Sevastopol

SWAG - Southwestern Army Group

NOTES

Abbreviations used in the notes (full details are in the bibliography):

DBFP   *Documents on British Foreign Policy*
DGK   *Direktivy Glavnogo komandovaniia Krasnoi armii*
DKF   *Direktivy komandovaniia frontov Krasnoi Armii*
DSV   *Dekrety Sovetskoi vlasti*
DVP   *Dokumenty vneshnei politiki SSSR*
GV   Bubnov (ed.), *Grazhdanskaia voina*
GVE   *Grazhdanskaia voina: Entsiklopediia*
IIGV   *Iz istorii grazhdanskoi voiny*
KPSSRR *Kommunisticheskaia partiia Sovetskogo Soiuza v rezoliutsiiakh i resheniiakh*
KVR   Trotsky, *Kak vooruzhalas' revoliutsiia*
ORS   Denikin, *Ocherki russkoi smuti*
PRO   Public Record Office, London
PSS   Lenin, *Pol'noe sobranie sochinenii*
TP   Meijer (ed.), *Trotsky Papers*

1 Triumphal March of Soviet Power

1 Gavrilov and Kutuzov, pp. 87–91.
2 *PSS*, 6: 127.
3 Service, 1979, p. 36; Rigby, 1979, pp. 59–62.
4 Keep, 1976, p. xi.
5 Radkey, 1963, pp. 283, 308, 466.

2 Railway War

1 *GVE*, p. 247.
2 *ORS*, 2: 224.
3 *PSS*, 36: 233–234; *ORS*, 2: 223.
4 Population figures here and below are mostly 1980 estimates by Poliakov and Kiselev. See also Pipes, 1964, and Lorimer.

5 Reshetar, p. 141.
6 Pidhainy, p. 597.
7 Puntila, p. 108.
8 Upton, p. 396.
9 Upton, p. 475.
10 *PSS*, 36: 5; *KVR*, 1: 105.

3 Obscene Peace

1 Trotskii, 1930, 2: 64.
2 Fokke, p. 207.
3 *Protokoly TsK*, pp. 168–169; *PSS*, 35: 250.
4 Hoffmann, 1929, pp. 206–207; *PSS*, 36: 26.
5 *KPSSRR*, 2: 26–27.
6 Freund, p. 251.
7 Krastyn', 1962, p. 62.
8 Freund, pp. 252–253.
9 *PSS*, 36: 10.

4 Allies in Russia

1 Trotskii, 1930, 2: 118; *Protokoly TsK*, p. 208.
2 Lockhart, p. 231.
3 *PSS*, 37: 2; *KVR*, 1: 221.
4 Maksakov and Turunov, p. 168.
5 Bunyan, 1976, p. 91.
6 *KVR*, 1: 363.
7 *PSS*, 37: 3.
8 McCullagh, p. xi.

5 Volga Campaign

1 *PSS*, 50: 116.
2 Aralov, p. 107; Nenarokov, p. 107.
3 *DKF*, 1: 412.
4 Trotsky, 1930, 2: 127; *DGK*, pp. 104–105.
5 Petrov, 1930, pp. 35–36; Lebedev, pp. 153, 158.
6 *DGK*, pp. 107–108; Krastyn', 1962, pp. 105–110.
7 *KVR*, 1: 105.
8 Kliatskin, 1965, pp. 182–183; Kakurin, 1925: 1: 135.
9 Spirin, 1965, p. 12; *GV*, 2: 93, 95; Bonch-Bruevich, p. 258.

10 *KVR*, 1: 151.
11 Aralov, pp. 21–22; Kliatskin, 1965, pp. 160–161.
12 *KVR*, 2: 110–113.
13 Vatsetis, 1977, p. 52; Stalin, *Soch.*, 4: 211–212; GV, 2: 58.
14 *GV*, 2: 87; DKF, 4: 51–52, 54–55.
15 Klimushkin, p. 85; Spirin, 1968, p. 258.
16 Petrov, 1930, p. 48; Klimushkin, pp. 63–64.
17 Nenarokov, pp. 174–184.
18 *PSS*, 50: 146; *DKF*, 4: 31, 38, 48, 286–289.
19 Trotskii, 1930, 2: chap 33; Lebedev, pp. 175–183.
20 *PSS*, 50: 178; Trotskii, 1930, p. 131; *TP*, 1: 155–157, 252; Trotsky, 1969, 2: 89–90.
21 Janin, p. 46.
22 Berk, 1973, p. 458.
23 *TP*, 1: 117.
24 Petrov, 1930, p. 38; *KVR*, 1: 262.

6 Sovdepia

1 In August 1918, after the Germans had completed their advance and the Soviet eastern front had stabilized, the following provinces, or parts of them, were in the Soviet zone.
    North: Novgorod, Olonets (most), Petrograd, Pskov (most), Vologda. *Central Industrial Region*: Iaroslavl, Kostroma, Moscow, N. Novgorod, Tver, Vladimir. *Central Agricultural Region*: Kaluga, Kursk (most), Orel, Penza, Riazan, Tambov, Tula, Voronezh (most). *Urals*: Perm (part), Viatka. *Volga*: Astrakhan, Kazan (part), Samara (part), Saratov, Simbirsk (most). *Ukraine*: Chernigov (part). *West*: Mogilev (part), Smolensk, Vitebsk (part). (*IKPSS: Atlas*, p. 53).
    The 1917 population of this region was about 59 million (Gaponenko and Kabuzan, pp. 102–103). The Red population also included several million cut off in the north Caucasus and Turkestan. Red Troops soon after August 1918 regained control of all of Kazan, Simbirsk, and Samara provinces, which they held for the rest of the Civil War. So the overall "Sovdepia" population was at least 60 million.
2 Shanin, pp. 137–138.
3 *PSS*, 37: 140.
4 *PSS*, 36: 217–218, 294.
5 *PSS*, 34: 305–309, 38: 155.
6 *PSS*, 43: 379. For a recent example of the contrary interpretation see Cohen, 1972, p. 193.
7 *PSS*, 35: 250, 44: 222; Trotsky, 1976, pp. 21–23.
8 Medvedev, chap. 11.
9 Stalin, *Soch.*, 4: 123–124.
10 Medvedev, p. 177.
11 *PSS*, 34: 313, 38: 145.
12 Trotskii, 1930, p. 79; Rigby, 1979, p. 224; Duval, 152–71, 260–71, 325–32.

13   Gimpel'son, 1982; Stalin, *Soch.*, 4: 216; Rigby, 1979, p. 62; *PSS*, 45: 376;
     Trotsky, 1972, p. 113; Orlovsky, pp. 35–66.
14   Service, 1979, p. 109.
15   Leggett, p. 114; Trotskii, 1920, p. 57.
16   Leggett, p. 130; *PSS*, 26: 311, 50: 106, 142–144.
17   Latsis, 1920, p. 75; Leggett, pp. 109, 111–113.
18   Trotsky, 1959, p. 80.
19   Kovalenko, 1967, p. 390.
20   Latsis, 1920, p. 75.

7   Cossack Vendée

1   Dobrynin, 1921, p. 57.
2   Stalin, *Soch.*, 4: 118.
3   *TP*, 1: 106.
4   *TP*, 1: 136; Kakurin, 1925, 1: 238.
5   *ORS*, 3: 149, 151; Kakurin, 1926, p. 54.
6   *ORS*, 3: 228.
7   *ORS*, 3: 210.
8   *ORS*, 3: 211.
9   *ORS*, 3: 262–263, 4: 45–48.
10   *KVR*, 1, 335.

8   Siberia and the Urals

1   Kennan, 2: 413.
2   Snow, p. 222; Berk, 1971, pp. 122–123, 479.
3   Trotskii, 1924, pp. 88–89.
4   Berk, 1971, p. 111.
5   *DKF*, 1: 411.
6   Gins, 1: 131, 197, 199, 201; *GVE*, p. 537; Boldyrev, pp. 32, 103.
7   Fleming, p. 99; Bunyan, 1936, pp. 362–365.
8   *Dopros*, pp. 161–188; Boldyrev, pp. 105, 116.
9   Boldyrev, p. 109; Janin, 31.
10   Ullman, 1961, pp. 279, 281.
11   Piontkovskii, pp. 284–286; Chamberlin, 2: 478.
12   Boldyrev, p. 83.
13   Churchill, p. 97.

9   Revolution on the March

1   *PSS*, 37: 150, 164.

2 *DKF*, 1: 468–469.
3 *DGK*, p. 147.
4 *TP*, 1: 431, 457, 516.
5 *DSV*, 5: 259–261.
6 Bonch-Bruevich, p. 340; *DKF*, 4: 51, 55–56, 61–62; Kakurin, 1925, 2: 41.
7 *PSS*, 37: 164, 38: 263; Degras, 1956, 1: 52.
8 *KVR*, 1: 372; *PSS*, 37: 99.
9 *IIGV*, 2: 382; *PSS*, 50: 285–286.
10 *PSS*, 37: 164; Trotskii, 1920, p. 117; *DGK*, pp. 148, 162.
11 *DVP*, 1: 628–630, 2: 57–60.
12 Trotskii, 1920, p. 117.
13 *DBFP*, ser. 1, vol. 3: 310–311.
14 *DSV*, 2: 91–95; Degras, 1956, 1: 2; *KPSSRR*, 2: 37, 39.
15 *ORS*, 5: 21, 35.
16 Carley, 1983, 162.
17 Gilbert, 4/1: 609; *FRUS: Paris Peace Conference*, 4: 120–123; *IIGV*, 2, 5–15; *DBFP*, ser. 1, vol. 3: 310.
18 *KVR*, 2/1: 188.

10   Kolchak's Offensive

1 *TP*, 1: 258–260.
2 "Report on the Work of the British Military Mission to Siberia, 1918–1919," 10 Dec. 1919 (hereafter cited as "Siberia Report"), PRO, WO 32/5707, p. 7; Grondijs, p. 73; Budberg, 15: 331–332.
3 Budberg, 15: 330; Gins, 2: 42, 440.
4 Budberg, 13: 199.
5 Gins, 2: 119, 183–186.
6 Gins, 2: 151; Filat'ev, p. 139.
7 Chamberlin, 2: 478.
8 Stalin, *Soch.*, 4: 190–194, 197–224; Kakurin, 1925, 2: 167; *TP*, 1: 308.
9 *DGK*, 161, 163; *KVR*, 2/1: 32; *DKF*, 1: 758.
10 *DGK*, pp. 553–555, 563; Kakurin, 1925, 2: 188–189; Kamenev, 1957, p. 256; *PSS*, 50: 328.
11 Stalin, *Soch.*, 4: 199; Vatsetis, 1958, p. 42; *TP*, 1: 322.
12 "Siberia Report," Appendices A and C.
13 Gins, 2: 128.
14 "Siberia Report," pp. 16–17.
15 "Siberia Report," p. 16, Appendices B and K; Spirin, 1957, pp. 89–91.
16 Eikhe, 1960, p. 42; Vatsetis, 1958, p. 42.
17 Gins, 2: 36; Eikhe, 1960, p. 291, n. 69.
18 Filat'ev, p. 51; Janin, pp. 133, 164.
19 "Siberia Report," Appendix D; Eikhe, 1960, p. 205.
20 *DKF*, 4: 54–57; "Siberia Report," Appendix D.
21 *KPSSRR*, 2: 88; *KVR*, 2/1: 335; *DGK*, p. 313; *DKF*, 4: 60.
22 Sakharov, 1923, p. 98.

11 Omsk and Arkhangelsk

1 *PSS*, 50, 328.
2 *DBFP*, 1st ser., vol. 3: 362–364.
3 Budberg, 14: 327.
4 *DGK*, pp. 580–582; *PSS*, 51: 50.
5 Budberg, 15: 527; Gins, 2: 362.
6 "Siberia Report", pp. 3, 5; Smirnov, 238; Gins, 2: 261–262; Petrov, 1930, 108–110; Sakharov, 116–126.
7 Filat'ev, pp. 62–64; Budberg, 15: 341; "Siberia Report," Appendix C.
8 *DBFP*, 1st Ser., vol. 3: 330–332, 362–364.
9 Spirin, 1957, p. 186; *DKF*, 4: 98, 101–102.
10 Filat'ev, p. 81; *DKF*, 4: 111; *GVE*, pp. 412–413.
11 Smirnov, 241–242; Eikhe, 1966, p. 313; Budberg, 15: 269.
12 *IIGV*, 2: 722; Long, p. 349.
13 Long, p. 398.
14 Ironside, p. 202.

12 Armed Forces of South Russia

1 *ORS*, 4: 113; Kakurin, 1925, 2: 59.
2 *TP*, 1: 262; *DKF*, 1: 685–686.
3 *KVR*, 2/1: 26–27.
4 *ORS*, 4: 106–107.
5 *KPSSRR*, 2: 33–34; *DGK*, p. 249; Vatsetis, 1977, p. 73.
6 *DKF*, 4: 56; Dobrynin, p. 111; Poliakov, 1962, p. 309.
7 Dobrynin, p. 111.
8 Krasnov, 1922b, pp. 205, 221.
9 Krasnov, 1922b, p. 204.
10 Krasnov, 1922b, p. 205.
11 Krasnov, 1922b, pp. 210–212, 251–253.
12 *DGK*, p. 161.
13 *KPSSRR*, 2: 94; "Final Report of the British Military Mission, South Russia," n.d. (ca. March 1920) (hereafter cited as "South Russia Report II"), PRO, WO 33/971, p. 94.
14 "South Russia Report II," pp. 43–47, 139; "Report on the British Military Mission, South Russia," 8 October 1919 (hereafter cited as "South Russia Report I"), PRO, FO 371/3979, pp. 24–26.
15 Bernshtam, 1979, pp. 301–302; Spirin, 1968, pp. 322–324; *KVR*, 2/1: 174, 186; *ORS*, 5: 78; *DGK*, p. 802, n. 82.
16 *DGK*, p. 338; Krastyn', 1978, p. 308.
17 *KVR*, 2/1: 349.
18 *DGK*, p. 337; *KVR*, 2/1: 237; *DKF*, 4: 56, 60, 63, 70; *ORS*, 5: 74, 104, 118.
19 *ORS*, 5: 72–75.
20 *DKF*, 2: 256; *KVR*, 2/2: 194.
21 *DGK*, p. 337.

22 Vrangel', 1: 161–162.
23 *ORS*, 5: 106.
24 *TP*, 1: 644.
25 *ORS*, 5: 117.
26 Dreier, p. 83.
27 *KVR*, 2/1: 388.
28 *TP*, 1: 470; *KPSSRR*, 2: 94–109.
29 *DGK*, pp. 161, 338; *KVR*, 2/1: 253; *TP*, 1: 578–581, 590–593.
30 *DGK*, pp. 438–439.
31 *DGK*, pp. 429–433, 462–463, 466; *KVR*, 2/1: 301–303.
32 *KVR*, 2/1: 303.
33 Trotskii, 1930, 2: 186–189; Vrangel', 1: 196–197, 258.

13   Armed Camp

1 *PSS*, 37: 200; Trotskii, 1930, 2: 180; *Leninskii sbornik*, 37: 137.
2 *TP*, 1: 590–593; Gusev, p. 216.
3 Kamenev, 1963, p. 17; Knox, 352.
4 *GV*, 2: 95–96; Iovlev, 1968, 31; Spirin, 1965, 14.
5 *DKF*, 4: 254–255; *GV*, 2: 123.
6 Vatsetis, 1977. 72–75; Kritskii, 1926, 274.
7 Kliatskin, 1965, p. 421.
8 *PSS*, 37; 97–100; Bernshtam, 1979, pp. 297–300; *DGK*, pp. 151, 327; *DKF*, 4: 480–482.
9 Vatsetis, 1977, p. 74; *DGK*, pp. 60–61, 70–71, 149; *GV*, 2: 87.
10 Olikov, pp. 30–31.
11 Gusev, pp. 59–60, 130–132; *GV*, 2: 15–16, 86n; *DKF*, 4: 275.
12 *GV*, 2: 60, 67, 148; Gusev, 69; "South Russia Report II," pp. 85–86.
13 Vatsetis, 1958, p. 71; Golovin, 1939, 2: 7, 13, 19, 31, 41; *DKF*, 4: 386.
14 *GV*, 2: 373, 406; *DGK*, p. 320; *KVR*, 2/2: 12.
15 *GV*, 2: 21, 314.
16 *GV*, 2: 264.
17 *PSS*, 38: 146; *KPSSRR*, 2: 77–83.
18 Gladkov, 1976, p. 376; Malle, p. 407.
19 *GV*, 2: 395; Malle, p. 502; Kritsman, p. 204.
20 *KPSSRR*, 2: 42.
21 Rigby, 1968, p. 68.
22 *KPSSRR*, 2: 76–77.
23 *PSS*, 39: 504 n. 88; Rigby, 1968, pp. 77–78.
24 Leggett, p. 181; "South Russian Report II," p. 96.
25 Latsis, 1920, p. 75.
26 Maiskii, pp. 345, 352.

14   Turning Point

1 Kritskii, 1936, pp. 139–40; "South Russia Report II," pp. 55–56.

2 *DKF*, 2: 102; *DGK*,. p. 378; Rodzianko, p. 44.
3 Drujina, p. 133; Rodzianko, pp. 120, 129.
4 Drujina, p. 62.
5 Drujina, pp. 66, 74.
6 *General Iudenich*, p. 43; *DKF*, 4: 480.
7 *KVR*, 2/1: 82.
8 *PSS*, 39: 282–284; *TP*, 1: 796; Kakurin, 1925, 2: 333.
9 Trotskii, 1930, 2: 158, 159–160; *KVR*, 2/1: 383, 462, n. 79; *TP*, 1: 716–719.
10 Drujina, p. 128; *GVE*, p. 404.
11 Kamenev, 1957, p. 262; Trotskii, 1930, 2: 154–155, 189; *TP*, 1: 692; Kamenev, 1963, p. 94; Kakurin, 1925, 2: 337–338.
12 *KVR*, 2/1: 428.
13 Trotskii, 1930, 2: 155; *General Iudenich*, p. 10; Rodzianko, pp. 93–94.
14 *DGK*, pp. 475–476; *PSS*, 39: 206; *TP*, 1: 686–690, 710–716.
15 Trotskii, 1930, 2: 188; Trotsky, 1969, 2: 119; Voroshilov, 1934, pp. 53–54; *PSS*, 51: 50; Stalin, *Soch.*, 4: 275–277.
16 *DKF*, 4: 463–464.
17 Egorov, 1931, pp. 148, 151, 164, 179; Kakurin, 1925, 2: 318; Budennyi, 1: 249–251.
18 Vrangel', 1: 161, 258; *ORS*, 5: 117; *KVR*, 2/1: 302.
19 Vrangel', 1: 160; Kakurin, 1925, 2: 245; Lehovich, pp. 404–405; *ORS*, 5: 111.
20 *ORS*, 5: 109, 117; Kakurin, 1925, 2: 245.
21 Lukomskii, pp. 157–158; *ORS*, 5: 235–236; Egorov, 1931, p. 140.
22 Lukomskii, pp. 201–202; "South Russia Report II," p. 56.
23 Vrangel', 1: 257; "South Russia Report II," p. 5.
24 Vrangel', 1: 290; *IIGV*, 2: 518–519.
25 *ORS*, 5: 118.
26 Kenez, 1977, pp. 166–177; Shekhtman.
27 *ORS*, 5: 302.
28 Kenez, 1977, p. xiii.
29 *ORS*, 5: 154.
30 Anishev, p. 255.
31 Kritskii, 1936, p. 149.
32 *ORS*, 5: 234–235; Kritskii, 1926, p. 269.
33 Olikov, p. 27.
34 *ORS*, 5: 126.
35 *ORS*, 5: 231; Kritskii, 1926, p. 282
36 *DKF*, 4: 105–106, 108–110; "South Russia Report II," pp. 8, 15; Kakurin, 1925, 2: 306.
37 *DKF*, 4: 108–110.
38 "South Russia Report II," p. 29.

15 End of Denikin

1 Dreier, p. 85; *ORS*, 5: 261n; "South Russia Report II," p. 60.
2 *KVR*, 2/1: 287–288; *DKF*, 4: 121.
3 Kamenev, 1963, p. 140; Vrangel', 1: 256.

4   Budennyi, 1: 399.
5   *DKF*, 4: 123; *GVE*, p. 529; "Evacuation of Novorossiisk," 2 April 1920, PRO, WO 32/5718.
6   *DGK*, p. 350
7   *ORS*, 5: 294.
8   Kamenev, 1963, pp. 66–69.
9   Kritskii, 1936, p. 159.
10 "Evacuation of Novorossiisk"; Kakurin, 1926, p. 147; *DKF*, 3: 314.
11 *ORS*, 5: 342.
12 Lehovich, pp. 259, 296; *ORS*, 5: 364.
13 Jeffery, p. 135.
14 Stalin, *Soch.*, 4: 380.
15 *DGK*, pp. 736–737.
16 *DGK*, pp. 733–735.
17 *TP*, 2: 376, 378–380; Trotsky, 1969, 2: 46–47.
18 *TP*, 2: 200–202.

16   Storm over Asia

1   Kakurin, 1925, 2: 357.
2   Churchill, 1929, p. 250.
3   Smirnov, p. 310; *TP*, 2: 30–34; Gins, 2: 198.
4   *PSS*, 51: 137.
5   *TP*, 1: 620–627, 675.
6   *PSS*, 51: 89.
7   Safarov, 86.
8   *TP*, 2: 208–210.

17   Consolidating the State

1   *DKF*, 4: 220–227.
2   *DKF*, 4: 386.
3   Trotskii, 1930, 2: 197–202; Dobb, p. 149.
4   Carr, 2: 261–262.
5   Bukharin, pp. 138–139.
6   Carr, 2: 271; Malle, pp. 506–507; Trotskii, 1920, pp. 128–129; Nove, p. 76.
7   Atkinson, pp. 228–229.
8   Rigby, 1968, p. 52; Kenez, 1985, p. 168.
9   Leggett, pp. 184–185.
10 *KVR*, 2/2: 307; Stalin, *Soch.*, 4: 355, 359, 360–361.

18   Polish Campaign

1 *KPSSRR*, 2: 182–185; *DGK*, pp. 607, 676–677.
2 Egorov, 1929, p. 15.
3 Ullman, 3: 47; Davies, 1972, pp. 91–95.
4 Trotskii, 1930, 2: 191–193.
5 *TP*, 2: 166–168; Stalin, *Soch.*, 4: 320–322; Kamenev, 1963, p. 165.
6 Zamoyski, p. 20; Davies, 1972, pp. 194, 197–200, 220–225; Urlanis, 1960, pp. 181, 185; *KVR*, 2/2: 141; *TP*, 2: 174.
7 Trotskii, 1930, 2: 192–193; Trotsky, 1969, 2: 126–133; *DGK*, p. 704–705, 711; *DKF*, 3: 256.
8 *PSS*, 51: 285–286; Zetkin, p. 22.
9 *TP*, 2: 264; *DKF*, 4: 161–162; *GV*, 2: 88; Davies, 1972, p. 200.
10 Davies, 1975, p. 178; *KVR*, 2/2: 153.
11 Trotskii, 1930, 2: 194–195; *KVR*, 2/2: 116.
12 *DGK*, pp. 610–612.

19   Crimean Ulcer

1 Kenez, 2: 267.
2 Rakovskii, 1921, p. 32.
3 *KPSSRR*, 2: 186–187; Kakurin, 1925, 2: 373; *DKF*, 3: 153.
4 *TP*, 2: 260–262; *DGK*, p. 628.
5 Vrangel', 2: 190.
6 *TP*, 2: 324–326, 347.
7 *KVR*, 2/2: 220; Vrangel', 2: 44, 180–182.
8 Vrangel', 2: 86–87.
9 *PSS*, 51: 293; *KVR*, 2/2: 218–219.
10 Kakurin, 1925, 2: 385.
11 *DKF*, 3: 495.
12 *DKF*, 3: 510, 513.
13 Vrangel', 2: 230, 242.
14 *PSS*, 42: 74, 52: 6; Mel'gunov, 1979, pp. 66–71.
15 Lukomskii, 2: 237.
16 Vrangel', 2: 306.

Conclusion

1 *PSS*, 42: 1; *Pravda*, no. 250, 7.11.20, p. 1.
2 Kollontai, p. 170; Timoshenko, pp. 158–159; Atkinson, pp. 179–185; *TP*, 2: 518–520.
3 *TP*, 2: 494–496, 554; *PPS*, 40: 12.

4   *PSS*, 40: 241.
5   Lebedev, p. 152.
6   Churchill, p. 234.
7   *PSS*, 41: 48; *KVR*, 3/2: 185.
8   Pilsudski, p. 222; *KVR*, 3/1: 60.
9   Carr, 3: 97–98; Kautsky, pp. 180, 198, 207, 231.
10 Trotskii, 1930, 2: 180; Stalin, 1947, p. 6.
11 Stalin, *Soch.*, 6: 336n; *KVR*, 2/1: 463, n. 85; Lunacharsky, p. 68.
12 Gorn, p. 363; Gins, 2: 464.
13 *TP*, 2: 552–554.
14 Gins, 1: 97.
15 Sakharov, p. 112; *ORS*, 5: 298.
16 Sakharov, pp. 177, 314.
17 *ORS*, 4: 245.
18 Pipes, 1964, 296; *ORS*, 5: 304.
19 *ORS*, 5: 139.
20 Stalin, *Soch.*, 4: 283; *PSS*, 34: 226.
21 Sakharov, p. 180.
22 Kritsman; Urlanis, 1960, pp. 180–188, 304–308, 399–401; Poliakov, p. 208.
23 Urlanis, 1960, pp. 187–188; Kritskii, 1936, p. 6; Poliakov, p. 208.
24 Urlanis, 1960, pp. 305–307.
25 Latsis, 1921, p. 9; Chamberlin, 2: 75; Leggett, pp. 466–467; Conquest, 1971, p. 11.
26 Maksudov, p. 231.
27 Lorimer, p. 41; Volkov, p. 185; Maksudov, pp. 198, 231.
28 Volkov, pp. 190–191; Lorimer, p. 40; *Bol'shaia Sovetskaia entsiklopediia*, vol. 5 (1930), col. 786.
29 Lorimer, p. 41; Urlanis, 1968, pp. 21–22; Volkov, p. 238; Maksudov, p. 231.
30 *PSS*, 34: 225–226; Urlanis, 1960, p. 145.
31 Malle, pp. 506, 508–511; Nove, pp. 86, 94.
32 Kritsman, p. 162.

BIBLIOGRAPHY

The bibliography that follows falls into two main parts: a Bibliographical Essay and an Alphabetical Bibliography.

A full bibliography of the Civil War remains to be compiled; it would be much longer than this present volume. I have tried to cover most topics *and* to introduce sources of the four main types: Western (mostly English-language), early Soviet (from the 1920s), emigre, and post-1956 Soviet.

The first part of the bibliography, the Bibliographical Essay, suggests the most useful sources for various topics and is intended to supplement the end-notes. Sources in the Bibliographical Essay are given with the first author's surname and a condensed form of the title; full details are in the Alphabetical Bibliography. Giving a condensed version of the title will, I hope, be more helpful than just giving the author and date would have been; for one thing, the language in which the source is written is usually clear. (When writing about "class enemies" Soviet authors seem obliged to entitle their work "*razgrom* [destruction] of this" or "*krakh* [failure] of that"; this formula has been left out in the abbreviated form in the Bibliographical Essay, and minor Russian grammatical changes have been made.)

Bibliographical Essay

The more general works, which cover all or most of the Civil War, are dealt with in the first part ("A.1," etc.); narrower studies are cited in connection with the relevant chapters. It is important to check part "A" for the major sources, as some of them are useful for nearly all chapters.

A.1. Bibliographies

Mazour, *Writing of History*, contains a substantial though now dated discussion; Erickson, "Pens", makes more specialized comments. Many of the early published sources are listed in Slavik's *Bibliografiia* of the Prague emigre archive (1938). On the Soviet side there is Naumov, *Letopis'*. The new Civil War encyclopedia (*Grazhdanskaia voina: Entsiklopediia*) has an extensive Soviet-oriented bibliography.

A.2. General Histories

There are not many general histories of the Civil War in English. Chamberlin, *Russian Revolution*, although it dates from 1935, is generally still regarded as the best. Footman, *Civil War*, and Bradley, *Civil War*, are short and somewhat selective.

Soviet histories tend (rather surprisingly, given their Marxist-Leninist basis) to separate political-economic events and the military campaigns. They have also suffered, at least since 1930, not so much from a Marxist interpretation as from nationalism and from an "official" approach. In general they are weak on their enemies. The most recent Soviet history is Azovtsev *et al.*, *Grazhdanskaia voina* (1980-1986). The previous version, *Istoriia Grazhdanskoi voiny* (1938-1960) had a checkered history, but the three post-Stalin volumes are of some value. A broader (thematic) perspective is attempted in Spirin, *Klassy i partii*, and, more recently, Korablev, *Zashchita*, and Golub, *Revoliutsiia zashchishchaetsia*. The *Entsiklopediia*, mentioned above, is very useful, although it says something about the slow progress of Soviet historiography that there are no entries for Trotsky, Bukharin, and other "oppositionists"—forty-five years after they were killed.

Two earlier official histories, written in the 1920s, are very good, although they both concentrate on military aspects. The first, Colonel Kakurin's two-volume *Kak srazhalas' revoliutsiia*, is the best military narrative (there is a condensed version, *Strategicheskii ocherk*). The second work, *Grazhdanskaia voina*, was produced under the general supervision of A. S. Bubnov *et al.*; vol. 1 includes 23 memoirs on particular episodes, vol. 2 has excellent articles about aspects of the Red Army, and vol. 3—largely by Kakurin again—outlines the whole war. A stimulating early Soviet book that combines military and political aspects is Anishev, *Ocherki*.

There is no satisfactory emigre general history, although General Denikin, the main leader of the southern Whites, produced a very impressive five-volume account, *Ocherki Russkoi smuty*; it is both a memoir and a general survey. The first volume deals with 1917 (and has been translated as *Russian Turmoil*); vols. 2–3 deal with 1918, vols. 4–5 with 1919–1920; an abridged translation is *White Army*. The Kadet politician-historian Miliukov wrote *Rossiia na Perelome*. For an example of the latest emigre generation see the highly eccentric but richly documented works of Bernshtam, "Storony" and "Smysl'"; the reply by Maksudov, "Internatsionalisty," is also of interest, and both are discussed in Jansen, "International Class Solidarity."

The year 1918 is the only one to have a number of general histories; the Civil War seems to wear authors down very quickly. Golovin, *Kontrrevoliutsiia*, and Zaitsov, *1918*, are emigre works; *Year One* is by an independent radical, Serge; and *1918g* is by the dean of Soviet revolution specialists, I. I. Mints.

Baedeker's Russia: 1914, recently reprinted, is an invaluable companion for the Civil War campaigns. Some of the best maps are in Kakurin, *Kak srazhalas' revoliutsiia*, *Istoriia KPSS: Atlas*, and Stewart, *White Armies*; the *Entsiklopediia* has perhaps the most accessible set.

A.3. General Collections of Documents

Chamberlin, *Russian Revolution*, contains many valuable documents in translation. Also useful are Bunyan and Fisher, *Bolshevik Revolution*, on the winter of 1917–1918, and Bunyan, *Intervention*, on the rest of 1918. The most interesting general Soviet collection is Piontkovskii, *Grazhdanskaia voina*. There are some nuggets, too, in the post-1956 Soviet general collections; two volumes on the winter of 1917–1918, *Triumfal'noe shestvie*, are the postscript to a series on 1917; they are followed by the three volumes of *Iz istorii Grazhdanskoi voiny*. Important material was published in the 1920s in the periodical *Krasnyi arkhiv*, and there were other documents in the post-Stalin *Istoricheskii arkhiv*. Lenin's writings, both theoretical and what might be called 'operational,' are of great importance because they relate to all aspects of high policy and have been published in a relatively complete form. In the latest (5th) edition (*PSS*), Civil War material is in vols. 35–41 and 50–52 (correspondence); in the English translation, *Collected Works*, vols. 26–32 contain the relevant general works, and 35, 36, 42, and 44 the correspondence and drafts.

A.4. Soviet Politics

Schapiro, *Origins*, introduces the Bolsheviks and their domestic opponents; see also his posthumous *1917*. Carr, *Bolshevik Revolution*, gives a different but wide-ranging view. Helgesen, "Party-State Monolith", provides further detail, and for Lenin's perspective see Kleubort "Lenin/State."

Rigby, *Lenin's Government*, is an excellent introduction to Soviet central government, and especially to Sovnarkom; another wide-ranging account is Pietsch, *Revolution und Staat*. The basic state documents have been published in *Dekrety*. For local administration there are Abrams, "Local Soviets," Anweiler, *Soviets*, and Renehan, "Local Soviet Government." Sakwa, "Moscow," gives an interesting case study, and Getzler, *Kronstadt*, deals in detail with a famous but atypical soviet. The basic modern Soviet sources are Kovalenko, *Sovety* (1967) and Gimpel'son, *Sovety* (1968); for the social composition of the administration there is Gimpel'son, *Rabochii klass v upravlenii* (1982).

The secret police, the Cheka, is now well covered by Gerson, *Secret Police*, and Leggett, *Cheka*; Sofinov, *Ocherki*, is a Soviet account. See also the near-contemporary pamphlets by the Chekist Latsis, *Chrezvychainye komissii* and *Dva goda*. Mel'gunov, *Krasnyi terror*, is by a historian-victim. *Iz istorii VChK* and *Vnutrennye voiska* provide documents.

On the Bolshevik/Communist party the standard general history is Schapiro's *Communist Party*; Service, *Bolshevik Party*, is the best treatment of the general period. The latest official account is *Istoriia KPSS*; vol. 3 covers the Civil War. Rigby, *Communist Party Membership*, is definitive. See also Adelman, "Development/Apparat." Lipitskii, *Voennaia deiatel'nost'*, covers the party leadership's military role. Daniels, *Conscience*, covers intraparty debates. The basic collection of documents is *Kommunisticheskaia Partiia S. S. v r. i r.*; some of these are available in translation in *Resolutions and Decisions*. See also *Partiia* (1962).

On "mobilization" by state and party there is Kenez, *Propaganda State*; see also Tumarkin, "Myth of Lenin."

A number of biographical works contain much on the functioning of the Soviet regime. Ulam, *Lenin*, and Shukman, *Lenin*, are the standard Western works; the relevant volume of Service, *Lenin: A Political Life*, when it appears, will no doubt give fullest details. Harding, *Lenin's Political Thought*, and Meyer, *Leninism*, cover the theoretical side. Trotsky, *O Lenine/On Lenin*, presents unique insights. See also the articles in Schapiro and Reddaway, *Lenin*. Details of Lenin's administrative role in mid-Civil War are given in Iroshnikov, *Predsedatel'*. On the military side see Kuz'min, *Lenin vo glave*, and Korablev, *Lenin/Zashchita*.

Trotsky's autobiography is *Moia zhizn'/My Life*; Deutscher, *Prophet Armed*, is the standard biography, while Knei-Paz, *Thought*, covers ideas (including Trotsky's post-mortem on the revolutionary period). The fullest treatment of Trotsky's military role, although mainly theoretical, is Heyman, "Leon Trotsky." Other leading Bolsheviks are covered in Cohen, *Bukharin*, Duval, "Sverdlov," Oppenheim, "Rykov," and Tucker, *Stalin*. Lunacharsky, *Revolutionary Silhouettes*, and Haupt and Marie, *Makers*, are valuable collective biographies, while Rigby, "Soviet Political Elite," is a good broad analysis.

A.5. Soviet Economy

Nove, *Economic History*, is the standard introduction. Malle, *Economic Organization*, now gives the most detailed account of the period, but see also Szamuely, *First Models*, and the classic discussions in Dobb, *Economic Development*, and Carr, *Bolshevik Revolution*. The early Soviet accounts of Kritsman, *Geroicheskii period*, and Miliutin, *Ekonomicheskoe razvitie*, are still of interest; Gladkov, *Sovetskaia ekomomika*, is the current general history. Much work has been done in America on the organization of the economy; see especially Roberts, "War Communism," Buchanan, "Soviet Economic Policy" (on VSNKh), Holman, "War Communism," and Remington, *Building Socialism*. Of the more specialized Soviet works see Gimpel'son, *Voennyi kommunizm* (1973), and *Velikii oktiabr'* (1977).

Kovalenko, *Oboronaia promyshlennost'*, is the basic source on the war industries. A good case study of a major industrial sector is Husband, "Textile Industry." Bunyan, *Forced Labor*, contains important documents on labor policy. There is, of course, much on agriculture in the general economic histories; see also Atkinson, *Land Commune*, Channon, "Peasant Revolution," and Shanin, *Awkward Class*. Kingston-Mann, *Lenin*, looks at ideological factors. Pershin *Agrarnaia revoliutsiia*, gives a classic Soviet survey.

Scheibert, *Lenin an der Macht*, presents the fullest picture of social change; also useful is Gimpel'son, *Sovetskii rabochii klass* (1974). See also the new interpretation in Koenker, "Urbanization and Deurbanization".

A.6. Red Army

The best general campaign histories are given in A.2. Among the most important sources on the campaigns and the state of the army are the published command documents. *Direktivy Glavnogo komandovaniia* and the first three volumes of *Direktivy Komandovaniia frontov* give a great mass of orders and reports, often very candid, from the highest operational levels of the Red Army.

Vol. 4 of *Direktivy Komandovaniia frontov* is a unique collection of tables of strength, details of supply, lists of commanders, etc. The best English-language introductions to the Red Army are Erickson, *Soviet High Command*, and Seaton, *The Soviet Army*. Fedotoff-White, *Growth*, is still useful. The first part of Hagen's thesis, "School," is relevant to the Civil War, and he has interesting things to say about the implications of militarization. The best Soviet introduction to Red Army organization is Kliatskin, *Na zashchite;* the second volume of Bubnov (ed.), *Grazhdanskaia voina*, is also a most important source. Benvenuti, *Bolscevichi*, will soon be translated into English, and there is also Ritter, *Kommunemodell*. Rapoport, *High Treason*, an example of the latest samizdat/emigre generation, gives a longer-term view and is interesting on some episodes.

Lipitskii, *Leninskoe rukovodstvo*, is good on strategic direction. See also S. Gusev's essays in his *Grazhdanskaia voina*. Voroshilov, "Stalin," is mainly important for historiographical reasons. For Lenin's role there is Korablev, *Lenin i sozdanie* (1970), and Erickson's essay in Schapiro and Reddaway, *Lenin*. For foreign volunteers see Zharov and Ustinov, *Internatsional'nye chasti*, and, from a hostile perspective, Maksudov, "Internatsionalisty." On the commissars and morale see the documents in *Partiino-politicheskaia rabota*. Kharitonov, *Obmundirovanie*, deals with uniforms and insignia.

Trotsky's collected military writings, *Kak vooruzhalas' revoliutsiia*, a most important source, are now available in a full and well-annotated English translation by Pearce, *How the Revolution Armed;* the first three parts deal with the Civil War; they help make up for Trotsky's neglect in the rest of the Soviet literature. The material Trotsky took abroad with him in 1929 was published in two volumes of Meijer (ed.), *Trotsky Papers;* while the collection is far from comprehensive, these documents provide invaluable insights and have extremely useful notes.

On the senior Red commanders, there is a Western biography, Germanis, *Oberst Vacietis*, and a Soviet biography with documents, Krastyn', *Glavnokomanduiushchii . . . Vatsetis*. Fragments of Vatsetis's memoirs have appeared in several places, including the samizdat *Pamiat'*. Rather surprisingly, no full biography of Colonel Kamenev has appeared, but his *Zapiski* contains many details, as well as reprints of important writings. Kamenev's limited memoirs comprise "Vospominaniia." Republished *Izbrannye* of Frunze and Tukhachevskii are a convenient source of material. Jacobs, *Frunze*, includes in passing some interesting comments on Civil War campaigns. Simpkin, *Tukhachevskii*, is forthcoming.

A.7. The Whites

The thesis by Dacy, "White Russian Armies," is an intelligent and well-written overview. Stewart, *White Armies*, and Luckett, *White Generals*, are really intended for the general reader. Kenez, "Ideology," is a useful summary of what passed for White "ideas." The memoir by Margulies, *God interventsii*, is unusual in giving a first-person account of south Russia, the Baltic, Paris, and London.

Kenez's two-volume *South Russia* is the best Western overview of any of the White regions. It is complemented by Lehovich's excellent biography of

BIBLIOGRAPHY

General Denikin, *White against Red. Ocherki*, by Denikin himself, is best on the south. Other important White military memoirs on the south over the whole period of the Civil War are Lukomskii, *Vospominaniia/Memoirs* and Vrangel', *Vospominaniia/Always with Honor.* Sokolov, *Pravlenie*, is a good inside account of Volunteer civil administration. Procyk, "Nationality Policy," and Mal't, "Krest'ianstvo" and "Rabochie," cover important aspects of southern White "internal" policy. Aleksashenko, *Krakh Denikinshchiny*, is the most substantial modern Soviet account; see the earlier Kin, *Denikinshchina.* Lower-level memoirs of the White movement by participants include Shteifon, *Krizis Dobrovol'chestva*, and Shkuro, *Zapiski.* There are many White unit-histories; a good example is Kritskii, *Kornilovskii udarnyi polk.*

The other main White front, Siberia and the Urals, is not so well served by modern Western accounts. White, *The Siberian Intervention*, though dated, is a reasonable survey of many aspects. Fleming, *Fate/Kolchak* is beautifully written. On the other hand, the Russian-language material, both Soviet and emigre, is better than for the east than for the south. There is the large-scale emigre survey by Mel'gunov, *Tragediia admirala Kolchaka.* Filat'ev, *Katastrofa*, gives a good military survey by a relatively disinterested White participant. Eikhe, *Oprokinutyi tyl'*, was written by a Soviet participant with an axe to grind, but is a substantial work. Spirin, *Razgrom armii Kolchaka*, is useful, and for a very recent overview there is Ioffe, *Kolchakovskaia avantiura.* Aver'ev, "Agrarnaia politika," gives an early view of the peasant policies of the eastern anti-Bolshevik governments.

Many participants of the Civil War in the east left memoirs. Gins, an important civilian official, produced *Sibir', soiuzniki*, a detailed account of the administration. General Budberg's sharply written notes, "Dnevnik," are excellent on the Far East in 1918 and the inside workings of Kolchak's government in 1919. Sakharov, a senior combat commander, left outspokenly reactionary memoirs, *Belaia sibir'.* Petrov, *Ot Volgi*, an account by a middle-level commander, is remarkable for its long chronological scope. Fedorovich, *General Kappel'*, is a comrade's account of the outstanding White commander in the east. Dotsenko, *Struggle for Democracy*, is an SR memoir, and unusually, is available in English. On the Bolshevik side there is a frank early collection of memoirs edited by Smirnov, *Bor'ba.*

A.8. *Civilian Anti-Bolsheviks*

Schapiro, *Origins*, is probably the best short account in English of the crushing of the Bolsheviks' opponents in the center. In the last few decades study of opposition groups has resumed in the USSR. Golinkov, *Antisovetskoe podpol'e*, covers internal opposition in general, and various groups are discussed in the essays in Mints (ed.), 1984, *Neproletarskie partii.* On the right see Ivanov, *Kontrrevoliutsiia*, for the 1917 background, then Ioffe, *Monarkhicheskaia kontr-revoliutsiia.* The best Western study of any opposition party throughout the Civil War is Rosenberg on the Kadets, *Liberals*; the Soviet counterpart is Dumova, *Kadetskaia kontrrevoliutsiia.*

For the non-Bolshevik socialists there are Radkey, *Agrarian Foes*, and *Sickle*; they are the best introduction to the Socialist-Revolutionaries but stop early in 1918. A longer-ranging Soviet account is Gusev, *Partiia eserov.* Jansen, *Show*

Trial, is the best English-language account of the SRs' later activities. Mel'gunov, *Chaikovskii*, is the biography of a key figure who was prominent in several areas. (For sources on the Left SRs see chap. 3, below.) The Mensheviks have had rather better coverage in the West than the SRs: essays in Haimson (ed.), *Mensheviks*, and his *Russian Review* articles, "Mensheviks"; the thesis by Brovkin, "Menshevik Opposition," and his "Political Comeback." Getzler's *Martov*, on the leader of the Menshevik Left, is good for the Civil War years. Avrich, *Anarchists*, gives documents and some discussion of the libertarian Left; Kanev, *Anarkhizm*, is a Soviet survey. Makhno's peasant "anarchist" movement is now covered in depth in English by Malet, *Makhno* and Palij, *Anarchism of . . . Makhno*.

A.9. Nationalities

Pipes, *Formation*, is still the best overview; Carr, *Bolshevik Revolution*, provides the theoretical/constitutional background. The details of the Nationalities Commissariat are in Blank, "Unknown Commissariat." Kulichenko, *Natsional'nyi vopros*, surveys Bolshevik policy, while Mints (ed.), 1980, *Neproletarskie partii*, has articles on many nationalist parties; see also the selected documents, *Sovetskoe sodruzhestvo*.

The best English survey on the Ukraine in the Civil War period is still Reshetar, *Ukrainian Revolution*. Borys, *Sovietization*, Mace, *Communism/National Liberation*, Majstrenko, *Borot'bism*, and Motyl, *Turn to Right*, give scholarly treatment of various aspects, as do the articles in Hunczak (ed.), *Ukraine*. *Ukraine: Concise Encyclopedia* is packed with information. Suprunenko, *Ocherki*, provides a general Soviet account; a vast number of documents are given in *Grazhdanskaia voina na Ukraine*.

Belorussia is dealt with in some depth in English by Lubachko, *Belorussia*. On the Baltic states in general the older survey by Page, *Formation*, still provides a useful summary, and von Rauch, *Baltic States*, gives a German viewpoint. Lithuania is dealt with by Senn, *Emergence*, and Latvia by Bilmanis, *History*. Finland has the monograph by Smith, *Finland*, and Kholodkovskii, *Finliandiia*. The *Memoirs* of a key figure, Mannerheim, are available in English. For the Transcaucasus see chap. 15, below; for Central Asia see chap. 16.

A.10. The Cossacks

Longworth, *Cossacks*, gives a wide-ranging introduction; Karmann, *Freiheitskampf*, is very detailed on the southern cossacks. R. H. McNeal, *Tsar and Cossack*, provides important historical background. See also the memoirs of Tschebotarioff, *Russia*, on the Don, and Starikov and Medvedev's biography of the Red Cossack, *Philip Mironov*. *Quiet Flows the Don* and *The Don Flows Home to the Sea*, Sholokhov's classic cossack novels, are available in English. Soviet documents on the overall political situation in 1917–1920 are in *Bor'ba za v. s. na Donu*. Interesting military memoirs by Don leaders are Dobrynin, *Bor'ba*, Poliakov, *Donskie kazaki*, and especially Ataman Krasnov's long article, "Vsevelikoe voisko." On the Kuban see the documents in *Bor'ba za s. v. na Kubane*. Akulinin, *Orenburgskoe . . . voisko*, and Zuev, *Orenburgski kazaki*, are solid accounts by cossack participants. On the remarkable adventures of the Ural Host see Akulinin, 'Ural'skoe . . . voisko."

A.11. International Relations

Carr, *Bolshevik Revolution*, and Ulam, *Expansion and Coexistence*, are two surveys that take in the overall pattern of Soviet foreign policy, although from different points of view. The current Soviet overall account is *Istoriia vneshnei politiki*. The early years of the Foreign Commissariat are covered by Uldricks, *Diplomacy and Ideology*. Important translations are available in Degras, *Soviet Documents*; the fullest current collection is the standard *Dokumenty vneshnei politiki*. For the Komintern see chap. 9.

Bradley, *Allied Intervention*, gives a general survey. Gaworek, "Allied Economic Warfare," covers the blockade. For a fresh discussion of Allied, especially American, purposes there is Gardner, *Safe for Democracy*. Coates and Coates, *Armed Intervention*, is an earlier critique. Brinkley, *V.A./Allied Intervention*, is a scholarly work on Allied-White relations in south Russia.

British policy over the whole period of the Civil War is covered in the three-volume work by Ullman, *Anglo-Soviet Relations*. There are British documents in Watt/Lieven, *Soviet Union*, and (on post-Armistice developments) in *Documents on British F.P.* Jeffery, *British Army*, gives a useful perspective on Britain's other military/imperial problems. See Graubard, *British Labour*, for domestic pressures. French policy, once a gap in research on Allied policy, is dealt with in Wandycz, *Eastern Allies*, Hovi, *Cordon Sanitaire*, and Carley, *Revolution and Intervention*. The standard work on American policy, by George Kennan, was originally entitled "Soviet-American Relations, 1917–1920," but only *Russia Leaves* and *Decision* actually appeared, covering the period up to the Armistice. The American-published documents are still the best, *FRUS*. On the German role see below, under chap. 3.

Chap. 1. Bolshevik Takeover in Central Russia

Suny, "Social History," gives a stimulating discussion of recent writing, as well as a summary of the social history approach. For general background see Chamberlin, *Russian Revolution*, Fitzpatrick, *Russian Revolution*, Schapiro, *1917*, or Service, *Russian Revolution*. Haimson, "Social Stability," and Pipes, *Old Regime*, are helpful for understanding the general historical background.

Rabinowitch, *Bolsheviks*, is the most thorough discussion of the October armed uprising in Petrograd; see also Daniels, *Red October*. Medvedev, *October Revolution*, is stimulating on the revolution and its consequences. Mel'gunov, *Kak Bol'sheviki/Bolshevik Seizure*, has an interesting argument and covers the vitally important week *after* 25 October; the Russian original elaborates on the Moscow events. The standard Soviet account is now Mints, *Istoriia Velikogo Oktiabria*. See also Startsev, *Krakh Kerenshchiny*. Krasnov, "Na vnutrennem fronte," is a colorful account by a leader of the counterrevolutionary forces. Important documents on the takeover and early running of Soviet Russia are those of the Petrograd MRC, *Petrogradskii V.-R. K.*

The voting figures for the Constituent Assembly elections are in Spirin, *Klassy i partii.* For a Western discussion see Radkey, *Election;* Lenin's own late-1919 analysis in *PSS*, vol. 40 (pp. 1–24), is interesting.

For the aspirations of society in general see Ferro, *October,* and, especially, Keep, *Russian Revolution.* Smith, *Red Petrograd,* gives the best treatment of the important Petrograd workers. The workers' militia are covered by Collins, "Russian Red Guard," and Wade, *Red Guards.* On worker dissatisfaction with the Bolsheviks see Rosenberg, "Russian Labor," and the material in Bernshtam, *Nezavisimoe rabochee dvizhenie.*

The massive works on the front-line army, *Russkaia armiia,* and rear garrisons, *Zakhvat vlasti,* by the emigre historian Frenkin are very important. There is no comparable source in English, although Wildman, *Russian Imperial Army,* is a perceptive introduction; it is to be hoped that Wildman's work will soon be extended to the second half of 1917.

For the early Soviet state see Gorodetskii, *Rozhdenie,* and Iroshnikov, *Sozdanie.* The soviet protocols published in Keep, *Debate,* are important.

For the political alternatives to Bolshevism, see A.8, above. Fedotov, *Russian Church,* and Curtiss, *Russian Church,* give some details of a neglected subject. Mayzel, *Generals and Revolutionaries,* provides background on the army. Jones's "Officers/October" and "Officers and Soviets" are valuable.

For the initial Allied response see, in addition to the general sources, Kettle, *Allies.*

More is made of the comparison with Germany in the article by Mosse, "February Regime."

Chap. 2. Spreading the Revolution

See chap. 8, below, for Siberia, chap. 11 for north Russia; see A.10, above, for the cossacks, and A.7 for the Volunteer Army. Kirienko, *Krakh kaledinishchiny,* is a Soviet account of the first stage on the Don. Kenez, *Civil War/1918* (1971), the best work on the Volunteer Army, is also good on the cossacks.

Background to the national minorities is in A.9. For the Transcaucasus see chap. 15, for Central Asia see chap. 16. Poliakov and Kiselev, "Chislennost'," is a recent computation of the size of various ethnic groups. Arens, "Revolutionary Developments," gives a good background on the early period in Estonia. Pidhainy, *Formation,* is the most complete English source on the creation of the Ukrainian Republic; Antonov-Ovseenko, *Zapiski,* is especially important for the "railway war." Finland has now received definitive English treatment in Upton, *Finnish Revolution.*

Chap. 3. Soviet Russia and the Central Powers

Of general books on Soviet foreign policy in 1917–1918 the best is Debo,

Revolution and Survival; see also Pearce, *Haig/Lenin,* for the role of the war. Baumgart, *Deutsche Ostpolitik,* is the most important source on German policy. Wheeler-Bennett, *Brest-Litovsk,* is still of interest. Chubar'ian, *Brestskii mir,* gives a Soviet interpretation. Trotsky discussed his central role in various versions of his memoirs, especially *Moia zhizn'/My Life* and *O Lenine/On Lenin.* The minutes of the Bolshevik Central Committee, *Protokoly TsK/Bolsheviks,* are very important; see also *Sedmoi s"ezd* for the emergency March party congress. The Left Communist objections to Brest-Litovsk are discussed in Daniels, *Conscience,* and Cohen, *Bukharin.* For the German military view there is Hoffmann, *War Diaries,* and for the Austrians, Czernin, *World War.*

German military operations are outlined in *Weltkrieg;* Petrov, *Otrazhenie,* gives a Soviet overview. Bonch-Bruevich, the senior "Soviet" general in the first months, wrote interesting memoirs on the period, *Vsia vlast'.* Antonov-Ovseenko, *Zapiski,* is a basic source for operations in the south. Erickson, "Origins," discusses the impact on army organization.

For "self-determination," Fedyshyn, *Germany's Drive,* covers the effect of Brest on the Ukraine. Doroshenko, *Ukrainian Hetman State,* attempts a defense of Skoropadsky.

Interesting material on post-Brest relations between Moscow and Berlin is available in Freund, *Unholy Alliance.* The best surveys of the July 1918 Left SR uprising are Fel'shtinskii, *Bol'sheviki i levye esery,* and Spirin, *Avantiura.* For background there are two works by the Left SR Steinberg, *Spiridonova* and *Workshop.* The eccentric view that the affair was a Leninist provocation is advanced in Katkov, "Assassination." On the Latvian Riflemen there is background in English in Ezergailis, *Latvian Impact,* and Jansen, "International Class Solidarity." Krastyn (ed.), *Latyshskie strelki,* includes extracts from Vatsetis; Krastyn', *Istoriia latyshskikh strelkov,* is the fullest history.

Chap. 4. The Allies in Russia

See sources for A. 11 and chap. 3. A much-used memoir is that of the British representative in Moscow, Lockhart, *British Agent.*

The most comprehensive English-language account of the Czechoslovak Corps in this period is Fic, *Revolutionary War* and *Bolsheviks/Czechoslovak Legion;* a third volume, on the situation after May 1918, is forthcoming. See also *Légion tchécoslovaque* by Bradley. Klevanskii, *Chekhoslovatskie internatsionalisty,* gives the Soviet perspective.

For north Russia see chap. 11, below. For the murky Iaroslavl affair there are the testimony in Shutskever, "Soiuz zashchity," the memoirs of the ringleader, Savinkov, *Bor'ba s Bol'shevikami* and the account of his 1924 trial, *Protsess.*

Chap. 5. The Volga Campaign

The best survey in English of the politics on the Komuch side is Berk, "Coup d'Etat"; some of this is summarized in his "Democratic Counterrevolution." For a Soviet view see Garmiza, *Eserovskie pravitel'stva.* For rare documents see

321

Bernshtam (1982). The emigre collection, *Grazhdanskaia voina na Volge*, contains the memoirs of Klimushkin, one of the major leaders of Komuch. Memoirs of Brushvit, Cecek, Klimushkin, Lebedev, and Nikolaev were printed in vols. 8/9 and 10 of the Prague *Volia rossii*. A classic account by a Menshevik Komuch leader who eventually went over to the Reds is Maiskii, *Demokraticheskaia kontrrevoliutsiia*. On Izhevsk there is Berk, "Class Tragedy," and the early Soviet account, Sapozhnikov, "Izhevsko-Votkinskoe vosstanie"; documents are in Bernshtam (ed.), *Ural i Prikam'e*.

The best recent Soviet history of the fighting is Nenarokov, *Vostochnyi front*. A good anti-Bolshevik military account of the Kazan campaign is Stepanov, "Simbirskaia operatsiia"; on the other side there is Tukhachevsky's article in his *Izbrannye*. Petrov, *Ot Volgi*, is good on the Komuch Army, and there is Fedorovich, *Kappel'*. The Sviiazhsk episode, a central part of the Trotsky legend, is dealt with in Trotsky, *Moia zhizn'/My Life*, Gusev, "Sviiazhskie dni," and Reisner, "Kazan'" and "Sviiazhsk."

For general works on the Red Army see A.6, above. For 1918 the memoirs of General Bonch-Bruevich, *Vsia vlast'*, and Aralov, *Lenin vel*, are especially valuable. On the important question of officer recruitment see Spirin, "Sozdaniie," and Iovlev, "Leninskaia politika."

Chap. 6. Sovdepia

General works on politics and economic development are covered under A.4, A.5, and chap. 1. Medvedev, *October Revolution*, is good on the period up to the summer of 1918.

Chap. 7. Cossack Vendée

See A.7 for the Volunteer Army and A.10 for the cossacks. Tucker, *Stalin*, and Seaton, *Stalin*, discuss the Tsaritsyn affair. Sukhorukov, *XI Armiia*, includes the north Caucasus battles of 1918–1919.

Chap. 8. Siberia and the Urals

Snow, *Bolsheviks*, is the best introduction to the "first" Soviet era in Siberia. There is much unique material in Maksakov and Turunov, *Khronika*. Morley, *Japanese Thrust*, covers the beginnings of Tokyo's involvement. For America, there is Unterberger, *Siberian Expedition*.

The best English-language survey of the political conflict between Komuch and the Siberian government is Berk, "Coup d'État" (see also the sources for chap. 5). The protocols of the Ufa State Conference are the emigre-published "Ufimskoe . . . soveshchanie" (1929); other documents appeared in the Soviet "Ufimskoe soveschanie" (1933). Rosenberg, *Liberals*, includes the Siberian

Kadets. See the general sources in A.7 and A.8 and also General Boldyrev's memoirs, *Direktoriia*.

There is no full biography of Kolchak, but see a naval colleague's short account (in Russian), Smirnov, *Kolchak*. At his 1920 "trial" (in *Dopros/Testimony*) Kolchak only had time to testify about his background and his activities in 1918.

Chap. 9. Sovdepia and the Outside World

See A.9 and chap. 2 for the national background of the borderlands. German 1919 military activities are detailed in *Ruckführung des Ostheeres* and the two volumes on the northwest, *Feldzug im Baltikum* and *Kämpfe im Baltikum*. There is a good American book on the Ukraine in this period, Adams, *Bolsheviks*. Antonov-Ovseenko, *Zapiski*, covers his campaign in depth.

For plans for European revolution see also A.11. Hulse, *Forming*, introduces the Komintern; see also Carr, *Bolshevik Revolution*. The documents are in Degras, *Communist International*, and the multivolume series currently being published, *The Communist International in Lenin's Time*. Temkin, *Ot vtorogo*, is a recent Soviet account.

See A.11 and chap. 4 above for Allied intervention, and especially Ullman and Carley. Mayer, *Politics and Diplomacy*, and Thompson, *Russia, Bolshevism*, present the events of 1919 from different viewpoints. McNeal, "Conference of Jassy," is best for this episode. Churchill, *Aftermath*, is the colorful account of a leading interventionist; Gilbert, *Churchill*, discusses his role and publishes related documents.

Chap. 10. Kolchak's Offensive

See the White accounts mentioned in A.7. The account of the French army's representative, Janin, *Ma Mission*, is valuable on the Allied role and on the military-political situation. Eikhe, *Ufimskaia avantiura*, is a Soviet commander's archive-based account of Kolchak's offensive.

Chap. 11. Omsk and Arkhangelsk

There is a large Soviet literature on the Siberian partisans. Footman, "Siberian Partisans," is a Western introduction, El'tsin, "Krestian'skoe dvizhenie," an early Soviet account.

Long, "North Russia," is the best general account of the Civil War in that region. The local Red commander, General Samoilo, wrote memoirs, *Dve zhizni*, and also, with Sboichakov, a general history of the northern campaign, *Pouchitel'nyi urok*. Tarasov, *Bor'ba s interventami*, is a Soviet military monograph. General Miller published a brief account, "Bor'ba . . . na Severe," but the memoirs of Marushevskii, "God na Severe," Dobrovol'skii, "Bor'ba za vozrozhdeniie," and Sokolov, "Padenie", are more interesting. For the British in 1919 see the memoirs of the British commander, Ironside, *Archangel*, and the documents in *Evacuation*.

Chap. 12. Armed Forces of South Russia

The basic sources on the Volunteer Army and the southern cossacks were given in A.7 and A.10, while A.6 gives the Red Army background. The north Caucasus campaign and the breakout are best covered, from the White side, by Denikin, *ORS*, and Vrangel, *Vospominaniia*; for a modern Soviet account of the north Caucasus disaster see Sukhorukov, *XI armiia*.

Chap. 13. The Armed Camp

Most of the material on the Red Army is given under A.6. or Chap. 5. Kritskii, "Krasnaia armiia", has some fascinating insights based on captured Red Army documents. Olikov, *Dezertirstvo*, is frank on desertion. For the Defense Council see Kublanov, *Sovet*.

The development of the state and the economy in 1919 is covered by sources given under A.4. and A.5; see also the records of the pivotal Eighth Party Congress, *Vos' moi s"ezd*.

Chap. 14. The Turning Point

Simonov, *Razgrom denikinshchiny*, gives an early Soviet appraisal of events in the south. Colonel Egorov was an interested party, but his *Razgrom* is valuable. On the role (or non-role) of the Poles see Denikin, *Kto spas*. The political failures of the White movement are dealt with by the sources in A.7. Shekhtman, *Pogromy*, documents White atrocities.

The best English-language source on the Baltic Whites is still Drujina's thesis, "North-West Army"; like the Siberian campaign, the Baltic is much more fully covered in Russian. The memoirs of Colonel Rodzianko, *Severo-Zapadnaia armiia*, provide the best White military history of the campaign, by the operational commander; there are also the memoirs of Gorn, *Grazhdanskaia voina*, and the journalistic account by Kirdetsov, *U vorot*. Little was written about the commander of the army, but see the essays in *General . . . Iudenich*. *Bor'ba za Petrograd* is an early Soviet collection with material on Trotsky and Zinoviev's role. Soviet accounts from the 1920s include Kornatovskii, *Bor'ba*, and Geronimus, *Razgrom Iudenicha*; Pukhov, *Petrograd ne sdavat'!*, is a more modern monograph. Serge, *Conquered City*, gives an excellent feel of besieged Petrograd. Fedotov, "Na dal'nikh postupakh," is good on White politics; some documents on the White government appeared in "Obrazovanie."

Chap. 15. End of Denikin

Agureev, *Belogvardeiskie voiska Denikina*, is a solid post-Stalin campaign history of Denikin's last months. On the Red Cavalry see the memoirs of Budenny, *Proidennyi put'*. Rakovskii, *V stane belykh*, is the account of a well-informed White journalist. The "Greens" are recalled by one of their leaders, Voronovich, in "Mezh dvukh ognei."

The Transcaucasus is a region especially well served by English-language literature. The standard introduction is still Kazemzadeh, *Struggle for Transcaucasia*; Pipes, *Formation*, is also useful for Soviet policy. Soviet surveys include Mints (ed.), *P. s. v. v Zakavkaz'e*; for the military dimension see Kadishev, *V Zakavkaz'e*.

Turning to particular regions, the dynamics of revolution in 1917–1918 are dealt with in Suny, *Baku Commune*. On Azerbaidzhan see Zenkovsky, *Pan-Turkism*, and Swietchowski, *Russian Azerbaijan*. For a western account of the Georgian events see Lang, *Modern History*. Armenia receives perhaps the fullest scholarly treatment of any "Russian" minority, in the works of Hovannisian, *Road to Independence* and *Republic of Armenia*; Walker, *Armenia*, provides a smaller-scale survey.

Chap. 16. Storm over Asia

Many of the sources for A.7 and chaps. 8, 10, and 11 are relevant for the final Siberian period. Grondijs, *Cas-Koltchak*, prints documents on Kolchak's last months. Smith, *Vladivostok*, is a substantial academic work on the agony of the White movement in the Far East.

The best introduction to events in Central Asia is Park, *Bolshevism in Turkestan*. Zenkovsky, *Pan-Turkism*, is also very useful. For a recent Soviet survey there is Mints (ed.), *P. s. v. v. srednei azii*. Safarov, *Kolonial'naia revoliutsiia*, is a remarkable Bolshevik critique of the Tashkent government. Becker, *Russia's Protectorates*, covers Bukhara and Khiva, Ellis, *"Intervention" in Transcaspia*, the British role. The protocol of the Baku Congress of Peoples of the East is translated in *Congress*; see also the account by White, "Communism." White, "Asian Revolution," gives a good brief introduction to Soviet policy in the region.

Chap. 17. Consolidating the State

See Erickson, "Militia Army," for later Red Army developments. On the economy the sources are mainly in A.5. For the debates of 1920 see Daniels, *Conscience*, Day, *Trotsky*, Cohen, *Bukharin*, and the protocol of the 9th party congress, *Deviatyi s"ezd*. Bunyan, *Forced Labour*, documents labor militarization. Litvinova, *Revoliutsionnye komitety*, discusses the role of Revcoms in the reintegration of Belorussia, the Ukraine, and eastern Siberia.

Chap. 18. The Polish Campaign

Davies, *White Eagle*, is the best political-military history of the Polish war; another recent account, strongest on the military side, is Zamoyski, *Marchlands*. Pilsudski's 1924 military memoirs are now available in English, *Year 1920*. On the diplomatic background see vol. 3 of Ullman, *Anglo-Soviet Relations*, Wandycz, *Soviet-Polish Relations*, and Carley, "Politics of Anti-Bolshevism." Kakurin and Melikov, *Voina s belopoliakami*, is the standard Soviet military history; a more recent general account is Kuz'min, *Poslednyi pokhod*. See also the substantial analysis by S. S. Kamenev in his *Zapiski*. Tukhachevsky wrote memoirs of his campaign; these are available in his *Izbrannye* and have recently been translated into English (in Pilsudski). Egorov's memoirs, *L'vov-Varshava*, provide an important inside view, and there is much in Budenny, *Proidennyi put'*. Stalin's role is covered in Seaton, *Stalin*, and Tucker, *Stalin*. For the flavor of the war see the "Red Cavalry" stories in Babel, *Collected Stories*.

Chap. 19. Crimean Ulcer

The best English-language introduction is Kenez, *South Russia/1919–1920* (1977); Ross, *Vrangel'*, is an excellent Russian-language survey written abroad. Vrangel's own account, *Vospominaniia/Always with Honor* is invaluable. For Vrangel's biography see the collection of articles edited by Lampe, *Vrangel'*. Treadgold, "Ideology," outlines Vrangel's doctrine.

The journalistic account of Rakovskii, *Konets belykh*, is useful. Pipes wrote a biography of a leading official, *Struve. Krasnyi arkhiv* published several collections of documents relating to Vrangel's policies.

Vrangel's battles are described at length in his memoirs, and also those of one of his commanders, General (fon-) Dreier, *Krestnyi put'*. Kritskii, *Kornilovskii udarnyi polk*, is also good. On the Red side see Budenny, *Proidennyi put'*. Korotkov, *Razgrom Vrangelia*, is a Soviet military monograph.

Conclusion

For the impact of the Revolution see Laqueur, *Fate*, and Pethybridge, *Social Prelude*; Fitzpatrick, "Civil War," is the most interesting recent discussion.

Bibliography

Abrams, Robert (1966). "The Local Soviets of the RSFSR, 1918–1921." Columbia Univ. Ph.D. thesis.

Adams, Arthur E. (1963). *Bolsheviks in the Ukraine: The Second Campaign, 1918–1919*. New Haven.

Adelman, Jonathan R. (1982). "The Development of the Soviet Party Apparat in the Civil War: Centre, Localities, and Nationality Areas." *Russian History* 9, pt. 1: 86–110.

Agureev, K. V. (1961). *Razgrom belogvardeiskikh voisk Denikina: (Oktiabr' 1919–mart 1920 goda).* Moscow.

Akulinin, I. G. (1937). *Orenburgskoe Kazach'e Voisko v bor'be s bol'shevikami, 1917–1920.* Shanghai.

—— (1927). "Ural'skoe Kazach'e Voisko v bor'be s bol'shevikami." *Beloe Delo* 2: 122–47.

Aleksashenko, A. P. (1966). *Krakh denikinshchiny.* Moscow.

Anishev, A. I. (1925). *Ocherki istorii grazhdanskoi voiny 1917–1920.* Leningrad.

Antonov-Ovseenko, V. A. (1924–1933). *Zapiski o grazhdanskoi voine.* 4 vols. Moscow.

Anweiler, Oskar (1974). *The Soviets: The Russian Workers Peasants and Soldiers Councils, 1905–1921.* New York.

Aralov, S. I. (1962). *Lenin vel nas k pobede: Vospominaniia.* Moscow.

Arens, Olavi (1976). "Revolutionary Developments in Estonia in 1917–18 and their Ideological and Political Background." Columbia Univ. Ph.D. thesis.

Atkinson, Dorothy (1983). *The End of the Russian Land Commune 1905–1930.* Stanford.

Aver'ev, V. (1929). "Agrarnaia politika kolchakovshchiny." *Na agrarnon fronte* 1929, 6: 24–45, 8: 23–44.

Avrich, Paul, ed. (1973). *The Anarchists in the Russian Revolution.* London.

Azovtsev, N. N., et al. (1980–1986). *Grazhdanskaia voina v SSSR.* 2 vols. Moscow.

Babel, Isaac (1974). *Collected Stories.* Harmondsworth.

Baedeker, Karl (1971). *Baedeker's Russia: 1914.* London.

Baumgart, Winfried (1966). *Deutsche Ostpolitik 1918: Von Brest-Litovsk bis zum Ende des Ersten Weltkrieges.* Vienna & Munich.

Becker, Seymour (1968). *Russia's Protectorates in Central Asia: Bukhara and Khiva, 1865–1924.* Cambridge, Mass.

Benvenuti, Francesco (1982). *I Bolscevichi e l'Armata Rossa, 1918–1922.* Naples.

Berk, Stephen M. (1971). "The Coup d'Etat of Admiral Kolchak: The Counterrevolution in Siberia and Eastern Russia 1917–1918." Columbia Univ. Ph.D. thesis.

—— (1973). "The Democratic Counterrevolution: Komuch and the Civil War on the Volga." *Canadian-American Slavic Studies* 7: 443–459.

—— (1975). "The 'Class Tragedy' of Izhevsk: A Working-Class Opposition to Bolshevism in 1918." *Russian History* 2: 176–190.

Bernshtam, M. S. (1979). "Storony v grazhdanskoi voine 1917–1922 gg. (Problematika, metodologiia, statistika)." *Vestnik Russkogo khristianskogo dvizheniia* 128: 252–357.

—— ed. (1981a). *Nezavisimoe rabochee dvizhenie v 1918 godu: Dokumenty i materialy: Narodnoe soprotivelenie kommunizmu v Rossii.* Paris.

—— (1981b). "Smysl Kommunisticheskogo unichtozheniia narodov: Iz istorii demograficheskoi i biosotsial'noi revoliutsii v SSSR." *Novyi zhurnal* 1981: 162–215.

—— ed. (1982). *Ural i Prikam'e (noiabr' 1917–ianvar' 1919): Dokumenty i materialy: Narodnoe soprotivlenie kommunizmu v Rossii.* Paris.

Bilmanis, Alfred (1970). *A History of Latvia.* London.

Blank, Stephen (1979). "The Unknown Commissariat: The Soviet Commissariat of Nationalities 1917–1924." Univ. of Chicago Ph.D. thesis.

Boldyrev, V. G. (1925). *Direktoriia Kolchak Interventy: Vospominaniia.* Novoniko-laevsk.
Bonch-Bruevich, M. D. (1957). *Vsia vlast' Sovetam: Vospominaniia.* Moscow.
Bor'ba za Petrograd: 15 oktiabria–6 noiabria 1919 goda (1920). Petrograd.
Bor'ba za Sovetskuiu vlast' na Kubani v 1917–1920 gg. Sbornik dokumentov i materialov (1957). Krasnodar.
Bor'ba za vlast' Sovetov na Donu 1917–1920 gg.: Sbornik dokumentov (1957). Rostov.
Borys, Jurij (1980). *The Sovietization of Ukraine 1917–1923: The Communist Doctrine and Practice of National Self-Determination.* Edmonton.
Bradley, John F. N. (1965). *La Légion Tchécoslovaque en Russie 1914–1920.* Paris.
———— (1968). *Allied Intervention in Russia.* London.
———— (1975). *Civil War in Russia 1917–1920.* London.
Brinkley, George A. (1966). *The Volunteer Army and Allied Intervention in South Russia, 1917–1921: A Study in the Politics and Diplomacy of the Russian Civil War.* Notre Dame.
Brovkin, Vladimir (1983). "The Mensheviks' Political Comeback: The Elections to the Provincial City Soviets in Spring 1918." *Russian Review* 42: 1–50.
———— (1984). "The Menshevik Opposition to the Bolshevik Regime and the Dilemma of Soviet Power, October 1917–January 1919." Princeton Univ. Ph.D. thesis.
Bubnov, A. S., et al., eds. (1928–1930). *Grazhdanskaia voina 1918–1921.* 3 vols. Moscow.
Buchanan, Herbert R. (1972). "Soviet Economic Policy for the Transition Period: The Supreme Council of the National Economy 1917–1920." Indiana Univ. Ph.D. thesis.
Budberg, Aleksei (1923–1924). "Dnevnik." *Arkhiv Russkoi Revoliutsii* 12: 197–290, 13: 197–312; 14: 225–341, 15: 254–345.
Budennyi, S. M. (1958–1973). *Proidennyi put'.* 3 vols. Moscow.
Bukharin, N. I. (1980). *Ekonomika perekhodnogo perioda.* Letchworth.
Bunyan, J., ed. (1967). *The Origins of Forced Labor in the Soviet State, 1917–1921: Documents and Materials.* Baltimore.
————, ed. (1976). *Intervention, Civil War, and Communism in Russia: April–December 1918: Documents and Materials.* New York.
Bunyan, J., and Fisher, H. H., eds. (1961). *The Bolshevik Revolution, 1917–1918: Documents and Materials.* Stanford.
Bykov, P. M. (1926). *Poslednie dni Romanovykh.* 2d ed. Sverdlovsk; English ed.: (1934). *The Last Days of Tsardom.* London.
Carley, Michael J. (1976). "The Politics of Anti-Bolshevism: The French Government and the Russo-Polish War, December 1919–May 1920." *Historical Journal* 19: 163–189.
———— (1983). *Revolution and Intervention: The French Government and the Russian Civil War 1917–1919.* Kingston and Montreal.
Carr, E. H. (1966). *The Bolshevik Revolution.* 3 vols. Harmondsworth.
Chamberlin, William H. (1965). *The Russian Revolution: 1917–1921.* 2 vols. New York.
Channon, John (1983). "'Peasant Revolution' and 'Land Reform': Land Redistribution in European Russia, October 1917–1920." Univ. of Birmingham [England] Ph.D. thesis.
Chubar'ian, A. O. (1964). *Brestskii mir.* Moscow.
Churchill, Winston S. (1929). *The Aftermath.* London.

Coates, W. P., and Coates, Z. (1935). *Armed Intervention in Russia 1918–1922*. London.

Cohen, Stephen F. (1972). "In Praise of War Communism: Bukharin's 'Economics of the Transition Period'." In *Revolution and Politics in Russia: Essays in Memory of B. I. Nicolaevsky*, edited by Alexander Rabinowitch et al., pp. 192–203. Bloomington.

—— (1974). *Bukharin and the Bolshevik Revolution: A Political Biography, 1888–1938*. London.

Collins, David (1975). "The Origins, Structure, and Role of the Russian Red Guard." Univ. of Leeds Ph.D. thesis.

Congress of Peoples of the East: Baku, September 1919: Stenographic Report (1977). Edited and translated by Brian Pearce. London.

Conquest, Robert (1971). "The Human Cost of Soviet Communism." In "Document 92–36, Committee on the Judiciary, U.S. Senate." Washington.

Curtiss, John S. (1953). *The Russian Church and the Soviet State, 1917–1950*. Boston.

Czernin, O. (1919). *In the World War*. London.

Dacy, Donald A. (1972). "The White Russian Movement." Univ. of Texas Ph.D. thesis.

Daniels, Robert V. (1960). *The Conscience of the Revolution: Communist Opposition in Soviet Russia*. Cambridge, Mass.

—— (1968). *Red October: The Bolshevik Revolution of 1917*. London.

Davies, Norman (1972). *White Eagle, Red Star: The Polish-Soviet War, 1919–20*. London.

—— (1975). "The Genesis of the Polish-Soviet War." *European Studies Review* 5: 47–68.

Day, Richard B. (1973). *Leon Trotsky and the Politics of Economic Isolation*. New York.

The Debate on Soviet Power: Minutes of the All-Russian Central Executive Committee of Soviets: Second Convocation, October 1917–January 1918 (1979). Translated and edited by John L. H. Keep. Oxford.

Debo, Richard K. (1979). *Revolution and Survival: the Foreign Policy of Soviet Russia, 1917–18*. Toronto.

Degras, Jane, ed. (1951). *Soviet Documents on Foreign Policy*. Vol. 1. London.

—— (1971). *The Communist International 1919–1943: Documents*. Vol. 1. London.

Dekrety Sovetskoi vlasti (1957–1980). Vols. 1–10. Moscow.

Denikin, A. I. (1921–1926). *Ocherki Russkoi Smuty*. 5 vols. Paris; English abridgements: (n.d.). *The Russian Turmoil*. London; (1930). *The White Army*. London.

—— (1937). *Kto spas sovetskuiu vlast' ot gibeli?* Paris.

Deutscher, I. (1954). *The Prophet Armed: Trotsky 1879–1921*. New York.

Deviatyi s"ezd RKP(b): Mart–aprel' 1920 goda: Protokoly (1960). Moscow.

Direktivy Glavnogo komandovaniia Krasnoi Armii (1917–1920): Sbornik dokumentov (1969). Moscow.

Direktivy komandovaniia frontov Krasnoi Armii (1917–1922 gg.): Sbornik dokumentov (1971–1978). 4 vols. Moscow.

Dobb, Maurice (1928). *Russian Economic Development since the Revolution*. London.

Dobrovol'skii, S., (1921). "Bor'ba za vozrozhdenie Rossii v Severnoi oblasti." *Arkhiv Russkoi revoliutsii* 3: 5–146.

Dobrynin, V. (1921). *Bor'ba s bol' shevizmom na iuge Rossii: Uchastie v bor'be Donskogo kazachestva: Fevral' 1917–Mart 1920 (Ocherk)*. Prague.

Documents on British Foreign Policy 1919–1939 (1949–1962). 1st Series, Vols. 3, 11, 12. London.

Dokumenty vneshnei politiki SSSR (1957–1959). Vols. 1–3. Moscow.

Dopros Kolchaka (1925). Edited by K. A. Popov et al. L.; English ed.: Varneck, E., and Fisher H. H., eds. (1935). *Testimony of Kolchak and Other Siberian Materials.* Stanford.

Doroshenko, Dmytro (1973). *The Ukrainian Hetman State of 1918.* Winnipeg.

Dotsenko, Paul (1983). *The Struggle for Democracy in Siberia, 1917–1920: Eyewitness Account of a Contemporary.* Stanford.

Dreier, V. fon- (1921). *Krestnyi put' vo imia rodiny: Dvukhletniaia voina krasnogo severa s belym iugom 1918–1920 goda.* Berlin.

Drujina, Gleb (1950). "The History of the North-West Army of General Iudenich." Stanford Univ. Ph.D. thesis.

Dumova, N. G. (1982). *Kadetskaia kontrrevoliutsiia i ee razgrom (Oktiabr' 1917–1920 gg.).* Moscow.

Duval, Charles (1978). "Iakov M. Sverdlov: Founder of the Bolshevik Party Machine 1885–1919." Unpublished.

Egorov, A. I. (1929). *L'vov-Varshava: 1920 god: Vzaimnodeistvie frontov.* Moscow.

—— (1931). *Razgrom Denikina 1919.* Moscow.

Eikhe, G. Kh. (1960). *Ufimskaia avantiura Kolchaka (Mart–aprel' 1919 g.): Pochemu Kolchaku ne udalos' prorvat'sa k Volge na soedinenie s Denikinym.* Moscow.

—— (1966). *Oprokinutyi tyl'.* Moscow.

Ellis, C. H. (1963). *The British "Intervention" in Transcaspia: 1918–1919.* Berkeley.

El'tsin, V. (1926). "Krest'ianskoe dvizhenie v Sibiri v period Kolchaka." *Proletarskaia revoliutsiia* 2 (49): 5–48, 3 (50): 51–82.

Erickson, John (1962). *The Soviet High Command: A Military-Political History, 1918–1941.* London.

—— (1969). "The Origins of the Red Army." In *Revolutionary Russia: A Symposium.* Edited by Richard Pipes, pp. 286–328. Garden City, New York.

—— (1974). "Some Military and Political Aspects of the 'Militia Army' Controversy, 1919–1920." In *Essays in Honour of E. H. Carr,* edited by C. Abramsky and B. Williams, pp. 204–228. London.

—— (1986). "Pens versus Swords: a Study of Studying the Russian Civil War, 1917–22." In *Warfare, Diplomacy and Politics: Essays in Honour of A. J. P. Taylor,* edited by Chris Wrigley, pp. 120–37. London.

"The Evacuation of North Russia, 1919" (1920). Cmd. 818. London.

Ezergailis, Andrew (1983). *The Latvian Impact on the Bolshevik Revolution: The First Phase: September 1917 to April 1918.* Boulder.

Fedorovich, A. (1967). *General Kappel'.* Melbourne.

Fedotoff-White, D. (1944). *The Growth of the Red Army.* Princeton.

Fedotov, B. F. (1971–1972). "Na dal'nikh postupakh k Krasnomu Piteru." *Voprosy istorii* 1971, no. 1: 122–131, 1971, no. 2, 108–115, 1972, no. 9: 143–154.

Fedotov, G. P. (1928). *The Russian Church since the Revolution.* London.

Fedyshin, Oleh S. (1971). *Germany's Drive to the East and the Ukrainian Revolution, 1917–1918.* New Brunswick.

Die Feldzug im Baltikum bis zur zweiten Einnahme von Riga: Januar bis Mai 1919 (1937). Berlin.

Fel'shtinskii, Iu. G. (1985). *Bol'sheviki i levye esery: Oktiabr' 1917–iiul' 1918: Na puti k odnopartiinoi diktature.* Paris.

Ferro, Marc (1980). *October 1917: A Social History of the Russian Revolution.* Leningrad.

Fic, Victor M. (1977). *Revolutionary War for Independence and the Russian Question: Czechoslovak Army in Russia 1914–1918.* New Delhi.

—— (1978). *The Bolsheviks and the Czechoslovak Legion: the Origin of Their Armed Conflict: March–May 1918.* New Delhi.

Filat'ev, D. V. (1985). *Katastrofa Belogo dvizheniia v Sibiri: 1918–1922: Vpechatleniia ochevidtsa.* Paris.

Fitzpatrick, Sheila (1982). *The Russian Revolution.* Oxford.

—— (1985). "The Civil War as a Formative Experience." In *Bolshevik Culture: Experiment and Order in the Russian Revolution,* edited by Abbott Gleason et al., pp. 57–76. Bloomington.

Fleming, Peter (1963). *The Fate of Admiral Kolchak,* London.

Fokke, D. G. (1930). "Na stsene i za kulisami Brestskoi tragikomedii (Memuary uchastnika . . .)." *Arkhiv Russkoi revoliutsii* 20: 5–207.

Footman, David (1956). "Siberian Partisans in the Civil War." *St. Antony's Papers, Soviet Affairs,* no. 1: 24–53.

—— (1961). *Civil War in Russia.* London.

Frenkin, M. (1978). *Russkaia armiia i revoliutsiia: 1917–1918.* Munich.

—— (1982). *Zakhvat vlasti bol'shevikami v Rossii i rol' tylovykh garnizonov armii: Podgotovka i provedeniie oktiabr'skogo miatezha: 1917–1918 gg.* Jerusalem.

Freund, Gerald (1957). *Unholy Alliance: Russian-German Relations from the Treaty of Brest-Litovsk to the Treaty of Berlin.* London.

Frunze, M. V. (1957). *Izbrannye proizvedeniia,* 2 vols. Moscow.

[FRUS] *Papers Relating to the Foreign Relations of the United States.* (a) *1918: Russia* (1931–1932). 3 vols. (b) *1919: Russia* (1937). (c) *The Paris Peace Conference* (1942–1947). 13 vols. (d) *1920* (1936). Vol. 3. Washington.

Gaponenko, L. S., and Kabuzan, V. M., (1961). "Materialy sel'skokhoziaistven-nykh perepisei 1916–1917 gg. . . ." *Voprosy istorii* 1961, no. 6: 97–115.

Gardner, Lloyd C. (1984). *Safe for Democracy: The Anglo-American Response to Revolution, 1913–1923.* Oxford.

Garmiza, V. V. (1970). *Krushenie eserovskikh pravitel'stv.* Moscow.

Gavrilov, L. M., and Kutuzov, V. V. (1964). "Perepis' Russkoi armii 25 Oktiabria 1917 g." *Istoriia SSSR* 1964, 2: 87–91.

Gaworek, Norbert H. (1970). "Allied Economic Warfare against Soviet Russia from November 1917 to March 1921." Univ. of Wisconsin Ph.D. thesis.

General-ot-infanterii Nikolai Nikolaevich Iudenich (1931). Paris.

Germanis, Uldis (1974). *Oberst Vacietis und die lettischen Schützen im Weltkrieg und in der Oktoberrevolution.* Stockholm.

Geronimus, A. (1929). *Razgrom Iudenicha: Partiia, rabochii klass i Krasnaia armiia v bor'be za Petrograd: Voenno-politicheskii ocherk.* Moscow and Leningrad.

Gerson, Lennard D. (1976). *The Secret Police in Lenin's Russia.* Philadelphia.

Getzler, Israel (1967). *Martov: A Political Biography of a Russian Social-Democrat.* Cambridge.

—— (1983). *Kronstadt 1917–1921: The Fate of a Soviet Democracy.* Cambridge.

Gilbert, Martin (1967, 1977). *Winston S. Churchill: 1917–1922.* Vol. 4 and Vol. 4: Companion (Parts 1 and 2). London.

Gimpel'son, E. F. (1968). *Sovety v gody inostrannoi interventsii i grazhdanskoi voiny.* Moscow.

THE RUSSIAN CIVIL WAR

Gimpel'son, E. F. (1973). *Voennyi kommunizm: Politika, praktika, ideologiia*. Moscow.
—— (1974). *Sovetskii rabochii klass 1918–1920: Sotsial'no-politicheskie izmeniia*. Moscow.
—— (1977). *Velikii oktiabr' i stanovlenie sovetskoi sistemy upravleniia nardonym khoziaistvom (noiabr' 1917–1920 gg.)*. Moscow.
—— (1982). *Rabochii klass v upravlenii Sovetskim gosudarstvom: Noiabr' 1919–1920 gg.* Moscow.
Gins, G. K. (1921). *Sibir', soiuzniki i Kolchak: Povorotnyi moment russkoi istorii 1918–1920 g.g.* Peking and Kharbin.
Gladkov, I. A., et al. (1976). *Sovetskaia ekonomika v 1917–1920 gg.* Istoriia sotsialisticheskoi ekonomiki SSSR, vol. 1. Moscow.
Golinkov, D. L. (1978). *Krushenie antisovetskogo podpol'ia v SSSR.* 2d rev. ed. 2 vols. Moscow.
Golovin, N. N. (1937). *Rossiiskaia Kontr-revoliutsiia v 1917–1918 g.g.* Paris.
—— (1939). *Voennyia usiliia Rossii v mirovoi voine.* 2 vols. Paris.
Golub, P. A. (1982). *Revoliutsiia zashchishchaetsia: Opyt zashchity revoliutsionnykh zavoevanii Velikogo Oktiabria, 1917–1920.* Moscow.
Gorn, V. (1923). *Grazhdanskaia voina na severo-zapade Rossii.* Berlin.
Gorodetskii, E. N. (1965). *Rozhdenie Sovetskogo pravitel'stva: 1917–1918 gg.* Moscow.
Graubard, Stephen R. (1956). *British Labour and the Russian Revolution 1917–1924.* Cambridge, Mass.
Grazhdanskaia voina i voennaia interventsiia v SSSR: Entsiklopediia (1983). Edited by S. S. Khromov et al. Moscow.
Grazhdanskaia voina na Ukraine: Sbornik dokumentov i materialov (1967–1968). Edited by S. M. Korolivskii et al. 4 vols. Kiev.
Grazhdanskaia voina na Volge v 1918 g. (1930). Prague.
Grondijs, L. H. (1939). *Le Cas-Koltchak: Contribution à l'histoire de la Révolution russe.* Leiden.
Gusev, K. V. (1975). *Partiia eserov: Ot melkoburzhuaznogo revoliutsionarizma k kontrrevoliutsii.* Moscow.
Gusev, S. I. (1924). "Sviiazhskie dni (1918 g.)." *Proletarskaia revoliutsiia* 2 (25): 100–109.
—— (1925). *Grazhdanskaia voina i Krasnaia Armiia: Sbornik . . . statei.* Moscow.
Hagen, Mark L. von (1985). "School of the Revolution: Bolsheviks and Peasants in the Red Army, 1918–1928." Stanford Univ. Ph.D. thesis.
Haimson, Leopold H. (1964). "The Problem of Social Stability in Urban Russia, 1905–1917." *Slavic Review* 23: 619–642, 24: 1–22.
—— (1974). *The Mensheviks: From the Revolution of 1917 to the Second World War.* Chicago.
—— (1979–1980). "The Mensheviks after the October Revolution." *Russian Review* 38: 456–473, 39: 181–207, 462–483.
Harding, Neil (1981). *Lenin's Political Thought.* Vol. 2. London.
Haupt, Georges, and Marie, Jean-Jacques (1974). *Makers of the Russian Revolution.* London.
Helgesen, Malvin M. (1980). "The Origins of the Party-State Monolith in Soviet Russia: Relations between the Soviets and Party Committees in the Central Provinces, October 1917–March 1921." SUNY (Stony Brook) Ph.D. thesis.
Heyman, Neil M. (1972). "Leon Trotsky as a Military Thinker." Stanford Univ. Ph.D. thesis.

Hoffmann, Max von (1929). *War Diaries and Other Papers*. London.

Holman, Glenn Paul (1973). "'War Communism' or the Besieger Besieged: A Study of Lenin's Social and Political Objectives from 1918 to 1921." Georgetown Univ. Ph.D. thesis.

Hovannisian, Richard G. (1967). *Armenia on the Road to Independence: 1918*. Berkeley.

―――― (1971, 1982). *The Republic of Armenia*. 2 vols. Berkeley.

Hovi, Kalervo (1975). *Cordon Sanitaire or Barrière de l'Est? The Emergence of the New French Eastern European Alliance Policy 1917–1919*. Turku.

Hulse, James W. (1964). *The Forming of the Communist International*. Stanford.

Hunczak, Taras, ed. (1977). *The Ukraine, 1917–1921: A Study in Revolution*. Cambridge, Mass.

Husband, William R. (1984). "The Nationalization of the Textile Industry of Soviet Russia, 1917–1920: Industrial Administration and the Workers during the Russian Civil War." Princeton Univ. Ph.D. thesis.

Ioffe, G. Z. (1977). *Krakh rossiiskoi monarkhicheskoi kontrrevoliutsii*. Moscow.

―――― (1983). *Kolchakovskaia avantiura i ee krakh*. Moscow.

Iovlev, A. M. (1968). "Razrabotka i osushchestvlenie leninskoi politiki v otnoshenii spetsialistov staroi armii (1917–1920 gg.)." *Voprosy istorii KPSS* 1968, no. 4: 30–43.

Ironside, Edmund (1953). *Archangel, 1918–1919*. London.

Iroshnikov, M. P. (1966). *Sozdanie sovetskogo tsentral'nogo gosudarstvennogo apparata. Sovet Narodnykh Komissarov i narodnye komissariaty, oktiabr' 1917–ianviar' 1918 g.* Moscow and Leningrad.

―――― (1980). *Predsedatel' Sovnarkoma i Soveta Oborony V. I. Ul'ianov (Lenin): Ocherki gosudarstvennoi deiatel'nosti v iiule 1918–marte 1920 g.* Moscow.

Istoriia grazhdanskoi voiny v SSSR (1938–1960). 5 vols. Moscow.

Istoriia Kommunisticheskoi Partii Sovetskogo Soiuza (1968). Vol. 3, parts 1–2. Edited by P. N. Pospelov et al. Moscow.

Istoriia Kommunisticheskoi Partii Sovetskogo Soiuza: Atlas (1977). 2d rev. ed. Moscow.

Istoriia vneshnei politiki SSSR: 1917–1975 (1976). Vol. 1. Edited by A. V. Berezkin et al. Moscow.

Ivanov, N. Ia. (1977). *Kontrrevoliutsiia v Rossii v 1917 godu i ee razgrom*. Moscow.

Iz istorii grazhdanskoi voiny v SSSR: 1918–1922: Sbornik dokumentov i materialov (1960–1961). 3 vols. Moscow.

Iz istoriia Vserossiisskoi Chrezvychainoi komissii: 1917–1921 gg.: Sbornik dokumentov (1958). Edited by G. A. Belov et al. Moscow.

Jacobs, Walter D. (1969). *Frunze: The Soviet Clausewitz 1885–1925*. The Hague.

Janin, M. (1933). *Ma Mission en Siberie: 1918–1920*. Paris.

Jansen, Marc (1982). *A Show Trial under Lenin: The Trial of the Socialist Revolutionaries, Moscow, 1922*. Leiden.

―――― (1986). "International Class Solidarity or Foreign Intervention? Internationalists and Latvian Rifles in the Russian Revolution and the Civil War." *International Review of Social History* 31: 68–79.

Jeffery, Keith (1984). *The British Army and the Crisis of Empire 1918–22*. Manchester.

Jones, David R. (1970). "The Officers and the October Revolution." *Soviet Studies* 28: 207–223.

―――― (1977). "The Officers and the Soviets, 1917–1920: A Study in Motives."

Soviet Armed Forces Review Annual 1: 176–187.

Kadishev, A. V. (1960). *Interventsiia i grazhdanskaia voina v Zakavkaz'e.* Moscow.

Kakurin, N. (1925–1926). *Kak srazhalas' revoliutsiia.* 2 vols. Moscow and Leningrad.

——— (1926). *Strategicheskii ocherk grazhdanskoi voiny.* Moscow and Leningrad.

Kakurin, N. E., and Melikov, V. A. (1925). *Voina s belopoliakami 1920 g.* Moscow and Leningrad.

Kamenev, S. S. (1957). "Vospominaniia o Vladimire Il'iche Lenine." In *Vospominaniia o Vladimire Il'iche Lenine,* vol. 2., pp. 249–265. Moscow.

——— (1963). *Zapiski o grazhdanskoi voine i voennom stroitel'stve: Izbrannye stat'i.* Moscow.

Die Kämpfe im Baltikum nach der zweiten Einnahme von Riga: Juni bis Dezember 1919 (1938). Berlin.

Kanev, S. N. (1974) *Oktiabr'skaia revoliutsiia i krakh anarkhizma (Bor'ba partii bol'shevikov protiv anarkhizma 1917–1922 gg.).* Moscow.

Karmann, Rudolf (1985). *Der Freiheitskampf der Kosaken: Die weisse Armee in der Russischen Revolution 1917–1920.* Puchheim.

Katkov, George (1962). "The Assassination of Count Mirbach." *St. Antony's Papers* 12: 53–93.

Kautsky, Karl (1973). *Terrorism and Communism.* New York.

Kazemzadeh, Firuz (1951). *The Struggle for Transcaucasia (1917–1921).* New York.

Keep, John L. H. (1976). *The Russian Revolution: A Study in Mass Mobilization.* London.

Kenez, Peter (1971). *Civil War in South Russia, 1918: The First Year of the Volunteer Army.* Berkeley.

——— (1977). *Civil War in South Russia, 1919–1920: The Defeat of the Whites.* Berkeley.

——— (1980). "The Ideology of the White Movement." *Soviet Studies* 32: 58–83.

——— (1986). *The Birth of the Propaganda State: Soviet Methods of Mass Mobilization, 1917–1929.* Cambridge.

Kennan, George (1956). *Russia Leaves the War.* London.

——— (1958). *The Decision to Intervene.* London.

Kettle, Michael (1981). *The Allies and the Russian Collapse: March 1917–March 1918.* London.

Kharitonov, O. V., ed. (1969). *Illiustrirovannoe opisanie obmundirovaniia i znakov razlichiia Sovetskoi armii (1918–1958 gg.).* Leningrad.

Kholodkovskii, V. M. (1975). *Finliandiia i Sovetskaia Rossiia, 1918–1920.* Moscow.

Kin, D. (1926). *Denikinshchina.* Leningrad.

Kingston-Mann, Esther (1983). *Lenin and the Problem of Marxist Peasant Revolution.* Oxford.

Kirdetsov, G. (1921). *U vorot Petrograda (1919–1920 gg).* Berlin.

Kirienko, Iu. K. (1976). *Krakh kaledinshchiny.* Moscow.

Kleubort, Daniel (1977). "Lenin on the State: Theory and Practice after October." Univ. of Chicago Ph.D. thesis.

Klevanskii, A. Kh. (1965). *Chekhoslovatskie internatsionalisty i prodannyi korpus: Chekhoslovatskie politicheskie organizatsii i voinskie formirovanie v Rossii: 1914–1921 gg.* Moscow.

Kliatskin, S. M. (1965). *Na zashchite Oktiabria: Organizatsiia reguliarnoi armii i militsionnoe stroitel'stvo v Sovetskoi respublike: 1917–1920.* Moscow.

Knei-Paz, Baruch (1978). *The Social and Political Thought of Leon Trotsky.* Oxford.

Knox, Alfred (1921). *With the Russian Army, 1914–1917.* 2 vols. London.

Koenker, Diane (1985). "Urbanization and Deurbanization in the Russian Revolution and Civil War." *Journal of Modern History* 57: 424–450.

Kollontai, Aleksandra (1977). *Selected Writings.* Westport, Conn.

Kommunisticheskaia Partiia Sovetskogo Soiuza v rezoliutsiiakh i resheniiakh s"ezdov, konferentsii i plenumov TsK (1970). Vol. 2. Moscow.

Korablev, Iu. I. (1970). *V. I. Lenin i sozdanie Krasnoi Armii.* Moscow.

——— (1979). *V. I. Lenin i zashchita zavoevanii Velikogo Oktiabria.* 2d rev. ed. Moscow.

Korablev, Iu. I., et al., eds. (1982). *Zashchita Velikogo Oktiabria.* Moscow.

Kornatovskii, N. A. (1929). *Bor'ba za Krasnyi Petrograd (1919).* Leningrad.

Korotkov, I. S. (1955). *Razgrom Vrangelia.* Moscow.

Kovalenko, D. A. (1970). *Oboronnaia promyshlennost' Sovetskoi Rossii v 1918–1920 gg.* Moscow.

Kovalenko, D. A., et al. (1967). *Sovety v pervyi god proletarskoi diktatury: Oktiabr' 1917 g.–noiabr' 1918 g.* M.

Krasnov, P. N. (1921). "Na vnutrennem fronte." *Arkhiv Russkoi revoliutsii* 1: 97–190.

——— (1922). "Vsevelikoe Voisko Donskoe." *Arkhiv Russkoi revoliutsii* 5: 190–321.

Krastyn', Ia. P. (1972). *Istoriia latyshskikh strelkov (1915–1920).* Riga.

Krastyn', Ia, P., et al., eds. (1962). *Latyshskie strelki v bor'be za Sovetskuiu vlast' v 1917–1920 godakh: Vospominaniia i dokumenty.* Riga.

——— (1978). *Glavnokomanduiushchii vsemi vooruzhennymi silami respubliki I. I. Vatsetis: Sbornik dokumentov.* Riga.

Kritskii, M. A. (1926). "Krasnaia armii na iuzhnom fronte v 1918–1920 gg." *Arkhiv Russkoi revoliutsii* 18: 254–300.

——— (1936). *Kornilovskii udarnyi polk.* Paris.

Kritsman, L. (n.d.). *Geroicheskii period velikoi russkoi revoliutsii.* Moscow.

Kublanov, A. L. (1975). *Sovet Rabochei i Krest' ianskoi Oborony (noiabr' 1918–mart 1920 g.).* Leningrad.

Kulichenko, M. I. (1963). *Bor'ba Kommunisticheskoi partii za reshenie natsional'nogo voprosa v 1918–1920 godakh.* Khar'kov.

Kuz'min, N. F. (1958a). *Krushenie poslednego pokhoda Antanty.* Moscow.

——— (1958b). *V. I. Lenin vo glave oborony Sovetskoi strany (1918–1920 gg.).* Moscow.

Lampe, A. A. fon- (1938). *Glavnokomanduiushchii russkoi armiei general baron P. N. Vrangel' . . .: Sbornik statei.* Berlin.

Lang, David M. (1962). *A Modern History of Georgia.* London.

Laqueur, Walter (1967). *The Fate of the Revolution: Interpretations of Soviet History.* London.

Latsis, M. Ia. (1920). *Dva goda bor'by na vnutrennem fronte: Populiarnyi ocherk. . . .* Moscow.

——— (1921). *Chrezvychainye komissii po bor'be s kontrrevoliutsiei.* Moscow.

Lebedev, V. I. (1928). "Iz arkhiva V. I. Lebedeva." *Volia rossii* 8/9: 50–212.

Leggett, George (1981). *The Cheka: Lenin's Political Police.* Oxford.

Lehovich, Dimitry V. (1974). *White Against Red: The Life of General Anton Denikin.* New York.

Lenin, V. I. (1962–1965). *Polnoe sobranie sochinenii.* 5th ed. Vols. 35–41, 50–52. Moscow; English ed.: (1964–1970). *Collected Works.* Vols. 26–31, 35, 36, 42, 44. London.

Lipitskii, S. V. (1973). *Voennaia deiatel'nost' TsK RKP(b) 1917–1920*. Moscow.
—— (1979). *Leninskoe rukovodstvo oboronoi strany: Sozdanie i deiatel'nost' vysshikh organov rukovodstva oboronoi Sovetskoi respubliki, 1917–1920*. Moscow.
Litvinova, G. I. (1974). *Revoliutsionnye komitety v gody grazhdanskoi voiny.* Moscow.
Lockart, R. H. Bruce (1932). *Memoirs of a British Agent*. London.
Long, John W. (1972). "Civil War and Intervention in North Russia, 1918–1920." Columbia Univ. Ph.D. thesis.
Longworth, Philip (1969). *The Cossacks*. London.
Lorimer, Frank (1946). *The Population of the Soviet Union: History and Prospects.* Geneva.
Lubachko, Ivan S. (1972). *Belorussia under Soviet Rule, 1917–1957*. Lexington.
Luckett, Richard (1971). *The White Generals: An Account of the White Movement and the Russian Civil War.* Harlow, England.
Lukomskii, A. S. (1922). *Vospominaniia*. 2 vols. Berlin. Eng. ed.: (1974) *Memoirs of the Russian Revolution*. Westport, Conn.
Lunacharsky, Anatoly V. (1967). *Revolutionary Silhouettes*. London.
McCullagh, Francis (1922). *A Prisoner of the Reds: The Story of a British Officer Captured in Siberia*. London.
Mace, James E. (1983). *Communism and the Dilemmas of National Liberation: National Communism in Soviet Ukraine, 1918–1933*. Cambridge, Mass.
McNeal, Robert H. (1963). "The Conference of Jassy: An Early Fiasco of the Anti-Bolshevik Movement." In *Essays in Russian and Soviet History in Honour of Geroid Tanquary Robinson*. Edited by John S. Curtiss, pp. 221–36. Leiden.
—— (1987), *Tsar and Cossack, 1855–1914*. London.
Maiskii, I. (1923), *Demokraticheskaia kontrrevoliutsiia*. Moscow.
Majstrenko, Iwan (1954). *Borot'bism: A Chapter in the History of Ukrainian Communism*. New York.
Maksakov, V. and A. Turunov (1926). *Khronika grazhdanskoi voiny v Sibiri (1917–1918)*. Moscow and Leningrad.
Maksudov, M. (1980). "Internatsionalisty i russkaia revoliutsiia." *Vestnik Russkogo Khristianskogo Dvizheniia* 131: 221–262.
—— (1981). "Losses Suffered by the Population of the USSR 1918–1958." *The Samizdat Register II*. Edited by Roy Medvedev, pp. 220–276. London.
Malet, Michael (1982). *Nestor Makhno in the Russian Civil War*. London.
Malle, Silvana (1985). *The Economic Organization of War Communism, 1918–1921.* Cambridge.
Mal't, M. (1924a). "Denikinshchina i krest'ianstvo." *Proletarskaia revoliutsiia* 1 (24): 140–157, 4 (27): 144–177.
—— (1924b). "Denikinshchina i rabochie." *Proletarskaia revoliutsiia* 5 (28): 64–85.
Mannerheim, K. G. (1953). *The Memoirs of Marshal Mannerheim*. London.
Margulies, M. S. (1923). *God interventsii*. 3 vols. Berlin.
Marusheskii, V. V. (1926). "God na Severe." *Beloe delo* 1: 16–61, 2: 21–61, 3: 15–52.
Mayer, Arno J. (1968). *Politics and Diplomacy of Peacemaking: Containment and Counterrevolution at Versailles, 1918–1919*. London.
Mayzel, Matitiahu (1979). *Generals and Revolutionaries: The Russian General Staff during the Revolution: A Study in the Transformation of a Military Elite*. Osnabruck.
Mazour, Anatole G. (1971). *The Writing of History in the Soviet Union*. Stanford.

Medvedev, Roy (1979). *The October Revolution.* London.
Meijer, Jan M., ed. (1964, 1971). *The Trotsky Papers: 1917–1922.* The Hague and London.
Mel'gunov, S. P. (1929). N. V. *Chaikovskii v gody grazhdanskoi voiny (materialy dlia istorii russkoi obshchestvennosti 1917–1925 g.g.).* Paris.
———— (1930–1931). *Tragediia admirala Kolchaka: Iz istorii grazhdanskoi voiny na Volge, Urale i v Sibiri.* 3 vols. (in 4). Paris.
———— (1951). *Sud'ba Imperatora Nikolaia II posle otrecheniia: Istoriko-kriticheskie ocherki.* Paris.
———— (1953). *Kak bol'sheviki zakhvatili vlast': Oktiabr'skii perevorot 1917 g.* Paris; Eng. ed.: (1972). *The Bolshevik Seizure of Power.* Santa Barbara.
———— (1979). *Krasnyi terror v Rossii.* New York.
Meyer, Alfred (1957). *Leninism.* Cambridge, Mass.
Miliukov, P. N. (1927). *Rossiia na perelome: Bol'shevistskii period russkoi revoliutsii.* 2 vols. Paris.
Miliutin, V. P. (1929). *Istoriia ekonomicheskogo razvitiia SSR.* Moscow and Leningrad.
Miller, E. K. (1928). "Bor'ba za Rossiiu na Severe: 1918–1920 g.g." *Beloe delo* 4: 5–11.
Mints, I. I. (1977–1979). *Istoriia Velikogo Oktiabria.* 2d ed. Vols. 2–3. Moscow.
———— (1982). *God 1918y.* Moscow.
———— ed. (1984). *Neproletarskie partii Rossii: Urok istorii.* Moscow.
Mints. I. I., et al. (1967). *Pobeda Sovetskoi vlasti v Srednei Azii i Kazakhstane.* Tashkent.
———— (1971). *Pobeda Sovetskoi vlasti v Zakavkaz'e.* Tbilisi.
———— (1980). *Neproletarskie partii i organizatsii natsional'nykh raionov Rossii v Oktiabr'skoi revoliutsii i grazhdanskoi voine: Materialy konferentsii.* Moscow.
Morley, James W. (1957). *The Japanese Thrust into Siberia, 1918.* New York.
Mosse, W. E. (1968). "The February Regime: Prerequisites for Success." *Soviet Studies* 19: 100–108.
Motyl, Alexander J. (1980). *The Turn to the Right: the Ideological Origins and Development of Ukrainian Nationalism, 1919–1929.* Boulder.
Naumov, V. P. (1972). *Letopis' geroicheskoi bor'by: Sovetskaia istoriografiia grazhdanskoi voiny i imperialisticheskoi interventsii v SSSR.* Moscow.
Nenarokov, A. P. (1969). *Vostochnyi front 1918.* Moscow.
Nove, Alec (1969). *An Economic History of the USSR.* London.
"Obrazovanie severo-zapadnago Pravitel'stva" (1922). *Arkhiv Russkoi revoliutsii* 1: 295–308.
Olikov, S. (1928). *Dezertirstvo v Krasnoi armii i bor'ba s nim.* Leningrad.
Oppenheim, Samuel A. (1972). "Aleksei Ivanovich Rykov (1881–1938): A Political Biography." Indiana Univ. Ph.D. thesis.
Orlovsky, Daniel (n.d.). "State Building in the Civil War Era: The Role of the Lower Middle Strata." Unpublished.
Page, Stanley W. (1959). *The Formation of the Baltic States: A Study of the Effects of Great Power Politics upon the Emergence of Lithuania, Latvia, and Estonia.* Cambridge, Mass.
Palij, Michael (1976). *The Anarchism of Nestor Makhno, 1918–1921: An Aspect of the Ukrainian Revolution.* Seattle.
Park, Alexander G. (1957). *Bolshevism in Turkestan, 1917–1927.* New York.
Partiia v period inostrannoi voennoi interventsii i grazhdanskoi voiny (1918–1920

godu): Dokumenty i materialy (1962). Edited by L. M. Spirin. Moscow.
Partiino-politicheskaia rabota v Krasnoi Armii: Dokumenty (1961, 1964). 2 vols. Moscow.
Pearce, Brian (1986). *How Haig Saved Lenin.* London.
Pershin, P. N. (1966). *Agrarnaia revoliutsiia v Rossii.* Vol. 2. Moscow.
Pethybridge, Roger (1974). *The Social Prelude to Stalinism.* London.
Petrogradskii Voenno-revoliutsionnyi komitet: Dokumenty i materialy (1966–1967). Edited by D. A. Chugaev et al. 3 vols. Moscow.
Petrov, P. P. (1931). *Ot Volgi do Tikhago Okeana v riadakh belikh, 1918–1922 g.g.* Riga.
Petrov, V. I. (1980). *Otrazhenie stranoi sovetov nashestviia germanskogo imperializma v 1918 godu.* Moscow.
Pidhainy, Oleh S. (1966). *The Formation of the Ukrainian Republic.* Toronto.
Pietsch, Walter (1969). *Revolution und Staat: Institutionen als Träger der Macht in Sowjetrussland 1917–1922.* Cologne.
Pilsudski, Jozef (1972). *Year 1920 and Its Climax Battle of Warsaw* [sic]. New York.
Piontkovskii, S., ed. (1925). *Grazhdanskaia voina v Rossii (1918–1921 g.g.): Khrestomatiia.* Moscow.
Pipes, Richard (1954). *The Formation of the Soviet Union: Communism and National-ism: 1917–1923.* Cambridge, Mass.
——— (1977). *Russia under the Old Regime.* Harmondsworth.
——— (1980). *Struve: Liberal on the Right, 1905–1944.* Cambridge, Mass.
Plaksin, R. Iu. (1968). *Krakh tserkovnoi kontrrevoliutsii: 1917–1923.* Moscow.
Poliakov, I. A. (1962). *Donskie kazaki v bor'be s.bol'shevikami.* Munich.
Poliakov, Iu. A. (1986). "O chislennosti naseleniia Strany Sovetov posle okonchaniia grazhdanskoi voiny." In *Istoricheskii opyt Velikogo Oktiabria,* edited by S. L. Tikhvinskii, pp. 205–211. Moscow.
Poliakov, Iu. A, and Kiselev, I. N. (1980). "Chislennost' i natsional'nyi sostav naseleniia Rossii v 1917 godu." *Voprosy istorii* 1980, no. 6: 39–49.
Procyk, Anna (1973). "Nationality Policy of the White Movement: Relations between the Volunteer Army and the Ukraine." Columbia Univ. Ph.D. thesis.
Protokoly Tsentral'nogo Komiteta RSDRP(b): Avgust 1917 g.-fevral' 1918 g. (1958). M.: Eng. ed.: (1974). *The Bolsheviks and the October Revolution: Minutes of the Central Committee.* London.
Protsess Borisa Savinkova (1924). Berlin.
Pukhov, A. S. (1960). *Petrograd ne sdavat'!: Kommunisty vo glave oborony Petrograda v 1919 g.* Moscow.
Puntila, L. A. (1975). *The Political History of Finland 1809–1966.* London.
Rabinowitch, Alexander (1976). *The Bolsheviks Come to Power: The Revolution of 1917 in Petrograd.* New York.
Radkey, Oliver H. (1950). *The Election to the Russian Constituent Assembly of 1917.* Cambridge, Mass.
——— (1958). *The Agrarian Foes of Bolshevism: Promise and Default of the Russian Socialist Revolutionaries, February to October 1917.* New York.
——— (1963). *The Sickle under the Hammer: The Russian Socialist Revolutionaries in the Early Months of Soviet Rule.* New York.
Rakovskii, G. N. (1920). *V stane belykh.* Constantinople.
——— (1921). *Konets belykh.* Prague.
Rapoport, Vitaly, and Rapoport, Iuri Alexeev (1985). *High Treason: Essays on the History of the Red Army, 1918–1938.* Durham.

Rauch, Georg von (1974). *The Baltic States: The Years of Independence: Estonia, Latvia, Lithuania, 1917–40*. London.
Reisner, L. (1922). "Kazan' (leto i osen' 1918 goda)." *Proletarskaia revoliutsiia* 12: 180–196.
———— (1923). "Sviiazhsk." *Proletarskaia revoliutsiia* 18/19: 177–189.
Remington, Thomas F. (1984). *Building Socialism in Bolshevik Russia: Ideology and Industrial Organization, 1917–1921*. Pittsburgh.
Renehan, Thomas J. (1984). "The Failure of Local Soviet Government, 1917–1918." SUNY (Binghamton) Ph.D. thesis.
Reshetar, J. S. (1972). *The Ukrainian Revolution, 1917–1920: A Study in Nationalism.* New York.
Resolutions and Decisions of the Communist Party of the Soviet Union (1974). Edited by Richard Greger. Vol. 2. Toronto.
Rigby, T. H. (1968). *Communist Party Membership in the USSR, 1917–1967*. Princeton.
———— (1971). "The Soviet Political Elite 1917–1922." *British Journal of Political Science* 1: 415–436.
———— (1979). *Lenin's Government: Sovnarkom, 1917–1922*. Cambridge.
Ritter, Gerhard (1965). *Das Kommunemodell und die Begründung der Roten Armee im Jahre 1918*. Berlin.
Roberts, Paul C. (1970). "'War Communism': A Reexamination." *Slavic Review* 29: 238–261.
Rodzianko, A. P. (1920). *Vospominaniia o Severo-Zapadnoi Armii*. Berlin.
Rosenberg, William G. (1974). *Liberals in the Russian Revolution: The Constitutional Democratic Party, 1917–1921*. Princeton.
———— (1985). "Russian Labor and Bolshevik Power After October" and "Reply". *Slavic Review* 44: 213–238, 251–256.
Ross, Nikolai (1982). *Vrangel' v Krymu*. Frankfurt/Main.
Ruban, N. V. (1968). *Oktiabr'skaia revoliutsii i krakh men'shevizma (mart 1917–1918 g.)*. Moscow.
Die Ruckführung des Ostheeres. (1936). Berlin.
Safarov, G. (1921). *Kolonial'naia revoliutsiia (Opyt Turkestana)*. Moscow.
Sakharov, K. V. (1923). *Belaia Sibir'*. Munich.
Sakwa, R. (1984). "The Communist Party and War Communism in Moscow, 1918–1921." Univ. of Birmingham [England] Ph.D. thesis.
Samoilo, A. A. (1958). *Dve zhizni*. Moscow.
Samoilo, A. A., and Sboichakov, M. I. (1962). *Pouchitel'nyi urok: Boevye deistviia Krasnoi Armii protiv interventov i belogvardeitsev na Severe Rossii v 1918–1920 gg.* Moscow.
Sapozhnikov, N. (1924). "Izhevsko-Votkinskoe vosstanie (avgust–noiabr' 1918 g.)." *Proletarskaia revoliutsiia* 8/9 (31–32): 5–42.
Savinkov, B. V. (1920). *Bor'ba s bol'shevikami*. Warsaw.
Schapiro, Leonard (1955). *The Origins of the Communist Autocracy: Political Opposition in the Soviet State: First Phase, 1917–1922*. London.
———— (1970). *The Communist Party of the Soviet Union*. 2d rev. ed. London.
———— (1984). *1917: The Russian Revolutions and the Origins of Present-Day Communism*. London.
Schapiro, Leonard, and Reddaway, Peter, eds. (1967). *Lenin: The Man, the Theorist, the Leader: A Reappraisal*. London.
Scheibert, Peter (1984). *Lenin an der Macht: Das russische Volk in der Revolution*

1918–1922. Weinheim.

Seaton, Albert (1976). *Stalin as Warlord*. London.

Seaton, Albert, and Seaton, Joan (1986). *The Soviet Army: 1918 to the Present*. London.

Sed'moi ekstrennyi s"ezd RKP(b), mart 1918 god: Stenograficheskii otchet (1962). Moscow.

Senn, Alfred E. (1959). *The Emergence of Modern Lithuania*. New York.

Serafimovich, A. (1935). *The Iron Flood*. London.

Serge, Victor (1972). *Year One of the Russian Revolution*. London.

—— (1978). *Conquered City*. London.

Service, Robert (1979). *The Bolshevik Party in Revolution: A Study in Organisational Change 1917–1923*. London.

—— (1986). *The Russian Revolution 1900–1927*. London.

Shanin, Teodor (1972). *The Awkward Class: Political Sociology of Peasantry in a Developing Society: Russia 1910–1925*, Oxford.

Shekhtman, I. B. (1932). *Pogromy Dobrovol'cheskoi Armii na Ukraine (K istorii antisemitizma na Ukraine v 1919–1920 g.g.)*. Berlin.

Shkuro, A. G. (1961). *Zapiski belogo partizana*. Buenos Aires.

Sholokhov, Mikhail (1967). *And Quiet Flows the Don*. Harmondsworth.

—— (1970). *The Don Flows Home to the Sea*. Harmondsworth.

Shteifon, B. (1928). *Krizis dobrovol'chestva*. Belgrade.

Shukman, Harold (1966). *Lenin and the Russian Revolution*. London.

Shutskever, A., ed. (1923). " 'Soiuz zaschity rodiny i svobody' i Iaroslavskii miatezh 1918 g." *Proletarskaia revoliutsiia* 10 (22): 202–232.

Simpkin, Richard (1986). *Deep Battle: The Genius of Marshal Tukhachevskii*. Oxford.

Simonov, B. (1928). *Razgrom denikinshchiny: Pochemu my pobedili v Oktiabre 1919 g*. Moscow and Leningrad.

Slavik, Ia., ed. (1938). *Bibliografiia russkoi revoliutsii i grazhdanskoi voiny (1917–1921): Iz kataloga biblioteki RZI Arkhiva*. Prague.

Smirnov, I. N., et al., eds. (1926). *Bor'ba za Ural i Sibir': Vospominaniia i stat'i uchastnikov bor'by s uchredilovskoi i kolchakovskoi kontr-revoliutsiei*. Moscow and Leningrad.

Smirnov, M. I. (1930). *Admiral Aleksandr Vasil'evich Kolchak (Kratkii biograficheskii ocherk)*. Paris.

Smith, C. Jay (1958). *Finland and the Russian Revolution, 1917–1922*. Athens, Ga.

Smith, Canfield F. (1975). *Vladivostok under Red and White Rule: Revolution and Counter-Revolution in the Russian Far East, 1920–1922*. Seattle.

Smith, Stephen (1983). *Red Petrograd: Revolution in the Factories, 1917–1918*. Cambridge.

Snow, Russell E. (1977). *The Bolsheviks in Siberia 1917–1918*. London.

Sofinov, P. G. (1960). *Ocherki istorii VChK (1917–1922 gg.)*. Moscow.

Sokolov, Boris (1923). "Padenie Severnoi oblasti." *Arkhiv Russkoi revoliutsii* 9: 5–90.

Sokolov, K. N. (1921). *Pravlenie generala Denikina (Iz vospominanii)*. Sofia.

Sovetskoe sodruzhestvo narodov: Ob"edinitel'noe dvizheniie i obrazovanie SSSR: Sbornik dokumentov: 1917–1922 (1972). Edited by L. S. Gaponenko et al. Moscow.

The Soviet Union: 1917–1939 (1984). Series A, vols. 1–3. Edited by D. C. Watt and D. Lieven. British Documents on Foreign Affairs: Reports and Papers from the Foreign Office Confidential Print. Part II. Edited by K. Bourne and D. C. Watt. Frederick, Maryland.

Spirin, L. M. (1957). *Razgrom armii Kolchaka*. Moscow.

—— (1965). "V. I. Lenin i sozdanie sovetskikh komandnykh kadrov." *Voenno-istoricheskii zhurnal* 1965, no. 4: 3–16.

—— (1968). *Klassy i partii v grazhdanskoi voine v Rossii (1917–1920 gg.)*. Moscow.

—— (1971). *Krakh odnoi avantiury: Miatezh levykh eserov v Moskve 6–7 iiulia 1918 g.* Moscow.

Stalin, I. V. (1947a). "Otvet tov. Stalina." *Bol'shevik* 1947, no. 3: 6–8.

—— (1947b). *Sochineniia*. Vols. 4, 6. M; Eng. ed.: (1953). *Works*. Vols. 4, 6. Moscow.

Starikov, S., and Medvedev, R. (1978). *Philip Mironov and the Russian Civil War*. New York.

Startsev, V. I. (1982). *Krakh kerenshchiny*. Leningrad.

Steinberg, I. (1935). *Spiridonova: Revolutionary Terrorist*. London.

—— (1953). *In the Workshop of the Revolution*. London.

Stepanov, A. P. (1926). "Simbirskaia operatsiia." *Beloe delo* 1: 83–95.

Stewart, George (1933). *The White Armies of Russia: A Chronicle of Counter-Revolution and Allied Intervention*. New York.

Sukhorukov, V. T. (1961). *XI Armiia v boiakh na Severnom Kavkaze i Nizhnei Volge (1918–1920 gg.)*. Moscow.

Suny, Ronald G. (1972). *The Baku Commune: 1917–1918: Class and Nationality in the Russian Revolution*. Princeton.

—— (1983). "Toward a Social History of the October Revolution." *American Historical Review* 88: 31–52.

Suprunenko, N. I. (1966). *Ocherki istorii grazhdanskoi voiny i inostrannoi voennoi interventsii na Ukraine*. Moscow.

Swietochowski, Tadeusz (1985). *Russian Azerbaijan, 1905–1920: The Shaping of a National Identity in a Muslim Community*. Cambridge.

Szamuely, Laszlo (1974). *First Models of the Socialist Economic Systems: Principles and Theories*. Budapest.

Tarasov, V. V. (1958). *Bor'ba s interventami na severe Rossii (1918–1920 gg.)*. Moscow.

Temkin, Ia. G., and Tupolev, B. M. (1978). *Ot Vtorogo k Tret'emu Internatsionalu*. Moscow.

Thompson, John M. (1966). *Russia, Bolshevism and the Versailles Peace*, Princeton.

Timoshenko, V. P. (1932). *Agricultural Russia and the Wheat Problem*, Stanford.

Treadgold, Donald W. (1957). "The Ideology of the White Movement: Wrangel's 'Leftist Policy from Rightist Hands'." *Harvard Slavic Studies* 4: 481–497.

Triumfal'noe shestvie Sovetskoi vlasti (1963). Edited by D. A. Chugaev et al. 2 vols. Moscow.

Trotskii, L. D. (1920). *Terrorizm i kommunizm*. Petrograd; Eng. ed: (1975). *Terrorism and Communism*. London.

—— (1923–1925). *Kak vooruzhalas' revoliutsiia: Na voennoi rabote*. 3 vols. (in 5). Moscow; Eng. ed.: (1979–1981). *How the Revolution Armed: Military Writings and Speeches*. 5 vols. London.

—— (1924). *O Lenine: materialy dlia biografa*. 2d ed. Moscow; Eng ed.: (1971). *On Lenin: Notes toward a Biography*. London.

—— (1930). *Moia zhizn'*. 2 vols. Berlin; Eng. ed.: (1975). *My Life: An Attempt at an Autobiography*. Harmondsworth.

Trotskii, L. D. (1959). *Trotsky's Diary in Exile 1935*. London.
—— (1967). *The Revolution Betrayed: What is the Soviet Union and Where is It Going?* London.
—— (1969). *Stalin: An Appraisal of the Man and His Influence*. Vol. 2. London.
—— (1972). *Writings of Leon Trotsky (1932–1933)*. New York.
Tschebotarioff, Gregory P. (1964). *Russia, My Native Land*. New York.
Tucker, Robert C. (1974). *Stalin as Revolutionary: 1879–1929: A Study in History and Personality*. London.
Tukhachevskii, M. N. (1964). *Izbrannye proizvedeniia*. 2 vols. Moscow.
Tumarkin, Nina (1985). "The Myth of Lenin during the Civil War Years." In *Bolshevik Culture: Experiment and Order in the Russian Revolution*. Edited by A. Gleason et al., pp. 77–92. Bloomington.
"Ufimskoe gosudarstvennoe soveshchanie" (1929). Edited by A. F. Iziumov. *Russkii istoricheskii arkhiv* 1: 57–280.
"Ufimskoe soveshchanie i Vremennoe sibir'skoe pravitel'stvo" (1933). *Krasnyi arkhiv* 61: 58–81.
The Ukraine: A Concise Encyclopedia (1963, 1971). 2 vols. Toronto.
Ulam, Adam B. (1968). *Expansion and Coexistence: The History of Soviet Foreign Policy, 1917–1967*. London.
—— (1969). *Lenin and the Bolsheviks: The Intellectual and Political History of the Triumph of Communism in Russia*. London.
Uldricks, Teddy J. (1979). *Diplomacy and Ideology: The Origins of Soviet Foreign Relations, 1917–1930*. London.
Ullman, Richard H. (1961–1972). *Anglo-Soviet Relations, 1917–1921*. 3 vols. Princeton.
Unterberger, Betty M. (1969). *America's Siberian Expedition, 1918–1920: A Study of National Policy*. New York.
Upton, Anthony (1980). *The Finnish Revolution: 1917–1918*. Minneapolis.
Urlanis, B. Ts. (1960). *Voiny i narodonaselenie Evropy*. Moscow.
—— (1968). "Dinamika naseleniia SSSR za 50 let." In *Naselenie i narodnoe blagosostoianie*, edited by D. L. Broner, pp. 20–43. Moscow.
[Vatsetis, I. I.] (1958). "Doklady I. I. Vatsetis V. I. Leninu (fevral'–mai 1919 g.)," *Istoricheskii arkhiv*, no. 1, pp. 41–75.
—— (1962). "Vospominaniia." *Voenno-istoricheskii zhurnal* 1962, no. 4: 70–79.
—— (1977). "Grazhdanskaia voina: 1918 god." *Pamiat'* 2: 7–81.
Vnutrennie voiska Sovetskoi respubliki: 1917–1922 gg.: Dokumenty i materialy (1972). Edited by I. K. Iakovlev et al. Moscow.
Volkov, E. Z. (1930). *Dinamika narodnonaseleniia SSSR za vosem'desiat let*. Moscow.
Voronovich, N. (1922). "Mezh dvukh ognei." *Arkhiv Russkoi revoliutsii* 7: 53–183.
Voroshilov, K. (1934). "Stalin i krasnaia armiia." In *Lenin, Stalin i Krasnaia armiia: Stat'i i rechi*, pp. 41–61. Moscow.
Vos'moi s"ezd RKP(b), mart 1919 goda: Protokoly (1959). Moscow.
Vrangel', P. N. (1969). *Vospominaniia*. Frankfurt/Main; Eng. ed: P. N. Wrangel (1957). *Always with Honor*. New York.
Wade, Rex A. (1984). *Red Guards and Workers' Militias in the Russian Revolution*. Stanford.
Walker, Christopher (1980). *Armenia: The Survival of a Nation*. London.
Wandycz, Piotr S. (1962). *France and Her Eastern Allies 1919–1925: French-Czechoslovak-Polish Relations from the Paris Peace Conference to Locarno*. Westport.

Wandycz, Piotr S. (1969). *Soviet-Polish Relations 1917–1921*. Cambridge, Mass.
Der Weltkieg: 1914 bis 1918 (1942). Vol. 13. Berlin.
Wheeler-Bennett, John W. (1938). *Brest-Litovsk: The Forgotten Peace, March 1918*. London.
White, J. D. (1971). "The Revolution in Lithuania 1918–1919." *Soviet Studies* 23: 186–200.
White, John Albert (1969). *The Siberian Intervention*. New York.
White, Stephen (1974). "Communism and the East: The Baku Congress, 1920." *Slavic Review* 33: 492–514.
——— (1984). "Soviet Russia and the Asian Revolution, 1917–1924." *Review of International Studies* 10: 219–232.
Wildman, Allan K. (1980). *The End of the Russian Imperial Army: The Old Army and the Soldiers' Revolt (March–April 1917)*. Princeton.
Zaitsov, A. (1934). *1918 god: Ocherki po istorii russkoi grazhdanskoi voiny*. Paris.
Zamoyski, Adam (1981). *The Battle for the Marchlands*. Boulder.
Zenkovsky, Serge A. (1960). *Pan-Turkism and Islam in Russia*. Cambridge.
Zetkin, Klara (1929). *Reminiscences of Lenin*. London.
Zharov, L. I. and V. N. Ustinov (1960). *Internatsional'nye chasti Krasnoi armii v boiakh za vlast' sovetov v gody inostrannoi voennoi interventsii i grazhdanskoi voiny v SSSR*. Moscow.
Zuev, A. V. (1937). *Orenburgskie kazaki v bor'be s bol'shevizmom: 1918–1922 g.g.: Ocherki*. Kharbin.

SUPPLEMENTARY BIBLIOGRAPHY

The following gives some of the important works that have appeared since *The Russian Civil War* was first published. A format similar to that of the original biography has been used, i.e. an essay-type general section ("B.1," etc.) and an alphabetical list with full bibliographical details.

B. 1. Bibliographies

Frame, *Revolution*, is a useful, if now a little dated, listing of English-language sources. For a discussion of new writing in Russia see Davies, *Soviet History* (1989 and 1997). Acton, *Rethinking*, provides an introduction to the historiography of 1917. Tormozov, *Beloe dvizhenie*, is now the fullest study of the historiography of the Whites.

B.2. General Histories

The collapse of Communism led to much re-interpretation of its origins, and an understanding of the 1917 Revolution is important for an understanding of the Civil War of 1917–1920. Medvedev in a short new book, *Russkaia Revoliutsiia*, argues that the two events should not even be seen as separate, and—while I do not agree with everything Medvedev writes—this is the general argument of my own *Russian Civil War* (see p. 289).

A range of articles on 1917 and its consequences may be found in Cherniaiev, *Anatomiia*, Frankel, *Revolution*, Service, *Society and Politics*, and Tiutiukin, *1917*. Poliakov, *Velikii oktiabr'*, and *Rossiia 1917*, with their contributions by leading Soviet specialists, show the early impact of Gorbachev's glasnost on the historiography of the revolution; in this connection see also Spirin, *Rossiia*. Broad points about the nature of the Revolution and Civil War in the context of Russian history can be found in Daniels, *End*, and in a related discussion, "Dynamics" with George Enteen and Lewis Siegelbaum. See also Suny, "Revision," Haimson, "Problem," and Smith, "Writing." For a survey of émigré literature see Ushakov, *Istoriia*.

344

SUPPLEMENTARY BIBLIOGRAPHY

A number of important general works on the Civil War period (in some cases including 1917) have now appeared in English, including Figes, *People's Tragedy*, Lincoln, *Red Victory*, Pipes, *Russian Revolution*, and Pipes, *Russia under the Bolshevik Regime*. Russian works of the same type include Buldakov, *Smuta*, and Medvedev, *Russkaia Revoliutsiia*. Swain, *Origins*, provides an original discussion of the early period of the Civil War. A number of important overviews have been made by the doyen of the older generation of Russian Civil War specialists, Iu. A. Poliakov, see "Gradzhdanskaia voina" (1990, 1992a, 1992b). An important "round-table "discussion by Russian historians is translated as "Civil War," the original appeared in *Otechestvennaia istoriia* in 1993 (issue no. 3). See also the range of contributions by Russian and Western historians, plus published memoirs and comments, in Poliakov and Igritskii, *Perekrestok*.

Many themes concerning the Civil War are covered in the various specialist essays in Acton, *Critical Companion*, Jackson, *Dictionary*, and Shukman, *Blackwell Encyclopedia*; these reference books might be the interested reader's first port of call. A useful new Russian reference work is Volobuev, *Politicheskie deiateli*.

B.3. General Collections of Documents.

The most significant top-level source is Pipes, *Unknown Lenin*. Several important episodes are covered by the documents in Butt, *Russian Civil War*. Published diaries provide further primary material, notably Got'e, *Time*, and Dune, *Notes*.

B. 4. Soviet Politics

The relevant volumes of Service's monumental biography, *Lenin*, are now available. On the theoretical side see also Harding, *Leninism*. Kowalski, *Conflict*, deals with the debates of 1917–1918.

The early consolidation of state power is discussed in Smirnov, *Tretii s"ezd*, and Gorodetskii, *Rozhdenie*. On the adminstrative system more generally see Dmitrienko, *Formirovanie*, Izmoznik, "Kontrol'," and Trukan, *Put'*. The Cheka is covered in Portnov, *VChK*, and in new western works: Andrew and Gordievsky, *KGB*, and Dziak, *Chekisty*. Fel'shtinskii, *Krasnyi terror*, is based on White investigation of Red Terror. Ross, *Gibel'*, and Steinberg and Khrustalev, *Fall*, deal with the execution of the Imperial family. Litvin, *Terror*, and Litvin, "Terror," should be taken as general works, since they cover both Reds and Whites.

For regional case studies, see Sakwa, *Soviet Communists* (Moscow), McAuley, *Bread* (on Petrograd), Friedgut, *Iuzovka*, and Kuromiya, *Donbas*. On the underground opposition to Bolshevik rule see Brovkin, *Behind*.

On the elite see Gimpel'son, "Upravlentsy", and Mawdsley and White, *Political Elite*. New biographies include Khlevniuk, *Shadow* (Ordzhonikidze), and three biographies by Volkogonov, *Lenin*, *Stalin*, and *Trotsky*.

Geldern, *Bolshevik Festivals*, Rosenberg, *Bolshevik Visions*, and Stites, *Revolutionary Dreams*, deal with cultural policy. On the neglected topic of church-state relations see Odinstev, *Gosudarstvo i tserkov'*.

345

B.5. Soviet Economy

Relevant general histories include Gregory, *Before*, Davies, *From Tsarism*, and Davies, *Economic Transformation*. On the all-important problem of food supply there is Lih, *Bread*.

The theme of War Communism has been explored in Bradley, "War Communism," Dmitrienko, "Voennyi kommunizm", and Pavliuchenkov, *Voennyi kommunizm*.

Fitzpatrick, *Russia*, Koenker, *Party*, and Siegelbaum and Suny, *Making*, are collections of essays covering many aspects of social history in this period. On working class aspirations see Aves, *Workers*, and Shkliarevsky, *Labour*. For the textile industry there is Husband, *Revolution*. Danilov, *Rural Russia*, Kabanov, *Krest'ianskoe khoziaistvo*, Kingston-Mann and Mixter, *Peasant Economy*, serve as a general introduction to the peasantry. Figes, *Peasant Russia*, takes the Volga as a case study. Pavliuchenkov, *Krest'ianskii brest*, Patenaude, "Peasants," and Poliakov, *Perekhod*, discuss the role of the peasants in War Communism, with Frenkin, *Tragediia*, discussing rural revolt. Important documents on the Cheka's efforts to control the countryside are published in Berelovich and Danilov, *Sovetskaia derevnia*. For the third "class," the intelligentsia, see Read, *Culture*, and Fitzpatrick, *Cultural Front*.

The growing literature of the place of women in this period includes Clements, *Women*, Goldman, *Women*, and Wood, *Baba*.

Sokolov, *Golos*, is a remarkable collection of reactions to the Civil War (and other events) from the perspective the ordinary inhabitant of Russia.

B.6. Red Army

For the important role of the army in 1917–1918 see Wildman, *End*, vol. 2, and the documents in Korablev, *V voennykh okrugakh*; the developments were important for both the Red and White armies. Meanwhile research on the Red Army in the Civil War period proper has expanded, with general works on the social structure of the Red Army: Benvenuti, *Bolsheviks*, and Von Hagen, *Soldiers*. The neglected topic of conscripted officers is now dealt with in Kavtaradze, *Spetsialisty*, and there is useful background in Volkov, *Ofitserskii korpus*. Insights into the critical military debate at the 8th Party Congress in March 1919 are given in the transcript of the secret military session, "Deiatel'nost TsK'." Nenarokov, *Revvoensovet*, is a collection of important studies on the Soviet high command. Figes, "Red Army" deals with conscription, using archival sources. On the Red Cavalry see Brown, "Communists," and Genis, "Pervaia Konnaia." On losses see Krivosheev, *Grif*, and my own brief discussion in Acton, *Critical Companion* (pp. 102f).

B.7. The Whites

Bornevskii, *Beloe delo*, Fediuk, *Belye armii*, Rybnikov and Slobodin, *Beloe dvizhenie*, Slobodin, *Beloe dvizhenie*, Ustinkin, *Tragediia*, and Zimina, *Beloe dvizhenie*, are general treatments of the White movement. There are useful reprints of White memoirs, with short modern commentaries, in the multi-volume *Beloe delo*. Kladving, *Belaia gvardiia*, is a substanial handbook on the organisation of the various White armies, with biographies of the main leaders. The formerly orthodox—and still nationalist—*Voenno-istoricheskii zhurnal* has in the 1990s taken a great interest in the White movement.

Ushakov and Fediuk, *Belyi iug*, covers the southern armies; Fediuk, *Belye*, Ioffe, *Beloe delo*, and Venkov, *Antibol'shevistskoe*, are on the early period. Lazarski, "White Propaganda" is about Denikin but could apply to other armies. Putych, *Spravochnik*, is a detailed guide to the commanding personnel of the southern armies. On relations with the Ukrainians see Procyk, *Russian Nationalism*; on this important question of White relations with the minorities see also Tormozov, *Natsional'nyi vopros*. The main southern leader is discussed in depth in Cherkasov-Georgievskii, *Denikin*, Ippolitov, *Kto vy?*, and Kozlov, "Denikin." Koehler, *Our Man*, is an interesting American memoir about south Russia, and especially the Crimea, in 1920.

The position concerning Kolchak and the Siberian counter-revolution has improved greatly since 1987, with two major Western studies in the form of Pereira, *White Siberia*, and Smele, *Civil War*. Both are stronger on the political and economic side than the military; the social side of the army is dealt with in Voinov, "Ofitserskii korpus." The collection of documents edited by Collins and Smele, *Kolchak*, is also valuable. The early period in Siberia is covered by Lar'kov, *Nachalo*. For the Supreme Leader himself see Bogdanov, *Admiral Kolchak*. See also the new version of the interrogation of the captured Kolchak and his mistress in Drokov, "Podlinnyie protokoly."

Goldin, *Belyi sever*, and Goldin, *Zabroshennye*, cover events in north Russia. Tsiklon, *Beloe dvizhenie*, the Far East. The Baltic, the most neglected of the White theatres, is now discussed in Mints, *Pribaltika*, Shishkin, *Interventsiia*, and Smolin, *Beloe dvizhenie*.

The emigration, once ignored in Russian sources, is now a fashionable research topic. See *Russkaia voennaia emigratsiiai*, Domin, 'Voennoe zarubezh'e", and Ushakov, *Istoriia*.

B. 8. Civilian Anti-Bolsheviks

For general background on this important topic see Brovkin, *Behind*, and Zevelev, *Istoriia*.

Menshevik studies remain healthy. The 1917 background is further covered in Galili, *Menshevik Leaders*, and Galili, *Mensheviki*. Brovkin, *Dear Comrades*, comprises Menshevik reports of local conditions. The most important new source on SRs is Jansen, *Socialist–Revolutionary Party*. Gusev, *Bogoroditsa*, is a biography of Mariia Spiridonova. Alekseev, *Kritika*, is indirectly valuable on SR ideas.

Verstiuk, *Makhno*, covers the best known of the 'Green' movements. See Danilov and Shanin, *Antonovshchina*, Esikov and Protasov, "Antonovshchina," and Samoshkin, "Antonov" for the Antonov movement in Tambov province. On the other main uprising of 1921, at the Kronshtadt naval base, see Kozlov, *Tragediia*, Naumov and Kosakovskii, *Kronshtadt*, and Shchetinov, "Za kulisami."

B.9. Nationalities

Suny, *Revenge*, is a refreshing study, partly informed by the strength of national feeling revealed from the late 1980s. Subtelny, *Ukraine*, is a new general work on a most important region. Soviet policy is covered in Smith, *Bolsheviks*; on Stalin's role in this see Blank, *Sorcerer's Apprentice*.

B.10. Cossacks

The phenomenon of "de-cossackisation," the first example of mass terror, is discussed in Genis, "Raskazachivanie."

B.11. International Relations

Debo, *Survival*, continues to 1921 his excellent discussion of Soviet foreign policy. For a Russian introduction informed by Perestroika see Nezhinskii, "Vneshniaia politika." McDermott and Agnew, *Comintern*, is the newest work on the Third International. Fel'shtinskii, *Krushenie*, focuses on Brest-Litovsk. Moscow's policy in the Polish war is analysed in Fiddick, *Russia's Retreat*; see also Lenin's candid discussion of the war in Pipes, *Unknown Lenin*.

A survey of the intervention, with some new insights, is Somin, *Stillborn Crusade*; also interesting is Fogelsong, *America's Secret War*.

Alphabetical Bibliography

Acton, Edward, et al., eds. (1997). *Critical Companion to the Russian Revolution, 1914–1921*. London.
Acton, Edward (1990). *Rethinking the Russian Revolution*. London.
Alekseev, G. D. (1989). *Kritika eserovskoi kontseptsii Oktiabr'skoi revoliutsii*. Moscow.
Andrew, Christopher and Gordievsky, Oleg (1990). *KGB: The Inside Story of its Foreign Operations from Lenin to Gorbachev*. London.
Aves, Jonathan (1996). *Workers against Lenin: Labour Protest and the Bolshevik Dictatorship 1920–22*. London.
Beloe delo. Izbrannye proizvedeniia v 16 knigakh (1993). Moscow.
Benvenuti, Francesco (1988). *The Bolsheviks and the Red Army, 1918–1922*. Cambridge.
Berelovich, A. and Danilov, V. (1998). *Sovetskaia derevnia glazami VChK–OGPU–NKVD 1918–1939. Dokumenty i materialy*. Vol. 1 (1918–1922). Moscow.
Blank, Stephen (1994). *The Sorcerer as Apprentice: Stalin as Commissar of Nationalities, 1917–1924*. Westport CN.
Bogdanov, K. A. (1993). *Admiral Kolchak*. St Petersburg.
Bortnevskii, V. G. (1993). *Beloe delo. Liudi i sobytiia*. St Petersburg.
Bradley, Joseph, ed. (1994). "War Communism." *Russian Studies in History* 33.

Brovkin, Vladimir N. (1994). *Behind the Front Lines of the Civil War: Political Parties and Social Movement in Russia, 1918–1922.* Princeton.

Brovkin, Vladimir, N., ed. (1997). *The Bolsheviks in Russian Society: The Revolution and the Civil Wars,* Yale.

—————— (1991). *Dear Comrades: Menshevik Reports on the Bolshevik Revolution and the Civil War.* Stanford.

Brown, Stephen (1995). "Communists and the Red Cavalry: The Political Education of the Konarmiia in the Russian Civil War, 1918–20." *Slavonic and East European Review* 73/1: 61–81.

Buldakov, V. (1997). *Krasnaia smuta: Priroda i posledstviia revoliutsionnogo nasiliia.* Moscow.

Burbank, Jane (1986). *Intelligentsia and Revolution: Russian Views of Bolshevism, 1917–1921.* Oxford.

Butt, V. P., et al., eds. (1996). *The Russian Civil War: Documents from the Soviet Archives.* Basingstoke.

Cherkasov-Georgievskii, Vladimir (1999). *General Denikin.* Smolensk.

Cherniaev, V. Iu., et al., eds. (1994). *Anatomiia revoliutsii: 1917 god v Rossii: Massy partii, vlast'.* St Petersburg.

"The Civil War in Russia: A Roundtable Discussion" (1994). *Russian Studies in History* 32/4: 73–95.

Clements, Barbara E., (1997). *Bolshevik Women.* Cambridge.

Collins, David and Smele, Jonathan (1988). *Kolchak i Sibir': Dokumenty i issledovaniia, 1919–1926.* White Plains, NY.

Daniels, Robert V. (1993). *The End of the Communist Revolution,* New York.

Danilov, V. P. (1988). *Rural Russia under the New Regime.* London.

Danilov, V. and Shanin, T., eds. (1994). *Antonovshchina: Krest'ianskoe vosstanie v Tambovskoi gubernii v 1919–1921 gg.: Dokumenty i materialy.* Tambov.

Davies, R. W. (1989). *Soviet History in the Gorbachev Revolution.* Basingstoke.

—————— (1997). *Soviet History in the Yeltsin Era.* Basingstoke.

Davies, R. W., ed. (1990). *From Tsarism to the New Economic Policy: Continuity and Change in the Economy of the USSR.* London.

Davies, R. W., et al., eds. (1994). *The Economic Transformation of the Soviet Union, 1913–1945,* Cambridge.

Debo, Richard K. (1990). *Survival and Consolidation: The Foreign Policy of Soviet Russia, 1918–1921.* Montreal.

"Deiatel'nost Tsentral'nogo Komiteta partii v dokumentakh (sobytiia i fakty): Mart 1919 g. VIII s"ezd RKP(b): Stenogramma zasedenii voennoi sektsii s"ezda 20 i 21 marta 1919 goda i zakrytogo zasedenii s"ezda 21 marta 1919 goda" (1989). *Izvestiia TsK KPSS* 9–11.

Dmitrenko, V. P. (1990). "'Voennyi kommunizm', NEP ..." *Istoriia SSSR* 3: 3–26.

Dmitrienko, V. P., ed. (1992). *Formirovanie administrativno–komandnoi sistemy.* Moscow.

Domin, I. V. (1995). "Russkoe voennoe zarubezh'e: dela, liudi, i mysli (20–30–e gody)", *Voprosy istorii* 7: 109–120.

Drokov, S. V. ed. (1994). "Podlinnye protokoly doprosov admirala A. V. Kolchaka i A. M. Timirevoi", *Otechestvennye arkhivy* 5: 84–97; 6: 21–57.

Dune, Eduard M. (1993). *Notes of a Red Guard,* Urbana IL.

"The Dynamics of Revolution in Soviet History: A Discussion" (1995). *Russian Review* 54/3: 315–351.

Dziak, John J. (1988). *Chekisty: A History of the KGB.* Lexington MA.

Esikov, S. A. and Protasov, L. G. (1992). "'Antonovshchina': Novye pokhody." *Voprosy istorii* 6–7: 47–57.

Fediuk, V. P. (1996). *Belye: Antibol'shevistskoe dvizhenie na iuge Rossii, 1917–1918 gg.* Moscow.

—— (1991). *Belye armii, chernye generaly.* Iaroslavl'.

Fel'shtinskii, Iu. G., ed. (1992). *Krasnyi terror v gody Grazhdanskoi voiny: Po materialam Osoboi sledstvennoi komissii po rassledovaniiu zlodeianii bol'shevikov.* London.

Fel'shtinskii, Iurii (1991). *Krushenie mirovoi revoliutsii, Ocherk 1–i. Brestskii mir: Oktiabr' 1917 – noiabr' 1918.* London.

Fiddick, Thomas C. (1990). *Russia's Retreat from Poland, 1920: From Permanent Revolution to Peaceful Coexistence.* New York.

Figes, Orlando (1989). *Peasant Russia, Civil War: The Volga Countryside in Revolution (1917–1921).* Oxford.

—— (1996). *A People's Tragedy: The Russian Revolution, 1891–1924.* London.

—— (1990). "The Red Army and Mass Mobilization during the Russian Civil War, 1918–1920," *Past and Present* 129: 168–211.

Fitzpatrick, Sheila (1992). *The Cultural Front: Power and Culture in Revolutionary Russia,* Ithaca.

Fitzpatrick, Sheila et al., eds. (1991). *Russia in the Era of the NEP: Explorations in Soviet Society and Culture.* Bloomington.

Fogelsong, D. S. (1995). *America's Secret War against Bolshevism: US Intervention in the Russian Civil War, 1917–1920.* Chapel Hill.

Frame, Murray (1995). *The Russian Revolution, 1905–1921: A Bibliographic Guide to Works in English,* London.

Frankel, Edith R., et al., eds. (1992). *Revolution in Russia: Reassessments of 1917.* Cambridge.

Frenkin, M. (1987). *Tragediia krest'ianskikh vosstanii v Rossii 1918–1921 gg.* Jerusalem.

Friedgut, Theodore H. (1994). *Iuzovka and Revolution: Politics and Revolution in Russia's Donbass, 1969–1924.* Princeton.

Galili i Garcia, Ziva (1989). *The Menshevik Leaders in the Russian Revolution: Social Realities and Political Strategies.* Princeton.

Galili, Z. et al., eds. (1994–1996). *Men'sheviki v 1917 godu.* 3 vols. Moscow.

Geldern, J. von (1993). *Bolshevik Festivals, 1917–1920.* Berkeley.

Genis, V. L. (1994). "Pervaia Konnaia armiia: Za kulisami slavy." *Voprosy istorii* 12: 64–77.

—— (1994). "Raskazachivanie v Sovetskoi Rossii." *Voprosy istorii* 1: 42–55.

Gimpel'son, E. G. (1997). "Sovetskie upravlentsi: politicheskii i nravstvennyi oblik (1917–1920 gg.)." *Otechestvennaia istoriia* 5: 44–54.

Goldin, V. I. ed. (1993). *Belyi sever, 1918–1920. Memuary i dokumenty.* 2 vols. Arkhangel'sk.

—— (1997). *Zabroshennye v nebytie: Interventsiia na Russkom Severe (1918–1919) glazami ee uchastnikov.* Arkhangel'sk.

Goldman, Wendy (1993). *Women, the State and Revolution: Soviet Family Policy and Social Life, 1917–1936.* Cambridge.

Gorodetskii, E. N. (1987). *Rozhdenie Sovetskoi gosudarstva, 1917–1918.* Moscow.

Got'e. I. V. (1988). *Time of Troubles: The Diary of Iurii Vladimirovich Got'e.* London.

Gregory, Paul R. (1995). *Before Command: An Economic History or Russia from Emancipation to the First Five Year Plan.* Princeton.

Gusev, K. V. (1992). *Eserovskaia bogoroditsa.* Moscow.

Hagen, Mark von (1995). *Soldiers of the Proletarian Dictatorship: The Red Army and the Soviet Socialist State, 1917–1930.* Ithaca.

Haimson, Leopold (1988). "The Problem of Social Identities in Early Twentieth Century Russia." *Slavic Review* 47/1: 1–20.

Harding, Neil (1996). *Leninism: A Critical Introduction*, Macmillan.

Husband, William (1990). *Revolution in the Factory: The Birth of the Soviet Textile Industry, 1917–1920*. New York.

Ioffe, G. Z. (1989). *Beloe delo: General Kornilov*. Moscow.

Ippolitov, G. M. (1999). *Kto vy, general A. I. Denikina? Monograficheskoe issledovanie politicheskoi, voennoi i obshchestvennoi deiatel'nosti A. I. Denikina v 1890–1947 gg*. Samara.

Izmozik, V. S. (1997). "Politicheskii kontrol' v Sovetskoi Rossii. 1918–1928 gody", *Voprosy istorii* 7: 32–53.

Jackson, George, ed. (1989). *Dictionary of the Russian Revolution*. New York.

Jansen, Marc, ed. (1989). *The Socialist-Revolutionary Party after October 1917: Documents from the PS-R Archives*. Amsterdam.

Kabanov, V. V. (1988). *Krest'ianskoe khoziaistvo v usloviiakh "voennogo kommunizma."* Moscow.

Kavtaradze, A. G. (1988). *Voennye spetsialisty na sluzhbe Respubliki Sovetov 1917–1920 gg.*, Moscow.

Khlevniuk, Oleg V. (1995). *In Stalin's Shadow: The Career of "Sergo" Ordzhonikidze.* Armonk.

Kingston-Mann, E. and Mixter, T., eds. (1991). *Peasant Economy, Culture, and Politics of European Russia, 1800–1921*. Princeton.

Kladving, V. V. (1999). *Belaia gvardiia*. St Petersburg.

Koehler, Hugo (1991). *Our Man in the Crimea. Commander Hugo Koehler and the Russian Civil War*, edited by P. J. Capelotti. Columbia SC.

Koenker, Diane R., et al., eds. (1989). *Party, State, and Society in the Russian Civil War: Explorations in Social History*. Bloomington.

Korablev, Iu. I., ed. (1988). *Revoliutsionnoe dvizhenie v voennykh okrugakh: Mart 1917 g. – mart 1918 g*. Moscow.

Kowalski, Ronald (1991). *The Bolshevik Party in Conflict*. Pittsburgh.

——— (1997). *The Russian Revolution 1917–1921*. London.

Kozlov, A. I. (1995). "Anton Ivanovich Denikin." *Voprosy istorii* 10: 54–73.

Kozlov, V. P., et al., eds. (1999). *Kronshtadtskaia tragediia 1921 goda: Dokumenty*. 2 vols. Moscow.

Krivosheev, G. F., et al., eds. (1993). *Grif sekretnosti sniat: Poteri vooruzhennykh sil SSSR v voinakh, boevykh deistviiakh i voennykh konfliktov: Statisticheskoe issledovanie*. Moscow.

Kuromiya, Hiroaki (1998). *Freedom and Terror in the Donbas: A Ukrainian-Russian Borderland, 1870s–1990s*. Cambridge.

Lar'kov, N. S. (1995). *Nachalo grazhdanskoi voiny v Sibiri: Armii i bor'ba za vlast'*. Tomsk.

Lazarski, Christopher (1992). "White Propaganda Efforts in the South during the Russian Civil War, 1918–19 (the Alekseev-Denikin Period)," *Slavonic and East European Review* 70/4: 688–707.

Lih, Lars (1990). *Bread and Authority in Russia, 1914–1921*. Berkeley.

Lincoln, W. Bruce (1989). *Red Victory: A History of the Russian Civil War*. New York.

Litvin, A.L. (1993). "Krasnyi i belyi terror v Rossii 1917–1922," *Otechestvennaia istoriia*, no. 6, pp. 46–62.

——— (1995). *Krasnyi i belyi terror v Rossii 1918–1922 gg*. Kazan.

McAuley, Mary (1991). *Bread and Justice: State and Society in Petrograd, 1917–1922*. Oxford.

McDermott, Kevin, and Agnew, Jeremy (1996). *The Comintern: A History of International Communism from Lenin to Stalin.* Basingstoke.
Mawdsley, Evan and White, Stephen (2000). *The Soviet Elite from Lenin to Gorbachev. The Central Committee and its Members, 1917–1991.* Oxford.
Medvedev, Roi (1997). *Russkaia revoliutsiia 1917 goda: Pobeda i porazhenie bol'shevikov (k 80-letiu Russkoi revoliutsii 1917 goda).* Moscow.
Mints, I. I., ed. (1988). *Inostrannaia voennaia interventsiia v Pribaltike: 1917–1920 gg.* Moscow.
Naumov, V.P. and Kosakovskii, A. A., eds. (1997). *Kronshtadt 1921. Dokumenty o sobytiiakh v Kronshtadte vesnoi 1921 g.* Moscow.
Nenarokov, A. P., ed. (1991). *Revvoensovet Respubliki (6 sent. 1918 – 28 avg. 1923 g.).* Moscow.
Nezhinskii, L. N. (1991). "Vneshniaia politika Sovetskogo gosudarstva v 1917–1921 godakh: Kurs na 'mirovuiu revoliutsiiu' ili na mirnoe sosushchestvovanie?" *Istoriia SSSR* 6: 3–27.
Odinstev, M. I. (1991). *Gosudarstvo i tserkov' (istoriia vzaimootnoshenii 1917–1938 gg.).* Mosow.
Patenaude, Bertrand M. (1995). "Peasants into Russians: The Utopian Essence of War Communism." *Russian Review* 54: 552–570.
Pavliuchenkov, S. A. (1996). *Krest'ianskii brest, ili predystoriia bol'shevistskogo NEPa.* Moscow.
—— (1997). *Voennyi kommunizm v Rossii: Vlast' i massy.* Moscow.
Pereira, Norman (1996). *White Siberia: The Politics of the Civil War.* Montreal.
Pipes, Richard (1990). *The Russian Revolution, 1919–1989.* London.
—— (1994). *Russia under the Bolshevik Regime, 1919–1924,* New York.
Pipes, Richard, ed. (1996). *The Unknown Lenin: From the Secret Archive.* New Haven.
Poliakov, Iu. A. (1992a), "Grazhdanskaia voina v Rossii: Posledstviia vnutrennie i vneshnie," *Novaia i noveishaia istoriia* 4: 3–14.
—— (1992b), "Grazhdanskaia voina v Rossii: Vozniknovenie i eskalatsiia." *Otechestvennaia istoriia* 6: 32–41.
—— (1990), "Grazhdanskaia voina v Rossii (poiska novogo videniia)." *Istoriia SSSR* 2: 98–117.
—— (1987). *Perekhod k NEPu i sovetskoe krest'ianstvo.* Moscow.
—— (1987). *Velikii oktiabr': Problemy istorii.* Moscow.
Poliakov, Iu. A. and Igritskii, Iu. I., eds. (1994). *Grazhdanskaia voina v Rossii: Perekrestok mnenii,* Moscow.
Portnov, V. P. (1987). *VChK 1917–1922.* Moscow.
Procyk, A. (1995). *Russian Nationalism and Ukraine: The Nationality Policy of the Volunteer Army during the Civil War.* Edmonton.
Putych, N. (1997). *Biograficheskii spravochnik vysshikh chinov Dobrovol'cheskoi armii i Vooruzhennykh Sil Iuga Rossii (Materialy k istorii Belogo dvizheniia).* Moscow.
Read, Christopher (1990). *Culture and Power in Revolutionary Russia: The Intelligentsia and the Transition from Tsarism to Communism.* London.
—— (1996). *From Tsar to Soviets: The Russian People and Their Revolution, 1917–21.* London.
Rosenberg, William G., ed. (1990). *Bolshevik Visions: First Phase of the Cultural Revolution in Soviet Russia.* 2 vols. Ann Arbor.
Ross, Nikolai, ed. (1987). *Gibel' Tsarskoi sem'i: Materialy sledstviia po delu ob ubiistve Tsarskoi sem'i (avgust 1918 – fevral' 1920).* Frankfurt.
Rossiia 1917 g.: Vybor istoricheskogo puti (1989). Moscow.

SUPPLEMENTARY BIBLIOGRAPHY

Russkaia voennaia emigratsiia 20-kh – 40-kh godov: Dokumenty i materialy (1998–). Moscow.

Rybnikov, V. V. and Slobodin, V. P. (1993). *Beloe dvizhenie v gody grazhdanskoi voiny v Rossii: Sushchnost', evoliutsiia i nekotorye itogi.* Moscow.

Sakwa, Richard (1988). *Soviet Communists in Power: A Study of Moscow during the Civil War, 1918–1921.* Basingstoke.

Samoshkin, V. V. (1994). "Aleksandr Stepanovich Antonov." *Voprosy istorii* 2: 66–76.

Service, Robert (1991, 1995). *Lenin: A Political Life.* vol. 2, *Worlds in Collision.* vol. 3, *The Iron Ring.* Basingstoke.

Service, Robert, ed. (1992). *Society and Politics in the Russian Revolution.* Basingstoke.

Shchetinov, Iu. A. (1995). "Za kulisami Kronshtadtskogo vosstaniia 1921 goda." *Vestnik Moskovskogo universiteta: Istoriia* 2: 3–15, 3: 22–44.

Shishkin, V. A., ed. (1995). *Interventsiia na severo-zapade Rossii 1917–1920 gg.* St Petersburg.

Shkliarevsky, Gennady (1993). *Labour in the Russian Revolution: Factory Committees and Trade Unions, 1917–1918.* New York.

Shukman, Harold, ed. (1988). *Blackwell Encyclopedia of the Russian Revolution.* Oxford.

Siegelbaum. Lewis J., and Suny, Ronald G., eds. (1994). *Making the Workers Soviet: Power, Class, and Identity.* Ithaca.

Slobodin, V. P. (1996). *Beloe dvizhenie v gody grazhdanskoi voiny v Rossii (1917–1922 gg.).* Moscow.

Smele, Jonathan D. (1996). *Civil War in Siberia: The Anti-Bolshevik Government of Admiral Kolchak, 1918–1920.* Cambridge.

Smirnov, N. N. (1988). *Tretii Vserossiiskii s"ezd sovetov.* Moscow.

Smith, Jeremy (1999). *The Bolsheviks and the National Question 1917–23,* Basingstoke.

Smith, Steve (1994). "Writing the History of the Russian Revolution after the Fall of Communism," *Europe–Asia Studies* 46/4: 563–578.

Smolin, A. V. (1999). *Beloe dvizhenie na severo-zapade rossii: 1918–1920 gg.* St Petersburg.

Sokolov, A. K., ed. (1998). *Golos naroda: Pis'ma i otkliki riadovykh sovetskikh grazhdan o sobytiiakh 1918–1932 gg.* Moscow.

Somin, Ilya (1996). *Stillborn Crusade: The Tragic Failure of Western Intervention in the Russian Civil War, 1918–1920.* New Brunswick NJ.

Spirin, L. M. (1987). *Rossiia 1917 god: Iz istorii bor'by politicheskikh partii.* Moscow.

Steinberg, Mark D. and Khrustalev, Vladimir M., eds. (1995). *The Fall of the Romanovs: Political Dreams and Personal Struggles in a Time of Revolution.* New Haven.

Stites, Richard (1989). *Revolutionary Dreams: Utopian Vision and Experimental Life in the Russian Revolution.* New York.

Subtelny, Orest. (1994). *Ukraine: A History.* Toronto.

Suny, Ronald G. (1993). *The Revenge of the Past: Nationalism, Revolution, and the Collapse of the Soviet Union.* Stanford.

——— (1994). "Revision and Retreat in the Historiography of 1917: Social History and Its Critics." *Russian Review* 53/2: 165–182.

Swain, Geoffrey (1996). *Origins of the Russian Civil War.* London.

Tiutiukin, S. V., et al., eds. (1998). *1917 god v sud'bakh Rossii i mira: Oktiabr'skaia revoliutsia: Ot novykh istochnikov k novomu osmysleniiu.* Moscow.

Tormozov, V. T. (1997). *Beloe dvizhenie i natsional'nyi vopros.* Moscow.

——— (1998). *Beloe dvizhenie v grazhdanskoi voine. 80 let izucheniia.* Moscow.

Trukan, G. A. (1994). *Put' k totalitarizmu: 1917–1929 g.g.* Moscow.

Tsiklon, Iu. N. (1996). *Beloe dvizhenie na Dal'nem Vostoke*. Khabarovsk.

Ushakov, A. I. (1993). *Istoriia grazhdanskoi voiny v literatury russkogo zarubezh'ia*. Moscow.

Ushakov, A. I. and Fediuk, V. P. (1997). *Belyi iug: Noiabr 1919–noiabr 1920*. Moscow.

Ustinkin, S. V. (1995). *Tragediia beloi gvardii*. Nizhnii Novgorod.

Verstiuk, C. F. ed. (1991). *Nestor Ivanovich Makhno: Vospominaniia, materialy i dokumenty*. Kiev.

Venkov, A. V. (1995). *Antibol'shevistskoe dvizhenie na Iuge Rossii na nachal'nom etape grazhdanskoi voiny*. Rostov on Don.

Voinov, V. G. (1994). "Ofitserskii korpus belykh armii na vostoke strany (1918–1920 gg.)," *Otechestvennaia istoriia* 6, 51–64.

Volkogonov, Dmitry (1994). *Lenin: Life and Legacy*. London.

—— (1991). *Stalin: Triumph and Tragedy*. London.

—— (1995). *Trotsky: The Eternal Revolutionary*. London.

Volkov, S. V. (1993). *Russkii ofitserskii korpus*. Moscow.

Volobuev, P. V., et al. (1993). *Politicheskie deiateli Rossii, 1917. Biograficheskii slovar'*. Moscow.

White, James D. (1994). *The Russian Revolution, 1917–1921: A Short History*. London.

Wildman, Allan K. (1987). *The End of the Russian Imperial Army*: Vol. 2. *The Road to Soviet Power and Peace*. Princeton.

Wood, Elizabeth A. (1997). *The Baba and the Comrade: Gender and Politics in Revolutionary Russia*. Bloomington.

Zevelev, A. I., ed. (1994). *Istoriia politicheskikh partii Rossii*. Moscow.

Zimina, V. D. (1998). *Beloe dvizhenie i rossiiskaia gosudarstvennost' v period grazhdanskoi voiny*. Moscow.

INDEX

Alash-Orda 238
Alekseev, General M. V. 20, 22, 86, 95
Allied Powers 282–4;
    and North Russia 158–9;
    and Poland 253–4;
    and Russia in 1917–18 45–55;
    and Russia in 1918–19 116, 127–31;
    and Siberia 100, 109, 143–4, 153–4, 232;
    and South Russia 26, 166–8, 264, 266–7;
    and Transcaucasus 228
Amur Region 101, 234
anarchists 82
Anishev, A. I. 212
anti-Bolshevik underground 191–2, 247–8
Antonov Movement (Tambov) 245
Antonov-Ovseenko, V. A. 4, 19, 36, 120–1
Arkhangelsk 16–17, 49–52, 156–9
Armed Forces of South Russia. See White
    armies in South Russia
Armenia 23, 27, 226–9
Army, Tsarist/Provisional Government 6,
    10–12, 24, 34, 59–61, 63
Astrakhan 162
Austria-Hungary 29, 35, 40–1, 116
Avksentiev, N. D. 106–8
Azerbaidzhan 23, 27, 226–9

Baku 52, 228, 239
Bashkirs 22, 136, 142, 199
Basmachi 239
Belorussia 22, 24, 118–19, 251–3, 256–7
Belov, General G. A. 149
Bermondt-Avalov, Colonel P. R. 199
Bernshtam M. S. 181
Berzin, R. I. 102
Bessarabia 23, 27
Bialystok 255
Bliukher, V. K. 234
Bogaevsky, General A. P. 166, 222
Bogoslovsky, General 102
Boldyrev, General V. G. 104, 108–10, 145
Bolshevik national parties:
    Armenian 229;
    Azerbaidzhan 229;
    Georgian 229;

Latvian 122;
Lithuanian 122;
Ukrainian 120, 122, 212, 266
Bolsheviks 17, 189–190, 274, 289. *See also*
    Soviet Russia;
Central Committee of 32, 57, 80, 146,
    151, 163, 179, 200, 229, 252, 264;
and cossacks 168, 171–2, 212;
Dalbiuro of 233;
Democratic Centralists in 247;
Donbiuro of 212;
economic policies of 7–8, 9, 70–5, 138–9,
    273–4;
electoral support for 5–6, 101;
factions in 39, 80, 246–7;
international policy of, in 1917–18 8–9,
    31–3, 39–40, 43–6;
international policy of, in 1918–19 124–9;
international policy of, in 1919–20 239–41,
    254–5, 259–61, 276–7;
Kavbiuro of 228–9;
Komsomol and 246;
Left Communists in 39, 80;
membership of 7, 79, 190, 246;
national minority policy of 8, 23–5, 122–
    3, 228, 248–9;
organization of 6–7, 79–80, 122, 189–90,
    246;
Organizational Bureau of 189;
Party congress, 7th 37;
Party congress, 8th 90, 122, 139, 141,
    178–9, 186, 189;
Party congress, 10th 246;
peasant policy of 139, 273;
Politburo of 173, 176, 189, 203, 254, 259,
    265;
in Red Army 34, 36, 180;
Secretariat of 79–80, 189;
Sibbiuro of 139, 230;
and state administration 8–9, 36–7, 75–9,
    80–1, 190, 246–7, 273–4;
Trans-front Bureau of 212;
Turkbiuro of 238, 241;
underground organizations of, in White
    territory 102, 137–9, 212;

355

Workers' Opposition in 247
Bonch-Bruevich, General M. D. 34, 60, 66, 68–9
Brest-Litovsk negotiations 9, 31–5, 43–4, 277
Britain 52, 100, 109–10,128, 223, 239;
  and Baltic 116, 198–200;
  and Central Asia 238;
  and North Russia 156, 158–9;
  and Poland 253–4;
  and Siberia 143–4, 153–4, 232;
  and South Russia 129–30, 166–8, 196, 208, 214–15, 224, 267;
  and Transcaucasus 167, 227
Budberg, General A. 135–7,150–1, 155
Budenny, S. M. 202, 205, 220, 252, 269
Bukhara 238–9
Bukharin, N. I. 39, 45, 191, 244, 247
Bulak-Balakhovich, General S. N. 197
Bullitt, William 128–9
Buriats 17, 23

Carr, E. H. 245, 276
Caucasus 225–6
Cecek, Colonel S. 58
Central Asia 23–4, 235–41
Central ExCom (VTsIK) 9, 77, 188
Central Powers 31–5, 41–2, 116, 283
Chaikovsky, N. V. 52, 157
Chapaev, V. I. 134
Chechens 225
Cheka 40, 53, 81–3, 138, 181, 190–1
Cheliabinsk 47–8, 100, 149, 152
Chernigov 173
Chernov, V. M. 107, 110
Chicherin, G. V. 42
Chita 233–4
Church, Russian Orthodox 10, 12
Churchill, Winston 111, 130, 232, 275
Clemenceau, Georges 128
Comintern. See Komintern
Communist Party. See Bolsheviks
Conquest, Robert 286
Constituent Assembly 5, 14, 18, 96, 106–7, 110, 136. See also Komuch;
  elections to 5–6, 10, 12, 24, 25, 27, 101, 105;
  White proposals for new 150, 222
Cossacks 17–20, 86, 168, 171–2, 208–9, 222, 266. See also White armies in South Russia, White armies in Siberia;
  Amur 145;
  Don, in 1917–18 5, 12, 18–19, 36, 39, 85–9;
  Don, in 1918–20 163–6, 170, 220–1, 264, 270;
  Irkutsk 145;
  Kuban 5, 20, 36, 94–5, 209, 220–1, 268;
  Orenburg 5, 17–18, 68, 136–7, 142, 145, 149;
  Semirechie 145;
  Siberian 103, 107–8, 145, 149;
  Terek 20, 93, 162, 225–6;
  Transbaikal 103, 145;
  Ural 136–7, 142, 145, 149;
  Ussuri 145
Council of Public Men 248
Council for State Unity 211
Crimea 35, 130, 224, 262–71
Crimean Tatars 35, 263
Curzon Line 253
Czechoslovak Corps:
  uprising of 46–9, 53–4, 56–7, 67–8, 99–100;
  and Russian anti-Bolsheviks 105–6, 143, 232, 235

Dagestan 225–6
Dashnaks 27, 226
Davies, Norman 260
Defence Council (SRKO/STO) 187
Democratic Centralists 247
Denikin, General A. I. 12, 21, 210, 212, 280. See also White armies in South Russia; White governments in South Russia;
  as commander of Volunteer Army 93, 95–6;
  as commander of AFSR 165, 170–2, 205–8;
  and minorities 222, 281, 283;
  in 1920 221, 223–5
Denisov, General S. V. 87, 164–6
Directory (Omsk) 106. See also Provisional All-Russian Government
Directory (Ukrainian) 119–20, 129
Diterikhs, General M. K. 152, 231, 235
Dobb, Maurice 244
Don Army:
  in 1917–18 86–9;
  in 1918–19 163–6, 171, 172, 174–6, 207, 214;
  in 1920 224
Don Soviet Republic 20, 86
Donbas 19, 36, 170–1
Donets-Krivoi Rog Soviet Republic 36
Drozdovsky, Colonel M. G. 86, 95
Dukhonin, General N. N. 11
Dumenko, B. M. 171, 222
Dunsterforce 52
Dutov, General A. I. 17–18
Dvinsk 35, 251
Dzerzhinsky, F. E. 138, 260;
  as head of Cheka 80, 181, 190;
  and Perm investigation 62, 78, 133, 138, 140–1

Egorev, General V. N. 180
Egorlykskaia, battle of 223
Egorov, Colonel A. I. 19, 171, 204, 207;
  in Polish campaign 252, 257–8
Eideman, R. P. 268
Eikhe, G. Kh. 151, 230, 233
Ekaterinburg 82, 101–2, 110, 148
Ekaterinodar 20–1, 93, 166, 223
Ekaterinoslav 172, 212
Emigration 286–7
Estonia:
  in 1917–18 22, 24, 33, 38, 42;
  in 1918–19 116–17;
  and 1919 White offensives 196–201

Far Eastern Republic 233–5
Field Staff of Red Army 69
Filatev, General D. V. 137–8, 153
Finland 5, 22, 27–8, 32–3, 37–8;
  civil war in 27–9;
  and Soviet Russia 117, 201;
  and Whites 159, 198–9, 281
First Cavalry Army (Budenny) 220–3, 252, 256, 258, 269
Fleming, Peter 107
Foch, Marshal Ferdinand 130
France 47, 49, 51, 128, 283;
  and Siberia 144, 232;
  and South Russia 121, 129–30, 267;
  and Poland 253–4
Frunze, M. V. 140, 151, 240, 266, 269–70, 272

Gai, G. D. 252, 255–6
Gajda, General R. 100, 104, 134, 145, 148, 152
Gatchina 4, 200
Gekker, A. I. 229
Germans, minority in Russia 23
Germany 116, 256;
  and Baltic states 118, 199;
  revolution in 15, 124, 254;
  and Russia in 1917–18 31–5, 37, 40, 41–3, 86–8, 227
Georgia 23, 27, 42, 226–9
Gins, G. K. 135, 151, 278–9
Gittis, V. M. 163, 169, 200
Gold reserve, imperial 231–3
Golovin, General N. N. 153
Goltz, General R. von der 11, 126
Gorn, V. 278
Gortsy 225–6, 228
Greece 130
Greens 223, 228
Grigoriev, N. A. 121, 126, 130
Grishin-Almazov, General A. N. 177, 279

Gusev, S. I. 179, 183, 223

Helsinki 28–9
Hoffmann, General Max von 32, 35
Hungary 121, 124–7

Iakuts 17, 23
Iakutsk Region 234
Iaroslavl 50–1
India 239–40
Ingushes 225
Irkutsk 17, 101, 232–3
Ironside, General Edmund 57, 159
Italy 227
Ivanov-Rinov, General P. P. 152
Iudenich, General N. N. 196–7 See also
  White armies in the Baltic region;
  White governments in the Baltic region
Izhevsk uprising 65–6

Janin, General Maurice 109, 135, 143, 146
Japan 52, 100, 144, 233–5, 283
Jassy Conference 128
Jews 23, 79, 210
July 1918 Moscow uprising 40–1

Kadets 5, 12, 103, 135, 191, 278
Kakurin, Colonel N. E. 60, 123, 206–7
Kakhovka, battle of 268–9
Kakhovskaia, I. 212
Kaledin, General A. M. 18–20, 85
Kalinin, M. I. 188
Kalmykov, I. M. 137, 145
Kalnin, K. I. 94
Kamenev, L. B. 33, 117, 189
Kamenev, Colonel S. S. 132, 140, 204 278;
  as Eastern Army Group C-in-C 151;
  as Main C-in-C 175, 179–80;
  on Red Army 220–1;
  on strategy in 1919 156, 175–6, 201, 202–4;
  on strategy in 1920 222, 228–9, 255, 258, 261, 265, 269
Kaplan, F. 80
Kappel, General V. O. 57, 65, 67, 69, 142, 145, 230–1
Kastornoe, battle of 202–3
Kautsky, Karl 276
Kazakhs 23, 238–9
Kazan 56–9, 61, 65, 67
Kenez, Peter 211
Kerensky, A. F. 4, 9, 11, 13
Khabarovsk 17, 101, 235
Khanzhin, General M. V. 134, 141, 145, 152
Kharkov 26, 36, 120, 171
Kharlamov, Colonel S. D. 200

Kherson 35, 130, 172
Khiva 238–9
Khorvat 105
Khrushchev, N. S. 195
Khvesin, T. S. 169
Kiev 24–6, 35–6, 119–20, 221, 250–3
Kirgiz ASSR 238
Klimushkin, P. D. 64
Kniagnitsky, P. E. 169–70
Knox, General Alfred 108, 135, 142–3, 152–3,180
Kokand 238
Kolchak, Admiral A. V. 129, 159, 198. *See also* White armies in Siberia; White governments in Siberia; capture and death 231–3; as political leader 135–6, 149–50; seizes power 108–10; and strategy 143–5,152
Kollontai, A. M. 273
Komarow, battle of 256
Kombedy 71, 120
Komintern 124–7, 129, 239, 254
Komuch 49, 56, 63–5, 68, 103–6, 136, 192
Kornilov, General L. G. 8–9, 11–12, 20–1
Kornilov Regiment/Division 195–6, 202, 207, 212, 268, 285
Kostiaev, General F. V. 179
Kovno 118
Kozhevnikov, I. S. 169
Krasnoiarsk, 17, 231
Krasnov, General P. N. 4, 39, 87, 163–7
Krestinsky, N. N. 189
Kritsman, L. N. 285, 288
Krivoshein, A. V. 263
Kronshtadt uprising 245
Krylenko, N. V. 11–12, 34
Kuban 21, 92, 94–5, 222–4
Kun, Bela 125, 271
Kursk, 195
Kutepov, General A. P. 158, 224, 269

Labour Armies 230, 244
Laidoner, General J. 199
Lashevich, M. M. 178
Latsis, M. Ia. 286
Latvia:
  in 1917–18 22, 24, 32–3, 38, 41–2;
  in 1918–20 117–18, 199, 201
Latvian Riflemen 41, 57–9, 117–18, 202, 204, 268, 270
Lazo, S. G. 235
Lebedev, General D. A. 142, 144–5, 152
Lebedev, General P. P. 179–80
Lebedev, V. I. 64, 275
Left Communists in 39, 80

Left SRs 9, 14, 40–1, 77–8, 81, 192
Lehovich, D. V. 206
Lenin, V. I. 29, 34, 41, 80, 101, 272–5, 287; and Allied intervention 45–7, 53; and Brest-Litovsk 33, 36, 43–4; and economy 8, 73–4, 186, 244–5; and foreign relations 8, 36–7, 124, 129; general doctrine of 6–8, 288; and international revolution 27, 115–16, 126–7, 129, 240, 276; and 1918 eastern front 47; and 1918 southern front 21–2; and 1919 Baltic front 200–1; and 1919 eastern front 133, 148, 151; and 1919 southern front 166, 174–5, 203; on 1920 eastern front 233; and Polish campaign 254, 259, 261; and Red Army organization 36, 57, 62–3, 66–8, 178–9; and Red Terror 81–3, 247; and state adminstration 75–7, 79, 189, 273; and strategy 277–8, 283; and Vrangel 269–71
Lithuania 22, 32–3, 118, 201
Lithuanian-Belorussian SSR 118
Liundkvist, Colonel V. E. 200
Lloyd George, David 46, 128, 130–1, 223
Lockhart, R. Bruce 53
Lorimer, Frank 286–7
Losses caused by Civil War 285–8
Lukomsky, General A. S. 12, 207, 211, 222, 224, 271
Lvov, battle of 256, 258

Mai-Maevsky, General V. Z. 170, 172, 174, 196, 208, 221
Maisky, I. I. 64–5, 192
Makhno, N. I. 121, 168, 212–13, 266, 270
Maksudov, M. 286–7
Mamontov, General K. K. 88, 174–5, 220–1
Malle, Silvana 287
Manchuria 105
Mannerhein, General C. G. 28, 199
Markhlevsky, Iu. V. 205
Markov, General S. L. 12, 95
Martov, Iu. O. 247
Medvedev, Roy 74–5
Melgunov, S. P. 82, 248
Mensheviks 288;
  in 1917 13, 27;
  in 1918 39, 65, 77–8;
  in 1919 192;
  Georgian 226–7, 229;
  Siberian 232
Mikhail Aleksandrovich, Grand Duke 82

Mikhailov, I. A. 135
Military Opposition 141, 178–9
Miller, General E. K. 157–9
Minin, S. K. 90
Minsk 24, 35, 118–19, 251, 253, 256
Mirbach, Count Wilhelm 40
Mogilev 11–12, 35
Moldavian People's Republic 27
Mongolia 234
Moscow 4, 6, 34, 273–5
Moscow Directive (of Denikin) 172
Moscow, Soviet-Turkish Treaty of (1921) 227
Mountain ASSR 226
Muraviev, Colonel M. A. 4, 19, 26, 56–7
Murmansk 49–51, 158–9
Musavats 27, 226, 228, 240

Nadezhny, General D. N. 102, 200
National Center 191, 211, 247
national minorities question 8, 22–30, 37–9, 76, 116–24, 248–51, 281–3
New Economic Policy 74, 245
Nicholas II 10, 82–3, 100
Nikolaev 35, 172
North Caucasus Soviet Republic 93–4
North Russia 16, 49–52, 141, 155–60
Northern Army 38, 116–17, 196
Northwestern Army 196–202
Northwestern Government 197
Nove, Alec 245, 288
Novitsky, General F. F. 238
Novocherkassk 19–20, 86–7, 221

October Revolution 3–5, 17, 289–90
Odessa 27, 129–30, 172
Odessa Soviet Republic 27, 35
Olderogge, General V. A. 151, 230
Olonets 159
Omsk 100, 103, 106–9. See also Provisional All-Russian Government; White governments in Siberia;
coup in 108–9;
Red capture of 149, 152–3;
uprising in 135, 139
Ordzhonikidze, G. K. 223, 228–9
Orel 196
Orenburg 17–18, 132, 238
Orlovsky, Daniel 79

Pan-Turkism 239, 241
Panteleev 67
Paris Peace Conference 127–8, 130, 227
Parsky, General D. P. 61
peasants 120, 273, 278–9;
in Siberia 137–9;

on Volga 64–5, 139;
in 1917–18 5, 7–9, 13, 71–2, 75;
in 1918–20 186–7, 244
People's Army (Komuch) 57, 64–5, 67–8
Peoples of the East, Congress of 239
Pepeliaev, General A. N. 145
Perekop, battle of 268, 270
Perm 62, 82, 133, 148
Persia 239
Petliura, S. V. 119, 209–10
Petrograd 4–6, 19, 34;
defense of, in 1919 196–202;
Military-Revolutionary Committee 9, 11
Petrozavodsk 159
Piatakov, G. L. 120
Piatigorsk 93, 161
Pilsudski, Jozef 205, 251, 254, 257, 275
Pipes, Richard 282
Podtelkov, F. G. 19–20, 86
pogroms 210
Pokrovsky, General V. L. 209
Poland 22, 32–3, 285;
in 1919 118–20, 205, 281;
and war with Soviet Russia 250–61, 267, 275
Poliakov, Iu. A. 285
Political Center (Irkutsk) 232
Poltava 173
Pozern 151
Primorskaia Region 234–5
Prinkipo Conference proposal 127–8
prisoners of war 47, 101, 238
Provisional All-Russian Government (Omsk) 104, 106, 138
Provisional Government (1917) 4, 8, 10
Provisional Government of Autonomous Siberia 105
Provisional Government of the Northern Region 156. See also White governments in North Russia
Provisional Siberian Government 103–6
Pskov 38, 116, 196

Rada, Ukrainian 24–6, 35, 38
Radkey, Oliver 13–14
Rakovsky, Kh. G. 120
Red Army 101, 178–85, 275–6. See also 1st Cavalry Army; Latvian Riflemen; Red Army Groups:
cavalry in 220–1;
command staff in 60–1, 169–70, 178–80, 242;
commissars in 62, 69, 141, 180, 242;
conscripts in 62–3, 66, 182–3, 242–3;
deployment of 60, 123, 181, 243;
desertion from 182–3, 200;

discipline in 69, 140–1, 151, 180–1;
equipment of 63, 182–5, 243;
foreigners in 47–8, 101, 238;
formation of 34, 36–7, 42, 59–63, 68–9;
internal role of 181, 243;
international role of 125–6;
losses of 285–6;
military districts of 60, 146–7, 154, 214;
and Military Opposition 141, 178–9;
national armies in 117, 120–1, 123, 127, 169, 171;
political organization of 69, 180, 242;
Republic RevMilCouncil (RVSR) of 69, 151, 179;
Screens in 36, 51, 60;
staffs of 60–1, 69;
strength of 63, 69, 123, 125–6, 181–4, 214, 242–3;
supply of 63, 184–5, 187, 273–4;
Supreme Military Council of 60;
uniforms of 185;
unit organization of 183;
Universal Military Training (Vsevobuch) in 63, 182, 242
Red Army Groups (Fronts):
Caspian-Caucasus 123, 161–3;
Caucasus, 221–4;
Eastern 41–2, 56–9, 66–9, 89, 102, 123, 132–3, 139–41, 146–51, 154, 230;
Northern 116–17;
Southeastern 214, 221–2;
Southern 69, 89–92, 97–8, 123, 163–4, 168–77, 202–5, 214, 269–71;
Southwestern 252, 256–9;
Turkestan 226;
Ukrainian 120–1, 123, 127;
Western 69, 118–19, 196–202, 252–6, 258–9
Red Guard 6
Red Terror 53–4, 80–3, 163, 190–1, 247–8, 274
Republic RevMilCouncil (RVSR) 69, 151, 179
RevComs 188, 196, 228, 230, 247, 255, 260, 271
Riga, Treaty of 256–7
Rigby, T. H. 77
Right (in Russian politics) 10–12, 107–10, 211, 278, 280
Rodzianko, General A. P. 197
Romanovsky, General I. P. 224
Rostov-on-Don 18–20, 36, 221
Rumania 23, 27
Russian Political Conference (Paris) 128
Rykov, A. I. 179, 187, 254, 278

Sablin, Iu. V. 19
Sakharov, General K. V. 145, 147, 152, 231, 280, 284

Samara 49, 56, 68, 104, 106
Samoilo, General A. A. 156–8
Saratov 58
Savinkov, B. V. 51, 267
Selivachev, General V. I. 175
Semenov, G. M. 103, 137, 144–5, 233–4
Sevastopol 35, 270
Shchepkin, N. N. 191
Shenkursk, battle of 156
Shkuro, General A. G. 94, 172, 202, 207, 222
Shliapnikov, A. G. 162
Shorin, Colonel V. I. 148–9, 175–7, 203, 222, 233
Siberia 16–17, 23, 99–111;
in 1918–19 134–46, 149–55;
in 1919–22 230–5
Siberian partisans 138, 150
Siberian Regional Duma 105
Siberian Regionalists 17, 102–3
Sidorin, General V. I. 171–2, 207, 222
Sikorski, General W. 255
Simbirsk 57, 68
Skachko, A. E. 169
Skliansky, E. M. 179
Skoblin, General N. V. 196
Skoropadsky, General P. P. 38, 119, 164
Slashchev, General Ia. A. 224, 268
Slaven, Colonel P. A. 67, 163
Smilga. I. T. 179, 223, 258, 278
Smirnov, I. N. 230
Sochi 224
Social Democrats. See also Bolsheviks; Mensheviks;
Finnish 28
Ukrainian 25
Socialist-Revolutionaries. See SRs
Sorokin, I. L. 94
Sovdepia 70. See also Soviet Russia
Soviet-German Supplementary Treaty 39, 42
Soviet Russia 70, 83–4, 273–4. See also Bolsheviks; Red Terror;
arms production of 184;
Central ExCom (VTsIK) of 9, 77, 188;
and cossacks 168, 171–2, 212;
Defence Council (SRKO) of 187–8;
economic policies of 7–9, 70–5, 138–9, 185–8, 243–6, 273–4, 287–8;
and food supply 71, 186–7, 243–6;
Interior Commissariat (NKVD) of 189–90;
international policy of, in 1917–18 8–9, 31–3, 39–40, 43–6;
international policy of, in 1918–19 115–16, 124–9;

international policy of, in 1919–20 239–41, 254–5, 259–61, 276–7;
and industrial organization 187, 244–5;
and labour mobilization 244–5;
losses suffered by 285–8;
national minority policy of 8, 23, 122, 228, 248–9;
and peasants 139, 186, 245–6, 273;
and Peasants' Soviets, Congress of 14;
political structure of 7, 9, 75–80, 122–3, 188–92, 246–9;
Rabkrin of 247;
soviets, local, of 8–9, 14, 77, 188–9;
and Soviets, 2nd Congress of 4, 7–9, 11;
and Soviets, 3rd Congress of 5, 37;
and Soviets, 4th Congress of 40;
and Soviets, 5th Congress of 40;
and Soviets, 6th Congress of 190;
and Soviets, 7th Congress of 247;
Sovnarkom of 7, 9, 77, 188;
Supreme Economic Council (VSNKh) of 187;
Turkkomissiia of 238, 241
Soviet-Polish War 250–61
Sovnarkom 7, 9, 77, 188
Special Council (Denikin) 96, 211, 222
SRs 279. See also Left SRs;
in 1917 5, 13–14, 17;
in 1918 39–40, 51, 56, 64, 77–8;
in 1919 192;
in 1920–21 223, 248
Siberian, 102, 104–7, 110–11, 136, 138, 231–2;
in Turkestan, 237;
Ukrainian 25, 120
Stalin, I. V. 28, 33, 75, 189, 220, 277–8, 288–9;
at Tsaritsyn 89–91, 94;
and Perm investigation 62, 78, 133, 138, 140–1;
and 1919 defense of Petrograd 196;
and 1919 southern front 203–4;
and Polish War 254, 258;
and national question 228, 240, 248–9
Stankevich, General A. V. 195
Stavka 11–12, 35
Stavropol 93
Stepanov, General N. A. 142, 145
Stogov, General N. N. 61
Struve, P. B. 263
Sukin, I. I. 135
Svec, Josef 68
Sverdlov, Ia. M. 36 7, 80, 82–3, 117, 188, 278
Sviiazhsk, battle of 67
Syrovy, General J. 104
Sytin, General P. P. 90

Tactical Center 248
Tadzhiks 23
Tallin 116
Taman Army 94
Tambov 174
Tampere, battle of 29
Tashkent 24, 237–8
Tauride SSR 35
Terek Soviet Republic 20
Tiflis 27, 229
Tikhon, Patriarch 10
Timoshenko, S. K. 220
Tomsk 17, 102, 231
trade unions 6, 245, 247
Transbaikal 100, 233–4
Transcaspia 238–9
Transcaucasus 5, 27, 33, 52, 226–9
Trotsky, L. D. 189, 277–8;
as Foreign Commissar, 32, 42, 50;
on internal policy, 74, 139, 243–5, 247;
on international situation, 46, 81, 125–8, 131, 240–1;
on national question, 120–1, 248, 282;
and 1918 eastern front, 48, 57–8, 67, 69, 102;
and 1918 southern front 29, 89–92;
and 1919 Baltic front 199;
and 1919 eastern front, 147;
and 1919 southern front, 162, 169, 171, 173–4, 176, 203–6;
and 1920 southern front 229, 266–7, 269;
and northern front 51;
and Polish War 254, 256–8, 260–1;
and Red Army organization 61–2, 178–9, 183–4, 220;
and Red high command 151, 175, 179;
on strategy, 140, 275, 288–9;
becomes War Commissar 59
Tsaritsyn, 19, 36, 88–92, 164, 172, 177, 221
Tsentrosibir 101
Tuapse 224
Tukhachevsky, M. N. 67–9, 149, 151, 169, 223;
and Polish campaign 252–3, 255–6, 258, 261
Turkestan 235–41
Turkey 41, 52, 227–9
Turkmens 23
Tver 188

Uborevich I. P. 268
Ufa 68, 105, 110, 132, 134
Ufa State Conference 105–7
Ukraine:
in 1917–18 22, 24–6, 32, 35–6, 38–9;
in 1918–19 119–21, 127, 129–30, 172–3;

in 1920 248, 250–1, 257, 266;
and Whites 209–10
Ulagai, General S. G. 221, 268
Ungern-Sternberg, Baron R. F. 234
Union for Defense of Fatherland and Free-
dom 51
Union for the Regeneration of Russia 106,
211, 248
United States 100, 144, 227, 235, 283
Urals 4, 7, 82, 101–2, 105, 137, 143, 149
Urals Provisional Government 105
Uralsk 132
Urlanis, B. Ts. 285–6
Uzbeks 23

Vareikis, I. M. 57
Vatsetis, Colonel I. I.:
on cossack policy 171–2;
dismissal of 175, 179;
as Eastern AG C-in-C 58–9;
as Main C-in-C 68, 89–90, 102, 278;
and Moscow uprising 41;
on Red Army 181–4;
on strategy 119, 121, 127, 140, 150–1,
163, 166, 169
Versailles Conference. See Paris Peace
Conference
Veshenskaia uprising 168, 171
Viatka 78
Vilna 118, 251, 253
Vinnichenko, V. K. 25, 119
Vinogradov, V. A. 106
Vladivostok 17, 52, 100, 234–5
Voitsekhovsky, General S. N. 232–3
Volkov. E. Z. 286
Vologda 46
Vologodsky, P. V. 103, 106, 108
Volsky, V. K. 64, 136, 192
Volunteer Army/Corps 20–2, 39, 58, 86,
92–8, 103, 164–5, 214, 222–4, 264. See
also White armies in South Russia;
in Donbas campaign 170–1;
in North Caucasus 161–3
Voronezh 88, 174, 202
Voroshilov, K. E. 89–91, 94, 169
Votkinsk uprising 139
Vrangel, P. N. 93, 158, 262–71. See also
White armies in South Russia; White
governments in South Russia;
as C-in-C Caucasus Army 172, 175, 177;
as C-in-C of Volunteer Army 221;
commands southern Whites 224–5;
and cossacks 209;
dismissal of 224;
and strategy 172–3, 206, 208, 220;

in winter of 1918–19 163, 171
Vsevolodov, General N. D. 170
VSNKh 9, 73, 187

War Communism, 73–4, 248–9
Weygand, General Maxime 253–4, 257
White armies 279–81, 285–6
White armies in the Baltic region:
Northern Army 38, 116–17, 196;
Northwestern Army 196–202;
West Russian Army 199
White armies in North Russia 155–60
White armies in South Russia 169. See also
Don Army; Kornilov Regiment/Divi-
sion; Volunteer Army/Corps;
Armed Forces of South Russia 142–4,
165, 172–3, 207–8, 219–25;
Caucasus Army 163, 172–5, 206;
Kuban Army 222;
population base of 213–14;
Russian Army (Vrangel) 262–71;
Turkestan Army 238
White armies in Siberia 132–55, 230–5. See
also People's Army:
Siberian Army 103–4, 107–8, 134, 142,
148;
Western Army 134, 142
White governments 280–1
White governments of Siberia 156–7, 159,
238. See also Provisional All-Russian
Government; Provisional Siberian
Government;
in 1919 134–8, 149–50;
in 1920–22 230–5;
population resources of 146
White governments of South Russia
and cossacks 164–5, 208–9;
and French 129;
policies of 210–13;
propaganda of 211;
under Vrangel 263, 265–6;
and Ukraine 209
Workers' Opposition 247
working class 5–7, 65–6, 72–4,187
Wrangel. See Vrangel

Yudenich. See Iudenich

Zenzinov, V. M. 106, 108
Zetkin, Klara 259
Zinoviev, G. E. 33, 200
Zhitomir 35
Zlatoust 149
Zhukov, G. K. 180, 220